Socratic Digest

Reprinted from five issues originally published
separately between the years 1943 and 1952

Joel D. Heck, Editor

Concordia University Press
Austin, Texas

Library of Congress Cataloging-in-Publication Data
Socratic Digest / Joel D. Heck, editor.
  Austin, TX: Concordia University Press, 2012
  240 p., 28 cm.
  "Reprinted from five issues originally published separately between the years 1943 and 1952"—T.p.

ISBN 978-1-881848-16-5

  1. Christianity--20th century—Periodicals. 2. Philosophy and religion. I. Lewis, C. S. (Clive Staples), 1898-1963. II. Oxford University Socratic Club. III. Heck, Joel D., 1948-

BR1.S62 2012
2012948235

Preface to the 2012 Edition

With the reprinting of the *Socratic Digest*, one more major document in Lewisiana becomes available to the general public. One *caveat*, however, should give many Lewis fans pause. The arguments and discussions recorded on these pages reflect the mature thought of many an Oxford don who was a specialist in his or her field. Many of these speakers were philosophers, reflecting an Existential, Platonic, Aristotelian, or Logical Positivist position or that of another system of thought. For those not conversant in twentieth-century philosophy, many of these essays will present a serious challenge to understanding the arguments of these writers.

For those who want to read many of the talks presented at the Socratic Club, however, whether clear or difficult, specialized or accessible, this *Digest* will serve them well. For those, especially, who want to read the actual essay that Elizabeth Anscombe presented in response to Chapter 3 of C. S. Lewis' 1947 book *Miracles* or who want to understand better the context in which Lewis wrote seven of his essays, some of which appear in different format than as they were later published, the *Socratic Digest* will provide that. For those who want to read the response of Unitarian Nicol Cross to Lewis' chapter in *Mere Christianity*, "The Shocking Alternative," this *Digest* provides that response. For those who want to know the issues of the day in Oxford during the 1940s, particularly for the Christian faith, the *Socratic Digest* is the answer. For those who want to read the notes taken on Charles Williams' argument in the first issue that free love is neither free nor love, the *Socratic Digest* provides it. For those who want to enjoy the give-and-take between H. H. Price and C. S. Lewis on the topic of a minimal religion or the importance of theism, this is where one will find that argument, and in the reading one will see the same Lewis who later proposed similar arguments in *Miracles*. Those who want to anticipate Lewis' inaugural lecture at Cambridge will enjoy his statement, "almost I'd sooner be a pagan suckled in a creed outworn" (p. 164), or this one, "When grave persons express their fear that England is relapsing into Paganism, I am tempted to reply, 'Would that she were'" (p. 229). Perhaps the chance to read such luminaries as G.E.M. Anscombe, Iris Murdoch, M. Gabriel Marcel, and D. M. MacKinnon will be reward in itself.

Some minor typographical changes have occurred for the sake of consistency. The cover of the various issues of the original *Socratic Digest* had different formats, so those differences have been eliminated. Punctuation, capitalization, and spelling have also been regularized, and the frequent use of hyphenated words has been updated (e.g., world-view appears as worldview; first-hand appears as firsthand). The original footnotes have been retained. Where the current editor included the translation of a foreign language phrase or some other note, those footnotes always begin with the words "Editor's Note (2012)."

With this edition we also supply a brief Table of Contents for the five volumes of the *Socratic Digest*:

Socratic Digest, No. 1, 1942–43	5–28
Socratic Digest, No. 2, 1943–44	29–56
Socratic Digest, No. 3, 1944–45	57–98
Socratic Digest, No. 4 (Double Number), 1947–48	99–192
Socratic Digest, No. 5, 1949–52	193–240

Joel D. Heck, Editor

Permissions

Extracts by C. S. Lewis copyright © C. S. Lewis Pte. Ltd. Reprinted by permission.

Permission to reprint the notes on M. Gabriel Marcel's essay has been granted by Présence de Gabriel Marcel, Paris.

Permission to reprint the article entitled "Reply to Mr. C. S. Lewis' Argument that "Naturalism" is Self-Refuting" by G.E.M. Anscombe has been granted by her daughter and literary executor, Dr Mary C Gormally.

Permission to reprint the fifth issue of the *Socratic Digest* has been granted by kind permission of the Philosophical Library, Inc., New York, New York.

Permission to reprint the article by Iris Murdoch, entitled "The Existentialist Political Myth" and originally published in the *Socratic Digest*, has been granted by kind permission of the Estate of Iris Murdoch.

All other copyright holders have been sought, but the editor has been unable to locate them.

SOCRATIC DIGEST

No. 1   1942–1943

CONTENTS

PAPERS AND SPEAKERS, 1942–1943	6
PREFACE	8
SOCRATES WAS A REALIST	10
THE FIRST MEETING	12
IS GOD A WISH-FULFILLMENT?	13
CAN SCIENCE RENDER RELIGION UNNECESSARY?	14
PURPOSE AND DESIGN IN NATURE	15
FREE WILL AND PREDESTINATION (in full)	16
CONSCIENCE AND MORAL FREEDOM	22
IF WE HAVE CHRIST'S ETHICS, DOES THE REST OF THE CHRISTIAN FAITH MATTER?	23
HOW WAS JESUS DIVINE?	24
ARE THERE ANY VALID OBJECTIONS TO FREE LOVE?	25
IS CHRISTIAN SEX MORALITY NARROW-MINDED AND OUT-OF-DATE?	25

Printed at the Oxonian Press, Ltd., 29 Queen Street, Oxford.

NOTE.—The selection of papers represented has been influenced by a variety of factors—e.g., historical interest, variety of subject matter, availability of the text, etc.—and the non-appearance of an outline of any paper is no reflection whatever on its interest or excellence—e.g., we would like to have included Mr. MacKinnon's paper on "Some Uses of the Word Rational," as it was of outstanding usefulness to the purposes of the Club, but pressure of work at the time of our going to press has prevented his having the leisure to expand the over-meager précis preserved in our Minutes. Likewise, Fr. d'Arcy's paper on the Existence of God does not lend itself to being fruitfully reduced to an outline, and lack of space precludes its reproduction in full. We would like to express our keen appreciation of the kindness of our speakers in giving us of their time and energy in the preparation of papers, and to thank them for subjecting themselves to being a one-man Brains Trust with such courtesy and patience.

OXFORD UNIVERSITY SOCRATIC CLUB

OFFICERS

President: C. S. LEWIS, M.A.   *Chairman*: STELLA ALDWINCKLE, M.A.

Secretaries and Treasurers:

1942	Hilary Term	Monica Shorten (Somerville)
		Patience Cunningham (St. Anne's)
	Trinity Term	Monica Shorten (Somerville)
		R. B. Joynson (Oriel)
	Michaelmas Term	M. Macnaughton-Smith (St. John's)
		J. M. Burch (Oriel)
1943	Hilary Term	Margaret Handover (St. Anne's)
		J. M. Burch (Oriel)
	Trinity Term	Margaret Handover (St. Anne's)
		J. M. Burch (Oriel)

PAPERS AND SPEAKERS
HILARY TERM, 1942

January 26th—Won't mankind outgrow Christianity in the face of the advance of science and of modern ideologies?
    R. E. HAVARD, M.D.
February 2nd—Is God a wish-fulfillment?
    Dr. WILLIAM STEVENSON
    (Assistant Director of the
    Institute of Experimental
    Psychology)
    C. S. LEWIS, M.A.
February 9th—Was Christ really any more than a great teacher and prophet?
    STELLA ALDWINCKLE, M.A.
February 16th—Skepticism and Faith
    W. B. MERCHANT, M.A.
    C. S. LEWIS, M.A.

February 23rd—Is Christian obscurantism hindering social progress?
    LORD ELTON
March 2nd—Are there any *valid* objections to free love?   CHARLES WILLIAMS
March 9th—Is prayer auto-suggestion?   Dr. L. W. GRENSTED

TRINITY TERM, 1942

April 29th—Some ambiguities in the use of the word "rational"   D. M. MACKINNON, M.A.
May 6th—Is it rational to believe in a 'personal' God?   Prof. W. G. DE BURGH
May 13th—Did Christ rise from the dead?   Rev. A. M. FARRER
    Prof. R. EISLER
May 20th—Can science render religion unnecessary?   Prof. H. A. HODGES
June 3rd—Has man a special place in the universe?   Dr. R. W. KOSTERLITZ

MICHAELMAS TERM, 1942

October 12th—Purpose and design in nature   Mr. J. Z. YOUNG
October 19th—Is a 'mechanistic' view of the universe scientifically tenable?
    Dr. MOTZ
October 26th—The concept of revelation   Mr. D. M. MACKINNON
November 2nd—How was Jesus divine?   Rev. A. M. FARRER
November 9th—Christianity and other world faiths   Prof. E. O. JAMES
November 16th—Christianity and Aesthetics, or "The Company accepts no liabilities"
    Mr. C. S. LEWIS
November 23rd—Is Christian sexual morality narrow-minded and out of date?
    Fr. GERALD VANN, O.P.

HILARY TERM, 1943

January 18th—Does Christianity foreclose philosophical enquiry?   Mr. D. M. MACKINNON
January 25th—What is prayer?   Rev. F. C. BRYAN
February 1st—Free will and Predestination   Prof. O. C. QUICK
February 8th—If we have Christ's ethics does the rest of the Christian faith matter?
    Mr. C. S. LEWIS
February 15th—Can the existence of God be proved?   Fr. D'ARCY, S.J.
February 22nd—Science and Faith   Dr. F. SHERWOOD-TAYLOR
March 1st—The political relevance of Christian metaphysics   Rev. Dr. V. A. DEMANT

TRINITY TERM, 1943

May 3rd—Is the New Testament reliable evidence?   Fr. KEHOE, O.P.
May 10th—Immortality   Rev. A. M. FARRER
May 17th—The Fall and the Unconscious   Dr. R. SCOTT-FRAYN
May 24th—Conscience and moral freedom   Dr. WILLIAM STEPHENSON
    Prof. L. W. GRENSTED

June 14ᵗʰ—Marxism and Christianity Prof. JOHN MACMURRAY
                                       Dr. COSSLETT
June 21ˢᵗ—Mysticism   DOM B. C. BUTLER, O.S.B.

SOCRATIC DIGEST

"Οὗτος μὲν οἴεταί τι εἰδέναι οὐκ εἰδώς, ἐγὼ δὲ ὥσπερ οὖν οὐκ οἶδα οὐδὲ οἴομαι."
—*Socrates*

"Εἴ τις δοκεῖ ἐγνωκέναι τι, οὔπω ἔγνω καθὼς δεῖ γνῶναι."
—*St. Paul*

"La dernière démarche de la raison est de reconnaître qu'il y a une infinité de choses qui la surpassent." —*Pascal*

PREFACE

Like a quietly efficient nurse arriving in a house confused by illness, or like the new general arriving at the siege of Ismail in Byron's *Don Juan*, our Chairman broke in (if she will pardon the word) during the autumn of 1941 on that welter of discussion which even in war-time makes up five-eighths of the night life of the Oxford undergraduate. By stages which must have been very swift (for I cannot remember them), we found that a new society had been formed, that it was attempting the difficult program of meeting once a week, that it was actually carrying this program out, that its numbers were increasing, and that neither foul weather nor crowded rooms (they were lucky who found seats even on the floor) would reduce the size of the meetings. This was the Socratic Club. Socrates had exhorted men to "follow the argument wherever it led them": the Club came into existence to apply his principle to one particular subject matter—the pros and cons of the Christian Religion.

It is a little remarkable that, to the best of my knowledge, no society had ever before been formed for such a purpose. There had been plenty of organizations that were explicitly Christian—the S.C.M., the Ark, the O.U.C.H., the O.I.C.C.U.—and there had been plenty of others, scientific or political, which were, if not explicitly, yet profoundly anti-Christian in outlook. The question about Christianity arose, no doubt, often enough in private conversation, and cast its shadow over the aesthetic or philosophical debates in many societies; but an arena specially devoted to the conflict between Christian and unbeliever was a novelty. Its value from a merely cultural point of view is very great. In any fairly large and talkative community such as a university there is always the danger that those who think alike should gravitate together into *côteries* where they will henceforth encounter opposition only in the emasculated form of rumor that the outsiders say thus and thus. The absent are easily refuted, complacent dogmatism thrives, and differences of opinion are embittered by group hostility. Each group hears not the best, but the worst, that the other group can say. In the Socratic all this was changed. Here a man could get the case for Christianity without all the paraphernalia of pietism and the case against it without the irrelevant *sansculottisme* of our common anti-God weeklies. At the very least we helped to civilize one another; sometimes we ventured to hope that if our Athenian patron were allowed to be present, unseen, at our meetings he might not have found the atmosphere wholly alien.

We also learned, in those motley—and usually stifling—assemblies where English boys fresh from public schools rubbed shoulders with elderly European *Gelehrten* in exile, almost any type of opinion might turn up. Everyone found how little he had known about everyone else. We of the Christian party discovered that the weight of the skeptical attack did not always come where we expected it; our opponents had to correct what seemed to us their almost bottomless ignorance of the Faith they supposed themselves to be rejecting.

It is (theoretically) a difficulty in the British Constitution that the Speaker of the House of Commons must himself be a member of one of the Parties. There is a similar difficulty about the Socratic. Those who founded it do not for one moment pretend to be neutral. It was the Christians who constructed the arena and issued the challenge. It will therefore always be possible for the lower (the less Athenian) type of unbeliever to regard the whole thing as a cunningly—or not even so very cunningly—disguised form of propaganda. The Athenian type, if he had this objection to make, would put it in a paper and read that paper to the Socratic itself. He would be welcome to do so—though I doubt whether he would have the stomach if he knew with what pains and toil the committee has scoured *Who's Who* to find intelligent atheists who had leisure or zeal to come and propagate their creed. But when all is said and done, the answer to any such suspicion lies deeper. It is not here that the honesty of the Socratic comes in. We never claimed to be impartial. But argument is. It has a life of its own. No man can tell where it will go. We expose ourselves, and the weakest of our party, to your fire no less than you are exposed to ours. Worse still, we expose ourselves to the recoil from our own shots; for if I may trust my personal experience no doctrine is, for the moment, dimmer to the eye of faith than that which a man has just successfully defended. The arena is common to both parties and cannot finally be cheated; in it you risk nothing, and we risk all.

Others may have quite a different objection to our proceedings. They may protest that intellectual discussion can neither build Christianity nor destroy it. They may feel that religion is too sacred to be thus bandied to and fro in public debate, too sacred to be talked of—almost, perhaps, too sacred for anything to be done with it at all. Clearly, the Christian members of the Socratic think differently. They know that intellectual assent is not faith, but they do not believe that religion is only "what a man does with his solitude." Or, if it is, then they care nothing for "religion" and all for Christianity. Christianity is not merely what a man does with his solitude. It is not even what God does with His solitude. It tells of God descending into the coarse publicity of history and there enacting what can—and must—be talked about.

C. S. Lewis

SOCRATES WAS A REALIST

One afternoon towards the end of the Michaelmas Term, 1941, a fresher (afterwards our first Secretary) was complaining that no one seemed ready to discuss the deeper agnostic questionings seriously. "The sermons and the religious clubs just take the real difficulties as solved—things like the existence of God, the divinity of Christ, and so on." As a one-time agnostic myself, I could understand and sympathize deeply. I asked her whether she knew others who felt as she did. "Yes, plenty." "Well, collect them together and we'll see what we can do." A startling notice forthwith appeared on Somerville notice-boards, exhorting "all atheists, agnostics, and those who are disillusioned about religion or think they are," to come to the East J.C.R. at an appointed hour. There they fulminated (I was told) for twenty minutes against the shortcomings of religious clubs and sermons. As a Daniel to the den of lions, I went a few days later to face this formidable assembly, prepared to be torn limb from limb. They proved to be consideration and courtesy itself, but their questions showed me where their needs lay. An open forum for the discussion of the intellectual difficulties connected with religion in general and with Christianity in particular was the obvious solution, and Mr. C. S. Lewis the obvious President. The interest aroused quickly spread to other colleges, and from the women's to the men's, and the Socratic Club came into being.

The Club, it must be explained, is intended for "realists," not for "escapists," for those, that is to say, who purpose to get at the truth about existence, if such there be, whatever the difficulty or the cost involved: it is not meant for the dilettante intellectual poseur who prefers to substitute abstract discussion about truth for the effort to live by it. Socrates who drank the hemlock is our patron. We have no time, at such a crisis in history, to use our minds to justify ourselves in avoiding costly decisions. Real thought leads on to action or to a way of living, as Socrates showed. We insist on being not rationalistic but rational.

Many, of course, of the undergraduates coming up are self-centered and narrow-minded enough to be out for their own interests only: some for "having a good time," others for winning a short-lived local glory by displaying their talents, and many wish to see no deeper into life than to envisage a good class in Schools and the avocation which is to follow. But there are others who already have some dim conception of self-fulfillment as distinct from self-expression, and who do not take lightly the privilege of coming up to the University: who mean to become rational and adult, and who stubbornly assume with Socrates that existence has some significance, and are prepared to wrestle with it till it yields its secret. To them skepticism is not enough. Their reason, and not only their desire, tells them as much. They insist on asking *ultimate* questions. But the Christian Faith as they have met it in conventional or hypocritical Christians, bad sermons or inefficient Scripture lessons at school, is worse than irrelevant: it is sentimental, escapist, impractical and superstitious. Self-respect and love of humanity drive them to atheism or agnosticism. Unless they can swallow the optimistic and over-simplified solution of Marxism, or rest content with some relative objective that avoids asking those ultimate questions, they are left without star or chart to steer by. They see the futility of a self-centered life; the more discerning among them come to realize the *spiritual failure of being successfully "ethical"*—even supposing that they can discover a philosophically satisfying sanction for ethics which the physicists tell them is "running down." It is for such ruthless "realists" that the Socratic primarily exists.

From the endless questions raised by such an approach, two main ones emerge: First, is existence significant at all? (for Socratics will have no truck with naïve "wish-fulfillment thinking," however urgent the personal need for an absolute objective may be). Secondly, if it is, and "ethical" living remains a spiritual bondage because it cannot deliver from the egocentric motive, is there any way out of that bondage? The Socratic meetings are designed to summon Reason to wrestle with the first problem, and to assess the relevance (if any) of the Christian Faith to its solution. The question is found to be not as simple as the undergraduate agnostic in the first flush of a gloriously dogmatic and anti-authoritarian atheism had decided in his or her VIth Form circle that it is. The speakers, Christian and non-Christian are specialists in their respective subjects, and give more than a popular insight into their several spheres of study. It begins to be realized that only a *conspectus* of the various types of data about life can give a balanced judgment: to go on concentrating on red patches or tables and chairs with the philosophers, or on atoms, hormones, equations or creedal definitions with the scientists, mathematicians and theologians, or on political and economic crises or the Unconscious with the historians, economists and psychologists, is not to be rational or scientific, but to believe in wearing blinkers. We of the Socratic insist on being *intellectually* respectable.

Thus after the first few somewhat bewildering meetings the issues at stake may begin to appear, and the complexity of their ramifications. Questions are raised but tantalizingly evade being finally answered. And now the problems of the universe are settled with a shade less finality over the beer mugs and the midnight oil. For, when all is said and done, it can be seen that ratiocination can give no more than probabilities in the matter of "truth about life." Sooner or later the perception may dawn on some that knowledge of such truth is not finally an intellectual judgment at all, and that the whole man must be involved, will and action as well as reason. But what we do expect the intellect to do is to clarify the issues, and that is an imperative task, for it is not only the undergraduate who finds it difficult to see what those issues are: the modern world is full, for instance, of impressively learned men and women (some of them Christians, too) who fail to perceive two complementary truths: that Christianity is organically bound up with ethics and *yet* that if it is reduced to being in essence no more than an ethical code, it ceases to be itself and therefore to have any relevance whatever to the fundamental human problem of spiritual bondage and moral failure.

To grasp the issues clearly, to probe beneath the surface of facile answers and false generalizations, to be impatient of the "worm's-eye view," and of the pigeon-hole mind, to be locked in mortal combat with Bulverism[1] and all its works, above all to scorn wishful-thinking and escapist cowardice—these are our Socratic tasks.

With the second main question, therefore (that as to the way out of the *impasse* created by the power of evil), the Socratic as such is not directly concerned. But for certain members who wished to have that question answered, a short weekend Conference was arranged at Jordans (March 13th to 16th). There some of them found that, on certain conditions, there *is* an answer, and that they had been right to trust their intuition that skepticism and cynicism are not finally justified any more in the twentieth century than in the first.

STELLA ALDWINCKLE

---

[1] NOTE.—We hope to give a diagnosis of this prevalent modern mental disease in our next issue.

THE FIRST MEETING

The first meeting of the Socratic Club was held in Somerville East J.C.R. on Monday, January 26th, at 8 p.m.

The Speaker: Dr. R. E. Havard, M.D.

The Subject: "Won't mankind outgrow Christianity in the face of the advance of Science and of Modern Ideologies?"

The Chairman opened the meeting with a brief description of the nature and aims of the Club. She said it had been formed for those who do not necessarily wish to commit themselves to Christian views but are interested in a philosophical approach to religion in general and Christianity in particular. It was pointed out that this was especially important today in view of the present war and the obvious bearing of creed on personal and social ethics.

The Chairman said that the Club was not interested in mere debating or in the conventional answers, but that its aim was rather to enable its members to think out an "intellectually respectable" philosophy of life. It was impossible for individuals to go deeply enough into the varied branches of knowledge whose evidence affects the issue so vitally, and too much time was wasted in arguing with those equally ignorant.

The speakers of the Socratic Club were to be chosen to introduce subjects of which they have made a careful study and about which they are willing and competent to attempt to answer questions.

The speaker was then introduced.

Dr. Havard said that he had himself deserted Christianity, in the face of the advance of science, for some years; and proceeded to give an account of his opinions at that time, and the reasons for his changed point of view.

He defined a Christian as one who believes that Christ was and is God, emphasizing that Christianity is a matter not only of morals, but of beliefs. As a scientist he had elevated the uniformity of Nature to an absolute principle, discarding all the supernatural in Christianity, although retaining an admiration for its ethics. After a study of the beliefs of the Roman Catholic Church his views had altered, and he came to the conclusion that to accept any other interpretation of events described in the Gospels was to raise greater difficulties than the ones arising from the traditional Christian interpretation. The speaker remarked that it was unlikely that such men as Thomas Aquinas, Thomas More, Erasmus, Pasteur, Ronald Knox or Archbishop Temple had failed to notice that God walking the earth as man seemed at first sight unlikely. After reading the Dialogues of Plato he doubted if modern man was superior to the Ancients just because he knew more of the physical world.

Talking of the so-called conflict between Science and Christianity, the speaker emphasized that they operated in different spheres. It was as if one man said: "It is very fine today"; and the other: "On the contrary, it is half-past four!" Hostility was more apparent between scientists and philosophers.

On the subject of the Menace of Modern Ideologies to Christianity, Dr. Havard pointed out that although all intellectual fashions seem to be irresistible in their day they do not outgrow the Christian Creed. Christianity was very unpopular in the first and third centuries, and unfashionable in the eighteenth—but it continued to survive.

In conclusion, the speaker gave it as his opinion that man's intellectual trust in the advances of science and in modern ideologies would not prove to be permanent.

A DISCUSSION followed.

The speaker was asked:

If he could equate the theory of Evolution with the accepted Roman Catholic creationist view?

If the soul evolved or if it occurred suddenly, and if so at what point?

If the fact that you admired a Christian proved that he was well-advised to be a Christian?

The speaker was reminded:

That the Roman Catholic Church had been an obstacle to science in the past and might continue to be so in the future.

That when a scientist postulates that he is able to understand the universe he means that he can understand the relevant facts *he* has selected, and in religious discussion it is impossible to be sure that all the relevant facts have been considered.

IS GOD A WISH-FULFILLMENT?

Dr. Stephenson and Mr. C. S. Lewis

Dr. Stephenson said that his position in regard to the question of the existence of God was one of neutrality, but that he held the accepted views of the psychological school of thought.

He said that believing, as he did, in the Law of the Conservation of Energy, he denied that it was possible for Man's ideas of religion to spring from his mind with no cause. They were a direct gratification of his aspirations, caused by a naturally developed need in him.

God was a dramatization of all the fears, hopes and longings arising in a child in regard to its parents. As the child realized the limits of his parent's power, he created a God in the outside world to deal with his difficulties.

It was pointed out that the history of man's religious tendencies was an unbroken sequence of the development of this need.

The culture of a country affects that country's idea of God. A normal development leads man to become a type such as the scientist or the artist, in whom are satisfied the natural needs he has recognized. Abnormal development leads to various complexes, positive sublimation or self-denial, irrational views and morbidity.

Mr. C. S. Lewis rose to reply.

He remarked that Dr. Stephenson had him at a disadvantage, for: (1) from the psychologist's point of view God was a wish-fulfillment, whether good or bad; (2) by speaking first he had proved that there was an explanation for the belief in God, on the basic assumption that God did not exist. Mr. Lewis asserted that he could explain away disbelief in God on the basic assumption that God did exist.

He said that it was essential to prove that it was an error to believe in God before explaining the cause of the error.

A Discussion followed.

The first was asked if there were not a significant difference between a belief in God and a need of God.

On being confronted with a belief in the Resurrection, the speaker said that he did not accept it as an historical fact. Naturally Man wished to believe in this more than in anything else. It is vital to his peace of mind.

The speaker was asked to explain why, on his view, (1) a child believed in God even if his father had died before his birth. (2) Many men had believed in an infinity of Gods. (Hardly caused by having an infinity of fathers!)

The speaker was reminded of the ego in man, of which psychologists knew little, and which might be equated with the eternal soul.

CAN SCIENCE RENDER RELIGION UNECESSARY?

Professor H. A. Hodges

Professor Hodges first spoke about the exact meaning of the title of his paper. He pointed out that he was not called upon to discuss whether science could show religion to be false, but whether it could undermine the necessity or utility of it. Erroneous beliefs might be useful and the truth was often useless. "Science," he said, in this context must have its widest meaning, so as to include not only the natural sciences, but also the social and historical sciences and the whole of modern knowledge.

The question in the title arose from a widespread feeling, first, that statements about God were not to be taken seriously, and were not so much false as boring; and second, that it was possible to "get along quite well without religious techniques," and that, therefore, though religion might once have been useful, it was not so now. After a man had reached this decision he experienced a feeling of relief at finding himself in a simpler and more unified world.

Professor Hodges defined religion as an active relationship with God, its nature depending on God's action rather than on man's. In Christianity, which did maturely what the other religions did less maturely, the relationship meant imitation of God as revealed in Christ, and it showed itself in an activity which had three aspects: the life of private devotion, the organized institutional life, and the life of free fluid groups. It was only healthy when these three elements were properly balanced. This was genuine pseudo-religions, e.g., religion as a giver of good luck, or of supernatural powers for selfish ends, or as a heightener of morale.

He then argued that science (i.e. modern knowledge) could not attack genuine Christianity, but that it had a very destructive effect upon the pseudo-religions. The luck, prosperity, and personal power techniques were discredited or shown to rest on something other than God. A new emotional attitude to the world, not of fear, but of power, was generated. In proportion as social stresses were removed, God as a policeman would be abandoned, and when psychotherapists succeeded in resolving frustration complexes and curing neurotic cases there would be no need for that kind of pseudo-religion.

Although it was only these secondary uses of religion on the wrong levels that were threatened by the advance of modern knowledge, to many people these constituted the whole of religion. For these people, therefore, religion would become incredible and uninteresting. They might find life tolerably satisfying without it, and yet that did not alter the fact that it could be even more full and satisfying with true religion.

PURPOSE AND DESIGN IN NATURE

Mr. J. Z. Young

Mr. Young began by apologizing for the fact that he was neither a philosopher nor a logician, and emphasized that he would treat the subject from the point of view of a biologist. It was also unlikely that he would come to any final conclusions. His paper was divided into three parts: the logical, the technical, and general observations. The second of these would bear the most weight as he was best equipped to deal with the technical aspect.

He defined the word "design" as pattern with a purpose, while pattern itself consists of a sequence of events. Purpose is apprehended by recognizing that the end is conceived by some other entity like ourselves; it implies striving and the persistence of an action through changing circumstances. In Nature, this persistence characterizes living organisms, and causes an increasing adaptation to increasingly varied environments. There is also in Nature a tendency to expand and increase the "bio-mass." The most important change takes place in nervous organization.

Mr. Young next said that, though the biologist does not make use of the concept of mind, it cannot be denied that something very like a mind is present in the higher mammals, and possible in varying degrees, in the lower organisms.

The expansion of life and the development of intelligence are laws of Nature. They do not provide adequate bases for the religious or moral codes. Although religious knowledge cannot be analyzed the biologist can examine it in the light of his technical knowledge. He finds much in religion that conflicts with this: for instance, the religious claim to absolute knowledge, and the suppression of the individual's status in the community; but he can respect the renunciation of power by religious organizations.

With regard to morals, over-strict codes had been put forward by moralists, many of whom failed to appreciate the complexity of life. In conclusion, Mr. Young said that the development of mind had not been fully reached, and to achieve its fuller penetration into our lives is one of our most important duties.

Mr. Lewis opened the discussion by agreeing with the speaker's definition of purpose, but pointed out that a mere repetition of effort is not in itself an adequate criterion. He disagreed with the moral assumption that we must expedite the tendency to increase the bio-mass simply because this tendency exists.

A general DISCUSSION followed in which it emerged that, although Mr. Young made use of moral judgments, they could not be derived either from biology or from astronomy.

FREE WILL AND PREDESTINATION

Prof. O. C. Quick

I have been asked to speak about Free Will and Predestination; and I must apologize if, after hearing what I have to say, you think I have come here under false pretences. The truth is that the actual problem of Free Will and Predestination in itself does not greatly interest me. For I cannot escape the intuition that it is not so much a real problem as a logical puzzle which conceals rather than expresses the fundamental problem which lies behind it. On that ground I thought at first of declining your kind invitation to speak about the subject. On second thought, however, I felt that, after all, that would be rather a mean evasion. At least I could try to explain why I do not think the problem of Free Will and Predestination is fundamental, and what I think the really fundamental problem is. And that is what I propose very diffidently to do. I emphasize the word "diffidently" because for the sake of clearness I propose to talk in an apparently dogmatic way. I must ask you therefore to forgive me if I approach my professed subject very obliquely, and if the relevance of my starting point is not immediately apparent. I propose (1) to say something of the theological background against which the Christian has to view the fact and the problem of human free will; (2) to consider the human foreground, the nature and implications of free will itself; (3) to relate the foreground to the background, and in so doing to define what I think the really fundamental problem to be.

(1) The Theological Background

In order to sketch this background, I will start by asking an apparently irrelevant question: what does it mean to say that man was originally created in God's image? Brunner in his book *Man in Revolt* has recently reminded us of an important distinction which patristic theologians, beginning with Irenaeus, drew in answering this question. They distinguished between two elements in the divine image, (*a*) the *imago* or εἰκών; (*b*) the *similitudo*, or ὅμοίωσις. The first, they said, consisted in the rationality and free will which constitute human nature as such. This *imago* was retained, substantially unaffected, after the Fall of man. The second, the *similitudo*, consisted in man's self-determination according to God's will and in the communion with God which went with it. This *similitudo* was enjoyed by unfallen man as a special gift of God's grace, and it was forfeited and lost by the Fall.

Like Brunner, though for very different reasons, I find this distinction and its consequences unsatisfactory. And I want to suggest an answer to the main question which seems to me simpler and which to some extent cuts across or even inverts the patristic distinction. Man's likeness to God consists primarily in his power of choice and of his purposive control over things. Within limits man can choose both the ends of his action and the means whereby he pursues them, and in so doing he exercises control over his environment, over nature, over his fellow creatures, and even over himself. He knows in his own experience what ownership and lordship mean. And thus, alone of all creatures, he possesses a limited and relative *independence* of his own, wherein he is like, though still unlike, the infinite Creator, who is dependent on nothing outside himself and can fashion and control all things according to his will.

Clearly the power of conscious choice resides in the individual man; and the Church has always maintained that it is the individual who is the bearer of God's image. Hence arises an obvious paradox. The very power in the individual which makes him godlike involves him in a capacity utterly ungodlike—i.e., the capacity to choose and do what is wrong. It is because the individual is godlike that he may be sinful. Only the creature made in God's image can really sin against God. To call animal instincts sinful is mere confusion of thought—unless indeed we suppose them to have been already perverted or disordered by the agency of some spirit already fallen and sinful. No doubt the animal nature with its instincts is the raw material of sin, the *fomes peccati* which the spark of willful rebellion kindles into actual sin. But the same nature is also the raw material of goodness, *fomes caritatis*, which willed obedience kindles into love. In themselves the instincts are morally neutral. It is the free and spiritual will, the highest element in human nature which is the source of virtue and vice. Christian theology owes a debt to the heresiarch, Apollinarius, for making this truth so clear.

But the paradox of man's godlikeness has deeper implications which take us to the heart of our subject. All things are utterly dependent on God, the author of all, the one absolute Owner and Lord. How can there be anyone except God who has any real independence at all? Theologians are obliged, I think, to answer that such a thing can only be because of the mysterious self-limitation of the Creator whereby he permits to his creatures free action of which he is not himself the efficient cause. (I shall return to that point presently.) But then they must surely go on to say that this equivocal position, in which godlikeness involves the capacity and possibility of rebellion against God, though it is man's beginning, cannot possibly be man's end. Man cannot rest in it eternally. God, we must say, has assigned to man such a position for a time and for a purpose, so that of his own free will he will surrender himself, with all that he has made his own, to God's love which gave him power so to give. From the beginning man's true end is not so much to be *godlike* as to find himself *in* God through the voluntary offering up and surrender of that real independence which, even in making him godlike, separated him initially from God and from his fellows.

This line of thought, you will notice, cuts across the patristic distinctions between the *imago* and the *similitudo*. From our point of view it is less important to distinguish two elements in the divine image than to distinguish man's initial stage before the Fall from his final state after redemption, man's beginning from man's end. In the first we find godlikeness, in the second perfection of communion with God. In the first we find fullness of responsibility, in the second fullness of *responsiveness* to God. In the first we find the freedom which accompanies responsibility, freedom of choice, of ownership and control. In the second we find the utterly unburdened and glorious liberty of the children of God, the perfect freedom of the child at home in his father's house.

But what of sin? And how does man's present sinful state affect his freedom? The possibility of sin, we have seen, is due to man's initial freedom of choice which makes him godlike. But this freedom or independence is evidently, like man's nature, finite and limited and therefore unlike God's. And inevitably the finitude of man's mind splits up the full unity and harmony of goodness, and makes different goods appear as in rivalry and competition with one another. Therefore man's initial freedom is freedom to choose between mutually exclusive alternatives. To choose one is to reject the others, and also to be responsible as well for the choice as the rejection. Hence this power of choice which in one aspect is freedom is in another aspect a burden (the migrating bird and the rich man). It belongs to a condition of being which is imperfect, unfulfilled, not final. "Ye therefore," said Christ, "shall be perfect, even as your Father which is in heaven is perfect." This saying contains both the precept and the promise of the gospel. But precept and promise alike can only be finally fulfilled when the burden of responsibility has wholly vanished in the complete responsiveness of communion. Meanwhile, man's will must be trained for final self-surrender by constantly choosing the higher good in preference to the lower.

We may, I think, rightly imagine that such training would have been necessary, even if man had never actually sinned. Nevertheless, in that case there would have been no such inner conflict and perplexity as we now experience. For man in his own pure nature would have discerned and chosen the higher good naturally by the unfailing help of God's supernatural grace. However that may be, we know, in the light of the Christian revelation, that the critical and crucial moment of man's choice must always come when the supreme good of love has to be absolutely preferred to the lower good of lordship, acquisition or self-assertion. In God and in the soul finally surrendered to God these two goods are perfectly one and harmonious, so that choice between them is not required or even possible. It is indeed only by the final and complete self-surrender of love that the soul can win its own royal lordship in Christ's Kingdom. But in man's initial state of finite independence, in which he must choose, the good of love and the good of lordship must present themselves to him as a dilemma; one must be taken and the other left. Sin is the choice which affirms the finite independent self, its lordship and acquisitiveness, against love and obedience to God. Once that fatal choice has been made, sin with its dire consequences of corruption has gained a foothold in human nature and the consequences are transmitted to every soul that is naturally born. Henceforth man's nature is marred. Not that there is no good left in him, or that the divine image or free will has been lost. But man's nature conditions the powers of his mind and will. And, the nature having been marred, man's discernment is insufficient and his will, at best, too weak to enable him to attain full self-surrender without a fresh and special intervention of redeeming grace. We may define the effect of the Fall on man's freedom by saying that, though man retains the capacity (δύναμις) to be a true son of God, he has lost the actual power (ἐξουσία). "There is no *health* in him." "To as many as received him to them gave he ἐξουσία to become sons of God, even to those who believe on his name."

(2) THE HUMAN FOREGROUND

So much for the theological background against which the Christian has to view the problem of human free will. Let us now turn to the purely human foreground itself.

What is a free action?

First, I think, we have to determine the relevant sense of the word action. In its widest sense action denotes simply causal efficacy in the concrete. Every instance of efficient causation is an action, and all existing entities, insofar as they are causes, may be said to act. Fire acts in burning, and water acts in quenching fire. A man also acts in lighting a fire or in quenching it with water. So far there is no difference between the animate and the inanimate agent.

But within this quite general meaning of the word action we have first to distinguish vital action from mechanical. The peculiarity of vital action may be described by saying that it involves some movement which cannot be wholly accounted for unless we suppose it to be determined in some degree by the future as well as by the past. The action of a billiard ball in striking another, or of an explosive in detonating, is mechanical, because we account for the action of the ball or the explosive solely by reference to what has happened to it. The action of a plant in growing towards the light, or of an animal in seeking food, is vital, not mechanical, insofar as we cannot wholly account for it without some reference to the effect which light will have on the plant or food on the animal.

Next, within the class of vital actions, we have to distinguish between the special characteristic of those which are purposive. An action is called purposive when we cannot wholly account for it unless we suppose it to be partly determined by some future possibility, consciously apprehended, towards the actualization of which it is directed.

Suppose a man knocks a boy down, and the boy gets up and runs away. The action of the boy in falling down is mechanical. His action in getting up and running away is vital. And it is also purposive, insofar as you suppose it to be determined by the boy's conscious apprehension that he will be safer at a distance.

Now free will is exercised only in purposive actions: and these require further analysis. When we act with a purpose and freely (*a*) we apprehend a future state of things that is to be brought about; (*b*) we decide to bring it about for some reason; (*c*) we initiate that series of causal movements which seems appropriate to bring it about. In every purposive action there are really five elements involved:—

(1). The actual state of things to be brought about—the object.
(2). That for the sake of which we desire to bring it about—the end.
(3). The desire for the end which moves our will in deciding to act—the motive.
(4). The series of movements initiated by the decision of the will—the process.
(5). The decision of the will itself.

Thus in the case just imagined: the object of the boy's action is to be at a distance from the man who struck him. The end is safety from another blow. The motive is the desire for safety. The process the movements of running. Or suppose I get up and shut the window. The object is the shutting. The end, perhaps, to exclude the draught. The motive my desire to exclude the draught. The process my bodily movements which terminate the shutting of the window.

But where is the freedom of the action, and in what does it consist? Speaking in terms of man's initial freedom, freedom from compulsion, freedom of alternative, I should say that freedom resides in the decision of the will, and it consists in the fact that the decision has no efficient cause, but is itself a fresh efficient cause introducing itself into the situation. That is what freedom of the will means. But we must be very careful to define exactly what we mean if we say that a free action is uncaused.

(1) We do not mean that it is unmotivated, or that it is without final cause or end. On the contrary, its whole character consists in the fact that it is done from a motive in order to realize an end. And undoubtedly the desires, nature and character of the agent operate all the time as efficient causes which have their proper and inevitable effects. They restrict the limits within which the will can choose, they, together with outward circumstances, set the conditions of his choice; they influence the decision itself. But they do not efficiently cause it. If they did, not only the freedom but the really purposive character of the action would vanish. It would be wholly caused by *vis a tergo*, like the movement of the billiard ball, it would be in the last resort mechanical.

(2) We do not mean that free action depends on any degree of uncertainty or unpredictability either (*a*) in the decision of the will itself, or (*b*) in the behavior of anything else.

(*a*) It is not true that the decision of free will, because it is uncaused, is unpredictable. A man does not become less free to choose, in proportion as his choices are predictable. On the contrary, my friend's freedom to accept a bribe is in no way diminished by the fact that I know him well enough to predict with certainty that he will not accept it. His freedom is impaired only if I seek to maintain that his upright character is the efficient cause of his decision to reject a bribe.

(*b*) As regards the behavior of other things, it is evident that a man's freedom of action depends entirely on its predictability. I cannot even light my pipe if I cannot depend on the behavior of the match, nor lift my hand if I cannot depend on the behavior of nerves and muscles. If the accomplishment of my purpose depends on the behavior of other free personal agents, I must be able to predict what that behavior under given conditions will be.

It seems then the whole connection which is often assumed to exist between freedom of the will and some kind of uncertainty, unreliability or unpredictability is really an illusion, the result of defective analysis. The illusion seems generally to be caused by confusing indeterminateness, or what Aristotle and St. Thomas called *passive potentiality*, with freedom. According to Aristotle primary matter is quite indeterminate, and it is capable of being determined by every possible variety of form. In the same way the character of a child, which as we say is still unformed, is relatively indeterminate; it is capable of a greater variety of changes and developments than that of an adult which is already formed and relatively fixed and stable. But in no case has such indeterminateness anything to do with freedom. Primary matter is not more free than the mind because it is more indeterminate; on the contrary, it is not free at all. And again the child, being relatively indeterminate, has less freedom of deliberate choice than the man. The child's instability of purpose makes his free actions both less predictable and less free. The freedom of the freely willed action consists not in any indeterminateness but in the fact that the act of the will is determined by the deliberate purposive choice of the agent and not by an efficient cause either inside or outside himself. In other words, the act of will, insofar as it is free, is determined by final, not by efficient causes: and it is the *expression*, not the effect, of the character. But it is not for that reason more uncertain or less predictable.

The confusion between indeterminateness and freedom becomes apparent, as it seems to me, in Berdyaev's doctrine of so-called meonic freedom, which is merely the indeterminateness of Aristotle's primary matter, but which, nevertheless, Berdyaev supposes in some inexplicable way to be the cause or ground of freedom in man.

Once this confusion is entirely cleared out of the way, the problem of the apparent conflict between divine predestination and human free will appears far less insoluble in principle.

(3) Relation of the Foreground to the Background

The truth of predestination lies primarily in the absoluteness of divine omniscience. God knows how all men will behave in all possible circumstances, and he knows the end of all and each. If we allow ourselves—as we can hardly help allowing ourselves sometimes—to speak as though the divine knowledge existed at a particular point in time, we may then say that God foreknows or can predict with certainty the behavior of every man in every event. It is God's knowledge which makes his purposes absolutely certain of achievement. God cannot be surprised by anything that happens. All the events in the whole universe will work out according to God's plan and design to the end which to his knowledge is certain.

The truth of human free will consists in the fact that the free and purposive decisions of the will are not effects of any efficient cause, and are not determined by efficient causes. This truth is in principle reconcilable with the other, if we suppose that God who is the first efficient cause of the being of all things, freely limits his own action as efficient cause so as to leave room for man's free will to choose and decide man's own purposive actions. Granted this self-limitation on God's part, the reality of human free will does not conflict either with the omniscience or with the omnipotence of God. For as to omniscience there is no conflict, unless we suppose (erroneously) that everything which is certainly predictable must be the effect of efficient causes. And as to omnipotence, omnipotence can only mean God's power to achieve his purpose in all things. And if, as I have previously suggested, the Creator's original purpose was that man should attain to eternal life through free and voluntary self-surrender to Himself, any action on God's part which supersedes or takes away human freedom is necessarily a sign of failure in God, and therefore of weakness rather than power. God's design in redemption is to save fallen man by *grace*, which does not and cannot act as an efficient cause of man's free decisions but only as an *influence* and an illumination which give man power to choose and decide rightly. It is simply a means of achieving after all, in spite of sin, the original purpose with which man was created. Even if some souls are to be eternally *lost*, the possibility of such perdition is understood by Christians as a witness to God's refusal to interfere with or contradict his original work of creation in making man free. Belief in hell is not anti-humanistic; it is the very proof of Christian humanism, because it safeguards to the uttermost the dignity of man as a free being who can determine his own destiny. The Christian will only contend that the final issue can never be such as to show that man had better not have been created. To conclude that μὴ θυναι τον ἅπαντα νικᾷ λόγον (best never to be born) is sheer paganism, even though the Savior himself said of an individual, "Good were it for that man if he had not been born."

I conclude that there is an insoluble mystery and problem in the relation of man to God. But the essence of that mystery does not really consist in the alleged conflict between divine predestination and human free will. Rather it lies in the antinomy between human *free will* and *createdness*, or in other words in the fact that any *creature* should be made in the true image and likeness of the Creator. As a creature, man, like any other creature, owes his whole being to the action of an efficient cause, God's will. And yet, insofar as he is free, man's decisions have no efficient cause at all. That is to say, this creature is not merely a creature; he bears the image and likeness of uncreatedness—he is a really originating and initiating cause of his own actions, it is that fact, and that alone, which gives him knowledge of creation, and of his own createdness, and of God his creator. But the paradox is extreme, and philosophers are hardly to be blamed for refusing to face it. They try desperately and in vain to find the source of man's freedom not in his likeness to God but at the other end of the scale in the indeterminateness of some primary matter out of which man is made. They might as well worship the Goddess τύχη or suppose that sheer indeterminateness can be the cause why things are thus determined. (Whitehead).

In truth, behind all metaphysics, there is one and only one fundamental problem, to which every other takes us back in the end. Is God made in the image of man, or man in the image of God? One or other proposition must be true. The first is the answer of Protagoras who said ἄνθρωπος μέτρον πάντων (man the measure of all things). It has been revived in modern times by multifarious forms of pragmatism and so-called humanism, which bear witness to the truth of Broad's rather malicious remark that all good fallacies go to America when they die. The second is the answer hinted at by Plato, first revealed to the Jews, and finally established by Christianity. It is not my task here to defend that answer. I have only tried to indicate that it is the basis of all Christian thought about the relations of God and man, including the problem of predestination and free will.

CONSCIENCE AND MORAL FREEDOM

Dr. Stephenson and Prof. Grensted

Dr. Stephenson first described the structure of our conscience as it exists from our earliest years. There is the superego which exists chiefly in the unconscious. It is superior only in harshness, setting itself up as a vicious judge which gives to such misdeeds as stealing a penny a fantastic moral importance.

Then there is the influence of society which makes a Scotch Puritan think thrift a virtue and an American admire pep. Thus a certain moral sense is developed, but Dr. Stephenson could not see in either of these influences any metaphysical significance.

He thought Justice and Truth could be found in a set of tertiary qualities which it is now thought have a reality of their own instead of that of mere association in our minds. Such are the smiling quality of a pleasant landscape, rough, cheerful, or graceful, and in the same way, he thought, the qualities of Truth and Justice.

To enable them to function freely the harsh superego and the influence of society must be eased, since at the moment they make a free act of will impossible. The superego can be opened up and indeed once this is done betterment immediately sets in. Dr. Stephenson admitted, however, that the superego was too deeply rooted for the individual to do this for himself.

Professor Grensted began by saying he did not disagree with Dr. Stephenson, but wished to add a complementary theory.

Conscience in his opinion indicated some maladjustment between the individual and his environment; sometimes the problem was a pseudo-conscience which set itself above the true conscience and from which the individual must be liberated. He would distinguish between the ego, the superego—a structure within the ego—and what he called the ego ideal, an integral part which he connected with the true conscience. In the ego ideal there is an immanent creative process which is challenged by an objective creative process and which will respond if the superego does not become a tyrant. For instance, a man should respond to the smiling quality in a pleasant landscape; if he does not this creative process is checked.

Free will does not lie where we often put it—in a power of choice—but in a real freedom—to respond or not to respond to the creative process.

In the discussion Dr. Senf protested against a refusal to go from science to metaphysics, pointing out that all natural science has sprung from theology.

Mr. Lewis also contributed an analysis of the three uses of the word conscience. First, one's judgment of what is good and evil; second, the sense of obligation to obey that judgment; and third, the emotional weight attached to obedience or disobedience to that judgment. The activity of the superego is evident in the third, and partly in the second, but apparently not in the first.

IF WE HAVE CHRIST'S ETHICS, DOES THE REST OF THE CHRISTIAN FAITH MATTER?

Mr. C. S. Lewis

Mr. Lewis first demonstrated the existence of a massive and immemorial moral law by listing precepts from Greek, Roman, Chinese, Babylonian, Ancient Egyptian, and Old Norse sources. By this account of the immutable laws of general and special beneficence, duties to parents and to children, of justice, good faith and of the law of mercy, three illusions were dispelled; first, that the expression "Christian moral principles" means anything different from "moral principles"; secondly, the anthropological illusion that the crude and barbarous man is the natural and normal man; and, thirdly, that the great disease of humanity is ignorance and the great cure, education. On the contrary, it is only too obvious that while there is massive and immemorial agreement about moral law, there is also a massive and immemorial inability to obey it.

In considering the remedy for the cleavage between human nature and generally accepted moral law, Mr. Lewis first separated from normal humanity those faddists, whether Epicureans, Communists or H. G. Wells, whose indefensible naivety forbade them to understand the actual condition of Man. The remainder of humanity would be divided into the ordinary mass of pagan mankind and Christians. Both these classes of men know the Moral Law and recognize their own inability to keep it. Both endeavor to deal with this tragic situation. The Pagan mysteries and Christianity are two alternative solutions, and whatever falls outside these two is simply naïve. Now the differentia of Christianity, as against pagan mystery religions, lies in its survival, its historical core, its combination of the ethical and the sacramental, its ability to produce that "new man" which all rites of initiation premise and finally its restraining effect upon a community under its domination.

The datum is the complete cleavage between human behavior and the code of morals which humanity acknowledges. And Christianity is the cure for this particular disease. For "excellent instructions" we have always had, the problem is how to obey them. To ask whether the rest of the Christian Faith matters when we have Christ's ethics presupposes a world of unfallen men with no need for redemption. "The rest of the Christian Faith" is the means of carrying out, instead of merely being able to discourse on, the ethics we already know.

HOW WAS JESUS DIVINE?

Rev. A. M. Farrer

The title of this paper means just what it says. It brings before you a consideration of how the divinity of Jesus may be understood by those who believe it. It does not touch the question why they should believe it.

"Divinity" in this context means "Godhead," and Godhead does not admit of degrees. No man can be raised to the station of God by the piling of virtues and miraculous powers upon his manhood. He might be dehumanized in this way, but he could not be divinized. He might become a god in the pagan sense, but he could not become God. Thus to say that the Man, Jesus, is divine is to say that in Him there is a unique union of manhood with the Godhead.

If we wish to understand such a union, our starting point must be what we know of the relation of the human to the divine within our own experience: this may provide a slight clue only, but it is the only clue we can possibly have for the exploring of the mystery. It is a mystery in any case, and those who will not have any mysteries may as well stop here. But they will not be wise. For the privilege of being human is the privilege of getting a baffling view of things divine, and those who refuse to see because they refuse to be baffled are merely refusing to be men because they cannot be God.

Our clue to this mystery is the act of prayer. This is itself a mystery, but a mystery closer to us, and in a manner more tangible. A man prays, then, that his will may be conformed to God's. He brings out and exercises whatever good aspirations he has. But merely to exercise them for oneself in the hope that they may coincide with the purposes of an absent Deity is not to pray at all. As the man prays, a change takes place. He begins by the attempt to link his own self-centered aspiration with God, but mysteriously the center and the basis of the act alters, and God's will expresses itself in him. Here lies a paradox: Unless our prayer is God's act of will it lacks the distinctive grace of prayer; unless it is an act of our will it has not the merit of being our prayer at all, but breathed through us without becoming ours. So far is this from being the case, that no act of will we ever make is so centrally and vividly our own as this act which God performs in us. This alone is what we really intend and really desire, this is when we are really ourselves. He who originally created us free is renewing our creation and our freedom.

Our prayers are incomplete. They are never pure, the divine act is always confused with elements of persisting self-will. Even if they were pure, they would not be our life. They are at best sincere resolutions, and resolution, we know to our cost, is not the same as performance. And when we do perform our resolutions, we do not carry with us into the field of action that mysterious God-centeredness which was the life of our prayer, we become once more centered in ourselves, external from God, and willing servants at the best.

Now if a man's life were united to God not merely at scattered points, at occasional acts of prayer, and then impurely, but purely and throughout, all of a piece, an unbroken union of wills, then this would be the life of a man, and yet would also be a life of God. God would not think this and that thought in him, He would live his life in him; this life would not be inspired, it would be divine, and the livers of it would be God and Man: and yet that Man would not be the less Man or the less himself, but most fully himself and most fully human.

This, then, is the only clue we seem to have for the understanding of the way in which Jesus is divine. A Christian will not, of course, accept this as a full account of the mystery, for it leaves open the question how such a union came about. But for Christians this is not open. The union did not happen through the heroic sanctity of a human will which was thrown up in the course of history; it could only happen by a special divine act, God making Himself such a Man, and living His life in Him from the start. And thus for the salvation of the world God brought into the world a perfect union of manhood with Godhead, so that this might adopt us, and carry us with it. And our incomplete acts of union with God are themselves the beginnings of the working of this adoption in us.

ARE THERE ANY VALID OBJECTIONS TO FREE LOVE?

Mr. Charles Williams

Mr. Williams first discussed the phrase "Free Love," asking if it was to mean "unconditioned amorousness." This, he said, was a meaningless phrase, as the emotions were influenced by intellectual and physical conditions, if not by a spiritual attitude.

The essence of emotional style lay in its capacity for definition. By following the immediate, momentary desires, instead of keeping in mind what he would call the "pattern," satisfaction was unlikely to be attained. (He pointed out that the Christian pattern need not necessarily be the one followed). It was a question whether the Pragmatic or Metaphysical was to dictate to the emotional movements.

Mr. Williams then discussed the other meaning of "Free Love" the right to seek for the most complete satisfaction by a series of trials. This theory assumes that there will be ultimately something satisfying for the individual. This does not guarantee that the same thing will be satisfying five minutes or five years later when the individual's views would have altered.

It was impossible to be "adult" in love unless the emotions or the moment could be accepted or rejected at will. Fidelity was the mark of such a power of will. Unless it operates under fixed conditions all that we mean by love would cease to be. If "Freedom" in "Free Love" meant freedom to be ruled by the emotions of the moment, and the "Love" meant the conscious pursuit of conscious felicity Mr. Williams emphasized that it was neither "Free" nor "Love."

IS CHRISTIAN SEX-MORALTIY NARROW-MINDED AND OUT-OF-DATE

Fr. Gerald Vann, O.P.

Fr. Vann first listed various modes of approach to sex:

People sometimes confuse hardboiled realism which is a good thing with narrow-mindedness, which isn't. For instance, there's the type of biological enthusiast with no nonsense about him, who won't have the activities of hormones romanticized for him, falling in love is just a biochemical reaction to appropriate stimuli; and so he believes in treating sex urges with scientific freedom and detachment. It's a point of view which seems to me very narrow-minded because it ignores all but a fraction of human nature. You cannot reduce Sibelius and Shakespeare and Michelangelo to scientific terms; and you cannot reduce the personality to vulgar fractions. Or again, there's the hearty hedonist who says: "I may not know much about morality, but I know what I like." He too is narrow-minded, to say the least, for he treats the human personality just as a child treats sweets. Then there's the more serious-minded lover, who is certainly not dissolute, but is, on the other hand, negatively dissoluble; because he cannot see any reason, once the flame of passion is spent, for acting as though it were not; tomorrow, for him, to pastures new. He too, I shall try to argue, is failing to see reality whole.

At the other extreme are the people who think not with their minds but with their emotions. To try to make marriage a life-sentence, to condemn the blessings of contraception, to try to force nature into unnatural formalisms and abstentions—this, they say, is cruel; and because it's cruel it's wrong. There are, of course, more serious arguments which cover much the same ground; I shall come to them presently; but this particular method of approach again seems to reduce human nature to a fraction of itself; at best it concentrates on one aspect of things and ignores others, and at worst it reduces the personality to the level of something out of Ethel M. Dell or Gertie Wentworth-James.

There is a third and far more attractive type of person, the joyous pagan that you find, say, in Herrick, or, in a very different way, in Norman Douglas. He is attractive because he really does love and worship beauty. But he interprets worship in a somewhat activist sense, and beauty in terms of consumption rather than production. He believes in gathering rosebuds while he may; and though he weeps as little as they—and he—droop and wither, he doesn't attempt to stop the rot.

All these attitudes recognize part only of human nature, because man is not to be regarded as a body and a mind, but as a body-mind, and so every action that he performs on one level of his being affects every other level. Each human personality is infinite in its possibilities, and so all those who cling to such attitudes as those described doom themselves to remain half men, never knowing the realities of life and love. 'The people who view sex simply in biological terms, or as a merely physical plaything, are missing its whole meaning, and therefore the whole meaning of life: they are dooming themselves never to know the deep human realities, to remain half-men. Nothing is more tiresome than to hear Casanova referred to as a great lover. There can have been few men who knew less about love than Casanova: he minced his pathetic pigmy path through the world and never, as far as one can gather, touched reality at all, never got outside the narrow, vacant shell of his own little ego. The lady-killer is exactly at the opposite pole to the lover; and they are not likely to meet.

But the Casanova type is sub-human for another reason. The individual he uses and discards is a human *person*. And there is a sort of infinity about a human person. The mind, as Aristotle said so long ago, becomes in a manner all things; and if the mind, then the whole personality. Every personality is in a sense infinite, every personality is also unique, a *mystery*. The Christian adds that every personality is potentially infinite in a far greater sense, since the destiny of man is to become one in knowledge and love not with all things merely but with the Maker of all things.

And because of this infinity, the primary duty of the lover is humility and reverence for the beloved, and no hedonism or promiscuity will allow for this: we are like the tripper who cannot contemplate a flower without wanting to grab and mawl it.

"The only possible attitude—*human* attitude—of human being to human being is one of reverence, of awe as towards a mystery. This surely is the difference between the wise and cultured man and the savage—whether he be a primitive savage or a modern civilized commercialized savage, a hard-boiled vulgarian. The troglodyte of the modern city, so suburban that he has forgotten what it means to be urbane—has lost what the child and the poet and the painter and the saint preserve, his sense of reverence for reality, and consequently his power to contemplate. He cannot adore, he can only grab. And the greater, the more holy the thing he brags, the deeper his degradation …. The soul of love-making is humility. And where sex is concerned you have to have a double reverence and humility: first, because there is no art without reverence, and love-making is an art in the simple sense of the making of what is good and true and beautiful; and secondly because its material is not stone or paint or sound, and not merely flesh, but the mysterious infinite of the person."

Thus the very fact that we live a many-leveled life makes love necessarily a matter for a lifetime, for on every level, different clashes of the will are to be expected, and never can it be said that two souls are completely tuned one to the other—and yet no other goal can satisfy love: those who make it an amusement will find that it ceases to amuse. "Love-making demands infinite patience and gentleness and care, and often heroic generosity; otherwise everything may be spoiled. Sexual pleasure is not a king in its own right. It is one element in a totality; and being one element only, it may not *rule*. It is one element in the integral worship of and joy in an integral person; if it is not that—if it is a dictator—then it is not human at all."

"Likewise, if by means of contraception lovers deliberately turn their life away from creation, that act will have a disastrous effect on the soul: an act turned away from its nature produces a monster. And "free love" which to the unthinking seems so normal and "natural," is really dilettantism, a refusal to take sex seriously, and indeed to take life seriously."

"Let me return for a moment to the charming pagan. You may perhaps feel that I have been treating all this with far too much heavy-footed solemnity. Let us be realists. Are we all to wear blinkers? What more natural than that youth and maiden happening to meet, and finding each other pleasing to the eye, should think it an acceptable idea to pop into bed for a space? Why shouldn't Cleon unravel the tangles in Neaera's hair? Why, indeed, to this last question. But I think there is a confusion over the word "natural." People say natural when they mean simply statistically normal; some people claim that there is no difference; but if by natural you mean what is according to the nature of a given thing, then there can be a world of difference. The statistically normal thing is what happens in the majority of cases or what the majority of people do …. Even if everybody in the world identified appreciation of beauty with sexual intercourse ("very artistic"), it would be normal, but it wouldn't be natural; and it wouldn't be natural because *human* sexual intercourse is so constituted as to be incompatible with dilettantism. If you are going to worship you have got to give your mind to it. No, let us have none of this blinker business; let us admire and reverence beauty wherever we can find it; let us by all means help the unfortunate Neaera with her hair. But do let us distinguish two totally different things. Do let us learn to admire rosebuds without having to keep plucking at them. (And it doesn't make it any better if the rosebud plucks back.) This is indeed only one example of our universal poverty: we have forgotten how to contemplate. We're like the millionaire who doesn't know a Rembrandt from a Picasso, but will rob, cheat and murder to get *possession* of either of them. Christian morality denies only to affirm; the promiscuous pagan affirms only to deny. Even on the most pedestrian common sense level you have to take your choice: either a river that is deep and powerful because it is banked and dammed, or a sprawling soggy marsh."

Father Vann finished by pointing out that Christianity did not deny the hardness of hard cases—such as congenital homosexuality—nor indeed was there any human solution for all problems, sexual or otherwise. But Christianity claimed that its morals were objective, a consequence of the natural order of things, and so acts were not wrong because they were forbidden, but forbidden because they were wrong. Therefore it was no use arguing from hard cases that these morals should be revoked. If you did, you would be in "an advanced stage of Canutism." If you believed in Christianity—or even without that belief—you believed that certain consequences would follow certain behavior. If man was really made to know, love and serve God, and so be happy, he would have to follow certain laws—the laws of morality—in working out his own destiny. "You have either got to accept the idea of objective moral principles and absolute standards, or else you must reject the idea of objectivity altogether, and then it is pointless to talk about morality at all. Catholic morality is objective, because it is based on the idea that things in general and man in particular have a definite nature and a definite purpose. So, as we have seen, it regards divorce and contraception, and so on, as wrong, and *always* wrong, not because forbidden by law, but in *themselves*. But that doesn't mean that it is harsh or hard-hearted or that it has no understanding of the tragedy of hard cases. The fact that it recognizes them and yet doesn't attempt to put them all right, that it doesn't make any attempt to smooth out every difficulty and provide a plush cushion for every worshipper, only means that it recognizes also that evil and suffering are inherent in human life as we know it, and that they have an immensely important—indeed an essential—part to play in the discovery and deepening of love. I have seen the Christian doctrine of redemption explained (by a non-Christian, needless to say) as a belief that the God-man did all the necessary suffering for us, vicariously, so that we needn't bother any further. It is funny the things people say. Suffering can help to reveal to us what we are, what man is, what God is, and what love is. That *is* the solution of the problem of suffering; it is its own solution. And that is why there *is* a Christian solution of the problems of sexual maladjustment, and so on, which is complete in a way that no humanist solution can ever be complete. For on the Christian view nothing need be lost or frustrated or useless; everything can be creative—creative of human love in the first place, and then creative of the final greatness and glory of man, his discovery of God. Your particular form of suffering may be sexual maladjustment or bereavement or inability to marry the person you love, or a thousand and one other things: the whole basis of Christian optimism is that God can and does use it to lead us to discover the abyss of our own hearts, and so to learn how to love, and to be worth loving.

That leads me to my final point. I have been trying mainly to show that Christian sex morality isn't a narrow obscurantist life-hating policy of repression. But there is bound to be something cold and repellant about morality until it is seen as a function of religion. We come from the Good, who is our home; but we come into evil, for "there hath passed away a glory from the earth." We have to try with toil and tears to make our way back. Morality is that way back, the way of love and worship. All our life is meant to be worship: worship, in union with the *one* we love, and the *many* we love, and the *earth* we love, of God who *is* Love.

NOTE.—Quotations from Fr. Vann's paper are included by courtesy of the Centenary Press, who are embodying the full text of the paper in a forthcoming book of wider scope by Fr. Vann.

EXTRA COPIES of this DIGEST (limited edition) are obtainable by post (1*s*. 2 ½ *d*. each) from STELLA ALDWINCKLE, 42 Leckford Road, Oxford.

SOCRATIC DIGEST

No. 2   JUNE, 1944

CONTENTS

PAPERS AND SPEAKERS, 1943-1944	31
EDITORIAL	32
SOCRATES	34
MORALS WITHOUT FAITH	35
CAN SCIENCE PROVIDE OUR ETHICS?	36
CHRISTIANITY AND PHILOSOPHY	38
CAN WE KNOW THAT GOD EXISTS?	39
REASON AND FAITH	41
"BULVERISM" (in full)	42
PHILOSOPHY TODAY (in full)	46
CONCERNING THE QUESTION: "JESUS, PROPHET, OR SON OF GOD?"	54

ONE SHILLING

Printed at the Oxonian Press, Queen Street, Oxford.

EDITOR'S NOTES

ACKNOWLEDGEMENTS. Our grateful thanks are due to all our speakers for their kindness and patience and the help they have given us: to the Principal of Pusey House and to St. Hilda's and Oriel J.C.R.'s for the loan of their Common Rooms: and to our printers for their personal interest and cooperation which make possible the appearance of DIGEST No. 2 at a time of serious understaffing.

SELECTION OF PRÉCIS. The selection this year has been governed by considerations indicated in the Editorial, the availability of the text and suitability of the papers to reduction. The omission of the précis of any paper is obviously no reflection on its interest or excellence—the task of selection, in fact, proves to be an invidious one.

ORDERS FOR "DIGEST." 1/- per copy, plus 2*d*. postage, for single copies, and appropriate postage for larger numbers, from Stella Aldwinckle, 42 Leckford Road, Oxford. Please send in your orders as soon as possible. The DIGEST appears annually in June.

LONDON SOCRATIC CLUB. This is to be launched in October under the presidency of Miss Dorothy L. Sayers (particulars from Miss Moore, 17 Cadogan Street, S.W.3, in close affiliation with the Oxford Socratic Club).

FUTURE DEVELOPMENTS. A lawyer, now at the War Office, has written as follows in comment on DIGEST No. 1 and the help he derived from Prof. Quick's paper in particular: "I am sure there must be thousands of educated people up and down the country, deeply interested in religion, but not knowing too much to be convinced by the Christian Faith and knowing too much to be entirely skeptical. What we need is the guidance of the expert." He goes on to suggest our printing more papers and the discussions in full. This is impossible in war-time, and undergraduate discussion would not necessarily meet older people's questions. But to meet such a need, if it exist, we have in mind the possibility of beginning a "Socratic Farm" after the war, immediately outside Oxford, combining a "Socratic" Library and Guest House for extra-Oxford and gone-down Socratics on holidays, with a Club House for undergraduate Socratics during term. Here Socratic conferences could be held in vacation. We would welcome the considered views of readers and their friends on whether such facilities would be welcomed (also any donations towards the Library, now in embryo!), and the names of any who would like to combine a country holiday with a Socratic Conference in the summer of 1945.

STELLA ALDWINCKLE

OXFORD UNIVERSITY SOCRATIC CLUB

"In view of the present struggle between a 'Christian' and a 'Nazi' order of society, this Club has been formed for those who do not necessarily wish to submit themselves to Christian views but are interested in a philosophical approach to religion in general and to Christianity in particular, in a spirit of free enquiry and in the light of modern thought and knowledge.

Informal discussion will follow the introduction of the subjects by speakers who will include both Christians and non-Christians."

OFFICERS

President: C. S. LEWIS, M.A.   *Chairman*: STELLA ALDWINCKLE, M.A.

Secretaries and Treasurers:

1943	Michaelmas Term	Pamela Lockett (St. Anne's)
		Joseph Butler (Trinity)
	Hilary Term	Martin Shearn (Magdalen)
		Joseph Butler (Trinity)
1944	Trinity Term	G. B. Preston (Magdalen)
		Rosemary Woolf (St. Hugh's)

PAPERS AND SPEAKERS
MICHAELMAS TERM, 1943

October 16th—Morals without Faith   Dr. FALK,
   Mr. C. S. LEWIS

October 25th—Reason and Faith   Fr. D'ARCY, S.J.
November 1st—Can we know that God Exists?   Rev. A. M. FARRER
November 8th—Christianity and Philosophy   Prof. L. W. HODGSON
November 15th—Science and Miracles   Mr. C. S. LEWIS
November 22nd—Buddhism   Mr. G. E. HARVEY
November 29th—Inspiration in Art in Scripture   Fr. KEHOE, O.P.

HILARY TERM, 1944

January 17th—The Concept of Reason   Mr. PICKARD-CAMBRIDGE
January 24th—On Being Reviewed by Christians   Dr. C. E. M. JOAD
   Mr. C. S. LEWIS
February 7th—"Bulverism," or The Foundations of 20th Century Thought
   Mr. C. S. LEWIS
February 14th—Materialism and Agnosticism   Mr. J. K. WHITE
   Mr. G. B. PRESTON
February 21st—Christianity and Psycho-Neurosis   Mr. JOHN LAYARD
February 28th—Can Science provide our Ethics?   Mr. WHITTERIDGE

March 3rd—The Significance of Reinhold Niebuhr for Contemporary Thought
                                                                Mr. D. M. MacKinnon

TRINITY TERM, 1944

April 24th—Socrates	Mr. J. K. Spalding
May 1st—"Explaining" the Universe	Mr. P. D. Medawar
	Rev. A. M. Farrer
May 8th—Free will and Determinism	Mr. L. Mannheim
	Mr. G. H. L. Andrew
May 15th—Philosophy Today	Prof. H. A. Hodges
May 22nd—Concerning the Question: "Jesus, Prophet or Son of God?"	
	Stella Aldwinckle
May 29th—Duty and Delight	Rev. P. J. Thompson
	Dr. Falk
June 5th—Is Institutional Christianity necessary?	Mr. C. S. Lewis

SOCRATIC DIGEST

"Οὗτος μὲν οἴεταί τι εἰδέναι οὐκ εἰδώς, ἐγὼ δὲ ὥσπερ οὖν οὐκ οἶδα οὐδὲ οἴομαι."
                                                                —*Socrates*

"Εἴ τις δοκεῖ ἐγνωκέναι τι, οὔπω ἔγνω καθὼς δεῖ γνῶναι."
                                                                —*St. Paul*

"La dernière démarche de la raison est de reconnaître qu'il y a une infinité de choses qui la surpassent."   —*Pascal*

EDITORIAL

The Socratic approach to the fundamental human questions evidently meets a need which is being felt beyond Oxford. Requests for last year's Digest were received from all over Britain and even from the U.S.A., Canada and Australia. But printing difficulties prevent our complying with requests to print more papers and discussions in full. The précis must inevitably prove somewhat indigestible to those who have not heard the papers, but they may serve at least to stimulate lines of thought and suggest new insights to the reader's mind.

It is easy to be deceived in this "rational" and "scientific" age into the prevalent intellectual attitude which is neither rational nor scientific in the fullest sense of those words, since it prefers to explain away, rather than to explain, many of the data that demand explanation in any attempt to assess the meaning of our human existence. Such an attitude, claiming to be "rational" and "scientific," and so creating the impression of being "realistic," has made our civilization a prey to philosophies of political expediency, technical success, "blood, race and soil."

Since the universe must be assumed to be intelligible in *some* sense of the word (or our thought could not be related to it at all), we must of course be rational in our approach to life, and related in some sense it indeed proves itself to be. Bridges designed by mental calculation don't break down: we can by reasoning discover "laws" of nature, and to a large extent order our smaller practical affairs. But for such purposes we do not need to probe very far: if our philosophy of life is to be relevant to what the universe and existence ARE in their nature, we must go further. Only so will our grappling with the major political, social, educational and personal problems be at least on the "right" lines. One cannot successfully drive a horse if one assumes its nature is that of a car. As the crucial phase of the Second World War opens, we ask ourselves, "Is scientific planning enough? Or are corrupted human wills a real factor in the impasse our civilization has reached, as the sages unite in telling us they are? If so, can reasoned planning and applied science alone cure our ills? Is even dialectical materialism *true*?" With such considerations at the back of our minds, Reason is here discussed, and also Faith, as *practical* issues.

But if science may not be enough to meet our practical problems, neither is mere pragmatism sufficient as a guide to truth, useful though it be as a pointer and check. The trouble about pragmatism is that in the nature of the case it cannot tell us what will work *in the long run*: only access to what the universe and existence ARE can do that—in principle. So as Socratics we have to begin further back—with the question about that access, *i.e.* with the possibility of knowing truth. The question before us is not "What type of philosophy is politically expedient, useful or imposing; theoretically neat, clever *or* new"—still less individually comforting—but: "What is *true*?" or rather: "*How do we come to know what is true?*"

This is, of course, a profoundly complex question, but disciples of Socrates are willing to take infinite pains over the asking and the attempted answering. A beginning may be made by reflection on the nature and function of Reason in at least its three aspects, discursive (διάνοια), apprehensive (νους), and practical (will), and its relation both to scientific knowledge (wider German sense) and to spiritual knowledge (if such there be).

This is the consideration loosely linking the diversity of the papers appearing in this DIGEST, arranged in an order such as to display some movements in this wrestling. It is these that lead us to ask: Is reason denied by faith—*or completed by it*? After all, what do we mean by "knowledge," by "certainty," by "true," and "truth"? (we speak as fools). What are or what should be their bases? (we speak as those whose wisdom is that they know they do not know.) To what extent do our imagined "rational" convictions and "scientific" certitudes rest on truly rational grounds? (we speak *ad hominem*). Are we sure we know what we mean by "reason," or that we grasp the nature of the distinctions between superstition, credulity, intellectual assent to beliefs, and Christian faith? If not, it is time for Socratics to press these questionings.

The issues are complex indeed and require the coordinated search of honest minds approaching them from different points of view. A wide divergence will be seen in particular between the two thinkers whose papers appear in full. As we look first over Mr. Lewis's shoulder, then over Prof. Hodges', old philosophical horizons meet with new ones, and the problems are sharpened into a new focus. It is in the tension between these points of view that certain aspects of the ancient Christian Faith may stand for some in a new light (an epistemological one). May truth not be *both* "about something" *and* "for persons" without losing its "objectivity"?

STELLA ALDWINCKLE

SOCRATES

Mr. K. J. Spalding

Mr. Spalding began by pointing out how indebted our civilization was to that of Ancient Greece and in particular to the life and thought of a single man of that time, Socrates. Unlike most thinkers of today, Socrates' main interest was man. The great magnetism of his personality caused many to regard him as a kind of "magician." He influenced all, either antagonizing them or enlisting their enthusiastic support. "He is the only one who ever made me ashamed," said Alcibiades. Socrates' views on many subjects could with advantage be seriously considered today (*e.g.*, If I have rights, you also have rights. If you respect men, ye see more in them than when you only like them).

Socrates found no man dull. Each man was an enigma, and had progressed insofar as he had attained to knowledge of himself. Socrates clearly showed most of those with whom he came into contact how little they knew about themselves and how their outward appearance in general deceived others much less than it deceived themselves. He made men seem strange to themselves until they began to suspect themselves as appearances whose real self was buried deep within.

The Conservatives and Sophists of that time objected so strongly to the undermining effect of Socrates' teaching on many of their contemporaries, especially the young men, that they eventually put him into prison and condemned him to death. Others, however, began to think deeply and undertook a search for the true self. In modern times Spinoza had found this self for periods of longer and longer duration by means of meditation. Most of us can catch only fleeting glimpses of it. Beginning by the Socratic method, we first of all love a particular beautiful body; then beauty is perceived in all things seen; then beauty in mind, in ideas, in laws and institutions, in sciences; thus extending our love up through all particular beauties until we reach the Beauty Absolute. This method taught by Socrates was based on first-hand direct experience. His reasonings were founded on fact and on a firm faith in the ancient traditional morality of Greece. Beauty could be experienced, not communicated.

Mr. C. S. Lewis opened the discussion. He pointed out that progress on the Socratic ladder was always upwards, that once human love had been passed by and the love of laws had been reached, there could be no returning down the ladder again to the love of individual persons: there was no sacramental system. This forms one of the main contrasts between Socratic thought and Christianity. Socrates thinks of man from man's point of view, and the Christian Faith teaches us of God descending the ladder in Christ to help man to knowledge of himself. The Christian believes that we need this help.

Discussion

The difference between what was meant by "intellect" by Socrates and what we mean nowadays was emphasized. The intellect, imagination and the emotions were then united. We have much to learn from the Greeks in this connection.

How much of Socratic thought was due to Plato? The discussion of this question eventually led on to the drawing of a parallel between Christ and Socrates, and it was pointed out that it was very interesting to study both the likenesses and the differences between the *Phaedo* and the Last Supper. Socrates' death struck one as an "interruption"; that of Christ as a sacrifice, deliberate and complete.

It was suggested that Socrates' main contribution was to teach us that truth is more important than life itself.

MORALS WITHOUT FAITH

Dr. W. Falk
Mr. C. S. Lewis

Dr. Falk spoke first of the two questions to which the subject referred: (1) Does subjection to a moral law mean anything more than being commanded by God? (2) Does obedience to God's laws imply obedience to some indispensable *lex naturae*?

Dr. Falk supported this second view implicit in the classical tradition and revived by 17th and 18th century moralists who desired to emancipate morals from religion. He referred briefly to the three main disruptive forces which had discredited the latter, and to the law of Nature which supplied the new basis for morals. He maintained, however, that this law of Nature, the dictate of Reason, could not be valid for all men at all times. This was the fundamental problem of moral philosophy. Dr. Falk then analyzed Natural Law, which implies:

(1) an imperative command, not simply volition;
(2) an impulse of our own will towards a desirable end;
(3) the possibility of following that impulse based on the Kantian "ought implies can."

The dualism between "want" and "must" is constituted by three modes of practical thinking—(1) directive; (2) elective; (3) selective—by means of which we project to ourselves the thought of what it is rationally necessary for us to do.

Dr. Falk's conclusions were that there is a natural foundation for morality, that there will always be some laws which are imposed on us from within regardless of whether they are also imposed on us from without, that we find them if we seek them, and that we must seek to find them.

In his reply, Mr. Lewis agreed with Dr. Falk that it was ruinous to base morality on a religion which did not offer any explanation for the performance of duties. Mr. Lewis's objections were based on a belief in objective values. Dr. Falk's three principles he considered tended to judge right and wrong actions merely on the grounds of their conformity with our natural dispositions.

Replying to Mr. Lewis, Dr. Falk asked if by objective values we meant objective eligibility. He maintained that the eligibility of an action rested on an impulse to perform it, a causal relation about which no demonstrative arguments were possible. Dr. Falk maintained that to say that a duty is obedience to the predominant impulse on reflection was not to deny the necessity for the scrutiny of one's actions. He admitted that practical difficulty of rationalizing the consequences of one's actions, but said that these could be ascertained by reference to the social good, and finally to our own lasting happiness.

CAN SCIENCE PROVIDE OUR ETHICS?
MR. WHITTERIDGE

PROF. HODGSON

[Dr. C. H. Waddington, who was to have addressed the Club, was prevented at the last moment from coming, and Mr. Whitteridge very kindly stepped into the breach.]

Mr. Whitteridge pointed out that science provides an increasing body of new facts which alter the range of our moral responsibilities—*e.g.* negligence about nutrition and prevention of disease amount to the manslaughter of those whom we could have saved by acting on our scientific knowledge. Whereas scientists ten to fifteen years ago, dominated by the attention paid to physics, accepted what might be called the neutrality of science in ethical matters, and it was then generally conceded that natural science on the one hand, and art and theology on the other, dealt with distinct and divided worlds, today this outlook had disappeared, and certain scientists were claiming to be able to supply a criterion for ethics from the findings of the empirical sciences.

Attention is being focused in agriculture on techniques to control and interpret a variety of interacting factors; in biology, on the extent to which an organism organizes itself, and on the new idea of there being different levels of organization within it, so that it may be possible to account for an organism by physics and chemistry plus organizing relations, which organizing relations are to be studied by scientific methods. Thus life, being explained in terms of these organizing relations, would cease to be mysterious, and vitalism becomes defunct. The same emancipation may be hoped for in psychology, which would then become a strict science working at a higher level and describe the activity of man's mind on the basis of neuro-physiological processes and their interrelations.

The claim is now being made that science must have a say in controlling the development of society by controlling its conditions. This raises the question of a criterion for the right and for the good. Certain scientists (notably Prof. Julian Huxley) claim that such a criterion can be empirically based by ascertaining the general direction of evolution, especially in man: anything which cooperates with this trend is right, that which hinders it is wrong. Our values can be derived from that which experience shows us to be "the more intrinsically and permanently satisfactory" to the nature of man and conducive to the construction of a society which respects the individual and encourages the actualization of new possibilities in evolution.

Mr. Whitteridge closed by pointing out that in Russia a society run on scientifically based ethics was already in being.

Prof. Hodgson opened the DISCUSSION. He welcomed the scientists' efforts to find some firm objective ground on which to base ethics, and pointed out that in this attempt they were in the company of such men as Socrates, Descartes and Kant. He deplored the exhibition of themselves made by the philosophers in the symposium "Science and Ethics" and accused them of not appreciating what such men as Dr. Waddington are getting at—*i.e.* a *basis* for ethics which need not itself be an ethical statement. He said that Dr. Waddington, Prof. Huxley and the theologians (as represented by Dr. Kirk) are agreed that conscience is not automatic and that the *mind* must be used to find out objectively what is right and wrong. The philosophical-theological criterion of right and wrong, as represented by St. Thomas Aquinas, is the nature of reality. To him Being is fundamental, and a good action is one which is in accordance with the nature of reality.

So the real issue between Dr. Waddington and Prof. Huxley on the one hand, and theology on the other, is about the nature of reality. Are causal systems the whole of reality, as the former hold, or only *part*, as the latter hold? Theologians believe, not on authority but on *empirical* grounds, that there are *reasons* as well as *causes*, and that there are *two orders of events*—(*a*) purposive, (*b*) caused. The causal system of the natural universe is seen as only *part* of God's creation, but, because it is such, scientific discoveries within it may *help* us to know what we ought to do, but cannot give the necessary ultimate criterion of good.

The following points were made in the DISCUSSION:

1. That both speakers seemed to *assume existing ethics* (*e.g.* it is wrong to murder).
2. That evolution *must* have an *end*, and this end cannot be determined *empirically*.
3. That evolutionary ethics have to *assume* that the end to which evolution tends is good.
4. That Science can derive the scientific virtues pragmatically.

Mr. Lewis wanted to know *how*, if one values evolution for its results (*e.g.* the preservation of the species), is one to decide that such results are a Good Thing? If nature is our criterion, since organic life is becoming extinct, there are only two commands in scientific ethics—murder and suicide.

CHRISTIANITY AND PHILOSOPHY

Professor Hodgson

Professor Hodgson began by considering the question "What is Philosophy?" He said that, first, metaphysics are basic to philosophy, *i.e.* metaphysics in its original sense as the study of what goes beyond physics. In natural science we consider how various objects fit together and are interrelated. As metaphysicians, however, we must go beyond these particulars and ask, "What does it all *mean*?" To regard metaphysics as nonsense is itself a metaphysical view, because it asserts that there is no meaning. Secondly, philosophy springs from a questioning attitude which insists on asking "why?" This attitude breeds philosophical systems—hypotheses about existence—constructed by taking some one feature and making it a key to the whole: *e.g.* by taking the principle of logical consistency one arrives at various types of idealism; by taking the natural order as key, at positivism; by taking the interplay of economic forces, at Marxism; and so on.

In the history of human thought, philosophy was constantly striving to reconcile the empirical and the formal elements in knowledge—the data given by experience with the rational principles by which we seek to order that experience. No philosophical system had yet succeeded in including all the data without distortion.

Christian philosophy, he said, is fundamentally empirical, since it takes as its key feature, not an abstract rational conception of God, but the movement of God to man in history rescuing creation from evil through Christ. Whereas Buddhism is applied metaphysics, starting from elucidatory dogmas, Christianity is an historic religion, generating metaphysics, starting from elucidatory facts (Whitehead). Although God is active everywhere and in all history, He is most characteristically revealed in the crisis of dealing with the power of evil through Christ.

Whereas Christian theology studies this key feature itself, and is therefore more scientific than philosophical, Christian philosophy attempts to understand and to interpret the whole of existence by means of this key. Since this key is revelational, Christianity is a religion of revelation.

Professor Hodgson took exception to the Thomist distinction between natural and revealed theology, and insisted that the logic of the argument both about the existence and the Trinitarian character of God is the same—God's revelation of Himself is given in Divine acts, in deeds rather than in words.

Christianity is a revealed religion because it is based on historic acts. Christianity says to philosophy: "You must interpret all the data, and omit none of the evidence, and that evidence includes God's historic acts."

An hour's lively Discussion followed.
Among the questions raised were the following:—

(1) Is God the creator of evil?
(2) Need philosophical questioning breed philosophies? And *must* there be answers?
(3) Is it not dangerous subjectivism to base philosophy on belief, since men's beliefs differ?
(4) How is one to account for the difference between the theologian's dogmatic attitude and the tentative attitude of the philosopher?

CAN WE KNOW THAT GOD EXISTS?

The Rev. A. M. Farrer
Mr. MacNabb

Mr. Farrer began by pointing out that the existence of intelligent agnostics confutes the contention that we can demonstrate the existence of God. If we cannot demonstrate His existence, is there any other way in which we can know that He exists? The way in which we know objects differs according to the ways in which they are related to our minds. God, as the object of our love, is unique, since, unlike all other objects of our knowledge, He is not only "out there," but also underlies our very existence. But, although our way of knowing God is unique, it can be said to be *more like* knowing a person than knowing, let us say, a carpet.

Mr. Farrer went on to argue that the knowledge of God is mediate as well as immediate. He is known through His creation as well as in our souls. But he strongly insisted that the knowledge of God from Creation is not inferential, since one cannot legitimately argue from finite objects to God, who is unique and infinite; nor can one argue from physical cause and effect, to God as First Cause in that sense of cause, since this would be to make God part of the physical system, like a Divine billiard player who gives the balls that first push from which they rebound forever, whereas the believer believes in God as *Sustainer* of the universe. One cannot arrive at the God of theism from de-theologized physics.

Nor can one argue from neutralized morals to get God back again into the system. If we de-theologize our facts we have gutted them: for the believer's hypothesis it is *part of the evidence* that God is in the world, or underlies it, every moment. As the truth cannot be told about any mental act without reference to the self, so truth about existence cannot be told without reference to the Creator. Thus arguments which uphold theism should not attempt to be demonstrative, but should examine whether the theistic way of regarding the world "lights up more of reality" than other ways, or not.

But if strict logical demonstration is not possible, can we exhibit the groundedness of finite things upon God? All we can do is to direct attention to that aspect of finite being which fails to satisfy our minds unless it is seen in one picture with the creative activity of God. So we exhibit the paradoxes of finitude; for example, that neither any finite thing nor the whole system of finites is self-explanatory—it could as well have been otherwise; or that all that any finite being is, can only hold on to existence at a pinpoint instant of present time. These things are not logical paradoxes; we feel them to be paradoxical only because they are naturally and properly seen on the background of an eternal and self-explanatory being, and if we exclude this divine background it clamors to be readmitted because it is really there and really coming to bear upon our minds through the finite things it creates and sustains. When the mind has, in consequence, re-plotted its view from the divine center, the resultant vision simply convinces us by its naturalness and fertility, and we cannot dream of relinquishing it for a return to a thinner and more shadowy interpretation of our existence.

Mr. MacNabb, in his reply, objected to the definition of knowledge as "the apprehension of objects," and pointed out that many of the things one knows are not *entities*, *e.g.* "it is raining," "2 + 2 = 4," etc. There must be a *double* acceptance in knowing. Can we accept the proposition that there is a God *and* accept that there are adequate grounds for such acceptance? There are different kinds of knowing and different grounds are accepted for different propositions. Mr. MacNabb further questioned the alleged "naturalness" and "fertility" of viewing natural phenomena as revealing God. He said that many have shaken themselves out of believing in God, but none out of the realistic way of viewing sensible appearances. He said that the discoveries of physics have been made on realistic and not on theistic assumptions. He suggested that it was intellectually wicked to suggest that there is no way out of such antinomies as the concepts of eternity and evil except by the theistic hypothesis, and he insisted one must continue to attempt to solve such antinomies *logically* until success is achieved. Such philosophical puzzles are bad grounds for arguing the existence of God.

Mr. Farrer, in his reply, agreed that verbal puzzles do not give grounds for taking refuge in the hypothesis of God: they are only of importance insofar as they are symptoms of our minds' grappling with a two-sided thing, *viz.* the finite which is grounded in infinity.

REASON AND FAITH

Rev. Father D'Arcy, S.J.

Father D'Arcy spoke first of various definitions of the term "belief," *e.g.* belief in self-evident propositions, and belief as implying trust or loyalty. He discussed the historical treatment of the subject, emphasizing its neglect by Aristotle, and referred us chiefly to Browning, Newman's "Grammar of Assent," and to Butler and William James.

Father D'Arcy then spoke of the "neurosis" of unbelief and its root in the egoistic will of "rationalism." Countering the oversimplification of the psychologists with their own weapons, he was led to convict the agnostic as materialistic, hedonistic and pessimistic.

The speaker returned to his discussion of Belief, as concerning things which lie beyond the sphere of immediate experience and of self-evident propositions. He maintained that religious belief was dependent on the evidence of things seen or written, like the "beliefs" of the scientist and the historian. In the same way, rational as opposed to irrational belief depended on the correlation and interpretation of the evidence. He referred us to the superabundance of evidence in everyday life which led us to certainty; to the recognition of a pattern, an internal consistency, which, he said, came from the "unity of indirect reference."

It was this recognition of unity and order, Father D'Arcy concluded, with which religious belief was concerned. Faith crowns reason if we do not restrict ourselves, as does the scientist, merely to a piecemeal examination of external evidence. In discussing religious belief and certain faith, we must always remember that this latter demands a special analysis of its own, as it has an object and motive which are supernatural, and it transcends reason the while it fortifies it.

The DISCUSSION was opened by Mr. John Marsh (Mansfield). He confined himself, not to a discussion of the difference of outlook between Father D'Arcy and himself (which was, as he explained, merely one of emphasis) but to an illustration of the first speaker's theory of indirect reference. He explained how the Bible supplied the basic evidence for belief. An attempt to discover what Christ was like from a study of what he did; the facts of his birth, death and resurrection could, he said, point out reasonable grounds for belief.

In the lively discussion which ensued, Father D'Arcy was asked if the problem of belief, for the agnostic, was not confined, not to belief in God, but to particular difficulties—*e.g.* predestination, immortality—which followed from a belief in a *personal* God? Father D'Arcy replied that such problems were common to believer and unbeliever alike, but that the conflict of reason, resulting from lack of coordination of evidence, precluded any solution for the agnostic.

Considerable doubt was expressed, not so much in the evidence which formed the basis of belief, as in the *interpretations* of that evidence. Their variety, it was urged, precluded certainty.

For the agnostic viewpoint, it was argued that morality without faith was not impossible, and, further, that the agnostic was not prepared to believe *only* in what he sees, but that he hesitated to express the *same certainty* about the transcendental, *i.e.* that it was difficult to give the same meaning to certainty when applied to immediate experience, logical implication, and so-called knowledge of spiritual truths and transcendent persons or Person.

"BULVERISM,"
or, The Foundation of 20th Century Thought

Mr. C. S. Lewis

It is a disastrous discovery, as Emerson says somewhere, that we exist. I mean, it is disastrous when instead of merely attending to a rose we are forced to think of ourselves looking at the rose, with a certain type of mind and a certain type of eyes. It is disastrous because, if you are not very careful, the color of the rose gets attributed to our optic nerves and its scent to our noses, and in the end there is no rose left. The professional philosophers have been bothered about this universal blackout for over two hundred years, and the world has not much listened to them. But the same disaster is now occurring on a level we can all understand.

We have recently "discovered that we exist" in two new senses. The Freudians have discovered that we exist as bundles of complexes. The Marxians have discovered that we exist as members of some economic class. In the old days it was supposed that if a thing seemed obviously true to a hundred men, then it was probably true in fact. Nowadays the Freudian will tell you to go and analyze the hundred: you will find that they all think Elizabeth [I] a great queen because they all have a mother-complex. Their thoughts are psychologically tainted at the source. And the Marxist will tell you to go and examine the economic interests of the hundred; you will find that they all think freedom a good thing because they are all members of the bourgeoisie whose prosperity is increased by a policy of *laissez-faire*. Their thoughts are "ideologically tainted" as the source.

Now this is obviously great fun; but it has not always been noticed that there is a bill to pay for it. There are two questions that people who say this kind of thing ought to be asked. The first is, Are *all* thoughts thus tainted at the source, or only some? The second is, Does the taint invalidate the tainted thought—in the sense of making it untrue—or not?

If they say that *all thoughts* are thus tainted, then, of course, we must remind them that Freudianism and Marxism are as much systems of thought as Christian theology or philosophical idealism. The Freudian and the Marxian are in the same boat with all the rest of us, and cannot criticize us from outside. They have sawn off the branch they were sitting on. If, on the other hand, they say that the taint need not invalidate their thinking, then neither need it invalidate ours. In which case they have saved their own branch, but also saved ours along with it.

The only line they can really take is to say that some thoughts are tainted and others are not—which has the advantage (if Freudians and Marxians regard it as an advantage) of being what every sane man has always believed. But if that is so, we must then ask how you find out which are tainted and which are not. It is no earthly use saying that those are tainted which agree with the secret wishes of the thinker. Some of the things I should like to believe must in fact be true; it is impossible to arrange a universe which contradicts everyone's wishes, in every respect, at every moment. Suppose I think, after doing my accounts, that I have a large balance at the bank. And suppose you want to find out whether this belief of mine is "wishful thinking." You can never come to any conclusion by examining my psychological condition. Your only chance of finding out is to sit down and work through the sum yourself. When you have checked my figures, then, and then only, will you know whether I have that balance or not. If you find my arithmetic correct, then no amount of vaporing about my psychological condition can be anything but a waste of time. If you find my arithmetic wrong, then it may be relevant to explain psychologically how I came to be so bad at my arithmetic, and the doctrine of the concealed wish will become relevant—but only *after* you have yourself done the sum and discovered me to be wrong on purely arithmetical grounds. It is the same with all thinking and all systems of thought. If you try to find out which are tainted by speculating about the wishes of the thinkers, you are merely making a fool of yourself. You must first find out on purely logical grounds which of them do, in fact, break down as arguments. Afterwards, if you like, go on and discover the psychological causes of the error.

In other words, you must show *that* a man is wrong before you start explaining *why* he is wrong. The modern method is to assume without discussion *that* he is wrong and then distract his attention from this (the only real issue) by busily explaining how he became so silly. In the course of the last fifteen years I have found this vice so common that I have had to invent a name for it. I call it Bulverism. Some day I am going to write the biography of its imaginary inventor, Ezekiel Bulver, whose destiny was determined at the age of five when he heard his mother say to his father—who had been maintaining that two sides of a triangle were together greater than the third—"Oh you say that *because you are a man*." "At that moment," E. Bulver assures us, "there flashed across my opening mind the great truth that refutation is no necessary part of argument. Assume that your opponent is wrong, and then explain his error, and the world will be at your feet. Attempt to prove that he is wrong or (worse still) try to find out whether he is wrong or right, and the national dynamism of our age will thrust you to the wall." That is how Bulver became one of the makers of the Twentieth Century.

I find the fruits of his discovery almost everywhere. Thus I see my religion dismissed on the grounds that "the comfortable parson had every reason for assuring the nineteenth century worker that poverty would be rewarded in another world." Well, no doubt he had. On the assumption that Christianity is an error, I can see easily enough that some people would still have a motive for inculcating it. I see it so easily that I can, of course, play the game the other way round, by saying that "the modern man has every reason for trying to convince himself that there are no eternal sanctions behind the morality he is rejecting." For Bulverism is a truly democratic game in the sense that all can play it all day long, and that it gives no unfair privilege to the small and offensive minority who reason. But of course it gets us not one inch nearer to deciding whether, as a matter of fact, the Christian religion is true or false. That question remains to be discussed on quite different grounds—a matter of philosophical and historical argument. However it were decided, the improper motives of some people, both for believing it and for disbelieving it, would remain just as they are.

I see Bulverism at work in every political argument. The capitalists must be bad economists because we know why they want capitalism, and equally the Communists must be bad economists because we know why they want Communism. Thus, the Bulverists on both sides. In reality, of course, either the doctrines of the capitalists are false, or the doctrines of the Communists, or both; but you can only find out the rights and wrongs by reasoning—never by being rude about your opponent's psychology.

Until Bulverism is crushed, reason can play no effective part in human affairs. Each side snatches it early as a weapon against the other; but between the two reason itself is discredited. And why should reason not be discredited? It would be easy, in answer, to point to the present state of the world, but the real answer is even more immediate. The forces discrediting reason, themselves depend on reasoning. You must reason even to Bulverize. You are trying to *prove* that all *proofs* are invalid. If you fail, you fail. If you succeed, then you fail even more—for the proof that all proofs are invalid must be invalid itself.

The alternative then is either sheer self-contradicting idiocy or else some tenacious belief in our power of reasoning, held in the teeth of all the evidence that Bulverists can bring for a "taint" in this or that human reasoner. I am ready to admit, if you like, that this tenacious belief has something transcendental or mystical about it. What then? Would you rather be a lunatic than a mystic?

So we see there is justification for holding on to our belief in Reason. But can this be done without theism? Does "I know" involve that God exists? Everything I know is an inference from sensation (except the present moment). All our knowledge of the universe beyond our immediate experiences depends on inferences from these experiences. If our inferences do not give a genuine insight into reality, then we can know nothing. A theory cannot be accepted if it does not allow our thinking to be a genuine insight, nor if the fact of our knowledge is not explicable in terms of that theory.

But our thoughts can only be accepted as a genuine insight under certain conditions. All beliefs have causes but a distinction must be drawn between (1) ordinary causes and (2) a special kind of cause called "a reason." Causes are mindless events which can produce other results than belief. Reasons arise from axioms and inferences and affect only beliefs. Bulverism tries to show that the other man has causes and not reasons and that we have reasons and not causes. A belief which can be accounted for entirely in terms of causes is worthless. This principle must not be abandoned when we consider the beliefs which are the basis of others. Our knowledge depends on our certainty about axioms and inferences. If these are the result of causes, then there is no possibility of knowledge. Either we can know nothing *or* thought has reasons only, and no causes.

[The remainder of this essay, which was originally read to the Socratic Club before publication in the *Socratic Digest*, continues in the form of notes taken down by the Secretary of the Club. This explains why it is not all in the first-person, as is the text proper.]

One might argue, Mr Lewis continued, that reason had developed by natural selection, only those methods of thought which had proved useful surviving. But the theory depends on an inference from usefulness to truth, of which the validity would have to be *assumed*. All attempts to treat thought as a natural event involve the fallacy of excluding the thought of the man making the attempt.

It is admitted that the mind is affected by physical events; a wireless set is influenced by atmospherics, but it does not originate its deliverances—we'd take no notice of it if we thought it did. Natural events we can relate one to another until we can trace them finally to the space-time continuum. But thought has no father but thought. It is conditioned, yes, not caused. *My* knowledge *that* I have nerves is inferential.

The same argument applies to our values, which are affected by social factors, but if they are caused by them we cannot know that they are right. One can reject morality as an illusion, but the man who does so often tacitly excepts his own ethical motive: for instance the duty of freeing morality from superstition and of spreading enlightenment.

Neither Will nor Reason is the product of Nature. Therefore either I am self-existent (a belief which no one can accept) or I am a colony of some Thought and Will that are self-existent. Such reason and goodness as we can attain must be derived from a self-existent Reason and Goodness outside ourselves, in fact, a Supernatural.

Mr Lewis went on to say that it was often objected that the existence of the Supernatural is too important to be discernible only by abstract argument, and thus only by the leisured few. But in all other ages the plain man has accepted the findings of the mystics and the philosophers for his initial belief in the existence of the Supernatural. Today the ordinary man is forced to carry that burden himself. Either mankind has made a ghastly mistake in rejecting authority, or the power or powers ruling his destiny are making a daring experiment, and all are to become sages. A society consisting solely of plain men must end in disaster. If we are to survive we must either believe the seers or scale those heights ourselves.

Evidently, then, something beyond Nature exists. Man is on the borderline between the Natural and the Supernatural. Material events cannot produce spiritual activity, but the latter can be responsible for many of our actions on Nature. Will and Reason cannot depend on anything but themselves, but Nature can depend on Will and Reason, or, in other words, God created Nature.

The relation between Nature and Supernature, which is not a relation in space and time, becomes intelligible if the Supernatural made the Natural. We even have an idea of this making, since we know the power of imagination, though we can create nothing new, but can only rearrange our material provided through sense data. It is not inconceivable that the universe was created by an Imagination strong enough to impose phenomena on other minds.

It has been suggested, Mr Lewis concluded, that our ideas of making and causing are wholly derived from our experience of will. The conclusion usually drawn is that there is no making or causing, only "projection." But "projection" is itself a form of causing, and it is more reasonable to suppose that Will is the only cause we know, and that therefore Will is the cause of Nature.

A DISCUSSION followed. Points arising:

All reasoning assumes the hypothesis that inference is valid. Correct inference is self-evident.

"Relevant" (re evidence) is a *rational* term.

The universe doesn't claim to be *true*: it's just *there*.

Knowledge by revelation is more like empirical than rational knowledge.

Question: What is the criterion of truth, if you distinguish between cause and reason?

Mr Lewis: A mountainous country might have several maps made of it, only one of which was a *true* one, i.e. corresponding with the actual contours. The map drawn by Reason claims to be that *true* one. I couldn't get at the universe unless I could trust my reason. If we couldn't trust inference we could know nothing but our own existence. Physical reality is an *inference* from sensations.

Question: How can an axiom claim self-evidence any more than an empirical judgment on evidence?

[The essay ends here, leaving this question unanswered.]

PHILOSOPHY TODAY

Professor H. A. Hodges

It is an empirical fact that philosophy ever since c. 1600 has been in a state of transition. There is disagreement among philosophers about why this is so, what the direction is, and what is now the goal of philosophy: but the fact of transition and the present crisis is widely admitted. That we are living in a period of "philosophy in crisis" is evidenced by the number of works published in modern times on philosophical method.

Since Descartes wrote his notable work on Method, philosophy has not lacked advocates of some procedure or other to redeem it from frustration. Descartes and Spinoza thought it could be done by "geometrizing" philosophy. Kant and Hegel and many more have had their own notion of method. Collingwood produced an essay on Philosophical Method which in his own judgment was the most satisfactory of all his philosophical writings. It is true the field of learning in general has been marked in modern times by a great growth of subjectivity and self-criticism, and the examination of one's own method is part of that process; but it has shown itself more conspicuously in philosophy than elsewhere. There is not much doubt what the method of physical science is: it is a field day if two philosophers are found to agree in method. But if the method of philosophy is in doubt that is because its aim is in doubt too. Where is philosophy going? Has it a future? Many people today are disposed to say, "No, philosophy has no future." Some philosophers are prepared to agree that it cannot survive without undergoing drastic changes. The very phrase a "philosophy of philosophy" coined by one of them is a pointer to the situation I am describing. When philosophy makes it its business not to do its job but to philosophize about its job, clearly something has gone wrong with the works. The sense of change is widespread, even though men differ as to what the change should be.

My intention is to review the history of philosophy and see if it suggests any pattern.

There have been three first-class revolutions in the conditions of human life. (1) The discovery of agriculture and the related arts which took place in unrecorded time—though that prehistoric epoch is not beyond the reach of the spade of the archaeologist. (2) The intellectual revolution in the first millennium B.C., associated with the beginnings of philosophy, religious reforms, the first systems of legal and political theory and the attempt to make thinking self-conscious and a force in history. The first fruit of this revolution in Europe was Hellenism. (3) The modern revolution—natural science, the machine age, industry, social revolution, large populations, large-scale administration, a worldwide outlook in social and intellectual life.

Philosophy took its origin in the second of these great revolutions, and that may help to suggest why we feel uneasy about it now, living as we do in the third of them. It comes from a time when the ideal of intellectual life was the sage (σοφός); the tendency today is to seek not the σοφός but the δεινός—the scientific technician, the man who "knows the gadgets," and he is certainly not a pretender to knowledge, he is no "sophist" in the bad sense: he does know what he claims to know. Well, philosophy has run its course for 2,500 years, and now it is being eclipsed by the scientist, technician and administrator.

This justifies us in treating the history of philosophy as a unit. If we look at it from the outside we find in it two main components: (1) Socratic criticism of life; (2) Speculation. The Socratic criticism of life deserves that name because it was embodied in the figure of Socrates. Socrates switched people's attention away from metaphysical or cosmological speculation to the criticism of life, *i.e.* of belief and conduct, and especially the principles which govern these.

Everyone is in fact governed by principles in thought and action: many people are not aware of these, and many suppose their principles to be other than they are. Socrates hammered into people's heads that nothing could be more important than to get clear on these things. And in the background there was something more than criticism—there was the hope that our principles of thought and conduct could be shown to have something objective about them, that they answered to something real in the build of the universe. That hope and faith were widespread, and still are. Socrates had that hope, though he was unable to prove even to his own satisfaction that the thing was so, *e.g.* that righteousness and honest thinking were in that sense objectively real; yet he believed it was so and imparted his faith to his disciples. But the immediate end of criticism is not to prove the objectivity of the principles of thinking and living, but to show what those principles are—in other words, "know thyself." And it is worthwhile to obey the Delphic maxim to know thyself even if the principles of human life do not govern the universe as a whole. Out of that kind of questioning comes a great deal of logic (the study of the principles of valid thinking), ethics and politics, aesthetics and the philosophy of religion. All these branches of philosophy reveal the effort to discover principles of order at work in the various fields of experience.

Speculation (or Metaphysics) is something much more bold, daring and constructive than Socratic criticism. It is based on impatience with fragmentary knowledge and half-truths. All our experience is fragmentary, but we conjecture that behind the fragments there is a coherent Whole, and we try to find out what it is. There is only one way of doing this, and that is by taking the facts and extending them by well-grounded conjecture—"extrapolating" them. The result is an apprehension of the Whole, Substance, Nature or the Absolute, in the contemplation of which we find our minds stabilized. This is called Metaphysics, and historically it is the part of philosophy in which philosophers have taken most interest. The history of philosophy is in effect a history of metaphysics. It shows what the prestige of metaphysics has been. The tendency to speculation is not confined to philosophers; it is found also in art and religion. That is why in Hegel and his followers, art, religion and philosophy are singled out and said to be three forms of the same thing. The reason is that the "metaphysical consciousness" discloses itself in all three forms. They tend to stabilize and unify the minds that indulge in them. We build up a picture of the world into something like a unifying symbol: the different metaphysical systems should be regarded in that way, *viz.* as unifying symbols. The metaphysician has projected into his system of thought the things he considers most important in life, so that his work is really a commentary on himself.

Metaphysics is like theology in that it talks mysterious language and delights in persuading people that things are not what they seem to be. The contrast between Appearance and Reality is one dear to the metaphysician. Dean Inge remarks in his Gifford Lectures that Plotinus (one of the greatest of all metaphysicians) transfigures life and the world for him no less than the New Testament. But philosophers always offer reasons (I do not say good reasons) for their metaphysics. The poet puts his work forward as vision; the theologian often says, "This is the Faith once for all delivered to the saints"; the philosopher says, "This I know, for I have proved it." One recalls the reply of Spinoza to a newly won convert to the Church of Rome who wrote him a letter, not in the best vein, reproaching him with "thinking that he had constructed the best philosophy": "I do not think I have constructed the best philosophy, but I know that I have discovered the true one." Metaphysics was originated by Plato. The great historical importance of Plato was that he made Socratic criticism and speculation an undivided whole. He made metaphysics the foundation of his criticism, and that combination of the two became the classic structure of philosophy down to this day. It is usual to begin the study of philosophy with logic (the enquiry into the principles of valid thought), to proceed to metaphysics, leading up through the study of the structure of matter and the natural universe to the supreme principle of Reality as a whole (usually conceived as "God"), and to descend from that height to moral and political theory, and to aesthetics if one happens to be interested. It is an impressive set of ideas. The history of philosophy is largely a variation of that great theme, though individual philosophers have laid the emphasis in different places, some finding the clue in metaphysics, some in ethics, others in religion, and others again in art.

Now philosophy makes a perpetual appeal to a type of mind which is alert and keenly interested in life and its problems but is not satisfied with the religious answers. To those who remain unconvinced by the traditional doctrines of religion, philosophy appears to be a godsend, doing more modestly what the theologian claims to have done for them by divine revelation or prophecy. And to the theologian's taunt that philosophers spend their time contradicting one another and themselves, the philosopher can rejoin with a devastating "*tu quoque*": in fact, the Babel of contradictions is louder among theologians than among philosophers.

Philosophy is in constant tension with religion on the one hand and with science on the other.

(1) With religion—partly because they compete over the same ground (the ultimate nature of Reality), and partly because religion takes its stand on revelation once for all delivered, while philosophy will have no truck with revelations and turns them into discoveries. To the religious man the activity of independent speculation and criticism is suspect even when he is capable of it: to the philosopher it is the breath of life. Religion needs philosophy against criticism from without and folly from within: it needs it as a discipline. But when it accepts the services of philosophy it admits a Trojan horse. If we look for the meaning of the Reformation we shall find it largely a purging of the religious world of the "damnable heresies" of philosophy which obscured or perverted the original deposit of Faith.

(2) With Science, because when philosophy claims to argue its point it lays itself open to criticism by people who have other (*i.e.* scientific) ways of arguing. Philosophy does not rest on the observation of particular facts. If any theory is such that its truth or falsity could make a difference to any particular fact, it is a scientific and not a philosophical theory. Science is empirical: the scientist argues from facts and figures and disdains what appear to him to be cloudy speculation.

In the intellectual climate of Greece and the Middle Ages philosophy flourished. But today the situation has changed. With the development of modern natural science have come new methods, new aims and ideals of thought. Of course if the work which the philosopher attempts to do is to be done at all, the philosopher must have at his disposal a great deal of non-philosophical knowledge: he must have, for example, physics and psychology. In the old days he did this work for himself amateurishly, but now physicists and psychologists do it, and in taking over this job they have removed what appeared to be final landmarks in philosophy. A discussion of some of the ways in which this challenge has shown itself involves a sketch of the history of modern philosophy.

Students of philosophy in the Universities are now taught the subject—as they are taught, say, literature—historically. It is unfortunate that the history of modern philosophy should be supposed to have stopped in the early months of 1781, when Kant had completed the first part of his *Critique of Pure Reason*. But history went on through the 19th century and still goes on today. Let us take a look at the way that stream of history has flowed. At the beginning of the 17th century Francis BACON makes a new start in logic and the theory of method: he challenged the

Aristotelian syllogism and started a new logic of induction which has gone on ever since. The old deductive logic had "compelled assent but not things"; the new inductive logic altered this and was made the foundation of modern natural science. (Knowledge is power, and what isn't power isn't knowledge.) During the course of the 17th century mighty edifices were built by GALILEO, BOYLE and NEWTON in physics and astronomy. As a result three fundamental assumptions in philosophy underwent drastic change:

(1) The concept of substance. Substance was a technical term in ancient and medieval philosophy. It was coined by Aristotle and given a fixed and definite meaning. In the 17th century it behaves as if it were drunk, in the 18th century it is found incapable, and after that it more or less disappears.

(2) The idea of cause and effect: this had a definite form in Plato and Aristotle and the philosophy of the Middle Ages. And it was a maxim of the scholastics that cause and effect stood in no essential relation to time: they were "simultaneous." In the 17th century philosophers began to speak of causality as a time-relation, and that is how we think today. It is plain that this involved a revolution in the old classical arguments for the existence of God, for those arguments were now translated into terms of the time-series, and this made nonsense of them.

(3) The concept of motion. The ancients and medievals all took for granted that motion was not a state of things but a departure from one state into another. But Galileo's first laws of motion amounted to denying this and affirming that it was a state.

In face of this challenge and tension arose the critical philosophy of the 18th century. Our own philosopher, John LOCKE, did succeed in his artless way in saying the right thing at that point. Before we start building our metaphysical system we should test our capacities for the job: we must, so to speak, examine the telescope before turning it on to the heavens. Locke announced the program, though he failed to carry it out. He also started the idea that much of this critique of knowledge was an examination of the meaning of words: it needs no great erudition to see how prominent a place this occupies in present day philosophical thinking. Locke was followed by BERKELEY, who did a good deal in asking the meaning of words: he asked what people meant when they talked about "existing." We always suppose we know what we mean when we say things exist, but Berkeley found a very paradoxical answer, which is contained in his famous thesis that *esse est percipi*. HUME and KANT were superficially antithetic, but they had much in common. They stood together on the following points:

(1) All our thinking depends on certain first principles, *e.g.* the principles of causality and regularity—that everything that happens has its cause and is an instance of a law. These principles cannot indeed be shown to be true; there is a logical flaw in every attempt to prove them either *a priori* or from experience. You have no *reason* to believe them except that unless you believe them you cannot think at all; as Ewing has put it, you have to choose between them and the asylum. At the same time, while the first principles make possible the growth of empirical knowledge on a certain level, when pushed to a limit they lead to unavoidable antinomies, and this fact, inherent in our cognitive faculty, defeats all attempts at a coherent metaphysic.

(2) Since speculative or metaphysical truth is not attainable, the center of gravity for the philosopher is no longer metaphysics but the study of the way the mind works. For Kant this meant a critique of reason, and for Hume it meant empirical psychology. Socratic criticism was back again in a new form, only this time it did not start from ethics but from the theory of knowledge.

(3) Both Hume and Kant stressed the importance of emotional and volitional attitudes in man. Hume said that "reason is and ought only to be the slave of the passions," and Kant insisted on the primacy of the practical reason, *i.e.* reason in conduct. The principles of thought are to be discovered in the foundations of life.

But philosophy did not stop there (although some of our contemporaries have not got there yet). FICHTE, standing on Kant's foundation, said that there were only two completely consistent philosophies in history, his own and Spinoza's, and which you believed depended on whether you were a good man or not. If you were a good man you would have a strong conviction of freedom and the reality of moral choice, and so you would tend to agree with Fichte: if you were not a good man you would follow Spinoza and be an out-and-out Determinist.

HEGEL, who has been much talked of for good and ill since BRADLEY, BOSANQUET and Edward CAIRD (the so-called "Oxford Idealists") took to spreading his ideas in this country at the end of the last century, saw that humanity itself was the true philosopher; he thought of the individual in terms of his historical conditions. Karl MARX, the most celebrated of all Hegelians, added that the economic system in which we lived was the most important of all the historical factors which conditioned man's life, and further that this was a truth which, once seen, must be acted on. "The philosophers have interpreted the world in various ways; the point, however, is to change it." At the same time in Denmark KIERKEGAARD, who was also something of an Hegelian—a theologian mixed up with a philosopher—was dominated by the realization that in life one is perpetually confronted by a tension which it is impossible to overcome, though we often endeavor to conceal it. Hegel had thought that Reality was an "interpenetration of opposites," and that truth is the synthesis of all contradiction: Kierkegaard said that life was a mass of contradictions, but that there was no synthesis. And if there is no synthesis, then you are compelled to make choices, "existential" choices, and in every case the choice is not something determined by the intellect, but something elected by the will of the chooser, and the task of the philosopher is to help people to choose wisely. DILTHEY, who died shortly before the last war and whose works, written in German, have not been translated into English, said that all systems of philosophy fall into three main types, each with an intelligible psychological foundation: as your character is, so your type of philosophy will be. Any given philosopher belongs to one of the three types, or is a hybrid of two of them, but never of all three. Dilthey went on to say that there was truth in each of the three types, but no one of them can be brought fully into line with the other two. They have the truth between them, but it is confounded with error in each of them. It is for the philosopher to study the three types and help people to realize to which type they belong. To analyze and expose these types is what Dilthey called "the philosophy of philosophy," and that is the position in which we now find ourselves.

No modern writer has gone deeper than this: the situation is full of challenge. The question forces itself: "What next?" I suggest that a threefold choice has to be made:

(1) Admit the breakdown of metaphysics. There is an unwillingness to do this, but some forms of Idealism and all forms of Positivism and Pragmatism are doing it. It does not mean that philosophy has broken down, but that it becomes Socratic criticism.

(2) As a consequence of this, separate philosophy from theology for the health of both. The alliance is possible only as long as one thinks one can arrive at God's existence by reason. It was not by philosophic reasoning that the Psalmist became aware that the heavens declared the glory of God in whom he already believed on other grounds. But to Anaxagoras the heavens declared the glory of reason, and it was he who, followed by Plato and Aristotle, found that the

facts of astronomy, as known and interpreted in classical times, carried with them a theistic implication, and it was the inferences built on this foundation which were incorporated into the great tradition of metaphysics. The foundations of modern astronomy, however, do not tend to such conclusions: no metaphysical theology is part of the import of our scientific discoveries today. This does not mean that theology is discredited: it only means that it can no longer lay its foundations in a philosophical science of Being or a philosophical cosmology. Recognition of this may lead to the discovery of its real foundations. It does not mean a collapse of theology but only of metaphysical theology.

(3) Acknowledge the relativity of all points of view (*i.e.* of all Collingwood's "presuppositions"). Here lies the deepest challenge of all. There is danger and difficulty in it, for it is not easy for people to recognize that all points of view are personal without flying off at the deep end and becoming aggressively dogmatic—putting on the brown shirt, or its equivalent. It does not mean that one idea is as good as another, and that we can do what we like. The challenge is to do justice to relativity without making it the basis of nihilism, and the way to do this is not the way of thinking but the way of choosing.

What are we going to do next? We have to answer this question seriously and choose, in this chaos of relativities, with a sense of responsibility. That then is the task, though it is a very different one from that which a great deal of current philosophy suggests.

Mr. Lewis opened the DISCUSSION and commented as follows:

(1) All human activity seems to be here reduced to a mode of self-expression or self-indulgence (*cf.* alleged "stabilizing" effects of metaphysics), except perhaps history (but *cf.* Powicke's Riddel Lectures: he despairs about really knowing the past). A different pattern of history will emerge from each man's history of philosophy. The trouble about skepticism is that you cannot be skeptical about everything at the same time, or you are reduced to silence.

(2) If truth is not objective but only personal, what is the "right" method of thinking in logic?

(3) What sort of health is possible, from this point of view, to philosophy and theology when they are separated? Such a separation would leave a concealed "waffling" in metaphysics, and just naked "waffling" in religion!

(4) How choose responsibly when you don't know to what or to whom you are responsible? On this view, why is theology not regarded as pure "waffle"?

Professor Hodges: These questions amount to a challenge to me to state my theory of knowledge. I can do so only in outline. It is dialectical (not precisely in the Hegelian sense). All experience is a conscious relation between a subject and an object, based upon a complex of adjustments and mutual conditionings. The relation insofar as conscious can subsist only insofar as the subject *recognizes* or *acknowledges* the presence of an object, and this recognition or acknowledgement is a complex intellectual-emotional-volitional attitude which the subject can refrain from taking; in which case the object which he does not acknowledge cannot be an object for him, and his experience is to that extent the poorer. The recognition or acceptance of a particular object or type of objects is justified in face of questioning insofar as this recognition or acceptance opens up a realm of experience, not accessible otherwise, in exploring which I continually make new discoveries, produce effects, and find things happening to me. Thus e.g. (1) Acceptance of a world other than my own consciousness and conforming to the scientific principle of uniformity opens up wide realms of discovery and action. (2) Acceptance of an order of persons having claims upon me (the basic attitude underlying morality) opens up another realm in which, again, I make discoveries and find things happening to me. (3) Acceptance of the object commonly called God has analogous results. In each instance the initial acceptance opens up possibilities of continuing exploration, whose results react upon myself and build up my mind, character and life-pattern. This fruitfulness in exploration is the essence and also the test of truth.

In ordinary life we make our basic acceptances unconsciously and get on with our exploring. The resulting growth of knowledge is a fact of life. Socratic criticism (here epistemology) cannot destroy or alter it, but can show us how it depends on the basic acceptance, how there are alternative sets of first principles which can be used to cancel one another out, how consequently there are no bedrock certitudes. This *bottomlessness* is also a fact of life and we have to learn to live with it. We can even conceive the possibility of a total paralysis of thought by withdrawal of all acceptances, a depth in which, as Mr. Lewis says, only silence is possible. A serious thinker will go down again and again into that silence, but he will not stay there. He will go on living, *i.e.* accepting, exploring, and knowing, but with a new awareness of what he is doing, and why. He will make his acceptance responsibly—by which I simply mean seriously.

The choice (insofar as there is a choice) between accepting and not accepting a particular type of object or set of first principles depends on the principle of fullness of life: i.e. the opening up of as many realms of experience as possible. This principle operates in determining our choice whether we are aware of it or not.

The above contains or implies the answers to Mr. Lewis' questions. It is he who talks of skepticism, not I. The systematic exploration of the various realms of experience is not waffling. Theology is an instance of such exploration, and so is Socratic criticism, but metaphysics is not, since it endlessly frustrates itself, and therefore it does theology no good to tie it up with metaphysics. The "right" way to think, which logic is to detect, is that which is fruitful in discovery. I have tried to show that the possibility of discovery depends on factors in the subject as well as in the object. It is not I who have inferred from this that no discovery is possible at all.

Fallacies lead to frustration in action, but right thinking does not. Evaluation is by action.

QUESTION: How "choose," when you don't know what are the two principles between which you choose?

PROFESSOR HODGES. "Fullness of life" is *the* principle, but principles need not all be conscious. It is part of Socratic criticism to make them conscious. Something is at work in me which I have not chosen, *i.e.* myself. I ask myself, "Why do I believe so and so?" and this is the fundamental passion behind philosophy as I practice it. It doesn't worry me to say that philosophy is a branch of applied psychology. I cannot calculate what experience will yield.

QUESTION: Is the kind of knowledge before your choice different from the knowledge after it?

PROFESSOR HODGES. No. Before you made a choice you were not conscious why you did it, but afterwards you know and are therefore more stable. The aim is the emergence of self-consciousness. An "existential" decision is one which makes you a different person, and such decisions need not be religious ones.

MR. LEWIS. Must I, for the sake of "fullness of life," give up the only "fullness of life" I care about—the belief in objective truth (*my* unextinguishable, or rather unextinguished, passion)? Only love of objective truth could make me accept what you say.

PROFESSOR HODGES. I speak to you as to a Christian: certain things cannot be known "in via"—this we must accept.

QUESTION: I thought Professor Hodges was denying objective truth to metaphysics only, not, e.g., to the principles revealed by epistemology.

PROFESSOR HODGES: There are three levels of thought. (1) Positive or empirical enquiry, scientific and historical, where on the basis of agreed presuppositions agreed results are reached. These are objective in the sense that they hold for all thinkers who accept the principles and weigh the evidence. (2) Socratic criticism, which discloses the principles on which (1) is based, showing the extent to which they rest on foundations in the nature of the thinking subject. Such principles can be shown to have a history, but are not individual fantasies. (3) Metaphysical construction, which is individual fantasy.

QUESTION. Can we *argue* about fundamental choices?

PROFESSOR HODGES: We can sometimes show that a principle holds for all possible subjects in like circumstances, and is in that sense objective.

MR. LEWIS: For all *possible* subjects or for all *human* subjects? Is truth *about* something or only *for* persons?

The discussion had reluctantly to be closed at 10.50 p.m.

CONCERNING THE QUESTION: "JESUS, PROPHET OR SON OF GOD?"

Stella Aldwinckle

This question is the most important that a human being can ask, since on the answer to it depends the possibility, or impossibility, of being *certain* whether our human existence has meaning and purpose or not. For if Christ was Son of God, there has been a Word from ultimate Reality spoken to men, who are not then left groping up towards a God who may not be there (*cf.* "wish-fulfillment" theories). This would seem to be the ultimate distinction between Christianity and other world faiths: the claim is that in *history*—*i.e.* in an *objective* act, not merely in some prophet's mystical experience—ultimate Reality has given man *certain* knowledge concerning the nature and purpose of human existence (*i.e.* in the "chaos of relativities" our basic first principle or major clue is given *to* us, not selected *by* us).

The differing of intelligent men in their answers to our question brings the truth of the Christian claim into doubt. Yet there is an alternative to the conclusion that this differing indicates that Christ's deity is fantasy, not fact, *i.e.* that it is FACT but that the *conditions for perceiving it* are absent in the deniers.

In any act of knowing we can differentiate subject, object and the relation between the two. Let a true judgment, or act of knowing, be defined here as one which corresponds to the fact, *i.e.* to that which is the case. Let facts be the objects of acts of knowing or perceiving. Is "Jesus, Son of God," a TRUE judgment? Some *different types of fact* were then distinguished—mathematical, scientific, historical, personal, aesthetic, moral, metaphysical.

The possibility of a knower perceiving facts of any type depends on his *powers*, and on the *training*, *condition* and *use* of those powers (*e.g.* compare the access to the fact or facts of a field lying in the sunlight of a lump of coal, a plant, an animal and a man respectively; or of a farmer, a huntsman, a jerry-builder, a botanist, or a mystic). A leading part is played by the *will* in perceiving facts: the will focuses *attention*, and selection from among the many potentially perceptible facts is made in accordance with the subject's *interests*, which are formed by what he *loves* and/or serves. So we see that even when facts are of the same kind, the subjective conditions in various knowers judging of them may preclude their perceiving them as facts.

False judgments are obviously likely concerning personal and moral facts where the will is biased (*e.g.* by jealousy or fear), but metaphysical judgments may also be viciously subjective (*cf.* Mr. Aldous Huxley as a young man *choosing* a philosophy of meaninglessness because at that time he did not wish to be moral). The judgment concerning the "metahistorical" fact of Christ's deity, if fact it be, uniquely invites the danger of a vicious subjectivity, since if it be fact it must drive a man, however altruistic and high-minded, from the last strongholds of his egocentricity—his right to himself and his self-esteem.

Impregnable mental presuppositions can shelter one from the possibility of perceiving such a disturbing fact as the deity of Christ: sincerity in face of it is bound to be costly indeed,

> A condition of complete simplicity
> (Costing not less than everything).

Many today, however, are willing for such sincerity.

If his deity be fact, *how far can unbiased reason achieve the conditions necessary for perceiving it as fact*? (1) It can deliver from the intellectual bondage of pseudo-scientific presuppositions which confuse analysis with explanation and assume that only the physically observable can be real. (2) It can give intellectual understanding of what Christ's deity meant to those who first judged it to be fact (Christ, the Act of the Living God, breaking into time from eternity to fulfill the Creator's purpose in creation, Judge and Savior from above, not evolved from below) and the grounds on which their faith rested: also of what it meant to the thinkers who carried out the gigantic intellectual task of rethinking their categories of unity and divinity in order to reconcile his deity (which they could not deny) with ethical monotheism (which they could no less deny). (3) Reason can deal with such critical questions as "Did Christ actually live?" "Are the New Testament documents *bona fide* reliable evidence?" "Does the evidence point to the Resurrection appearances being hallucinations?" etc., etc. (4) Reason can weigh certain pieces of evidence *taken together* and decide whether it is more reasonable, or less, to accept the deity of Christ as fact, to explain them *together*, than to adopt several other hypotheses to account for them severally:

(1) The complete change in character in the Eleven between the arrest of Christ and the preaching in Jerusalem seven weeks later.

(2) The emergence of faith in his deity among fanatically monotheistic Jews.

(3) The persistence of the Church through nineteen centuries in spite of gross corruption within and major persecutions without.

(4) The integrating power, in individuals and in communities, of faith in Christ as Son of God where it is living and not merely conventional.

(5) The character of Christ taken together with his claims (*aut Deus aut non homo bonus*).

Here the frontiers are reached of what reason can intelligently be expected to do—intellectual and provisional assent to his deity as the most reasonable hypothesis to account for the evidence. This is theory, a working hypothesis. But what we look for is knowledge, *i.e.* perception which carries its own conviction and is common to others' minds with our own, and is related to the rest of life as we find it. We reach "certainty" in theoretical and scientific judgments by theoretical reasoning because we have standards of reference to judge by—axioms of thought or "laws" formulated from facts of previous experience. But a unique fact has *ex hypothesi* no standard of reference. If Christ be Son of God he is not an instance of anything we have met before, and access to the knowledge of the fact of his deity *cannot* therefore be by reasoning. It is by "faith," the act of the whole man. Reason may show us *that it is reasonable*, not superstitious, to believe Christ divine, but the step of faith is the crucial condition for *perceiving* his deity.

Faith is suspect among many intellectuals because, not being rational in the usual sense, it is misunderstood as irrational. It is in fact the most fully rational act of which a man is by original nature capable. It demands integration of the whole man, escapes our usual convenient, *irrational* divorcing of theory and practice, involves both intellectual assent and a continued act of trust by unconditional surrender of the will to God. *It is a new or renewed power of cognition.* By it the deity of Christ is perceived and KNOWN AS FACT (either suddenly or gradually) proportionately with the knowledge of the nature of sin, reached, not theoretically, but by awareness and admission of one's own bondage to it. Without it his deity cannot ever be known (cf. Mat. xvi, 13-17). It is a gift, received through prayer, most often through contemplating and *obeying* Christ (Jn. xiv, 21-24). Its life is thus a cooperation between man and God. It is found to open up a new dimension of perception and experience (1 Cor. ii, 9-14; Eph. iii, 14-19: love as *cognitive power*). It is as though one were to move from a two-dimensional into a three-dimensional existence, totally incomprehensible from the two-dimensional point of view, incontrovertible FACT from the three-dimensional.

    This explanation may help to show how Christians can (and must) be dogmatic without being obscurantist in their asserting "Jesus, Son of God," as a TRUE judgment. The intellectual formulations ("theology") of their spiritual knowledge may differ widely; but about the FACT they are at one. New and common power of cognition gives access to otherwise imperceptible Fact. It is as though by the journey of faith they came to a strange country, a Brave New World, different from that known to everyone. And when they come back and talk about what they have seen, those who have not been there cannot understand their language ("it is foolishness unto them," 1 Cor. ii, 14). But their words make immediate sense to all who have taken the risk of going there too: the FACT and facts they speak of are *public* facts among them. Faith gives the kind of *certain* knowledge beside which all other certainty seems empty and insecure, and all other knowledge mere tentative description. It is by such spiritual cognition that we come to *know* that our existence has meaning and purpose.

SOCRATIC DIGEST

No. 3   1945

CONTENTS

Papers, Speakers and Study Group, 1944–45	59
The Grounds of Modern Agnosticism Prof. H. H. Price	60
Life and Matter Dr. V. P. Whittaker	73
Is Theology Poetry? Mr. C. S. Lewis	75
Can Myth be Fact? Dr. A. M. Farrer	83
It and Thou Rev. Douglas Vicary	90
Christian and Non-Christian Mysticism Rev. Gervase Mathew, O.P.	95

ONE SHILLING AND SIXPENCE

Printed at the Oxonian Press, Oxford

ORDERS FOR DIGEST
By post from: MISS PROUT, 13 Norham Gardens, Oxford. 1/6 per copy, plus 2d. for postage and envelope. Please send the money by postal order or check, NOT in stamps.

PUBLICATION
We apologize for the very belated appearance of this number, due to severe printing difficulties.

LONDON SOCRATIC
The founding of the London Socratic has had to be postponed owing to the resignation of the prospective Chairman and Secretary.

OXFORD UNIVERSITY SOCRATIC CLUB

"In view of the present struggle between a 'Christian' and a 'Nazi' order of society, this Club has been formed for those who do not necessarily wish to submit themselves to Christian views but are interested in a philosophical approach to religion in general and to Christianity in particular, in a spirit of free enquiry and in the light of modern thought and knowledge.

Informal discussion will follow the introduction of the subjects by speakers who will include both Christians and non-Christians."

OFFICERS

President: C. S. LEWIS, M.A.   *Chairman*: STELLA ALDWINCKLE, M.A.

Senior Treasurer: DR. F. PRINGSHEIM
Secretaries and Treasurers:

1944	Michaelmas Term	Valerie Pitt (St. Hugh's)
		Christopher Browne (Magdalen)
1945	Hilary Term	Valerie Pitt (St. Hugh's)
		Christopher Browne (Magdalen)
1945	Trinity Term	Valerie Pitt (St. Hugh's)
		Caryl Micklem (New College)

PAPERS AND SPEAKERS
MICHAELMAS TERM, 1944

October 23rd—The Grounds of Modern Agnosticism   Prof. H. H. PRICE
October 30th—Is belief in a personal God compatible with modern scientific knowledge?
         Dr. DAVID EVANS, Ph.D.
         Rev. A. M. FARRER
November 6th—Is Theology Poetry?   Mr. C. S. LEWIS
November 13th—Has Psychology "debunked" Sin?   Prof. L. W. GRENSTED
         BARBARA FALK
November 20th—Is Christian Sex morality out of date?   Fr. GERALD VANN, O.P.
November 27th—Rational and Irrational   Fr. D'ARCY, S.J.
December 4th—Life and Matter   Dr. V. P. WHITTAKER

HILARY TERM, 1945

January 29th—The Gospels: History or Legend?   Rev. J. N. D. KELLY
February 5th—Poetry and Truth   MICHAEL DALGLISH
         ANTONY CURTIS

SOCRATIC DIGEST

"Οὗτος μὲν οἴεταί τι εἰδέναι οὐκ εἰδώς, ἐγὼ δὲ ὥσπερ οὖν οὐκ οἶδα οὐδὲ οἴομαι."
—*Socrates*

"Εἴ τις δοκεῖ ἐγνωκέναι τι, οὔπω ἔγνω καθὼς δεῖ γνῶναι."
—*St. Paul*

"La dernière démarche de la raison est de reconnaître qu'il y a une infinité de choses qui la surpassent." —*Pascal*

THE GROUNDS OF MODERN AGNOSTICISM[2]

Prof. H. H. Price

I think that some of you will not like some of the things I am going to say this evening. Indeed, though it sounds discourteous, I rather hope you will not. A spirit of pious optimism, a simple faith that "it will be all right on the night" does not suit our situation at all. The night is here already—a very black night it is too—and things are not all right by any means. To change the metaphor, Western Civilization is suffering from a very dangerous disease, more dangerous perhaps than any which has afflicted it since the fall of the Roman Empire: a disease which may quite easily prove fatal. I am not referring to the war, nor to the political and economic troubles which are certain to follow it. Terrible as these things are, they are only symptoms, as has often been pointed out. What I refer to is the inner emptiness and lack of faith from which our civilization is suffering. No military victory, however crushing, and no amount of political and economic planning, national or international (even though backed by overwhelming force and blessed by the whole bench of bishops), is going to cure this disease. It is an open question whether it can be cured at all.

What makes the situation more tragic is, that it is our virtues, not our defects, which have brought us to this pass. We have got into it not through stupidity, and still less through wickedness, but by following the best light we had. I think that some pious and high-minded persons have failed to see this. But until they do see it, the pills and soothing syrups which they offer us will do more harm than good. The disease is different from what they think it is, and very much worse.

Dixit insipiens, Non est Deus. The fool hath said, there is no God. Certainly some fools have said so. But it by no means follows, nor is it true, that all atheists are fools, nor even that most of them are. Still less does it follow, and still less is it true, that most *agnostics* are fools—poor silly muddleheads, victims of elementary intellectual confusions. On the contrary, anyone who thinks they are is himself living in a fool's paradise. No doubt in the long controversy between Theists and Agnostics—as in any other matter of popular debate—a good deal of claptrap and nonsense has been uttered; and not only on one side, either. But the fact remains that the Agnostic has a case, and a very strong case. You must realize how strong it is, and submit yourself, as it were, to the impact of it, and then if you disagree with him you must give him a fair and full answer. I will not say exactly that you must meet him on his own ground. For you might think I meant that you must accept his premises just as they stand. If you did that,

---

[2] Editor's Note (2012): This essay also appeared in *Phoenix Quarterly*, Vol. 1, No. 1, Autumn, 1946, p. 25.

I suspect you would get the worst of it. I only mean that you must treat him with intellectual respect, and with emotional sympathy too, trying to put yourself in his shoes before you answer him. If you find him using a weak argument now and then (as you may, for no human being is always rational), do not pounce on him and claim the victory. Try first whether you cannot state his case better than he has stated it himself. Then, and not till then, give him your answer. And you must give it by pointing out that his premises, though perfectly true as far as they go, are incomplete, and that there are relevant facts which he has not attended to. Moreover, you must try to offer him some intellectual analysis of these facts; or, if this is too difficult (and certainly it is exceedingly difficult) at least you must tell him clearly where these facts are to be found, so that he may verify your statements for himself.

There is another point which we must realize. Not only is it true that Agnosticism is more prevalent among us than it has ever been before in our history. A more disquieting consideration is that it is specially prevalent among the most highly educated strata of the population. And most disquieting of all, because of its significance for the future—it is even more prevalent among the highly educated young than among their elders. In the period between the two wars, a university teacher was genuinely surprised if he found that one of his abler pupils was a convinced Christian, or even a convinced Theist (though he expected to come across occasional traces of a vague and sentimental piety among his third-class students), and in the later years of the inter-war period he was more surprised than in the earlier. It is possible, of course, that the present war has produced a certain change in this respect. There are some faint signs that it has. But they do not amount to very much, and it would be unwise to count on them: especially when we remember that during the last four years or so higher education itself has almost been at a standstill.

It is true of course that, in the English-speaking countries at least, the *ethical* teachings of Christianity are respected by nearly everyone, educated and uneducated alike. What is more, they are practiced, even in war-time, whatever the Bishops may say. It may even be true that they are practiced more widely than ever before in our history. But religious belief, even of the most undenominational kind, appears to be dying out. Not that it is being replaced by positive disbelief. Dogmatic Atheism is rare among us. (Is it not itself in its way a form of religion?) In English-speaking countries at any rate, it is almost confined to a handful of Marxists, and even they lay little stress upon it. The prevailing attitude of educated people, and especially of the younger ones, should rather be described as *non*-belief. Their thoughts and interests are confined to this world, to Physical Nature and their fellow men: that is, to their fellow men considered not as immortal spirits, but as more or less intelligent and more or less social animals inhabiting this planet. If there be any reality beyond this, it is taken for granted that nothing can be known about it; that there is not even evidence enough for forming an opinion. Indeed, some of the ablest of our contemporary philosophers maintain that the very question "Does God exist?" is meaningless, and therefore to answer either "Yes" or "No" is equally meaningless. This is pushing Agnosticism to its utmost limit. The Agnostics of the last century admitted freely that the question did have a meaning, and merely maintained that they and all mankind were ignorant of the answer. But if the question itself is nonsensical (like asking "How many miles is it from here to next Tuesday?"), we cannot even say that we are ignorant of the answer, for there is nothing to be answered.

What reasons are there for this Agnosticism? We may answer in one word: Science. Before I elaborate this answer, I am going to be nasty again, if you will forgive me. There seem to be some pious and high-minded persons who regard Science as something not very important, or important only in a practical sense—for the multiplication of comforts, the curing of diseases, and the provision of bigger and better engines of destruction. I think that such persons are mistaken. I would even say that they are guilty of a kind of treason against the civilization of which they are members. Science is the one great original achievement of modern Western Europe since the Renaissance. In all the other great departments of human endeavor—art, literature, religion, political organization—other peoples and other ages have surpassed us. But in the understanding of Physical Nature and its laws, and in the inventive genius which has turned that understanding to practical effect, we are quite unrivalled by any other civilization that we know of. This is our gift to mankind, a gift for which posterity will always thank us, long after our politics and our wars, our literature and our art, have been forgotten. Let no one underrate it. To be sure, there is nothing very grand in the mere passive acceptance and enjoyment of the mechanical and other devices which science has made available to us: trains, telephones, motorcars, aircraft, anesthetics, and so on. But to understand the laws of Nature, to be able to explain and predict natural phenomena, and use this understanding for controlling Nature's forces: these *are* achievements, and we are right to be proud of them. Knowledge is a good thing, not a bad thing; the power to control the physical forces of Nature is also a good thing, not a bad thing; and our civilization has extended both to a degree never before dreamed of. You may say, we have paid a very heavy price for these achievements; we have lost, or all but lost, our own souls in the process. I do not disagree. But my present point is that we have got something in exchange, and something of real value, however dearly we have paid for it. And if our civilization does not survive to enjoy it, there are others which will. This is what I meant when I said at the beginning that it is our virtues, not our defects, which have brought us to our present pass. It is precisely our greatest achievement, Science, which has been our undoing: not primarily because of the destructive powers which it puts into the hands of unscrupulous and predatory men—though these are terrible enough—but because it has led to that inner emptiness and lack of faith, in short to that Agnosticism, which is our fundamental, and as it seems all but incurable, disease. Let us see how this result has come about.

Science brings with it a certain way of conceiving the Universe, something which may be called the Scientific Outlook. With the extraordinary extension of scientific knowledge during the last hundred years, and the equally extraordinary advances in our control over the forces of Nature which have followed from it, the Scientific Outlook has gradually been more and more widely diffused among educated men, and exercises a profound influence even upon those who have no detailed acquaintance with the achievements of scientists. This outlook, whether or not it is *logically* inconsistent with religious belief (a point we shall consider later), does seem to be *psychologically* opposed to the religious temper and attitude; and when it prevails, religion tends to fade away through psychological inanition, quite apart from intellectual refutations. When well-meaning philosophers and theologians assure us, as they still do from time to time, that the ancient conflict between Religion and Science has now at last been settled, the cynical observer may well reply that it has indeed been settled: Science has won a complete and crushing victory. Perhaps the victory is not permanent; the complaints and warnings we sometimes hear about the growth of "Modern Irrationalism" suggest that it is not. Perhaps it is not absolutely complete. Our Agnosticism is not yet carefree and whole-hearted; a certain lingering regret for our lost faith still lurks in obscure corners of our minds. But who can deny that broadly speaking the cynic would be right? Nor is this collapse of Religion confined to Western Europe and America. It has already begun in Eastern countries, wherever Science and scientific technique have established a firm foothold.

The victory of Science over Religion, which now seems so complete, is only the last and most striking phase of a long historical development. For about three-and-a-half centuries Science has been gradually undermining the religious tradition of the Western World. Indeed, the process began even earlier, when Copernicus showed that the earth is not the center of the physical universe, but merely one planet among others. With the invention of the telescope and, later, of the microscope, it was found that the physical world is both enormously larger and vastly more complex than theologians had dreamed. At the end of the seventeenth century, Newton's theory of Gravitation gave the final blow to the old cosmology. In the eighteenth century, the miraculous elements in Christianity began to look more and more incredible, as more and more phenomena in Physics and Chemistry were brought under the reign of natural law. The early nineteenth century saw the beginnings of Biblical Criticism, which cast doubt on the infallible authority first of the Old Testament, and later, of the New. About the same time, the Geologists were able to show that the earth is far older than the author—or authors—of the Book of Genesis supposed. Then came the Darwinian theory of Evolution, which made it clear that the various species of plants and animals have developed over an enormous period of time from a small number of much simpler forms. This refuted the doctrine of the Fixity of Species, derived partly from the Book of Genesis, partly from Aristotle. What is more, it greatly weakened the Argument from Design, which had been the main basis of the Rational Theology of the eighteenth century. For Evolution, it now appeared, had been an appallingly wasteful process. A merciless and unceasing struggle for existence had been its main instrument, working upon a multitude of "spontaneous variations," all but a few of which failed to survive and to perpetuate themselves. Such a process suggested, not a good and wise Creator, but rather (as Professor Broad has said) an immensely prolific Demon, proceeding by trial and error methods, and utterly indifferent to the welfare of his creatures.

Then came a further blow. The Theory of Evolution was extended to Man himself. Man was no longer the "lord of Creation," made in the image of God. He was the descendant of beasts, first cousin to the apes, and ultimately derived, like all other living creatures, from the primitive amoeba. As physiology progressed, and the intimate correlation between mind and nervous system was more and more fully established, it began to appear clear that consciousness in all its manifestations, from the lowest to the highest, was merely a byproduct of physico-chemical changes in the brain. The human body, it seemed certain, was just one piece of matter among others (a particularly complicated one, no doubt) working according to physical and chemical laws, and transforming one form of physical energy into another. There was no room for the intervention of a "soul." Such an intervention would be an exception to the principle of the Conservation of Energy, and that principle sufficed to explain all the available facts.

Meanwhile, the Anthropologists were busy showing that the higher religions are not separated by any sharp line from the superstitions and magic rituals of primitive races. The religions of civilized mankind were merely the most systematic and reflective development of that Primitive Animism which sees a "spirit" in every tree and every stone, and explains thunderstorms and plagues by the anger of invisible supernatural beings. Even the most distinctive and most sacred features of Christianity itself could be paralleled from the superstitions of the heathen. The primitive cultures had their dying Saviors, their ceremonies of "eating the God," their judgment after death, their heaven and hell. Religion, considered as a social phenomenon, appeared to be a kind of cultural senility, a survival into civilized times, of the beliefs and practices appropriate to a more primitive and childlike age.

Finally, the Psychologists stepped in to complete the argument of the Anthropologists by applying it to the individual human being. By the study of emotional disorders, they were led to conclude that such primitive ways of feeling and thinking are still present in the mind of each one of us, though repressed into the Unconscious; and, insofar as Religion still has a place in the life of the civilized adult, they maintained that these childish thoughts and wishes are the unacknowledged source of its power and its appeal. The late Dr. Freud, possibly the greatest psychologist of our age, called his little book on Religion *The Future of an Illusion*.

Such seem to have been the main stages in the conflict between Science and the Christian tradition. In every one of those encounters Christianity has been the loser. It has had to abandon one position after another; and each time a certain proportion of its most intelligent and open-minded followers has gone over permanently to the enemy, until now only a mere remnant is left. Ever since the Darwinian controversy, the Churches have been more and more on the defensive; and their attempts to repress their intellectual qualms by plunging into social work of one sort or another, and even sometimes into political controversy, have deceived neither the outside public nor even themselves. It is a sad story; and, as I have said, we shall probably see it repeated, though at a more rapid pace, in the Middle East and the Far East, wherever European science and scientific technique have penetrated.

But is the story so sad? Some people will contend that it is not. What looks like the gradual extinction of Religion is really—so they maintain—its gradual and very painful purification. They distinguish between the *essence* of Religion, and the *accretions* which have gathered around it in the course of ages: accretions of custom, tradition, mythology and theological drama. The essence is belief in God and immortality. But among the accretions there are naturally many highly fallible beliefs and speculations. Religious tradition preserves and, as it were, petrifies the conceptions of Physical Nature and Human History which were current in the period when the tradition began. These conceptions get enrolled among its dogmas, and its creed is formulated in terms of them; they thus acquire a sacredness which does not intrinsically belong to them. And if in the course of time these conceptions are superseded and replaced by others which are more scientific and more in accordance with the facts, surely this is a gain to Religion, and not a loss? Is it not perverse and irrational to give up belief in God, merely because one has acquired a wider and deeper understanding of His works? Newton said that the aim of his own scientific investigations was "to think God's thoughts after Him." Why should not modern science say the same?

What is suggested by such thinkers, then, is in effect this: The specific dogmas peculiar to any one religious tradition (Christianity, say, or Islam) are indeed incompatible with Science and the Scientific Outlook. They originated in an unscientific and uncritical age, and they are so tied up with erroneous and superstitious beliefs about Nature and about Man that they must be abandoned. But Theism as such, it is suggested, is in no way inconsistent with Science. Indeed, if anything, Science supports it, by giving us a fuller insight into the wisdom and power of the Creator. Let us hold fast to the kernel and boldly throw the dry shell away.

Some such proposals as these have attracted many thinking people ever since the early days of the conflict between Science and Religion. Is it possible for an educated, modern man to accept them without sacrificing his intellectual honesty? If we have the welfare of our civilization at heart, we must hope that it is. For history, and not least the history of our own time, seems to show clearly that no civilization can endure for long without a religious basis; hence the saying that "If God did not exist, it would be necessary to invent Him."

But there are serious difficulties which must be faced. In the first place, the distinction between the essence of Religion and the inessential accretions, the metaphor of the kernel and the shell, is not altogether apt. It may fit the logic of the matter; but does it fit the psychology of it? The Biblical account of the Creation may be *logically* independent of Theism. It may be false that the world was created in seven days in the year 4004 B.C., and yet it may still be true that there is an all-powerful and benevolent Supreme Being. But the Christian Theist of the last century, brought up from earliest childhood to accept the infallibility of the Scriptures, could not so easily dissociate the two propositions. Beliefs which are logically independent of each other may have a psychological solidarity to the mind, and especially to the emotions, of the believer. If he is compelled to reject one part of the religious tradition in which he has been brought up—even a small and, as it seems, wholly inessential part—it will not be so easy for him to retain the rest. And if by an effort he does succeed in retaining the rest, he may find that the emotional force and warmth has somehow gone out of it; what was once religious faith is now only a cold intellectual assent, and is no longer capable of influencing feeling or conduct. Hence, for many temperaments, religious belief is a matter of all or nothing. Their attitude of reverence and trust is directed to a certain body of religious teaching as a whole; if one part is shattered, the rest will lose its hold upon them. And because they are themselves half aware of this danger, they fight tooth and nail, and against all the evidence, for the retention of traditional doctrines and practices which to the outsider appear quite secondary and unimportant. Thus from a psychological point of view, the Church was not wholly wrong when it persecuted Galileo for accepting the heliocentric astronomy of Copernicus, much as we may deplore the means which it adopted. For from a psychological point of view the Copernican astronomy was certainly the thin end of the wedge. Once doubt the dogma that the earth is the center of the physical universe, and soon you will be doubting all the other dogmas of Theology as well; and even if you do not doubt them, your belief in them will not have the same integrity and force it had before.

There is another side to this matter. The belief in God and in Immortality cannot easily form the whole content of anyone's religion. In themselves these two beliefs are too sublime and at the same time too abstract for the everyday tenor of our thoughts and feelings. The mind cannot dwell on them for long, but only by fits and starts, and soon turns away again—dazzled, if you like, by excess of light. There is need of an apparatus of devotional symbolism to bring the meaning of these dogmas home to us and to incorporate them, as it were, in our daily lives: parables and illustrations, life stories of saints or prophets, set forms of prayer or praise. Consider, for example, the immense part which the Psalms have played in the religious experience of Christians from the earliest days of the Church. Now here again the metaphor of kernel and husk is inappropriate. Within very wide limits it may not matter *what* devotional symbolism you have, but *some* devotional symbolism you must have. Even the mystic and the religious genius cannot wholly dispense with it. And if men are forced to discard an old and familiar symbolism, because it is inextricably mixed up with unhistorical and unscientific beliefs about the world (as many of the Psalms, for example, are), a new one cannot be invented in a moment. It is not something which can be made to order, by conscious effort; or, if it can, no one yet has the psychological knowledge which would be required for the purpose. We must wait for the new symbolism to grow, and the growth takes time. Meanwhile, religion is in a state of dangerous weakness, and may even fade away altogether.

Much the same thing applies to ritual. To speak, as some do, of "mere ritual," as if it were something utterly external and unimportant, shows a lack of psychological insight. In many minds at any rate, faith can hardly exist at all unless it is permitted to express itself, and as it were solidify itself, in ritual actions. The Society of Friends, the most deeply religious, perhaps, of all the Protestant Christian sects, provides us with an excellent illustration. Nominally, they reject all ritual. But actually the silence and stillness of a Quaker meeting is itself a most powerful and impressive ritual, as anyone who has witnessed it knows. Now if a particular form of ritual has to be discarded, because it is bound up with superstitious or magical views about the Universe and about Man's place in it, views which Science has shown to be false, a new and better one cannot be made to order. For ritual is a product not of the intellect or the conscious will, but of the Unconscious, whose workings we do not yet understand and do not yet know how to control. New forms of ritual have to grow; they cannot be deliberately invented—at any rate not yet. When the old form has gone, and the new one has not had time to grow, the religious consciousness suffers from a feeling of frustration and emptiness, if it manages to survive at all.

But we must turn to difficulties which are even more important than these. Is it really true that Theism, in its essentials, is *logically* compatible with Science and the Scientific Outlook, whatever psychological obstacles there may be? This is the crucial question. There are two sides to it, and we must discuss them separately.

First we must distinguish between Scientific *Method* on the one hand, and on the other the *particular conclusions* about Nature or Man which particular sciences have reached. Scientific Method seems to be based upon two assumptions. The first is that all events are subject to laws (It does not matter for our purpose whether the laws are "deterministic" or only "statistical.") If a miracle is by definition a breach of some natural law—and that is one widely accepted definition of the term "miracle"—then a belief in miracles cannot be anything but unscientific. Either the alleged miraculous event was unmiraculous after all, though the law which it exemplified may be a little known one: or else the witnesses who testify that it occurred were mistaken. The second assumption of Scientific Method is that laws can be discovered by the study of publicly observable[3] regularities. Laws can only be discovered by observation, not by pure thought, nor yet by trusting to the *ipse dixit* of any authority, human or superhuman. And the observations which establish them must be capable, in principle, of being *repeated* by any normal man who cares to take the necessary trouble. Private revelations, which other people cannot verify, may be true or may be false, but in either case they are excluded from science. Thus the laws which Occultists or Theosophists profess to have discovered about the human aura or the astral body do not form part of Science, because it is not possible for other people to verify for themselves the observations which the Occultists profess to have made. If some means of public verification is discovered some day, as possibly it may be, and if other people's observations are found to confirm what the Occultists allege, then the study of auras and astral bodies will become a branch of Science; but not till then.

If this account of Scientific Method is correct, is the adoption of that method inconsistent with Theistic belief? It is true, as we have said, that a Deity who intervened miraculously and suspended natural law could never be accepted by Science. But, although many Theists have in fact believed in such miraculous interventions, there is no logical reason why they should; that

---

[3] The word "observable" must be understood somewhat widely. It must cover some objects and events which are strictly speaking inferred rather than observed, for instance, electrons; and it must cover the thoughts and emotions of human beings, if Psychology is a science. Nevertheless these things are verifiable *by means of* observation, even though not in the strictest sense observable.

belief is in no way *essential* to Theism. Moreover, as we have also said, the events deemed to be miraculous may really be manifestations of laws hitherto unknown, and so not miraculous at all. It is also true, of course, that Scientific Method could never *establish* the existence of God. When Laplace said to Napoleon "I have no need of that hypothesis," he was right, if he meant that in his scientific work he had no need of it. For God is not an *observable* entity, and Science by its very nature is confined to what is observable. Nevertheless, if the existence of God can be established in some other way, Scientific Method can have nothing to say against it. Our reasons for believing in His existence must be *non*-scientific, from the nature of the case. But they are not on that account *un*scientific. There is no reason why the whole of Nature—the whole world of observable events, with all the laws of their occurrence—should not be unilaterally dependent upon a Spiritual Being who stands outside of Nature altogether. Scientific Method can never establish the existence of such a Being, but equally can never disprove it.

Thus Scientific Method as such is perfectly compatible with Theism. And as a matter of history, it grew up in a Theistic atmosphere, as the very phrase "laws of Nature" testifies. It was thought that the uniformities which observable objects display were due to the commands of the Author and Ruler of the Universe: that the entities of which Nature is composed behave as they do, because it was the Creator's good pleasure that they should behave thus and not otherwise.[4]

But when we turn from Scientific Method in general to the conclusions which particular sciences have reached, the matter is not so simple. We must bear in mind the distinction between the Physical Sciences and the Biological Sciences. There is nothing in Physics or Chemistry, in Astronomy or Geology, which is inconsistent with Theistic belief; though there is much, especially in the two last, which is inconsistent with the cosmological traditions of the early Hebrew, taken over—wisely or unwisely—by Christianity and, I presume, by Islam as well. Indeed, it may be held, as was suggested earlier, that these sciences have been beneficial to Theism, since they enlarge our ideas of the power and wisdom of the Creator. The Heavens declare the glory of God far more effectively to us than to the Psalmist, for whom they were only a sparkling dome a few miles above his head. And if the knowable universe is far vaster both in time and in space than our ancestors conceived possible, if there are worlds within worlds even in a grain of sand, far transcending what our unaided senses would suggest: yet on the other hand all is explained and reduced to order by a comparatively simple set of laws, capable of exact mathematical formulation.

Much the same might be said of the Biological Sciences up to a point; but only up to a point. That point is reached when they offer their account of human personality. It is true that the Theist can consistently accept the Darwinian theory of Evolution. As for the apparent wastefulness and mercilessness of the evolutionary process (which I mentioned earlier) are our human measures of economy necessarily the right ones? If Nature is "red in tooth and claw" as the poet says, we must remember that the death of one animal provides food without which another animal cannot live. It is true, too, that the Theist can consistently believe that the human *body* has been gradually evolved from sub-human and eventually from animal forms. But can he believe it of the human soul? Even if he could, there is Physiology to be reckoned with, and not merely Zoology. The Theist, as it seems to me, is irretrievably committed to the distinction

---

[4] *Cf.* the words of the well-known hymn "Praise the Lord, Ye Heavens adore Him":—
    Praise the Lord, for He hath spoken,
    Worlds His mighty voice obeyed;
    Laws, which never shall be broken,
    For their guidance He hath made.

between Soul and Body.[5] He is bound to be what is called a Psychophysical Dualist. But, it would be claimed, Physiology has abolished that distinction; it is unscientific and out of date. Ultimately, it is a mere relic of Primitive Animism, plausible enough, perhaps, in days when nothing was known about the nervous system, but now shown to be utterly untenable. Let us consider how this conclusion has been reached.

That "the soul" has *some* degree of dependence upon the body; that drugs, fatigue, illness, old age, affect our intellectual and emotional power; that our sensations depend upon our sense organs and are altered by their disorders—all this has been known for ages. But Science in the course of the last three centuries has shown how exceedingly intimate that dependence is, and has revealed in minute detail the precise machinery of it—the nervous system and brain. And with this, the very idea of the soul began to appear questionable. Why had such an entity ever been postulated? For two reasons: as a source for certain sorts of bodily movements, viz. voluntary movements; and as the subject of conscious processes—sensation, thought, emotion, desire.

But Science claims to be able to show that the energy expended in our bodily movements (including the ones we call "voluntary") is nothing but ordinary physical energy: it is not something which comes into the physical world from outside. The human body is a sort of heat engine. The chemical energy taken into it in the form of food and air is given out again in the form of muscular work; and it has been found that the account balances exactly—no more energy is given out than is taken in. Thus there is no need to postulate a soul to be the source of voluntary movements. What about the other function traditionally assigned to the soul, the function of being the subject of conscious processes? That conscious processes do occur is of course absolutely certain. But in view of their intimate dependence upon the body and especially the brain, why do we need to postulate a special *soul-thing* to be their subject? If all our intellectual and emotional attributes (yes, and our spiritual attributes too) depend upon the brain, surely it is the brain which *has* those attributes? The thing which is conscious, which has experiences, is surely just the brain itself, not some mysterious and unobservable "spiritual" entity. What is called Psycho-physical Dualism, insofar as it is tenable at all, must really be a dualism not of *entities*—a bodily thing on the one side, a soul-thing on the other—but only of *functions*. One and the same entity, the living human organism, and more particularly the living brain, exercises both functions. On this view, common sense language is more scientific than the Theistic metaphysicians. We say "I walk," "I think," "I am six feet high," "I feel cold," "I desire this or that," "I believe this or that," " I weigh twelve stone." There is a distinction here between physical and mental *attributes*; but the same *thing*, "I," possesses both types of attributes alike. Thus "soul" and "body," according to this view, are not two things at all, but two aspects of one thing, two ways in which it functions. And scientific investigation seems to have shown that the conscious mode of functioning is wholly dependent upon the physical mode of functioning. This view, commonly called "Materialism," more technically called "Epiphenomenalism," is the working view of Science, and has been for the last fifty years at least.

Now why should the Theist object to it? Is it really true that Theism is committed irretrievably to the traditional Dualism of soul and body? Or was that Dualism merely a piece of infantile science, which can now be replaced by something less naïve and more in keeping with the observable facts? I think the Theist *is* committed to it in principle, whatever refinements he might be prepared to accept in detail. He is committed to the view that Man is essentially a

---

[5] Or at least he is committed to the threefold division of the human personality into Body, Soul and Spirit; and for our purposes it is sufficient to insist on the distinction between Soul and Spirit on the one hand, Body on the other.

spiritual being, and that the body, including the brain, is nothing but the temporary instrument of the spirit. It is logically impossible, as well as psychologically difficult, for the Theist to give up the belief in personal immortality. He may indeed allow that the human spirit is not literally everlasting, and that its final destiny is to transcend the limits of finite personality and to be absorbed in the Infinite Consciousness. But however that may be, he is committed to the belief that human personality continues in existence long after the destruction of the physical body (which is what the word "immortality" normally means).

Why so? Because Theism holds that God is not merely all-powerful but all-good.

What has been called "the conservation of values" must therefore be a fundamental feature of His universe. No doubt our human measures of what is good and what is evil are often shortsighted and childish. There may be more value in tragedy, sometimes, than in humdrum comfort. But the fact remains that if the highest forms of human excellence are annihilated by death, if not merely individual human beings but even the human race itself is destined to final extinction (for the time must come when this planet will be too cold to support life): if all this is so, then undeniably the most valuable things we know are *not* "conserved." If this life on earth is the only life there is, we must conclude that the universe is indifferent to values. It may indeed still have an all-powerful being for its Author; but that Author cannot be the God of Theism, who is all-good as well as all-powerful.

It is true that some religious men have thought otherwise. Some Theists seem to have disbelieved in personal immortality, for example the early Hebrews, as certain of the Psalms bear witness. But that was because they misconceived the empirical facts. They thought, mistakenly, that virtue is always rewarded in this present life. "Never yet saw I the righteous forsaken, nor his seed begging their bread." Noble words, but how false! Probably they also thought, equally mistakenly, that the human race will continue to exist indefinitely, even though the individual human being comes to an end. The more reflective Theist, aware of the falsity of these two assumptions, must answer in the words of the Apostle: "Here have we no continuing city, but we seek one to come"; and again, "The things which are seen are temporal, but the things which are not seen are eternal." Religion, then, is irreconcilable with the materialistic account of human personality which is, or appears to be, an inescapable part of the Scientific Outlook: for Physiology appears to establish conclusively that consciousness is wholly dependent upon the brain. *Ubi tres medici, ibi duo athei*[6] was not said in vain.

Let us pause to review the course of our argument. We have seen that it *is* possible for the Theist to tear away the many accretions of dogma and mythology which have gathered round his central belief, if it is shown (as it has been shown) that they are inconsistent with the conclusions which Science has established. The process of tearing them away is psychologically very difficult, and even perilous. It is not like casting off the dry shell, leaving the kernel intact. It is more like a drastic surgical operation, which for the time being—and it may be a long time—is bound to reduce the vitality of the patient, and may even kill him altogether. However, if after all he survives, we may anticipate that eventually he will be stronger and more healthy than ever before; a new devotional symbolism may grow up, and a new body of ritual, upon which modern educated man may feed without intellectual dishonesty and without a divided will. But when it comes to the belief in human immortality, the surgery must stop. For that belief is not an accretion, but belongs to the very essence of Theism, as we have seen. Theism cannot agree to the materialistic account of human personality. It is bound to hold that Man is a twofold being,

---

[6] "Where you find three medical men, there you will find two atheists."

an immortal spirit using for a time a perishable body; it cannot admit that he is just a body endowed with consciousness, a consciousness which will be extinguished forever as soon as the body breaks up. And if Science teaches that he *is* no more than this, then Theism and Science cannot possibly be reconciled. This then is the real crux of the quarrel between Religion and the Scientific Outlook. Other disputes, whatever agony of soul they may cause, do not go down to the root of the matter. Hence it appears to very many thinking people that at this point they must make a final decision between the two outlooks; and, with whatever reluctance, they conclude that the Scientific Outlook is the one which an intellectually honest man must choose. Ironically enough, the Theist himself is bound to applaud their decision, although it goes against him. They are following the best light they have. If they chose otherwise, they would be sinning against the light as they see it.

Is there no solution to this tragic dilemma? The seriousness of the issue can hardly be exaggerated. As I have said already, nothing less is at stake than the whole future of Western Civilization, perhaps the whole future of civilized mankind. No civilization can flourish, or even survive for long, without a religious basis: if the progress of civilization itself is bound to destroy that basis, with the advance of scientific enlightenment, the outlook is indeed black.

I believe myself that there *is* a solution; but at present it is only dimly visible, and neither of the two antagonists is likely to welcome it. It is to be found, I suggest, in that new and as yet very immature branch of scientific investigation known as Psychical Research. Psychical Research is the attempt to apply scientific method to events and experiences which are, *prima facie*, "supernormal." Such events and experiences have been abundantly reported in all ages and countries, and not least in our own. But the reports were mixed up with so much superstition and credulity, with so much careless observation and so much downright fraud, that until about sixty years ago nobody thought it worthwhile to subject them to serious and conscientious scientific investigation.

However, at last the attempt was made,[7] and by now a good deal of careful work has been done; and, though much remains uncertain, there are some positive results which seem to be reasonably well established. Orthodox Science has taken very little note of them as yet; for the most part it has ignored the whole subject, and when it has not, has treated it with grave suspicion. The attitude of Religious Orthodoxy has been similar, except that it has been even more unfavorable. Nevertheless, if any unbiased person considers the very voluminous body of carefully sifted testimony which is now available, I do not think he can reasonably deny the reality of Telepathy and Clairvoyance at least; and he will hesitate to deny the possibility of Precognition, unintelligible as it may seem. The evidence for the existence of localized and sometimes recurrent Apparitions (very roughly speaking, the "ghosts" of popular parlance), some of which are perceptible to a number of percipients at the same time, is also good, though we are not by any means obliged to accept the Spiritualist explanation of them. *Poltergeist* phenomena are reasonably well attested, however we are to explain them. The physical phenomena of mediumship—the alleged capacity of some "mediums" to move physical objects at a distance without the use of any physical means—are still a matter of controversy among those best qualified to judge. The only opinion I should myself venture to express is this, that it would be unwise to suppose that *all* phenomena of the sort are fraudulent, even if a great many are. As for the alleged "spirit messages," no doubt quite a large number can be explained away

---

[7] Roughly speaking, we may say that it began with the foundation of the Society for Psychical Research (S.P.R.) in 1882.

by fraud or collusion or misreporting. But there is a large remainder which cannot. Of this remainder, many can be explained away if, but only if, the reality of Telepathy is first admitted. But there is still a residuum left which cannot be explained away except by stretching the telepathic hypothesis almost to breaking point, if not beyond it. And in their case a reasonable man should be prepared at least to consider the hypothesis that the "messages" are what they purport to be—communications from discarnate human intelligences.

However this may be, it is sufficient for my present argument if the reality of Telepathy and Clairvoyance be admitted; and I do not see how it can reasonably be denied. The implications of Telepathy and Clairvoyance are very far-reaching indeed. A universe in which they are possible is very different from the universe of the Materialist. In Telepathy, one mind exercises a direct influence upon another mind, without any known physical intermediary, and regardless of the spatial distance between their respective bodies. In Clairvoyance, a mind has a veridical "impression" of an object or event (often a distant one) without making use of the physical sense organs. These occurrences seem to show that though many of our experiences are directly dependent upon physico-chemical processes in the brain, there are some which are not. They suggest that the old Dualistic theory, which regarded the brain as the instrument—the somewhat imperfect instrument—of the soul, is after all correct, at any rate in its main lines; that consciousness is not a mere byproduct of the body, but can function independently of it, and sometimes does. If it can so function even in this life, why should it not continue to function in much the same way when the physical organism breaks up?

The brain may be what Bergson says it is, the organ of *l'attention à la vie*, the organ by which an immaterial spirit adapts itself to the conditions of life in a material environment. It may be an instrument adapted to receive and coordinate the physical stimuli which come to it through the sense organs, and to register them for future use: and likewise an instrument for initiating and coordinating the muscular movements which are responses to those stimuli. If the instrument is damaged, or enfeebled by disease, fatigue or old age, to that extent the spirit is out of touch with the physical world. If the organ is destroyed, the spirit loses touch with the physical world altogether, but may nonetheless continue to exist and to be conscious. Indeed the range of its consciousness may be greater for the loss. For the brain may be an impediment as well as an instrument. Telepathy and Clairvoyance, in which the brain apparently plays no part, are extensions and not restrictions of the normal consciousness.

I conclude then that Psychical Research, by establishing the reality of Telepathy and Clairvoyance, has already in principle demolished the materialistic theory of human personality. As a distinguished student of Psychical Research, Mr. Whately Carington, has said, the walls of Jericho are already down, if only we could see it. It is true that Telepathy and Clairvoyance have not yet received the official blessing of Science. Orthodox Science still looks askance at the work of Psychical Research, though perhaps its attitude is beginning to change a little. But eventually the new facts must tell. *Magna est veritas, et praevalebit.*[8] (At least that is my faith, though it is often sorely tried!) When that happens, the results of Psychical Research will be incorporated into the Scientific Outlook, and at the same time will revolutionize it from within, so that it will no longer be materialistic, as it is now. There will then be no inconsistency between Science and Theism as such; whatever inconsistency there may still be between Science and the particular dogmas or traditions which particular forms of Theism have inherited from an earlier and unscientific age.

---

[8] Editor's Note (2012): "Truth is great, and it will prevail."

It must of course be admitted that the mere removal of the inconsistency between Religion and Science is not by itself sufficient to restore Religion to its old place in the life of mankind. The Scientific Outlook, if transformed in the way I have indicated, would be *incompatible* with Theism: but as we remarked before, Science by itself can never *establish* Theism. Science is the study of observable Nature, including Human Nature, but the Author of Nature is outside its purview. As a man, the scientist may believe in Him; but as a scientist, he can say nothing about a Being who by hypothesis stands outside the observable order of Nature altogether. If Theism is to be accepted, there must be independent positive reasons for accepting it. But, as it happens, there are such reasons, and always have been. They are roughly described by the phrase "religious experience." That experience in one form or another, has never ceased; and if it is less prevalent now than in former times, that is precisely because it commits us to certain beliefs, notably the belief in human immortality, which Science in its present stage of development appears to refute. If this obstacle were to be removed, as I have argued it can be and will be, religious experience would have a free field once again, and its message would be listened to in quarters which now feel bound, in intellectual honesty, to shut their ears to it. It will then be possible for the Theist to accept the Scientific Outlook as a true revelation of the power and wisdom displayed by the Creator in His works, a power and wisdom vastly greater than our unscientific ancestors could conceive of. On the other hand, it will be possible for educated men to be Theists, without any mental reservations, without any sense of strain or of intellectual dishonesty. Let us hope that that time will come quickly. Until it comes, our whole civilization is weakened from top to bottom by the fatal rift between Religion and scientific enlightenment. When it does come, we shall have a new civilization superior not only in degree but in quality to any that mankind has known.

LIFE AND MATTER

Précis of paper by

Dr. V. P. Whittaker

Most people like to fit their convictions about human nature and the universe into some sort of more or less coherent system of ideas or "ideology." Now that traditional Christianity no longer appears intellectually respectable to many people, several modern ideologies have sprung up to meet this demand and the most popular of these seek to gain for themselves the prestige of science by claiming to be founded on the results of scientific investigation.

Both the philosophical and the scientific pretentions of these current "scientific" ideologies need to be scrutinized, but the speaker intended to confine himself to an examination of one of their scientific assumptions. It was assumed that such conceptions as "mind," "personality," "behavior," could be given a scientific explanation in terms of biology, and that "life" could in turn be explained in terms of physical laws derived originally from a study of non-living matter. This was equivalent to denying that psychology, or biology, could possess autonomous concepts peculiar to themselves, which were not reducible to the concepts of the physical sciences. The speaker, as a biochemist, was particularly interested in the relation of the physical and the biological sciences, and the question of whether or not the latter required modes of explanation which were not reducible to physical terms. He believed that while a unified science might ultimately be achieved, the assumption that this goal had already in principle been attained was unjustified, and he thought that the present metaphysical basis of science was inadequate for such a union.

It was, however, quite natural, if misleading, to think of the sciences as forming a kind of pyramid of which physics formed the base to which the various other sciences could ultimately be referred. Historically, many sciences, as they had ceased to be merely fact-finding and classificatory, had attempted to adopt, as their theoretical basis, the picture of the physical universe provided by physics. This tendency was illustrated by chemistry, which, ever since Mendeleef's great generalization of the Periodic Law, had turned increasingly to physics for an explanation of that law in terms of the physics of the atom. Biology too, mainly made up before 1840 of the fact-finding and classificatory sciences of natural history and morphology, has become since that date increasingly experimental and thus increasingly dependent on physics and chemistry for its theoretical conceptions. This process had culminated in the emergence of the science of biochemistry which claimed for its special province, the investigation of the chemical and physical basis of life and thus attempted to provide a bridge between the physical and biological sciences.

Too often, scientists and laymen alike forget that science rests on certain metaphysical assumptions which cannot be proved or disproved by purely scientific tests. These assumptions are of two kinds, ontological (e.g. such basic principles as those of Causality and the Uniformity of Nature), which are essential for any kind of scientific activity, and methodological, i.e. those which determine the experimental approach of a particular science and the theoretical structures erected on the experimental evidence. When fresh experimental results become increasingly difficult to fit into an existing theoretical structure or are found to be meaningless or contradictory from the point of view of that theoretical structure, it is a clear indication that the methodological assumptions of the science are inadequate, and must be revised. An example of a revolution of this kind is furnished by the history of physics during the first quarter of the present century during which time the methodological assumption that it was possible to reconcile the behavior of light, atoms and subatomic particles with a system of physical laws based on the behavior of matter in bulk was finally abandoned.

The idea that biological phenomena can be investigated by the methods of the physical sciences and incorporated into a theoretical structure provided by the physical sciences is a methodological assumption. Do we not in fact find that chaos and confusion in biology which inevitably results from an inadequate methodological basis? In support of his contention, the speaker instanced the long and fruitless controversies such as those between vitalism and mechanism, epigenesis and preformation, and the admissibility or otherwise of teleological explanations in biology. The problem of "control" was an acute one at the present time. In any physical experiment it was axiomatic that only one independent variable should be varied at a time. In the investigation of a living cell any attempt to control the system in this way would result in its death, since one of the most fundamental characteristics of a living system appears to be that it is a self-perpetuating steady state system of great complexity, which tends to adapt itself to changes in its environment. Prevent this adaptation from taking place and the system is no longer "alive." This limitation imposes great difficulties on the investigation of any process which demands an intact cell for its occurrence. It is sometimes possible to isolate a number of processes in a "dead" extract or other preparation, which fit together in some sort of unique manner and so give one confidence that this is what actually occurs in the living cell. This is how our knowledge of cellular respiration has been obtained. Other processes, e.g. photosynthesis, are more intimately related to the life of the cell; one is obliged to work with living tissue; the components of the mechanism are therefore impossible to isolate, and no complete picture can be built up. It is thus significant that whereas our knowledge of respiration is now fairly complete, our knowledge of photosynthesis is still extremely fragmentary.

In the face of these difficulties, many biologists now admit that there is a place in biological explanation for purely biological concepts such as "organization." Professor Whitehead has gone even further and maintained that the concept of "organism" must also be introduced into the physical sciences. It is therefore clear that any idea that the biological sciences can be absorbed into the physical sciences is facile. Similar considerations apply to the relation between biology and psychology, although owing to the less developed state of the latter science the methodological crisis is not so acute, and it may well be that before a unified science is finally achieved, such concepts as "mind," "personality" and "organism" will have to be accorded the same fundamental status as "matter" and "energy."

IS THEOLOGY POETRY?

Mr. C. S. Lewis

The question I have been asked to discuss tonight—"Is Theology Poetry?"—is not of my own choosing. I find myself, in fact, in the position of a candidate at an examination, and I must obey the advice of my tutors by first making sure that I know what the question means.

By Theology we mean, I suppose, the systematic series of statements about God and about man's relation to Him which the believers of a religion make. And in a paper sent me by this Club I may perhaps assume that Theology means principally Christian Theology. I am the bolder to make this assumption because something of what I think about other religions will appear in what I have to say. It must also be remembered that only a minority of the religions of the world have a theology. There was no systematic series of statements which the Greeks agreed in believing about Zeus.

The other term, Poetry, is much harder to define, but I believe I can assume the question which my examiners had in mind without a definition. There are certain things which I feel sure they were not asking me. They were not asking me whether Theology is written in verse. They were not asking me whether most theologians are masters of a "simple, sensuous, and passionate" style. I believe they meant, "Is Theology *merely* poetry?" This might be expanded: "Does Theology offer us, at best, only that kind of truth which, according to some critics, poetry offers us?" And the first difficulty of answering the question in that form is that we have no general agreement as to what "poetical truth" means, or whether there is really any such thing. It will be best, therefore, to use for this paper a very vague and modest notion of poetry, simply as writing which arouses and in part satisfies the imagination. And I shall take it that the question I am to answer is this: Does Christian Theology owe its attraction to its power of arousing and satisfying our imaginations? Are those who believe it mistaking aesthetic enjoyment for intellectual assent, or assenting because they enjoy?

Faced with this question, I naturally turn to inspect the believer whom I know best—myself. And the first fact I discover, or seem to discover, is that for me at any rate, if Theology is Poetry, it is not very good poetry.

Considered as poetry, the doctrine of the Trinity seems to me to fall between two stools. It has neither the monolithic grandeur of strictly Unitarian conceptions nor the richness of Polytheism. The omnipotence of God is not, to my taste, a poetical advantage. Odin, fighting against enemies who are not his own creatures and who will in fact defeat him in the end, has a heroic appeal which the God of Christians cannot have. There is also a certain bareness about the Christian picture of the universe. A future state and orders of superhuman creatures are held to exist, but only the slightest hints of their nature are offered. Finally, and worst of all, the whole cosmic story, though full of tragic elements, yet fails of being a tragedy. Christianity offers the attractions neither of optimism nor of pessimism. It represents the life of the universe as being very like the mortal life of men on this planet—"of a mingled yarn, good and ill together." The majestic simplifications of Pantheism and the tangled wood of Pagan animism both seem to me, in their different ways, more attractive. Christianity just misses the tidiness of the one and the delicious variety of the other. For I take it there are two things the imagination loves to do. It loves to embrace its object completely, to take it in at a single glance, and see it as something harmonious, symmetrical, and self-explanatory. That is the classical imagination; the Parthenon was built for it. It also loves to lose itself in a labyrinth, to surrender to the inextricable. That is the romantic imagination; the *Orlando Furioso* was written for it. But Christian Theology does not cater very well for either.

If Christianity is only a mythology, then I find the mythology I believe in is not the one I like best. I like Greek mythology much better, Irish better still, Norse best of all.

Having thus inspected myself, I next inquire how far my case is peculiar. It does not seem, certainly, to be unique. It is not at all plain that men's imaginations have always delighted most in those pictures of the supernatural which they believed. From the twelfth to the seventeenth century Europe seems to have taken an unfailing delight in classical mythology. If the numbers and the gusto of pictures and poems were to be the criterion of belief, we should judge that those ages were pagan, which we know to be untrue.

It looks as if the confusion between imaginative enjoyment and intellectual assent, of which Christians are accused, is not nearly so common or so easy as some people suppose. Even children, I believe, rarely suffer from it. It pleases their imagination to pretend that they are bears or horses, but I do not remember that one was ever under the least delusion. May it not even be that there is something in belief which is hostile to perfect imaginative enjoyment? The sensitive, cultured atheist seems at times to enjoy the aesthetic trappings of Christianity in a way which the believer can only envy. The modern poets certainly enjoy the Greek gods in a way of which I find no trace in Greek literature. "What mythological scenes in ancient literature can compare for a moment with Keats's *Hyperion*?" In a certain sense we spoil a mythology for imaginative purposes by believing in it. Fairies are popular in England because we don't think they exist; they are no fun at all in Arran or Conemara.

But I must beware of going too far. I have suggested that belief spoils a system for the imagination "in a certain sense." But not in all senses. If I came to believe in fairies, I should almost certainly lose the particular kind of pleasure which I now get from them when reading the *Midsummer Night's Dream*. But later on, when the believed fairies had settled down as inhabitants of my real universe and had been fully connected with other parts of my thought, a new pleasure might arise. The contemplation of what we take to be real is always, I think, in tolerably sensitive minds, attended with a certain sort of aesthetic satisfaction—a sort which depends precisely on its supposed reality. There is a dignity and poignancy in the bare fact that a thing exists. Thus, as Balfour pointed out in *Theism and Humanism* (a book too little read), there are many historical facts which we should not applaud for any obvious humor or pathos if we supposed them to be inventions; but once we believe them to be real, we have, in addition to our intellectual satisfaction, a certain aesthetic delight in the idea of them. The story of the Trojan War and the story of the Napoleonic Wars both have an aesthetic effect on us. And the effects are different. And this difference does not depend solely on those differences which would make them different as stories if we believed neither. The *kind* of pleasure the Napoleonic Wars give has a certain difference simply because we believe in them. A believed idea *feels* different from an idea that is not believed. And that peculiar flavor of the believed is never, in my experience, without a special sort of imaginative enjoyment. It is therefore quite true that the Christians do enjoy their world picture, aesthetically, once they have accepted it as true. Every man, I believe, enjoys the world picture which he accepts, for the gravity and finality of the actual is itself an aesthetic stimulus. In this sense, Christianity, Life-Force-Worship, Marxism, Freudianism all become "poetries" to their own believers. But this does not mean that their adherents have chosen them for that reason. On the contrary, this kind of poetry is the result, not the cause, of belief. Theology is, in this sense, poetry to me because I believe it; I do not believe it because it is poetry.

The charge that Theology is mere poetry, if it means that Christians believe it because they find it, antecedently to belief, the most poetically attractive of all world pictures, thus seems to me implausible in the extreme. There may be evidence for such a charge which I do not know of, but such evidence as I do know is against it.

I am not, of course, maintaining that Theology, even before you believe it, is totally bare of aesthetic value. But I do not find it superior in this respect to most of its rivals. Consider for a few moments the enormous aesthetic claim of its chief contemporary rival—what we may loosely call the Scientific Outlook,[9] the picture of Mr. Wells and the rest. Supposing this to be a myth, is it not one of the finest myths which human imagination has yet produced? The play is preceded by the most austere of all preludes: the infinite void, and matter restlessly moving to bring forth it knows not what. Then, by the millionth millionth chance—what tragic irony—the conditions at one point of space and time bubble up into that tiny fermentation which is the beginning of life. Everything seems to be against the infant hero of our drama—just as everything seems against the youngest son or ill-used stepdaughter at the opening of a fairy tale. But life somehow wins through. With infinite suffering, against all but insuperable obstacles, it spreads, it breeds, it complicates itself, from the amoeba up to the plant, up to the reptile, up to the mammal. We glance briefly at the age of monsters. Dragons prowl the earth, devour one another, and die. Then comes the theme of the younger son and the ugly duckling once more. As the weak, tiny spark of life began amidst the huge hostilities of the inanimate, so now again, amidst the beasts that are far larger and stronger than he, there comes forth a little naked, shivering, cowering creature, shuffling, not yet erect, promising nothing, the product of another millionth millionth chance. Yet somehow he thrives. He becomes the Cave Man with his club and his flints, muttering and growling over his enemies' bones, dragging his screaming mate by her hair (I never could quite make out why), tearing his children to pieces in fierce jealousy till one of them is old enough to tear him, cowering before the horrible gods whom he created in his own image. But these are only growing pains. Wait till the next act. There he is becoming true Man. He learns to master Nature. Science comes and dissipates the superstitions of his infancy. More and more he becomes the controller of his own fate. Passing hastily over the present (for it is a mere nothing by the time scale we are using), you follow him on into the future. See him in the last act, though not the last scene, of this great mystery. A race of demigods now rules the planet—and perhaps more than the planet—for eugenics have made certain that only demigods will be born, and psychoanalysis that none of them shall lose or smirch his divinity, and communism that all which divinity requires shall be ready to their hands. Man has ascended his throne. Henceforward he has nothing to do but to practice virtue, to grow in wisdom, to be happy. And now, mark the final stroke of genius. If the myth stopped at that point, it might be a little bathetic. It would lack the highest grandeur of which human imagination is capable. The last scene reverses all. We have the Twilight of the Gods. All this time, silently, unceasingly, out of all reach of human power, Nature, the old enemy, has been steadily gnawing away. The sun will cool—all suns will cool—the whole universe will run down. Life (every form of life) will be banished, without hope of return, from every inch of infinite space. All ends in nothingness, and "universal darkness covers all." The pattern of the myth thus becomes one of the noblest we can conceive. It is the pattern of many Elizabethan tragedies, where the protagonist's career can be represented by a slowly ascending and then rapidly falling curve, with its highest point in Act IV.

---

[9] I am not suggesting that practicing scientists believe it as a whole. The delightful name "Wellsianity" (which another member invented during the discussion) would have been much better than "the Scientific Outlook."

You see him climbing up and up, then blazing in his bright meridian, then finally overwhelmed in ruin.

Such a world drama appeals to every part of us. The early struggles of the hero (a theme delightfully doubled, played first by life, and then by man) appeal to our generosity. His future exaltation gives scope to a reasonable optimism, for the tragic close is so very distant that you need not often think of it—we work with millions of years. And the tragic close itself just gives that irony, that grandeur, which calls forth our defiance, and without which all the rest might cloy. There is a beauty in this myth which well deserves better poetic handling than it has yet received; I hope some great genius will yet crystallize it before the incessant stream of philosophic change carries it all away. I am speaking, of course, of the beauty it has whether you believe it or not. There I can speak from experience, for I, who believe less than half of what it tells me about the past, and less than nothing of what it tells me about the future, am deeply moved when I contemplate it. The only other story—unless, indeed, it is an embodiment of the same story—which similarly moves me is the *Nibelung's Ring. Enden sah ich die Welt*.[10]

We cannot, therefore, turn down Theology, simply because it does not avoid being poetical. All worldviews yield poetry to those who believe them by the mere fact of being believed. And nearly all have certain poetical merits whether you believe them or not. This is what we should expect. Man is a poetical animal and touches nothing which he does not adorn.

There are, however, two other lines of thought which might lead us to call Theology a mere poetry, and these I must now consider. In the first place, it certainly contains elements similar to those which we find in many early, and even savage, religions. And those elements in the early religions may now seem to us to be poetical. The question here is rather complicated. We now regard the death and return of Balder as a poetical idea, a myth. We are invited to infer thence that the death and resurrection of Christ is a poetical idea, a myth. But we are not really starting with the *datum* "both are poetical" and thence arguing "therefore both are false." Part of the poetical aroma which hangs about Balder is, I believe, due to the fact that we have already come to disbelieve in him. So that disbelief, not poetical experience, is the real starting point of the argument. But this is perhaps an oversubtlety, certainly a subtlety, and I will leave it on one side.

What light is really thrown on the truth or falsehood of Christian Theology by the occurrence of similar ideas in Pagan religion? I think the answer was very well given a fortnight ago by Mr. Brown. Supposing, for purposes of argument, that Christianity is true; then it could avoid all coincidence with other religions only on the supposition that all other religions are one hundred percent erroneous. To which, you remember, Professor H. H. Price replied by agreeing with Mr. Brown and saying, "Yes. From these resemblances you may conclude not 'so much the worse for the Christians' but 'so much the better for the Pagans.'" The truth is that the resemblances tell nothing either for or against the truth of Christian Theology. If you start from the assumption that the Theology is false, the resemblances are quite consistent with that assumption. One would expect creatures of the same sort, faced with the same universe, to make the same false guess more than once. But if you start with the assumption that the Theology is true, the resemblances fit in equally well. Theology, while saying that a special illumination has been vouchsafed to Christians and (earlier) to Jews, also says that there is some divine illumination vouchsafed to all men. The Divine light, we are told, "lighteneth every man." We should, therefore, expect to find in the imagination of great Pagan teachers and myth makers some glimpse of that theme which we believe to be the very plot of the whole cosmic story—the

---

[10] Editor's Note (2012): "I saw the world end."

theme of incarnation, death, and rebirth. And the differences between the Pagan Christs (Balder, Osiris, etc.) and the Christ Himself is much what we should expect to find. The Pagan stories are all about someone dying and rising, either every year, or else nobody knows where and nobody knows when. The Christian story is about a historical personage, whose execution can be dated pretty accurately, under a named Roman magistrate, and with whom the society that He founded is in a continuous relation down to the present day. It is not the difference between falsehood and truth. It is the difference between a real event on the one hand and dim dreams or premonitions of that same event on the other. It is like watching something come gradually into focus; first it hangs in the clouds of myth and ritual, vast and vague, then it condenses, grows hard and in a sense small, as a historical event in first century Palestine. This gradual focusing goes on even inside the Christian tradition itself. The earliest stratum of the Old Testament contains many truths in a form which I take to be legendary, or even mythical—hanging in the clouds, but gradually the truth condenses, becomes more and more historical. From things like Noah's Ark or the sun standing still upon Ajalon, you come down to the court memoirs of King David. Finally you reach the New Testament and history reigns supreme, and the Truth is incarnate. And "incarnate" is here more than a metaphor. It is not an accidental resemblance that what, from the point of view of being, is stated in the form "God became Man," should involve, from the point of view of human knowledge, the statement "Myth became Fact." The essential meaning of all things came down from the "heaven" of myth to the "earth" of history. In so doing, it partly emptied itself of its glory, as Christ emptied Himself of His glory to be Man. That is the real explanation of the fact that Theology, far from defeating its rivals by a superior poetry, is, in a superficial but quite real sense, less poetical than they. That is why the New Testament is, in the same sense, less poetical than the Old. Have you not often felt in Church, if the first lesson is some great passage, that the second lesson is somehow small by comparison—almost, if one might say so, humdrum? So it is and so it must be. That is the humiliation of myth into fact, of God into Man; what is everywhere and always, imageless and ineffable, only to be glimpsed in dream and symbol and the acted poetry of ritual becomes small, solid—no bigger than a man who can lie asleep in a rowing boat on the Lake of Galilee. You may say that this, after all, is a still deeper poetry. I will not contradict you. The humiliation leads to a greater glory. But the humiliation of God and the shrinking or condensation of the myth as it becomes fact are also quite real.

I have just mentioned symbol, and that brings me to the last head under which I will consider the charge of "mere poetry." Theology certainly shares with poetry the use of metaphorical or symbolical language. The first Person of the Trinity is not the Father of the Second in a physical sense. The Second Person did not come "down" to earth in the same sense as a parachutist, nor reascend into the sky like a balloon, nor did He literally sit at the right hand of the Father. Why, then, does Christianity talk as if all these things did happen? The agnostic thinks that it does so because those who founded it were quite naïvely ignorant and believed all these statements literally, and we later Christians have gone on using the same language through timidity and conservatism. We are often invited, in Professor Price's words, to throw away the shell and retain the kernel.

There are two questions involved here.

1. What did the early Christians believe? Did they believe that God really has a material palace in the sky and that He received His Son in a decorated state chair placed a little to the right of His own?—or did they not? The answer is that the alternative we are offering them was probably never present to their minds at all. As soon as it was present, we know quite well which

side of the fence they came down. As soon as the issue of Anthropomorphism was explicitly before the Church in, I think, the second century, Anthropomorphism was condemned. The Church knew the answer (that God has no body and therefore couldn't sit in a chair) as soon as it knew the question. But till the question was raised, of course, people believed neither the one answer nor the other. There is no more tiresome error in the history of thought than to try to sort our ancestors on to this or that side of a distinction which was not in their minds at all. You are asking a question to which no answer exists. It is very probable that most (almost certainly not all) of the first generation of Christians never thought of their faith without anthropomorphic imagery, and that they were not explicitly conscious, as a modern would be, that it *was* mere imagery. But this does not in the least mean that the essence of their belief was concerned with details about a celestial throne room. That was not what they valued, or what they were prepared to die for. Any one of them who went to Alexandria and got a philosophical education would have recognized the imagery at once for what it was, and would not have felt that his belief had been altered in any way that mattered. My mental picture of an Oxford college, before I saw one, was very different from the reality in physical details. But this did not mean that when I came to Oxford I found my general conception of what a college means to have been a delusion. The physical pictures had inevitably accompanied my thinking, but they had never been what I was chiefly interested in, and much of my thinking had been correct in spite of them. What you think is one thing; what you imagine while you are thinking is another.

The earliest Christians were not so much like a man who mistakes the shell for the kernel as like a man carrying a nut which he hasn't yet cracked. The moment it is cracked, he knows which part to throw away. Till then he holds on to the nut, not because he is a fool but because he isn't.

2. We are invited to restate our belief in a form free from metaphor and symbol. The reason we don't is that we can't. We can, if you like, say "God entered history" instead of saying "God came down to earth." But, of course, "entered" is just as metaphorical as "came down." You have only substituted horizontal or undefined movement for vertical movement. We can make our language duller; we cannot make it less metaphorical. We can make the pictures more prosaic; we cannot be less pictorial. Nor are we Christians alone in this disability. Here is a sentence from a celebrated anti-Christian writer, Dr. I. A. Richards.[11] "Only that part of the cause of a mental event which takes effect through incoming (sensory) impulses or through effects of past sensory impulses can be said to be thereby known. The reservation no doubt involves complications." Dr. Richards does not mean that the part of the cause "takes" effect in the literal sense of the word *takes,* nor that it does so *through* a sensory impulse as you could take a parcel *through* a doorway. In the second sentence "The reservation involves complications," he does not mean that an act of defending, or a seat booked in a train, or an American park, really sets about rolling or folding or curling up a set of coilings or rollings up. In other words, all language about things other than physical objects is necessarily metaphorical.

For all these reasons, then, I think (though we knew even before Freud that the heart is deceitful) that those who accept Theology are not necessarily being guided by taste rather than reason. The picture so often painted of Christians huddling together on an ever narrower strip of beach while the incoming tide of "Science" mounts higher and higher corresponds to nothing in my own experience. That grand myth which I asked you to admire a few minutes ago is not for me a hostile novelty breaking in on my traditional beliefs. On the contrary, that cosmology is what I started from. Deepening distrust and final abandonment of it long preceded my

---

[11] *Principles of Literary Criticism* (1924), Chap. XI.

conversion to Christianity. Long before I believed Theology to be true I had already decided that the popular scientific picture at any rate was false. One absolutely central inconsistency ruins it; it is the one we touched on a fortnight ago. The whole picture professes to depend on inferences from observed facts. Unless inference is valid, the whole picture disappears. Unless we can be sure that reality in the remotest nebula or the remotest part obeys the thought laws of the human scientist here and now in his laboratory—in other words, unless Reason is an absolute—all is in ruins. Yet those who ask me to believe this world picture also ask me to believe that Reason is simply the unforeseen and unintended byproduct of mindless matter at one stage of its endless and aimless becoming. Here is flat contradiction. They ask me at the same moment to accept a conclusion and to discredit the only testimony on which that conclusion can be based. The difficulty is to me a fatal one; and the fact that when you put it to many scientists, far from having an answer, they seem not even to understand what the difficulty is, assures me that I have not found a mare's nest but detected a radical disease in their whole mode of thought from the very beginning. The man who has once understood the situation is compelled henceforth to regard the scientific cosmology as being, in principle, a myth; though no doubt a great many true particulars have been worked into it.[12]

After that it is hardly worth noticing minor difficulties. Yet these are many and serious. The Bergsonian critique of orthodox Darwinism is not easy to answer. More disquieting still is Professor D. M. S. Watson's defense. "Evolution itself," he wrote,[13] "is accepted by zoologists not because it has been observed to occur or... can be proved by logically coherent evidence to be true, but because the only alternative, special creation, is clearly incredible." Has it come to that? Does the whole vast structure of modern naturalism depend not on positive evidence but simply on an *a priori* metaphysical prejudice? Was it devised not to get in facts but to keep out God? Even, however, if Evolution in the strict biological sense has some better grounds than Professor Watson suggests—and I can't help thinking it must—we should distinguish Evolution in this strict sense from what may be called the universal evolutionism of modern thought. By universal evolutionism I mean the belief that the very formula of universal process is from imperfect to perfect, from small beginnings to great endings, from the rudimentary to the elaborate, the belief which makes people find it natural to think that morality springs from savage taboos, adult sentiment from infantile sexual maladjustments, thought from instinct, mind from matter, organic from inorganic, cosmos from chaos. This is perhaps the deepest habit of mind in the contemporary world. It seems to me immensely unplausible, because it makes the general course of nature so very unlike those parts of nature we can observe. You remember the old puzzle as to whether the owl came from the egg or the egg from the owl. The modern acquiescence in universal evolutionism is a kind of optical illusion, produced by attending exclusively to the owl's emergence from the egg. We are taught from childhood to notice how the perfect oak grows from the acorn and to forget that the acorn itself was dropped by a perfect oak. We are reminded constantly that the adult human being was an embryo, never that the life of the embryo came from two adult human beings. We love to notice that the express engine of today is the descendant of the "Rocket"; we do not equally remember that the "Rocket" springs not from some even more rudimentary engine, but from something much more perfect and

---

[12] It is not irrelevant, in considering the mythical character of this cosmology, to notice that the two great imaginative expressions of it are *earlier* than the evidence; Keats's *Hyperion* and the *Nibelung's Ring* are pre-Darwinian works.
[13] Quoted in "Science and the B.B.C.," *Nineteenth Century,* April 1943.

complicated than itself—namely, a man of genius. The obviousness or naturalness which most people seem to find in the idea of emergent evolution thus seems to be a pure hallucination.

On these grounds and others like them one is driven to think that whatever else may be true, the popular scientific cosmology at any rate is certainly not. I left that ship not at the call of poetry but because I thought it could not keep afloat. Something like philosophical idealism or Theism must, at the very worst, be less untrue than that. And idealism turned out, when you took it seriously, to be disguised Theism. And once you accepted Theism, you could not ignore the claims of Christ. And when you examined them it appeared to me that you could adopt no middle position. Either He was a lunatic, or God. And He was not a lunatic.

I was taught at school, when I had done a sum, to "prove my answer." The proof or verification of my Christian answer to the cosmic sum is this. When I accept Theology I may find difficulties, at this point or that, in harmonizing it with some particular truths which are imbedded in the mythical cosmology derived from science. But I can get in, or allow for, science as a whole. Granted that Reason is prior to matter and that the light of that primal Reason illuminates finite minds, I can understand how men should come, by observation and inference, to know a lot about the universe they live in. If, on the other hand, I swallow the scientific cosmology as a whole, then not only can I not fit in Christianity, but I cannot even fit in science. If minds are wholly dependent on brains, and brains on biochemistry, and biochemistry (in the long run) on the meaningless flux of the atoms, I cannot understand how the thought of those minds should have any more significance than the sound of the wind in the trees. And this is to me the final test. This is how I distinguish dreaming and waking. When I am awake I can, in some degree, account for and study my dream. The dragon that pursued me last night can be fitted into my waking world. I know that there are such things as dreams; I know that I had eaten an indigestible dinner; I know that a man of my reading might be expected to dream of dragons. But while in the nightmare I could not have fitted in my waking experience. The waking world is judged more real because it can thus contain the dreaming world; the dreaming world is judged less real because it cannot contain the waking one. For the same reason I am certain that in passing from the scientific points of view to the theological, I have passed from dream to waking. Christian theology can fit in science, art, morality, and the sub-Christian religions. The scientific point of view cannot fit in any of these things, not even science itself. I believe in Christianity as I believe that the Sun has risen, not only because I see it, but because by it I see everything else.

CAN MYTH BE FACT?

Dr. A. M. Farrer

The word myth is used in several senses, and varies with one's anthropological theory. I ask no more than that my use of the word may be allowed to pass. A myth is a traditional tale which purports to describe real happenings, for example, that the Olympian Gods came down *incognito* and paid surprise calls on the householders of Lycia to see what entertainment they would get, and were driven from the door by all except Baucis and Philemon, whose unfeigned kindness they rewarded with material blessings, while overwhelming their inhospitable neighbors in a general inundation. But such a story does not commonly impress us by any very firm grip on historical reality; no one, probably, is prepared to date it, it floats uncertainly in the great ocean of previous time. Its interest lies not in its claim to historical truth, but in its expression of some universal idea, in this case the idea that the Gods preside over the rights of strangers, in serving whom we serve the heavenly powers; that care for the stranger pays in the end, for heaven will bless the hospitable man and blast the churl. The reason why myths become current and maintain their hold is the expressiveness of their symbolism and the importance of what they symbolize. They seem to obey in their style and formation certain profound laws of the human imagination, and to handle in their subject matter certain central concerns of the human heart, especially its social and religious concerns. For this reason they tend to conform to certain types and even to reappear in different cultures with an identical content. For example, we read in Genesis how the Lord God also came down to earth, mysteriously manifest in a group of three travelers, how Abraham and Sarah showed a hospitality equal to that of Baucis and Philemon, and were rewarded by a miracle of fertility, the birth of Isaac: whereas the wicked men of Sodom, attempting outrage against their heavenly guests, were overthrown with fire and brimstone. The story is here pinned on to the bituminous desert around the Dead Sea, as in its other form it was pinned to the Pisidian swamps.

Myths were presumably taken for historical fact by simple-minded antiquity. Men were not content with general principles—for instance, of hospitable duty and divine reward. They wanted to feel the conviction that these principles were the actual working forces of the universe; and they found the evidence for this in the record that at some time the powers in control of nature had expressed these principles in one perfectly clear, typical and significant event. The myth was a guarantee that man's beliefs were not mere ideals or aspirations, but the very laws of being. It was the same with ritual myths. The man of primitive culture has been taught that to perform a certain ceremony will bring him rain; he does his ceremony to the accompaniment of a recitation: such and such an old hero of his tribe had been taught the ceremony in the direst extremity of drought by a kindly god, had performed it, and been rewarded with abundance of water in that very day.

As civilization and sophistication proceed, men let go the historical belief in their myths. The first expression of this is a Euripidean indignation against the ancient imposture, but second thoughts bring a more mature attitude. Men become tired of kicking the fallen idols, when no one any longer worships them: it is better to pick them up while they have still some noses and ears among them and place them in museums of history and art. And so the myths robbed of the substance of historical fact are rescued by the pedagogue and the philosopher: they will serve as Sunday school lessons in piety or morals, and as allegorical pegs for preaching Stoics to hang their sermons on. It now becomes the business of the philosophers to unearth from the mythic form the profound but implicit wisdom of antiquity, and to state it explicitly as universal truth. The mythic story no longer guarantees the general truths, as it did to the simpler age: on the contrary, the general truths must now be proved in their own right, and the validity of the myth depends on them.

Things had reached this pass when civilized ears first heard of Christianity. The Christian story of redemption looked outwardly like a myth: it was born in the very age which was dissolving myths in allegory: yet it resisted such treatment, and claimed for itself to be the only myth that is hard historical fact.

That Christians defend the factual character of the story of redemption is obvious; it is not so obvious that they admit its mythical character too, and indeed the *word* "mythical" would commonly be rejected by them, for "mythical" suggests false, imaginary. We are using "mythical" in a somewhat special sense, we must confess: but in this sense of ours, Christian orthodoxy not only *admits* that the story of redemption is mythical; it *claims* that it is, and makes a special point of the claim. Take as your evidence that most orthodox theologian, St. Thomas Aquinas; no one suspects him of putting up useless novelties, of defending boyish paradoxes. And this is what he says (he is explaining the unique character of the biblical record). In the pages of the Bible, he tells us, we have, as in any other book, words which express historical facts, and by means of the words we get hold of the facts. This is the first layer of meaning, but there is another. For just as the words were used by the Evangelists to signify the facts, so the facts themselves had already been used by God to signify further facts, i.e. divine or supernatural facts; and as we use the evangelists' words to get hold of the historical facts, so we are to use these historical facts in order to get hold of the supernatural or divine facts which God has expressed through them. How is it possible, St. Thomas asks, that the facts of the Gospel history can be a language through which a further layer of facts is expressed? It follows, he replies, from the omnipotence of God's creative power. He controls facts no less completely, far more completely, indeed, than I control words. And so, as I shape my words to express my meaning, with what seems to me perfect freedom, in like manner God has what really is absolute freedom to shape historical events into an expression of his divine meaning. The conclusion from this is plain. Men may construct a myth expressive of divine truths as they conceive them, and the stuff of the myth will be words. God has constructed a myth expressive of the divine truths he intends to convey, and the stuff of the myth is facts. And this can very well be, because God's control of facts is infinitely more complete than our control of words: as it was in the beginning, he said the *word*, "Let there be light," and there was light. In this text of Genesis there is already human imperfection. We do not really mean that God first uttered a word, a noise in the air, or even the voiceless image of such a noise within his mind, and that then a second event, the light, obediently jumped into existence as your dog may jump into the room when you have whistled for him. There were not two events, first the speaking, then the shining. The shining of the light was itself the speech, the utterance of God: facts do not *obey* God's words, they *are* his words.

This sounds all very fine, and people can accept it in a certain sense without meaning in the least what St. Thomas and Christendom as a whole is trying to assert. People may say: When I say "God," I mean "Nature." Now it is obviously all right to say that all facts are Nature's words, through which she expresses to us her universal truths, which we call her laws. If my kettle boils at 100 degrees centigrade we have a fact which I cannot make, but Nature makes, and I can, in a poetical mood, describe this fact as a word through which Nature shouts into my ears:

> All water boils at a fixed heat:
> This is the rule, so do not hope to cheat.

> Fall into line, or eat your cabbage raw:
> May Heaven incline your heart to keep this law.

As there are physical laws of Nature, so there may be moral and spiritual laws; as physical facts are the words through which physical truths are dictated to us, so human facts are the words through which moral or even spiritual truths are dictated to us; the misery and self-frustration of bad men, and the serene happiness of saints, are all positive or negative evidence for the inexorable laws of our spiritual nature.

Quite so, and who denies it? But it is evidently not this that Christians mean when they describe the story of Christ as a factual myth. The difference is not difficult to grasp. Consider two sentences in both of which the verb "to express" is used. (*a*) Every commonplace event *expresses* the truth of universal laws; and (*b*) Such and such a poem *expresses* the feeling of springtime or first love. Now ask yourselves whether the word "expresses" in the two sentences means the same thing. Plainly it does not. A commonplace event expresses universal laws simply by conforming to them, but the poem expresses its subject by creating an uniquely appropriate symbol of it. Now when St. Thomas says that God, through His creative control over facts, has caused the Gospel events to signify to us realities beyond themselves, he means this second thing: he means that God has bent and shaped these particular facts into a perfectly expressive symbol of a unique truth he wished to convey to us. Guidebooks sometimes describe a cathedral or a palace as a "poem in stone," and in somewhat the same sense we call Christ's birth, life and death and resurrection a myth not in words, but in the flesh and blood of human history.

So far we have been doing little more than to define. This, we say, is what Christians mean: God is the only myth-maker who can make his myths out of hard fact; the story of our redemption is such a myth. Christians do believe this. But we are not supposed to be asking, Do Christians believe that myth and fact can coincide? That's too easy. We are supposed to be asking, Can it really happen? And we have got nowhere towards the answering of that question so far, except by reminding ourselves that God is almighty. This is scarcely even the beginning of an answer, being far too general. We may know that God is almighty, and therefore might do anything, but we are concerned not with what He might do, but with what He does. In fact, almighty power is seen to be exercised in sustaining the operations of Nature according to Nature's laws, and if we are asked to believe that God has worked in quite a different and special way, shaping the half-chaos of historical fact into the perfect expressiveness of a poem, turning the undramatic stuff of life into something more significant than Shakespeare's masterpieces, if we are asked to believe this, we are inclined to say: Show how it fits in with the rest of the world we know.

This is a reasonable challenge; we will try to take it up. The most satisfactory way to do so seems to be the historical way. It is alleged that a mythic pattern got a grip on actual fact in Jesus Christ's existence. Well, can we see this happening? Can we see where the mythic pattern came from, and how it was built into the facts? If we can watch the alleged process, we may be able to satisfy ourselves that it either is, or is not, the sort of thing that could take place.

If we look for *the* mythic pattern fulfilled in the gospel, we may well be baffled by the multitude of claimants; one of the astonishing things about this story is that it seems to fulfill, and more than fulfill, all the figures of myth conceived by all the prophets. We must confine ourselves to one. Let us take the Son of Man, since if there is one thing clearer than another, it is that Jesus applied this title to himself, and along with the title the myth for which it stood.

The myth of the Son of Man is no other, of course, than the story of Adam. Son of Man is a Hebrew expression which just means Man, with a special added emphasis on his human character by which he differs from beasts below or angels above; as we might say "a human being" to get the same emphasis. The Hebrew for the Son of Man is Ben-*Adam*. Adam, in the story, just because he is all mankind, is compared, not with other men, but with the beasts over whom he was set to rule, and the God in whose royal likeness he was created.

Now the myth of Adam is, to start with, a far more serious affair than the myth of Philemon and Baucis. Philemon and Baucis simply illustrate a general principle of hospitable duty and divine rewards. The myth no doubt added solidity to people's belief in the principle, as we supposed, but (clearly) they could have got on without the myth, the principle could have stood up by itself. The myth of Adam is a very different matter. It does not illustrate a principle, it expresses the whole fact of man's existence, created and fallen. It attempts to describe in its own mythic way a fact inescapably real. We cannot escape from the facts that man occupies a certain place in the order of being; and that he is acutely aware of failure to fill that place, of guilt, moral frustration, and of an inability to reconcile himself to the prospect of physical death. This is an actual situation, which really has come about, and the myth of Adam endeavors to describe it. You may quarrel with the description or the explanation it seems to give, but you cannot deny that the facts are facts, for those facts are you. There is (by contrast) only one indubitable historical fact that *Philemon and Baucis* deals with, and that is the existence of some particularly dismal swamps in Pisidia with a small and fertile island in the middle: and that is not what the myth is really about.

What is more, this is a myth which cannot be allegorized or evaporated into general statements without losing its force. Something happened (so the myth is telling us) in the relations between man and his creator. Well, the intelligent modern Christian is inclined to say: Quite so. Men, evolved from the ape or however else called by Providence into their rational and godlike state, gradually and piecemeal misused their newly born faculties, and so lost their innocence before civilization began. So our culture has sprung from a race, not of barbarians simply, but of crooked barbarians. Such a statement as this sounds very reasonable and harmless, far better than the tale about the apple. It is indeed a safe sort of statement, but like most safe statements it is an almost completely meaningless one. Whatever really happened between primitive man, his conscience and his God, it certainly was nothing like a textbook generalization, it was the individual drama of someone's existence. Even supposing that it happened piecemeal all over the world and in different men, if there were indeed many thousand Adams, every one of them was the Adam of his own soul, to each of them it was personal reality, none of them saw himself as the instance of a statistical generalization. So, if you want to have any idea about the reality of the dawn of human reason and the fall of man, you have got to see it in a living instance, and if you won't have the myth of Adam you have got to make up a novel for yourself to replace it. Try, by all means, but I wonder if you are likely to do better?

The myth of Adam is, of course, no mere novelistic attempt to describe what the experiences of the primitive man may have seemed like to him. It is an attempt to express the drama of his existence with a clarity of which he himself would have been incapable, to bring out better than he knew it its significance in the destinies of heaven and earth. And for this purpose it brings to bear every central and elementary symbol which human life affords. It handles the contrasting natures of man and beast, of man and God; the fountain and the desert; the charm of forbidden fruit, and the slippery hostility of the serpent; the pain of childbirth and the toilsome quest for bread; the shame of nakedness and the intricacies of sexual function; the image of God to which we are born, and the dust into which we resolve. How can all this various stuff of human existence be woven into a single symbol, expressed in words that fill three or four pages?

Well it just is so: the inspired human imagination is capable of this. It was not accomplished in a day: it was the work of ages; written and rewritten, the gross purged, the inessential dropped, new insights embodied.

On the fifth day of creation, this story tells, God had called up the monsters out of the sea, to dominate for their little hour, but on the sixth day he made man in his own image, and set him over all his works. This was the last creation, and man's the final dominion: he had no successor, for on the seventh day God rested from his works forever, and through that eternal Sabbath the empire of man should endure. Such was the creator's purpose: but then came the fall, when Adam, the viceregent of God, had put himself under the serpent. And indeed the men of later days looking about them saw that while Adam still in a manner reigned on earth, it was the image of the beast, not the image of God, that reigned in the heart of man, and especially in the throne of princes. When would the purpose of God be fulfilled? When would he put down the beast and enthrone the Son of Man, the Man in the image of God?

Such thoughts possessed the mind of the writer of Daniel. It is, says he, as though the stages of creation are being repeated in the stages of history; as though we have reached the fifth day, or age, the age of the monsters from the deep, for what more bestial, more monstrous, than the soulless idolatrous empires which one after another rise to crush the people of God? When shall we reach the sixth "day" of the world, when God will reveal the Son of Man and put the monsters down? And so, in his vision, he sees it. It is the fifth day: the four winds of heaven, the fourfold breath of God, break loose on the great sea, and up come the monsters, which are the heathen predatory empires, to work their wicked will. But the sixth day is to come. "I beheld till thrones were set, and one that was Ancient of Days did sit, his raiment white as snow, and the hairs of his head like pure wool: his throne was fiery flames, and the wheels thereof burning fire. And as for the beasts, their dominion was taken away, yet their lives were prolonged for a season and a time. I saw in the night visions, and behold there came with the clouds of heaven one like unto a Son of Man, and he came even to the Ancient of Days and they brought him near before him. And there was given him dominion, and glory, and a kingdom, that all the peoples, nations and languages should serve him; his dominion is an everlasting dominion that shall not be taken away, and his kingdom that shall not be destroyed."

So far we have seen the myth of the Son of Man, a myth, and nothing but that: a myth first used to decipher the past, and then thrown forward on to a shadowy screen in prophecy of the future; it has not yet grasped present fact, nor translated itself out of words into flesh and blood. Now we reach the crucial point, the point on which our present enquiry turns. Jesus, standing in the High Priest's court, accused of many things, is silent to most, but himself chooses the issue upon which he wills to die. Am I the Christ? "I am," he says, and adds from himself, not in answer to any charge: "And ye shall see the Son of Man sitting on the right hand of Almighty Power and coming with the clouds of heaven." He takes to himself the part of the promised Adam. He takes it: but how does he perform it? How do we see him *being* the myth?

The prophet who saw the vision of Daniel vii applied one part of the Adam story alone. God has decreed that the divine image in mankind must have the dominion: in other words, the Son of Man must reign. And this Jesus also says: he said it to the High Priest. But there is another part to the Adam story. Adam is not now on the throne, nor is he in Paradise, he is naked, ashamed in the wilderness of his self-chosen misery, plowing among thistles, and destined to die. The new Adam must take up his destiny where it is, and work his way through it and out on to the further side: otherwise put, the Son of Man must suffer. And this also Jesus says in so many words. He does not simply say it. No sooner has the voice of the baptism, "Thou art my beloved

Son," ceased ringing in his ears, than the spirit of his destiny carries him into Adam's wilderness to be with the beasts, as Adam was, and to be tempted by Adam's old enemy, and succored, as Adam was believed to have been, by the angels of God's grace. Where Adam fell, he stood. Do this and that, the serpent had said to Adam, and make yourself your own God. If thou art the Son of God, says the tempter to Christ, do this and that, show your divinity and claim it by self-chosen arbitrary acts of power: subject yourself to me, and possess yourself of the universal dominion promised to the Son of Man. No. Adam grabbed, but Christ renounced. The birds have nests and the foxes holes: the Son of Man hath not where to lay his head. Yet in that very state of renunciation he raised the standard of his kingdom, and God's. He solemnly founded a new mankind in a group of twelve apostles; in the name of the Son of Man, that is, the eternal judge, he forgave sins on earth. In the name of the Son of Man, whose dominion is to last through the Sabbath of eternity, he claimed jurisdiction over the token Sabbath kept by Israel on the seventh day: the Son of Man is lord of the Sabbath also; the man created on the sixth day rules the seventh, and subjects it to the laws of divine compassion. His royalty and his renunciation exist together absolutely, each heightening the other: the Son of Man hath dominion on earth, he says: and, presently, "the Son of Man came not to be ministered unto, but to minister, and to give his life a ransom for many." Because he is the fulfillment of Adam, he goes back behind Moses to the perfection of the Creator's first intention. For the hardness of your hearts, he says, Moses gave you such a commandment, but in the beginning it was not so: for it is written, Male and female created he them: therefore shall a man leave father and mother and cleave to his wife, and the two shall be one flesh: what God hath joined, let not man put asunder.

On Adam's day, Friday, the sixth day of the week, his humiliation was fulfilled. "Art thou the King of the Jews?" said Pilate, and in that title he died, having first been mocked with purple and crowned with thorns. He died and he reigned, as he had foreseen, through the fabled instrument of Adam's death, the tree of wood. On the seventh day, the Sabbath, his body rested from all its works, as God did from his, and on the first day of the new week, in rhythm with the beginning of God's creation, with the *fiat lux* which called light out of darkness, something happened to the women carrying perfumes, to Peter and the Twelve, which they did not doubt to call a new creation. For "that which is born of the flesh is flesh, and that which is born of the spirit is spirit: marvel not that I say unto thee, ye must be born anew."

Can myth be fact? The only answer we hoped to find to this question lay in another. Since it is the Christians who say that myth was and is fact, we ask, how do they say it came about? And what we have seen is the slow formation of the perfect, the typical myth of Adam, its taking up and projection into the future by such prophets as him we call Daniel: its acceptance by Jesus as the meaning of his destiny, so that he sets out to *be* that new Adam, the Son of Man. Now insofar as he lives this poem, it may seem as though all we have is a private obsession with an idea. That Jesus does not talk or behave like the obsessed is a point that has often been made, but let it pass. But when we come to the climax of his action, the myth gets out of hand: he, as a helpless victim, cannot make it any longer. Did then that Creator God, of whom St. Thomas Aquinas spoke, take up and finish the work, making the tormentors of Jesus and his fugitive disciples unknowing instruments of it: did he bend and shape historical fact by that control which is his alone, into the expressive completion of the redeeming mystery? Did he (above all) actually raise Jesus from the dead, and enthrone the Son of Man at the right hand of Almighty Power, so that the divine image might reign in a kingdom both of Man and God, through the union of redeemed men with the enthroned Christ?

These last questions are not answered except by faith, faith in almighty power and in the testimony of Christ's apostles, and so "Can myth be fact?" brings us back to omnipotence after all. But we began by assuming God's almightiness. What we set out to show was that in the alleged instance his almighty act was somehow one piece with the rest of his action in nature and in man: and this we have attempted to do. The revelation of the myth which is fact did not begin suddenly in the first century; it began when men, first reflecting on the paradoxes of their destiny, were inspired to start the weaving of the myth of Adam.

IT AND THOU

Rev. D. R. Vicary

I must say first of all that I have come to think about these things because I came through the University as a scientist who was also a Christian. I later took to Theology: and then, after that, I have been busy teaching both Science and what is usually called Divinity. While this, in itself, does not affect the truth or falsehood of what I shall say, it will perhaps help to illuminate the standpoint from which I start, and explain some of the gaps in what I say.

The sub-title of this paper (given to me), "Scientific Knowledge and Personal Knowledge," is, like most potted phrases, a convenience and liable to be misunderstood. The emphasis I want to make is not primarily on different kinds of knowledge. It is rather on the relation which exists between the one who knows and the object known—i.e., more on ways of knowing than on kinds of knowledge. Scientific knowledge and personal knowledge are not to be contrasted as knowledge of things and knowledge of persons—rather I want to speak of scientific knowledge in terms of the I—IT relationship and personal knowledge in terms of the I—THOU. First let us examine how we get scientific knowledge: let us go into the labs.

If it is a biological lab, there may be a dissection going on. But instead of the rabbit, dogfish or frog, let us suppose we are dissecting a man: call him George, if you like. We know him, his likes and dislikes, his conversation, the claims he makes upon us—all this knowledge is what I will call personal knowledge: there is nobody quite like George and this knowledge of him is conveyed to us in a personal relationship which of its very nature is unique. Now, in order to have him on the slab either he must consent to be so treated—i.e., as a thing—or we must hold him there against his will, again ceasing to respect what makes him a person—i.e., treat him as a thing. But now we have him duly chloroformed, we are in a position to dissect. We can discover the structure of his inside; we can discover the relation between the various organs and examine the nervous system; we can remove various parts for more detailed examination with stains and sections and microscopes. But George is dead. The old adage, "We murder to dissect," is true. Now this primitive illustration lays bare one aspect of scientific method—it moves away from the unique and personal and views its subject matter in abstraction. It is true that I needn't have put George on the slab—I could have examined the structure of the body by using a corpse from another source, but the knowledge I gain from it applied to George is not personal knowledge—it is what in George is common to all bodies. True it is valuable knowledge and is part of my awareness of him, but it is not the part which makes my awareness of him unique in a personal relationship.

The method of abstraction is common to all scientific experiment. If you want to investigate the velocity of a chemical reaction, you have a number of variable factors to consider such as temperature and concentration of the reacting substances. In order to proceed you have to make some of these factors constant while you investigate changes in the others with time. You eliminate a variable in order to know more about the system. After you have performed numbers of experiments using this method, you try to express them all at once by a correlation such as a mathematical equation containing all the variables. What we have got now is a generalization which we can apply to particular conditions. Abstraction and generalization, then, are of the very nature of scientific method. And we notice that they cannot contain the element of uniqueness, which characterizes the knowledge we have of a person *in* a personal relationship.

In the less mathematical sciences, there are other aspects of scientific method. We have already noted in the dissecting room that we correlate knowledge gained from the dissection with other similar knowledge. George is a vertebrate, a biped, and so on. And even the fact that I may know he is not a vegetarian is not so personal that I cannot class him as a carnivore. Thus, the generalization turns up in a non-mathematical form as a classification. Whitehead says "Classification is the halfway house between the immediate concreteness of the individual thing and the complete abstraction of mathematical notions."

A further point which need not occupy us long is that a great deal of our scientific knowledge comes to us by means of measurement—in terms of quantity; the perception of quality or value is excluded by the method. Now all these aspects of scientific method show how we get scientific knowledge in terms of an I—IT relationship. But you will see why I insisted at the beginning that the distinction between scientific knowledge and personal knowledge is not that between knowledge of things and knowledge of persons. There is knowledge of persons on the I—IT level—a convenient distinction might be to say it is knowledge about a person rather than direct knowledge of the person, though I don't like that distinction because the I—IT knowledge goes to make up our total awareness of a person.

Thus it is possible to treat a person as though the only kind of knowledge available is of the I—IT kind—i.e., to apply scientific method. For example, the method known as mass observation gives statistics about size of families, opinions about Mr. Churchill or drink, and so on. This knowledge tells us the probability that someone will hold certain views: but it tells us nothing about what we shall find out if we meet him—he is not a statistic, and the absurdity of thinking that by these means there is much enrichment on the personal level is made clear by Mr. Punch's picture of the average man having two and a half children. The statistics merely help our generalizations; the knowledge that comes in personal relationship includes the knowledge given in the I—IT relationship, but the total awareness is on the level of I—THOU.

The I—IT knowledge then is obtained by these methods which are analytical after the moment of perception. What then of the other ways of knowing in the relationship I—THOU? I have spoken of the total awareness of another person which may include the scientific knowledge. Does the knowledge which we call personal simply mean adding up the analyzed parts to make the whole once more? It is true that synthesizing intuition sees them all at once, but is that all which makes personal knowledge—i.e., knowledge of a person in relationship? The adding up of the parts, the abstracted bits does not give us the whole of personal knowledge for two reasons: first, the method by which the analysis was made has removed the quality of the personal, which cannot be re-manufactured, so to say—("all the king's horses and all the king's men ....")—to have the same force as it had in the moment of apprehension in which we were conscious of the other; secondly, the way in which we are aware of the other person indicates the personal knowledge given in the relationship I—THOU is *sui generis*.

To elaborate these two points: we have seen that in the analytical approach we ignore the uniqueness which makes personal relationship; we abstract information from the particular occasion and fit it into generalizations. When we put all this information together we do not put back the personal element, because it is not there to be put back—we strained it off, as it were. The collection of information put together is really on the level of gossip: it is knowledge *about* somebody rather than direct knowledge of him in relationship. Again we notice why I insisted that we are approaching knowledge through the relationship between the knower and the object of knowledge. The synthesis of remembered knowledge cannot create the relationship which originally existed when the knowledge was given—*the element of encounter is missing*: not only because the other is not there, but because I have changed in the meanwhile, having had some more moments of experience—personalities grow. How often do we say of a person whom we haven't seen for some time but meet by chance—"You wouldn't know him," and even when we might say "He hasn't changed" it is by way of reflection on the fact that both parties have passed through more experience. The time factor enters here.

So we pass to the second point—that knowledge of other persons in a personal relationship is *sui generis*. As Karl Heim puts it: "The knowledge which the I has of the Thou, making it possible for them to interpret a particular sound as a 'Word,' comes about through a mode of knowledge which precedes observation of contents." Well, we have seen the characteristics of the I—IT type of knowing—the type of scientific knowledge: what are the characteristics of this mode of knowing in a personal relationship, which, as Heim says, precedes observation of contents?

That there is a difference between knowledge about a person and knowledge by direct confrontation can be seen if we imagine this situation. I and a friend are discussing a third person in his absence. We talk about his character, his oddities, his likeable qualities, his tastes, his ambitions …. Now suppose he walks into the room. We cannot simply go on talking *about* him. But why? Some might say—it isn't decent to do a thing like that; but really the deep-seated reason is that we recognize that talking about him is treating him like anything else that might be in the room—the piano, a picture. It is not in personal relationship. When the man comes into the room, you address him because there is a new condition of knowing—a direct relationship. The person who is there presents himself as someone with a right to be talked *to*, not merely talked *about*.

Now, just as we tried to see how we get our scientific knowledge, let us try to see how a person is known in relationship: why he is there with his right to be talked *to*.

In the first place, it is well to notice that all our knowledge of others has the category of being shared—take it away and there is no longer that personal knowledge: that is why I find no difficulty in accepting the existence of other minds which I have assumed all along. The other person is someone whom we know to be not only capable of hearing what we say to him, but capable of attaching *meaning* to it. In that, we find that he or she has the same power as we have, of discursive reason—of observing contents. We know that we have something to put across, and our personal relationship does depend on how much is understood. That is why English people in particular shout in order to make themselves understood when speaking to a foreigner!

Secondly, we also expect that the other person is able to act on his apprehension of meaning. That is to say, we know of a will over against ours. But that will must be free. For example, one of Dorothy Sayers' stories has in it a safe, which will open if a word is spoken into a hidden microphone. The safe is capable of responding to certain sound vibrations—but it is not a person—it can only respond in one way, and there is no element of discernment in the response because it is not able to respond to any other word. But in a person, we assume that element of free response: we give him or her credit for free will. If we ignore this, then we treat him not as a person but as a thing. We appreciate this: for do we not speak of a person whose will is overridden in his relationship as a "doormat"—even the word "stooge" means that he is less than a person. He is being treated as a thing. That, I think, bears witness to our fundamental understanding in personal relationships that the real personal knowledge involves knowing a free will over against ours in a living tension. But if this relationship is to be real—involving friendship and trust—then our response involves a committal to the other. If we had not this element—we might only talk about the weather. But there is an element of committal which must be there if we are to respect his will. If we really respect his will, then we recognize that it is something inaccessible to us: it is there in its own right, not to be manipulated for our ends—that is to ignore it—but to be responded to in living fellowship. How then is this committal possible?

This is the third thing about personal knowledge—it involves the recognition that the will over against ours is subject to the same standards (to use Farmer's phrase) of unconditional worth or value. The very existence of the other person involves for us the recognition of the moral values. In the relationship of trust in which there is real committal to the other, there is the recognition of our own obligation as well as that of the other person to the same moral order. If we do not recognize this, then inevitably the relationship breaks down because if there is no external judgment on ourselves as well as the other, we have to erect ourselves as authoritative over the other and reduce him to the level of a slave—which is the I—IT relationship.

So these are the distinguishing features of the way we get personal knowledge in relationship—they involve the recognition of mutual obligation to standards of unconditional worth or value. These are elements of the I—THOU knowledge.

Again, let us look back and see how science, by using the methods of analysis, cannot tell us about the validity of this kind of knowledge. We observed that the method removed the element of uniqueness and spontaneity which are the hallmark of the personal: but this is carried into the whole worldview of pure science. The recognition of the freedom of others is not something which can occur on the I—IT level. Treat a person as a thing and you will not discover he has free will—the only way you can discover he has free will is by mutual trust in which you implicitly recognize that he has freedom of will. The deterministic picture of the world is based on a generalization from situations in which freedom of will has not been evident—a causal system has been assumed to apply to occasions of the exercise of will; yet these cannot be observed treating the person as an IT, and the knowledge gained on the I—IT level does not contain the will as personally active.

The next thing to consider is how the I—IT and I—THOU ways of knowing are dependent on one another—this way of labeling ways of knowing is very convenient, but it suggests too complete a dichotomy between IT and THOU when the IT kind of knowledge is about persons. It is true that we can distinguish between knowledge about a person and knowing a person; but how much does knowing about a person help our direct knowledge of him? We find that it does help a great deal. Suppose you are going to meet some eminent person. It will make a great deal of difference to the freedom of your converse with him if you know his interests and reputation, the kind of friends he makes, and whether all this squares with what he says about himself in *Who's Who*! The discursive activity of reason in building up generalizations can be of use. The personal way of knowing in relationship—the mode which preceded observation of contents, is helped if the contents are partly knowing already, although it needs the actual encounter with the other to make the I—THOU knowledge possible.

It is probable that primitive animism which saw spirits in all sorts of dead things like trees and stones was simply a projection based on analogy with man's own experience. It is when the encounter with a real person occurs that it is no longer analogy because there comes forth from the object, as it were, something in common to meet it. I expect some of you have been to a waxworks and have seen a figure in policeman's uniform, and you wonder whether it is a real policeman. Your first knowledge is based on I—IT relationship—he has a blue uniform, he has a face, he looks lifelike, he is, in fact, all you may have come to regard a policeman as, if you have had no dealings with the police and have never seen one except standing still. But suppose you go up to him and ask the time: you will then know whether he is a person or not because of the response. But you would never have tried to get that response if you had not first knowledge on the I—IT level about policemen. The I—IT knowledge does give a continuing basis to the I—THOU relationship, because it is part of the *I*. But if the I—THOU depends on the I—IT, no less does the I—IT depend on something involving the person's conscious continuance in time. Knowledge in pure science need not be of persons at all, but it depends on tradition among scientists. And even the very act of observing and method of correlating observations rest on assumptions about the tradition which is communication between persons.

That is why Whitehead in *Science and the Modern World* speaks about the unsolved problem left to us by the seventeenth century as the rational justification of the method of induction. If I correlate observations, I assume the continuity of myself and the order of the natural world. The community of scientists out of which the general body of scientific knowledge issues forth depends on the I—THOU relationship because the other observers are all assumed to be subject to the same conditions of perception and loyalty to truth. And it is very interesting that such scientific philosophers as Whitehead are emphasizing the understanding of the immediate moment of experience in its concreteness.

So then, the I—IT way of knowing and the I—THOU way both play their part in the communication of persons with one another. The I—THOU is an immediate relationship; knowledge on the I—IT level comes when the discursive reason, as it were, retreats from the situation to sort it out. The most helpful description of this process I have come across is Oman's, from immediate awareness into: apprehension, comprehension, and explanation; e.g., country walk—general awareness, all senses alert. See a movement—seek *apprehension*—it is a man on a bike. If we have never seen a bike before, we seek to understand how it works to *comprehend* the relation between the bike and the man riding it; then as it passes, we see it has no support from the sides, and we try to *explain* in terms of general scientific principles how balance is kept ... at each stage the scope of knowing is less. But it is important to realize that if the man on the bike is someone whom we recognize, and he gets off and speaks to us, then there is *new element*—direct relationship with a person. We have an I—THOU relationship and the knowledge of the person is on a different level from knowing how he rides his bike and how it works.

You may have noticed that I have been using an I—IT method in describing the I—THOU relationship. In order to describe it, I stand outside it. I would claim that this is valid just because of what I have said about the way these ways of knowing depend on each other in the individual mind. The qualities of personal relationship can be described *post eventum* as well as experienced. The fact that these qualities *still* have power to evoke response even when simply described is because we are persons and owe our existence to Personal Being. These qualities are always there because they come from that moral order which I said was a condition of a true personal relationship. So then, this is not simply an analysis of knowledge, but it is bound up with our very existence.

In conclusion, I want to point out one thing. This valuation of the personal, not merely as *sui generis*, but involving those qualities I have mentioned—freedom, commanding utter respect, together with the fact that we find ourselves mutually under obligation—this valuation of the personal is utterly Christian. It owes its existence to Christianity. We took our examples of personal relationship of trust from what we know is a relationship of love. But we also noticed that it was easy to slip out of that relationship into one with a slave or thing; when that happens to persons, it is the occasion of the expression of selfishness. So when we take the view of knowledge as including I—THOU as well as I—IT, the fact of evil comes into the picture. All the things commonly called sins involve treating the THOU as IT. The effect of this on our knowledge is that the THOU is a challenge to us, so we prefer knowledge on the IT level. That is one reason why we like gossip. It is also the reason why it is much easier to talk about God than to obey Him. And I could only talk about this subject at all hopefully, if the Living God, Eternal Thou, persisted in his encounter, and had undertaken the remaking of personal relationship with Himself and between men and women. The fact that I do speak hopefully is because I believe that He does so persist, and has in Christ begun the reconciling of the world to Himself—the remaking of the true I—THOU. This is something which has to be considered if one dares to include the personal as a way of knowledge.

CHRISTIAN AND NON-CHRISTIAN MYSTICISM

Rev. Gervase Mathew, O.P.

(This is not a verbatim report, but an attempt to reconstruct what the speaker said.)

The subject matter of this paper may be divided into sections:
I. The significance of the mystical elements in traditional Christianity.

II. A more detailed examination of the mystical theory of the Middle Ages, under these headings:
  (*a*) Knowledge by means of friendship.
  (*b*) The relationship between contemplation and charity.
  (*c*) The doctrine of the gifts of the Holy Spirit.
  (*d*) The particular application of these doctrines to the literature of the medieval mysticism, with special attention to the phrases "*Per modum actus,*" "*non per modum habitus,*" and "*quid quid recipitur, secundum modum recipientis recipitur.*"

III. The application of this theory and these doctrines to non-Christian mysticism, especially to Sufism and to tendencies within Hinduism.

IV. The consideration of counter hypotheses which would attribute the literature of mysticism to the force of literary convention, or pathological factors.

The mystical element in traditional Christianity is of permanent significance; without it, indeed, it is impossible to understand the history of Christian prayer, for by the possibility of mystical experience is meant the possibility of an intuitive approach to the Divine. The early Middle Ages took this for granted, and so there is, in their writing, a constant use, and significance given to the words contemplation and "*mystica cognitia.*" The word "Mystic," which was first used by Clement of Alexandria, became naturalized into Christianity from the third century onward. Clement of Alexandria had held that all mystics were of the faithful, but that not all the faithful were mystics. By mysticism was meant the initiation into the Mysteries; the gift of realization added to faith. To the Alexandrians the faithful believe, but the mystic both sees and experiences what he believes. The significant word is "seeing" and within the mystical tradition there are different forms of "seeing." There is the blinding apprehension of Godhead which, transcending all the concepts he had used, led St. Thomas to say, when asked to finish the

Summa: "Reginald, I cannot. All that I have written seems to me to be of straw." There is the sudden perception of the relationship between the Divine and created things, described by Julian of Norwich, when she tells how she saw Creation lying, small as a nut in Christ's hand. And there is the realization lying behind so much medieval hagiography, behind the stories of St. Martin and the Cloak, of St. Francis and the Leper, the realization of Christ present. There were, in fact, two classes of mystic; those, like St. Bernard and Richard Rolle, whose perception was Christocentric, and depended upon a realization of Christ, and those like St. Thomas Aquinas, whose experience would seem to have centered in the contemplation of the transcendent Godhead.

The experience of realization was not in any way bounded by considerations of hierarchy. Anyone might be capable of it, merchants and masters in theology, friars and enclosed nuns. It was coextensive with Christianity, and transcended the boundaries between the priest and the layman. This, although the experience itself was inexpressible in words or phrases, became a vital factor behind Catholic Theology. But one question the Middle Ages left unasked and therefore unanswered: If the experience is valid, and is coextensive with Christianity, how far is it possible outside Christendom? How far was the formalization of fourteenth-century Europe applicable to the mysticism which arose, at the same time, in Islam, in Persia and in South India?

In the thirteenth century the Thomist view of mystical experience slowly became the norm, and it was increasingly dominant during the fourteenth century. St. Thomas distinguished between knowledge gained "*per modum rationis*," and knowledge gained "*per modum amicitiae*." Mystical experience was knowledge through friendship, or, as it is alternatively phrased, "*cognitio per modum amoris*," or "*per modum compassionis*." Understanding of this doctrine is dependent upon an understanding of the medieval approach to friendship. By "*amicitia*" was meant self-giving, the union of two souls who know each other intuitively, in whose relationship there is not, as there is in acquaintanceship, the need for one to use inference or discursive reason in his knowing of the other. If this intuitive knowledge is possible between man and man, is it also possible between man and God? It was answered, that it was made so in the Incarnation, in which Christ had united man with the Godhead. Through Grace a man might, as a member of His mystical body, share in the divine Life. So there was, through Grace, a possibility of friendship between man and God. Charity in fact was "*amicitia*," the love of friendship between man and God, made possible solely through the Grace given at the Incarnation.

This share in Christ's life increases with the growth of charity, "*caritas*," that love of God for His own sake which reflects Christ's love for us, and the love for others which reflects Christ's love for them. With this growth in charity the possibility of direct knowledge grows stronger in us. As charity grows in us we grow in the power of contemplation through the gifts of the Holy Spirit, especially in the gift of wisdom, that is in the power of seeing things as God sees them, and in the gift of understanding, the power of seeing God through things: hence the varied forms of seeing which come through grace and faith, and flower with charity.

This theory is reflected in the mystical literature of the time. It was held that contemplation might be "*per modum actus*," or "*per modum habitus*." Knowledge "*per modum habitus*" is permanent, it demands perfect charity, and is given only when, by growth in charity, the soul is finally united to the Godhead. Such knowledge could only be possessed by saints, but realization might be experienced "*per modum actus*," in momentary glimpses by a soul not in a state of habitual perfect charity. The other principle clearly evident in the mystical literature is the Aristotelian doctrine, that whatever is received is received according to the nature of the recipient. When we become members of Christ's body, we are still ourselves. The life of Grace does not destroy but strengthens the natural capacities. Prayer means the raising of the mind and spirit to God, but it is the individual mind and spirit. Therefore the realization given to the individual is known in terms of his own preconceptions. So the knowledge of St. Francis and St. Bernard was knowledge through their preconceptions of the Incarnate Word, and that of the author of "The Cloud" and of Meister Eckhart through theirs of the will and the Godhead.

But how far are these doctrines applicable to the mystical literature of Persia and of India during the same period? They are tenable if the existence of grace is held to be wider than the knowledge of Christianity. There are parallels in the literature of the Persian Sufis to the literature of Western mysticism, especially to the "Cloud of Unknowing." In that of South India during the twelfth and thirteenth centuries there are close resemblances to the sixteenth century work of St. John of the Cross. The Western Scholastics in their disputes about the Silvestris, the wild man living in the woods, remote from the possibility of Christian revelation, were prepared to admit that he might possess some kind of mystical knowledge. He might be baptized with desire, and therefore awakened to the new life of charity and become possessed of the gifts of the Holy Spirit.

For such a kind of knowledge no great sanctity was necessarily implied, and, indeed, it is tenable that in the poetry of the Sufi the experience habitually expressed, however valid, is *per modum actus*," not "*per modum habitus*." There seemed to be two tendencies in Sufism, the one expressed in the words "For I am the wine drinker, and the wine, and the wine cup, in which is perceived the unity of God and Creation"; and the other expressing not the Immanence but the Transcendence of God, and the comparative unreality of created things. This distinction has also a key to Indian mysticism, and it may correspond to the distinction, in Christian mysticism, between Christocentric and Theocentric mystics. If the Indian is more conscious of the transcendence of God, it is because he knows in terms of his preconceptions.

These hypotheses presuppose, of course, a whole mass of traditional Christian doctrine, and there have been other explanations offered. There is the explanation which traces mysticism to a common literary convention, derived both in Persia and in Provence from Neo-Platonic writings. But, as it is not possible to argue from a convention in love poetry to the non-existence of love, so it is not possible to argue from a convention in mystical literature to the non-existence of mystical experience. The psychological and pathological explanations are not very convincing. The experience may sometimes be accompanied, as in the case of Margery Kemp, by hysterical phenomena, but the hysteria does not invalidate the experience. Even the recognized existence of pseudo-mysticism is surely rather an argument for the existence of the mysticism it travesties. For if it were all an hallucination why should this particular hallucination so haunt the human mind? There is in all men, to a greater or lesser degree, a desire for the Infinite, a desire for otherness which man attempts to satisfy with mirage, though the mirage never lasts. In every human being, as in every literature, there is a nostalgia, a homesickness. And a homesickness is in itself an argument for the existence of a home.

SOCRATIC DIGEST

Number Four   Double Number

CONTENTS

PREFACE   102

REPLY TO MR. C. S. LEWIS' ARGUMENT THAT
    "NATURALISM" IS SELF-REFUTING   103
  G. E. M. Anscombe
    Reply by C. S. Lewis

THE LIMITS OF POSITIVISM   110
  Dr. F. Waismann

AQUINAS AND NEWMAN ON THEISM   113
  Précis by A. D. Howell Smith
    Summary of Reply to Mr. Howell Smith by Dr. E. L. Mascall

DOES GOD EXIST?   118
  Dr. Austin Farrer

PLATO AND CHRISTIANITY   124
  Leslie J. Walker, S.J.

ARISTOTLE AND CHRISTIANITY   129
  Fr. F. C. Copleston, S.J.

BELIEF AND REASON IN PHILOSOPHY   130
  Mr. M. B. Foster

KARL BARTH ON FAITH AND REASON   140
  Rev. Daniel Jenkins

EXISTENTIALISM   145
  Ronald Grimsley

THEISM AND PERSONAL RELATIONSHIPS   153
  M. Gabriel Marcel
    Reply by Dr. L. W. Grensted

THE SCIENTIFIC WORLD OUTLOOK Dr. F. Sherwood-Taylor	155

RELIGION WITHOUT DOGMA?
    C. S. Lewis
        Reply by Professor H. H. Price
	157

THE DEITY OF CHRIST Principal Nicol Cross and Rev. T. M. Parker	172

DID THE RESURRECTION REALLY HAPPEN?
    Rupert E. Davies
        Reply by Rev. T. M. Parker
	175

THE NECESSITY OF CHRISTIAN MYSTICISM Fr. Conrad Pepler, O.P.	182
PSYCHIC RESEARCH AND ITS BEARING ON CHRISTIAN FAITH Dr. L. W. Grensted	188
THE OXFORD UNIVERSITY SOCRATIC CLUB—OFFICERS	190
MEETINGS, 1947-8	191

THREE SHILLINGS

Oxonian Press, Queen Street, Oxford

SOCRATIC CLUB ROOM AND LIBRARY

This is at Pin Farm House, South Hinksey, Oxford, the home of the Chairman, by kind permission of Miss Margery Ewen. It is close to beautiful walking country.

Discussion Teas are held here on Thursdays, 3:30—5:00 p.m. in the Trinity Term. Members and others are welcome to drop in any afternoon to read or rest (or inspect the farmyard!). From Michaelmas onwards we hope it will be possible to put people up for weekends, and for longer during Vacations.

HOW TO GET TO PIN FARM. It is about 20 minutes' cycling or 25 minutes' walking from Carfax—once you know the way.

Go past Christ Church along the ABINGDON ROAD until you reach LAKE STREET on your right. Go down this and along the footbridge over the Reservoir and over the railway, and continue along the willow walk into S. Hinksey village. At the CROSS KEYS bear left, and follow the road until it passes the Church. Then turn left down BARLEYCOT LANE, and the first double doors on your left lead into Pin Farm.

NOTE.—No. 8 'bus from the Town Hall runs every 10 minutes past Lake Street (Fare 1½d.).

ORDERS FOR THIS DIGEST

By post from: Mr. J. F. Goodridge, 27 St. John Street, Oxford. 3/- per copy, plus 3d. for postage and envelope.

SOCRATIC DIGEST

"Οὗτος μὲν οἴεταί τι εἰδέναι οὐκ εἰδώς, ἐγὼ δὲ ὥσπερ οὖν οὐκ οἶδα οὐδὲ οἴομαι."
—*Socrates*

"Εἴ τις δοκεῖ ἐγνωκέναι τι, οὔπω ἔγνω καθὼς δεῖ γνῶναι."
—*St. Paul*

"La dernière démarche de la raison est de reconnaître qu'il y a une infinité de choses qui la surpassent."
—*Pascal*

PREFACE

In a penetrating article entitled "Credulity,"[14] Dr. Farrer has underlined the importance of asking "untidy questions." He suggests that if men and women coming up to the University to read philosophy are trained to analyze such apparently trivial propositions as "There is a lamp-post in the High" in such a way as to equip them to tackle questions that are not trivial, such as the existence of God, their time will have been well spent. The prevailing philosophical fashion, however, seems to be rather to regard philosophy as an intellectual therapy (in some quarters), one by which a man can be cured of asking the ultimately important questions (the "untidy" ones), by so analyzing the structure and nature of language as to make such questions probably "meaningless" (an artificially restricted use of "meaning" having been laid down beforehand). These questions are thereby discredited for many a young philosopher trained in the art of resolving "metaphysical" questions into "linguistic muddles."

"In answering the ultimate (and therefore untidy) questions, the danger of becoming misled by words is certainly very great, and any discipline we can learn from the logicians will be invaluable in this field. But it will be a great pity if we allow our discrimination between genuine and false questions to be determined by consideration of logical form alone. There is no getting round our sense for what is real, and any philosophy which attempts to argue us out of it, rather than to provide us with the means of coming to grips with it, must be rejected as an opiate and an evasion."

Whatever the philosophical fashion may be, one thing is certain: men and women (including many of the most intelligent and philosophically able ones) will continue to ask the ultimate, the "untidy questions." It seems better that at the University these should be asked with the help of minds trained in such asking as well as against the background of contemporary developments in philosophy and science and in presence of the attacks of the skeptics. Hence the Socratic Club. However unsatisfactory the procedure may be from the point of view of getting any tidy answers (or even a tidy discussion), we continue to ask those questions because they are the human and the ultimately important ones, whose asking serves to keep philosophical fashion in perspective as well as to grope for a bridge between scientific and personal knowledge, between "reason" and "faith."

A glance down the list of papers read may amuse a philosopher who considers himself cured of the naïveté of asking "metaphysical" questions, or of entertaining the possibility that the Christian Faith may in any reputable sense be *true*. But it is just possible that such "naïveté" may be fundamentally of a piece with the childlikeness which Christ teaches us can open the Kingdom of God to a man, and it is also possible that the fragmentary and more than untidy intellectual answers to our untidy questions may remove misunderstanding and ignorance and so prepare the way for one here and another there to another kind of answer—that spiritual discovery which sets the questions in a new frame of reference, and so gives them an intelligibility in which scientific and personal knowledge both find their due place.

STELLA ALDWINCKLE

---

[14] See "Illuminatio" for Oct., 1947, published from No. 3 Holywell, Oxford.

A REPLY TO MR. C. S. LEWIS' ARGUMENT THAT "NATURALISM" IS SELF-REFUTING

G. E. M. ANSCOMBE

NOTE.—*I wish to acknowledge that I was very greatly helped in writing this paper by discussing it with Mr. Y. Smythies: naturally, he is not responsible for its faults.—G.E.M.A.*

[*A short version of Mr. Lewis' argument will be found in his paper "Religion without Dogma" on pp. 87-8 of this issue, which is also commented on by Prof. H. H. Price in his reply to that paper, section 4, p. 98. The argument in full, which Miss Anscombe is criticizing, is in "Miracles," Chapter III, "The Self-Contradiction of the Naturalist."*—EDITOR.]

I want to discuss your argument that what you call "naturalism" is self-refuting because it is inconsistent with a belief in the validity of reason. With this argument you propose to destroy "naturalism" and hence remove the determinist objection to miracles.

For my purpose it is not necessary to go into your description of "naturalism" or your claim that one must either believe it or be a "Supernaturalist"—i.e. believe in God. For you say that "naturalism" includes the idea that human thought can be fully explained as the product of natural (i.e. non-rational) causes, and it is this idea which you maintain is self-contradictory because it impugns the validity of reason, and therefore necessarily of any thinking by which it itself is reached.

What I shall discuss, therefore, is this argument: the hypothesis that human thought can be fully explained as the product of non-rational causes is inconsistent with a belief in the validity of reason.

You state it as a rule that "no thought is valid if it can be fully explained as the result of irrational causes," and you give examples to show that we all universally apply this rule:—We do not attend to the belief of a man with delirium tremens that the house is full of rats and snakes; we are less impressed by a man's gloomy views if we know he is suffering from a bad liver attack; the disruptive power of Marxism and Freudianism against traditional beliefs has lain in their claim to expose irrational causes for them.

About the first two examples I should like to say that it is only because we already know that men with delirium tremens see things that are not there, and that men with liver attacks take gloomier views of the situation than they would normally take, or than is reasonable, that we dismiss a man's belief by ascribing it to delirium tremens or to a liver attack when we know he has one of these complaints.

What sorts of thing would one normally call "irrational causes" for human thoughts?—If one is asked this, one immediately thinks of such things as passion, self-interest, wishing only to see the agreeable or disagreeable, obstinate and prejudicial adherence to the views of a party or school with which one is connected, and so on. Suppose one mentions such things, and then someone says: There are also tumors on the brain, tuberculosis, jaundice, arthritis, and similar things, one would rightly object that these do not belong in the same list as the others. They are not "irrational causes"; they are conditions which we know to go with irrational beliefs or attitudes with sufficient regularity for us to call them their causes.

You speak of "irrational causes," and by that you seem to mean "any cause that is not something rational." "Something rational" you explain by example: "such as (you say) argument from observed facts." You contrast the following sentences: (1) "He thinks that dog dangerous because he has often seen it muzzled and he has noticed that messengers always try to avoid going to that house"; (2) "He thinks that dog dangerous because it is black and ever since he was bitten by a black dog in childhood he has always been afraid of black dogs." "Both sentences," you say "explain *why* the man thinks as he does. But the one explanation substantiates the value of his thought and the other discredits it…. The difference is that in the first instance the man's belief is caused by something rational (by argument from observed facts) while in the other it is caused by something irrational (association of ideas)."

I am going to argue that your whole thesis is only specious because of the ambiguity of the words "why," "because," and "explanation." That ambiguity is illustrated here. The case of the man who is frightened by black dogs is unclear. Imagine the two following possibilities: (1) He says "That dog's dangerous." He is asked, "How do you know?" He says, "It's black: I was once bitten by a black dog." To this we reply: "That's not a good ground. We know enough about dogs to know that." (2) He says: "That dog's dangerous." He is asked, "How do you know?" But to this he gives no answer; he shakes his head, trembles, and says, "It's dangerous." Then either he, or someone else, says that he behaves like this because he was once bitten by a black dog. Then we can know that we need not pay attention to his belief; it already appeared groundless, from the fact that he could give no grounds; but now we are satisfied it is groundless because we understand it as the expression of a fear produced by circumstances which we know to give no good grounds for fear. It is here quite natural to speak of "irrational causes."

Similarly it is true that the Marxists and the Freudians claim to expose irrational causes for various traditional beliefs. The Freudian says that my belief in God is a projection of my infantile attitude towards my father. The Marxist says that many of my beliefs and reasonings arise from my considering things important that I should not consider important if I were not bourgeois, and neglecting other things which I should not neglect if I were not bourgeois; and that the whole point and significance of certain kinds of thinking is simply—by the very pretence of detachment that they make—to draw people away from relating their thoughts to the class struggle.

But by your equation of "irrational causes" with "non-rational cause," you are led to imagine that if the naturalist hypothesis (that all human behavior, including thought, could be account for by scientific causal laws) were true, human thought would all have been explained away as invalid; that if human beings could be shown to act according to such laws, their case would have been shown to be universally like the particular case of the man who is actuated by "irrational causes" and whose beliefs are groundless. This seems to me to be a mistake founded on various confusions you commit about the concepts of "reason," "cause" and "explanation"; and I hope by showing what the confusions are, to show that it *is* a mistake.

First, I want to examine your remark that we must believe in the validity of reason, and that we can see when a hypothesis is inconsistent with a belief in the validity of reason, and refute it by the consideration that it is inconsistent with that belief.

You can talk about the validity of a *piece* of reasoning, and sometimes about the validity of a *kind* of reasoning; but if you say you believe in the validity of reasoning itself, what do you mean? Isn't this question about the validity of reasoning a question about the validity of *valid* reasoning? Suppose that you are asked to explain "valid," how will you do it?—The most obvious way would be to show examples of valid and invalid reasoning, to make the objections which in the examples of invalid reasoning, show that the conclusion does not follow from the premises; in the cases of valid reasoning, to elucidate the form of the argument: if the piece of reasoning under consideration is elliptical, to add the statements which are required to enforce the conclusion.—Whether you would adopt this method or some other (though I do not know of any other), I suppose you think it *somehow* possible to explain to yourself or someone else what "valid" means, what the distinction between "valid" and "invalid" is? Now if the naturalistic hypothesis (that human thought is the product of a chain of natural causes) is proposed to you, you say: "But if this were so, it would destroy the distinction between valid and invalid reasoning." But how? Would it imply that you could no longer give the explanation you gave, point to and explain the examples, say which arguments proposed to you are valid and which invalid in just the same way as you did before the naturalistic hypothesis was supposed? "But," you may say, "though I should of course know which arguments to *call* valid, or which I should have *called* valid, I should not now feel any confidence that they were *really* valid." But what do you mean by "really valid"? What meaning of "valid" has been taken away from you by the naturalistic hypothesis? What *can* you mean by "valid" beyond what would be indicated by the explanation you would give for distinguishing between valid and invalid, and what in the naturalistic hypothesis prevents that explanation from being given and from meaning what it does?

You say that on this hypothesis there would be no difference between the conclusions of the finest scientific reasoning and thoughts a man has because a bit of bone is pressing on his brain. In one way, this is true. Suppose that the kind of account which the "naturalist" imagines, were actually given in the two cases. We should have two accounts of processes in the human organism. "Valid," "true," "false" would not come into either of the accounts. That shows, you say, that the conclusions of the scientist would be just as irrational as those of the other man. But that does not follow at all. Whether his conclusions are rational or irrational is settled by considering the chain of reasoning that he gives and whether his conclusions follow from it. When we are giving a causal account of his thought, e.g. an account of the physiological processes which issue in the utterance of his reasoning, we are not considering his utterances from the point of view of evidence, reasoning, valid argument, truth, at all; we are considering them merely as events. Just *because* that is how we are considering them, our description has in itself no bearing on the question of "valid," "invalid," "rational," "irrational," and so on.

Given the scientific explanation of human thought and action which the naturalist hypothesis asserts to be possible, we could, if we had the data that the explanation required, predict what any man was going to say, and what conclusions he was going to form. That would not mean that there was no sense in calling what he did say true or false, rational or irrational.

"But," you say, "this imagined explanation would show that what we said was not caused by reason but by non-rational processes. We may give arguments, but as everything we say will be fully explained by non-rational causes, (a) the idea that conclusions are derived from premises will be an illusion (hence I say that the explanation impugns the validity of reason) and (b) the idea that we think what we do because of reasoning, i.e. because we have reasoned, will be an illusion. Every thought will have been produced by a non-rational chain of causes and therefore not by such rational causes as observation and argument. So no thought will be worth anything."

I want to say that such an argument as this is based on a confusion between the concepts of cause and reason, which arises because of the ambiguity of such expressions as "because" and "explanation."

1) If I said: "You think this conclusion follows from these premises, but in fact the assertion of it is a physical event with physical causes just like any other physical event," would it not be clear that I was imagining the ground of a conclusion to be a kind of cause of it? Otherwise there would be no incompatibility: "this conclusion follows from these premises"

would be in no way contradicted by "the assertion of this conclusion is a physical event with physical causes like any other physical event." Even though all human activity, including the production of opinions and arguments, were explained naturalistically, that could have no bearing on "the validity of reason"—i.e. on the question whether a piece of reasoning were valid or not. Here I am speaking of "reason" in a non-psychological sense, in which "a reason" is what proves a conclusion. If we have before us a piece of writing which argues for an opinion, we can discuss the question: "Is this good reasoning?" without concerning ourselves with the circumstances of its production at all.

2) But you may say that you do not wish to call a reason—in this non-psychological sense—the cause of its conclusion; you may agree that the naturalistic hypothesis could not impugn "the validity of reason" in this sense, but say that it makes reason an ideal which we cannot attain; that it does impugn the validity of all *actual* human reasonings. For granted that the logical derivation of a conclusion from its premises could not be affected by any hypothesis, yet if *our reasonings* are to be valid *we* must derive the conclusions from the premises, in actual fact.[15] This introduces a psychological application of the concept of "reason" which is used if we ask the following questions about, e.g. a piece of writing that we are examining: "Granted that this is a piece of reasoning, did the man who wrote it actually *reason*? Was he really persuaded by this reasoning or by something else? Or—another possibility—did he really understand and mean this argument? Or did he perhaps write it down quite mechanically?—Here is a statement (which is even in fact correct), but did the man who wrote it himself assert it because of the good grounds which do exist for asserting it?" If we can answer "yes" to such questions as these we call the opinions in question "rational" or the man "rational" for holding them. And if we know that a man's opinions are not rational in this sense, we regard it as accidental if in fact they are worth attending to or true; we shall not expect to find them worth attending to, and if it is a question of information to be accepted on his word, we shall not accept it.

You argue that the naturalist hypothesis about human thinking implies that no human thinking is rational in this sense. For if a man produces what purports to be the conclusion of an argument, in order that what he says should be rational he must say it *because* he has reasoned; but the naturalist hypothesis says that he says it *because* of certain natural causes; and if these causes *fully* explain his utterance, if the chain of causes is complete, there is no room for the operation of such a cause as the man's own reasoning. So someone might say: "If I claimed to be able to kill a man by an act of will, and he died, but his death was fully explained by the fact that someone who had sworn to murder him shot him through the heart, that would demolish any claim to have killed him by an act of will."

Your idea appears to be that "*the* explanation" is everywhere the same one definite requirement: as if there were a fixed place for "*the* explanation" so that we can know, when it is filled, that if it has been correctly filled, the whole subject of "explaining this fact" has been closed. We understand the requirement antecedently to any knowledge of the kind of investigation that might be made, and once we see that the requirement has been satisfied, no further question can be asked.

But the concept of "explanation" has very varied applications, and the expression "full explanation" has reference only to the type of explanation that is in question. I may, for example, ask a man to explain to me his reasons for thinking something. He gives me an explanation. I may say: "That's not a full explanation; there must be more to it than that—for it explains, let us say, why you take a naturalistic view but not why your view is a physical or physiological

---

[15] I think this is the argument of Mr. Lewis' reply to me.—G.E.M.A.

naturalism; the arguments you have given are consistent with a psychological naturalism: tell me why you reject that." Now if I ask for this sort of investigation I am not making a *causal* enquiry at all: I am asking for grounds, not causes; and you can only have imagined that it was appropriate to speak of "causes" because the word "because" is used. Giving one's reasons for thinking something is like giving one's motives for doing something. You might ask me: "Why did you half-turn towards the door?" and I explain that I thought I saw a friend coming in, and then realized it was someone else. This may be the explanation although I did not at the time *say* to myself "Hello! There's so-and-so; I'll go and speak to him; oh no, it's someone else." So when I give the explanation it is not by way of observing two events and the causal relation between them.

The naturalistic hypothesis is that causal laws could be discovered which could be successfully applied to all human behavior, including thought. If such laws were discovered they would not show that a man's reasons were not his reasons; for a man who is explaining his reasons is not giving a causal account at all. "Causes," in the scientific sense in which this word is used when we speak of causal laws, is to be explained in terms of observed regularities: but the declaration of one's reasons or motives is not founded on observation of regularities. "Reasons" and "motives" are what is *elicited* from someone whom we ask to explain himself. Of course we may doubt that a man has told, or even made clear to himself, his real reasons and motives; but what we are asking for if we say so is a more searching consideration, not an investigation into such a question as: "Is this really an instance of the causal law which I have applied to it?"—and that is true even though, as is possible, we doubt him on grounds of empirical generalizations which we have made about people's motives and reasons for the action or opinion in question. Such generalizations are possible, and hence one can imagine a psychological naturalism which believes in the possibility of a complete scientific system of psychological causal laws of human behavior. It is important to realize that such a notion of psychological causality (which would arise from observing regularities in people's motives and mental processes) should be distinguished from the use of "because" in the *expression* of motives and mental processes.

It appears to me that if a man has reasons, and they are good reasons, and they are genuinely his reasons, for thinking something—then his thought is rational, whatever causal statements we make about him. Even though he give good reasons, however, we may detect in him such passions or such motives of self-interest in saying what he does that we say that it is not really "for these reasons" that he says it, and regard the reasons as a façade that he puts up to obscure his "real reasons": these "real reasons" being the kind of thing that I admitted as "irrational causes." And we rightly suspect and scrutinize carefully the reasoning that he offers. Or we may think him so dominated by "irrational causes" that it is not worthwhile to look at his reasoning at all: though the mere fact that he is actuated purely by these motives does not necessarily mean that he will not in fact be able to reason well.

So far I have only talked of a man's reasons in a sense in which: "He thinks so-and-so because of such-and-such a chain of reasoning" is in no way a causal statement. There is a kind of statement that I have not yet considered, which is in some sense causal. Suppose I ask someone why he believes something, and he begins to produce reasons, I may say: "Sorry, I didn't mean that—I know what reasons there are for believing as you do; what I meant to ask was what in actual fact, as a matter of history led you to this opinion, what *caused* you to adopt it." This is a quite intelligible question which anyone would know how to answer. It seems to me that you have not distinguished it, as it ought to be distinguished, from the question "What are your reasons?"—and that it is in virtue of his answer to the latter that a man or his opinions should be called rational, whatever his answer to the former. However as your argument stands, it says that human thought is discredited unless his answer to the former question ("What, as a matter of history, led you to this belief?") states the *occurrence* of reasoning; and you also argue that on the naturalist hypothesis an answer which does state the occurrence of reasoning cannot be true, because the naturalist hypothesis is that non-rational causes produce his opinions. I should also deny this part of your argument. For though it is natural to use the word "cause" here, the logic of "cause" as used here is different from its logic as used when we speak of causal laws. Suppose someone asks me for such a historical account of the mental processes which actually issued in my belief, and I give it to him. And suppose he then asks: "What reasons have you for calling the thing that you mention in answer to this question the *causes* of your belief?" At first I would imagine that he was accusing me of self-deception, saying, "Look into it more thoroughly and you will realize that you have not given a truthful account." But suppose he makes it clear that he is not suggesting anything of this kind; he does not doubt my account of my mental processes at all; but, given that they occurred just as I have related them, and that afterwards I held the opinion which I say resulted from them, he asks why I say that it did result from them, that they did produce it?—Would this not be an extraordinarily odd question? It makes it seem as if one made here a causal statement analogous to scientific causal statement, which would be justified by—roughly—appeal to observed regularities; but here, though it is natural, given the kind of question "What actually led you to this?" to speak of a "cause," yet the sense of "cause" as used here is not to be explained by reference to observed regularities: That is sufficient to show that this is one more case of the great ambiguity of "explanation," "why," "because," and "cause" itself. And therefore the discovery of scientific cause could not demonstrate the falsity of such assertions as "I thought so and so as a *result* of such-and-such consideration."

I do not think that there is sufficiently good reason for maintaining the "naturalist" hypothesis about human behavior and thought. But someone who does maintain it, cannot be refuted as you try to refute him, by saying that it is inconsistent to maintain it and to believe that human reasoning is valid and that human reasoning sometimes produces human opinion.

A causal explanation of a man's thought only reflects on its validity as an indication, if we know that opinions caused in that way are always or usually unreasonable.

REPLY

In his reply Mr. C. S. Lewis agreed that the words "cause" and "ground" were far from synonymous but said that the recognition of a ground could be the cause of assent, and that assent was only rational when such was its cause. He denied that such words as "recognition" and "perception" could be properly used of a mental act among whose causes the thing perceived or recognized was not one.

Miss Anscombe said that Mr. Lewis had misunderstood her and thus the first part of the discussion was confined to the two speakers who attempted to clarify their positions and their differences. Miss Anscombe said that Mr. Lewis was still not distinguishing between "having reasons" and "having reasoned" in the causal sense. Mr. Lewis understood the speaker to be making a terachotomy thus: (1) logical reasons; (2) having reasons (i.e. psychological); (3) Historical causes; (4) Scientific causes or observed regularities. The main point in his reply was that an observed regularity was only the symptom of a cause, and not the cause itself, and in reply to an interruption by the Secretary he referred to his notion of cause as "magical." An open discussion followed, in which some members tried to show Miss Anscombe that there was a connection between ground and cause, while others contended against the President that the test for the validity of reason could never in any event be such a thing as the state of the bloodstream. The President finally admitted that the word "valid" was an unfortunate one. From the discussion in general it appeared that Mr. Lewis would have to turn his argument into a rigorous analytic one, if his notion of "validity" as the effect of causes were to stand the test of all the questions put to him.

NOTE

I admit that *valid* was a bad word for what I meant; *veridical* (or *verific* or *veriferous*) would have been better. I also admit that the cause and effect relation between events and the ground and consequent relation between propositions are distinct. Since English uses the word *because* of both, let us here use *Because CE* for the cause and effect relation ("This doll always falls on its feet *because CE* its feet are weighted") and *Because GC* for the ground and consequent relation ("A equals C *because GC* they both equal B"). But the sharper this distinction becomes the more my difficulty increases. If an argument is to be verific the conclusion must be related to the premises as consequent to ground, *i.e.* the conclusion is there *because GC* certain other propositions are true. On the other hand, our thinking the conclusion is an event and must be related to previous events as effect to cause, *i.e.* this act of thinking must occur *because CE* previous events have occurred. It would seem, therefore, that we never think the conclusion *because GC* it is the consequent of its grounds but only *because CE* certain previous events have happened. If so, it does not seem that the GC sequence makes us more likely to think the true conclusion than not. And this is very much what I meant by the difficulty in Naturalism.

C. S. LEWIS

THE LIMITS OF POSITIVISM

DR. F. WAISMANN
(*Summary by M. G. Brock*)

Dr. Waismann began by referring to some of the many different shades of thought to which, at various times, the label Positivism had been given, such as Comte's theory of history and "loi des trios états," or his worship of the "Great Being." Lacking, however, any ambition to be a "Bishop of the Positivistic church," the speaker turned quickly to its philosophical aspect, defining it as "the denial of metaphysics and all search for first and final causes: the assertion that what matters is only positive facts and observable phenomena with the laws which govern them."

The first thinker in modern times who used a Positivistic kind of reasoning was Berkeley. Berkeley was puzzled about the idea of *substance*. To assume that the existence of a something which supports the qualities in a thing seems to be at least a psychological necessity. We cannot help referring to something *behind* phenomena. Here, then, is the point where the idea of a "thing" turns into the metaphysical conception of substance. (In this connection, Dr. Waismann touched on the doctrine of the Eucharist, that the substance of the elements is changed, but not the "accidents"). Berkeley does not mean to deny the reality of the external world, but only to give a proper account of what we *mean* when we speak of a body. He is opposed to the metaphysical interpretation which assumes an unseen bearer behind the experienced qualities. He insists that the whole meaning of our statements about material objects exhausts itself in stating certain regular relations (of coexistence and succession) between our sense perceptions. These relations constitute the whole being of material objects.

The speaker went on to show how the beginnings of a Positivistic way of thought were inherent in Berkeley's "Phenomenalism." In the Phenomenalist view, the existence of a material thing, and consequently of corporeal substance, can neither be shown in, nor logically deduced from, observation. If all the available evidence is insufficient to prove the existence of substance, and equally insufficient to refute it, then we are faced with the much graver issue as to whether there is any difference at all between affirming and denying its existence—apart from producing certain noises. Berkeley did not state this point explicitly, nor did he write of "meaninglessness"; but he did occasionally come near to the modern view. Commenting on the view that material objects have an "absolute existence," he wrote, "those words mark out either a direct contradiction, or else *nothing at all*. The 'absolute existence' of corporeal substance are words without a meaning." Here is the battle cry of the modern view.

Hume made a somewhat similar attack: he showed that the element of coercion, which we seem to feel in causal connection, is neither to be found in experience nor in logic. Notice the likeness between the attitude of Berkeley and that of Hume: neither substance nor a relation of necessitation which holds between particular events, are observable things; nor can they be inferred from what is given in sense experience. Both are "invisible rabbits." It is too simple a form of argument to say: "If you cannot refute me, I may stick to my view." *Is* it a view?—or a word sequence that masquerades as a view, a pseudo-proposition?

The core of Positivism may thus be expressed as: *the meaning of a sentence is the method of its verification*; or, more correctly: *a sentence means what it means in virtue of the way in which it can be verified*. Dr. Waismann then quoted, with passionate emphasis, from Wittgenstein, Schlick, and Carnap. The positivistic attitude has changed the whole attitude of thought of our time: philosophy becomes a therapy to cure you of asking silly questions. Logical Positivism is presumably so called because it shows how illogically people think who pursue philosophical questions, posing not problems but muddles felt as problems. A clean sweep seemed to have been made of the old questions, so that everything was now quite clear.

But, in A. N. Whitehead's words, as soon as we become perfectly clear about what we mean, we can be sure that some very important point has been left out. The speaker now avowed his own principles—reluctantly, since (as Corporal Trim said) "whatever he chose, the world would blame him." He wholeheartedly subscribed to the positivist criticism, but … there were several 'buts.'

Before describing his reservations, the speaker wanted to demolish any idea that it was possible to undo what had been done. We *must* apply positivist methods and logical rigor. The reservations may be summarized as follows:—

1. The looseness of the criterion of verifiability.

2. The mutability of the rules of logical grammar—rules on which Positivism relies when stigmatizing metaphysical statements as nonsensical. (The rise of alternative logics typifies this mutability.)

3. The systematic ambiguity of the word "meaningful," which can actually be applied on different levels and in different senses.

"Everything that can be said"—according to the Positivist—"can be said clearly." Dr. Waismann disagreed. Lack of clarity may be the writer's fault; but it may be due to the inadequacy, for his task, of existing terminology. There were, in his view, *different senses of "clarity,"* just as there were different types of fact, of statement, of experience, or of communication.

There was, said the speaker, a danger of clarity-neurosis: the Positivists, by continually stressing the need for clarity, have had a paralyzing effect upon imagination. There seems to be a rhythm between thought-ages in which new visions are born and ideas shaped, and ages in which the results so obtained are put to the test. Positivism embodies the spirit of the second kind of age.

Further, is the linguistic approach really adequate? An order of nature is established by observation, but its mystery is not dispelled by saying that we ourselves impose the law on nature. The status of the sciences seems to point to some intrinsic rationality in nature. If metaphysics is nonsensical, how is it that a series of noises, a rigmarole, has exerted such an influence on some of the greatest minds of the past? It is true that metaphysics usually inherits its emotional force from a decaying religion which preceded it: it sets up the conceptual scaffolding within which the thought of a period will move. But still there are certain metaphysical motifs which seem to have no reference to any particular period: we catch the same faint flavor in some of Kafka's stories as in Plato's cave.

In summary, Dr. Waismann concluded, Positivism shows a healthy distrust for the tricks of language, but also disregards the deeper layers of experience.

The Discussion

The discussion which followed this paper was opened by Mr. C. S. Lewis who, after questioning the historical correctness of certain things which Dr. Waismann had said about the doctrines of the Eucharist, began by expressing his sympathy with the Positivists in their "war to end war." They represented a tendency which in the past had often stung their opponents into metaphysics, for example in the case of the Sophists and Socrates. But we must not, he said, be too easily browbeaten by their attack, for, except in mathematics and the exact sciences, men are doomed always to use metaphorical language. The weakness of Hume's argument on causation was surely that, when he denied the reality of the coercion which we feel in causal connection, he was saying in effect that this feeling was *due to*—or caused by—our psychological mechanism: as if to say, "there are no such things as causes, and I will now explain the cause of this illusion." Mr. Lewis went on to say that we were *compelled* to think always in terms of causes; every transitive verb means "to cause in a particular way." Berkeley had not dragged theology in at the end simply because he was a bishop, but because he had thought of his writings as the basis of a simpler and firmer theology, in that only by means of his Theism could he avoid Solipsism. In Hume, on the other hand, we do reach a kind of instantaneous solipsism.

AQUINAS AND NEWMAN ON THEISM

(A précis by A. D. HOWELL SMITH, *Rationalist Press Association, of his own paper)*

Towards the end of the last century Pope Leo XIII recommended St. Thomas Aquinas as the safest guide to follow in philosophy as well as theology. Catholic theologians insist that the five proofs of the existence of God (*quinque viae* = "five ways"), set forth and expounded in Aquinas's *Summa Contra Gentiles* and *Summa Theologica* are so cogent that only prejudice or misunderstanding can cause anyone to reject them. Other apologists besides those who adhere to the Church of Rome plead for Theism along substantially the same lines as the "Angelic Doctor." The argumentation of St. Thomas is couched in a phraseology derived from Greek metaphysics, more especially from those of Aristotle, who had hitherto been regarded by the Catholic authorities with suspicion, Plato's philosophical outlook, which was so largely shared by St. Augustine and other Fathers of the Church, having been considered to be far more favorable to Christianity. Aquinas exposed the weakness of the "ontological" argument of St. Anselm of Canterbury, who maintained that the idea of a perfect being involves the existence of such a being. Aquinas inferred the existence of God from the nature of things, not from an infallible intuition which has no need to contemplate the creature in order to rise to a knowledge of the Creator.

The first of the five proofs is drawn from the fact of motion. In the universe many things are seen moving. That which moves can only be moved by another. Self-motion is impossible, for this involves a change of being, at one and the same moment both actual and possible. The denial of a prime mover implies an infinite regress of movers. But infinite regress gets rid of initiation and result, and leaves us only with intermediaries, which cannot transmit what they have not received and with no goal of transmission. Aquinas does not deny, except on the ground of revelation, the eternity of the universe; but the admission of this will not invalidate the argument. There must, in any case, be an eternal initiator of the whole sequence, not as simply making the first link, but as the sustaining cause of all the links in the chain of phenomena.

The second proof is from the nature of efficient cause. The idea of an infinite regress of causes is open to the same objection as an infinite regress of movements, for all causation involves motion. All causes would become intermediaries because there would be no initiating cause (the really efficient cause) and no ultimate effect. Hence there must be a first cause, itself uncaused.

Then we have the proof from contingency. Since all objects and events once did not exist, their existence is not necessary; their non-existence is as possible as their existence. Countless other worlds than ours are possible because they are conceivable. But there must be necessary being. There must be pure unconditioned existence, devoid of all potentiality—"pure act" (*purus actus*). Necessary being can have neither beginning nor end, neither limitation in space nor limitation in power. What is this necessary being but what religion calls God?

The fourth proof is from the grading of things in the scale of perfections. Since there is a hierarchy of lesser and greater (pointing to a greatest), of worse and better (pointing to a best), there must be One who realizes in himself eternally all the perfections of his creatures. Not, of course, after the same modes. Good gains for man—an enriched awareness or reality—that belongs to God, and infinitely more so. What the eye is to man, omniscience is to God. But the perfection of divine goodness can only be human goodness without human limitations; it cannot be qualitatively different.

The fifth proof is "from the governance of the world"—the teleological proof. Natural bodies, lacking intelligence, effect generally the best results. How could this happen unless supreme intelligence was controlling them and coordinating the enormous complexities of the phenomenal world to produce the whole grand harmony of nature?

St. Thomas Aquinas met with severe criticism from other philosophers of the Middle Ages, e.g., Duns Scotus and William of Occam. The latter denied that it was possible to prove the existence of God; belief in God must rest solely on revelation. And Kant is generally held to have destroyed the force of all "the five ways."

Let us now examine these famous proofs. Aquinas, like everybody of his age, accepted the Ptolemaic astronomy. All the heavenly bodies, attached to crystalline spheres, were believed to revolve round a fixed earth. These spheres were set in motion by yet another sphere, the *primum mobile* ("first to be moved"). Aquinas held that God commands an angel to set the *primum mobile* revolving; its revolution is communicated to all the other spheres. The distinction Aquinas draws between starting agent, intermediary, and ultimate result assumes that these terms have other than a relative significance. In an infinite series each of these terms can be applied to every unit of change in accordance with its position in the series. Science is concerned with the context of a phenomenon it arbitrarily isolates from phenomena in general. Rest and motion were held by St. Thomas to be mutually exclusive, but uniform rest and uniform motion are coordinates; it is only when we contrast one system with another that rest and motion become differentiated. One thing is at rest in relation to a second thing and moving in relation to a third. A boulder carried by an ice floe is both moving and at rest. Aquinas knew, of course, nothing of our modern conceptions of matter, which our physics tends to equate with energy. The atom is an area of ceaseless change, which we can only represent by means of mathematical formulae; it is not picturable like moving masses of super-atomic size. The problem of how motion started is a bogus problem.

Similar considerations invalidate Aquinas's argument from causation. Causation is a dynamic sequence—routines of change from state to state. A first cause, existing unchanged prior to producing an effect and remaining unchanged afterwards, is not what science, which is only the systematic analysis and synthesis of the data of common sense, means by cause.

The argument from contingency assumes that "necessary" and "contingent" are mutually exclusive characteristics. One can validly distinguish the actual from the potential. But what is actually a present thing is potentially a future thing. Pure potentiality, which is what St. Thomas means by his *materia prima*, is unthinkable. The relations under which they exist are for us absurd—an ultimate, inexplicable fact. To attribute these relations to the will of God only creates a gratuitous mystery. There is furthermore a confusion, in the argument, of objective with subjective possible. A centaur is possible in the sense that we can imagine it, and give embodiment to it in art. But if a centaur is an objective possibility, then at some time or other it has existed or will exist.

The argument from the grading of perfections ignores the fact that perfection is always a perfection *of kind*. Beauty and goodness out of a specific context are mere abstractions. Finite perfection raised to the infinite is a chimera. Aquinas's logic forces him to admit that even existence cannot be predicated univocally of God and creatures. He further states that God, being indefinable, belongs to no genus, and that "we must ... not allow him wisdom who exceeds all wisdom." These admissions carry with them implications that undermine his whole system.

The last of the five proofs is still a great favorite with both Catholics and Protestants. Its suppressed assumption, as J. M. Robertson points out in his *Letters on Reasoning*, is that designed adaptations have marks distinguishing them from adaptations that are undesigned, and that we know what an undesigned cosmos would be like—something far different from ours. Complexity of adaptations is involved in any cosmos that is a unity in diversity. Aquinas says that natural bodies, "though not always," effect the best results. The statement that the best results are generally achieved implies that other results would betray less wisdom in the driving force, or perhaps no wisdom at all. An undesigned order of things is then thinkable, and so, on Theistic premises, possible.

In noting design we start with a knowledge of man and his needs. Man exploits nature to satisfy those needs, and if we find an object hitherto unknown to us, which cannot serve any end, *except accidentally*, that is not human, we infer that it was expressly made for a human purpose, unlike honey or apples or trees, which do not primarily exist to minister to our wants.

If we had some *a priori* intimation, however imperfect, of God's purposes, and then discovered how admirably the cosmic processes were adapted to fulfill them, we might well speak of design. Out of a given context "end" and "means" are interchangeable terms.

Evil and good must be alike God's handiwork, if the cosmos has been designed by God. Animal suffering is real, however much ignorance and sentimentalism may have exaggerated it. And what of human suffering? Not all of it can reasonably be regarded as merited or as spiritually beneficial.

St. Thomas Aquinas, here following St. Augustine, argues that evil is only a privation; its existence is negative, and God cannot be the author of a negative. Unless, however, we *resent* the privation of good, we put a scoundrel in the same moral (or non-moral) category as a corpse; and if we do resent it, then evil becomes something more to us than the absence of a quality.

If evil is privation, evil is integral to phenomenal existence. God, then, in willing phenomenal existence is willing evil—is willing that which gives finite expression to his own perfection. But evil, to the finite, is a limitation that frustrates and threatens it with destruction, and against which the finite revolts. Thus regarded, evil cannot exist for God. St. Augustine and St. Thomas Aquinas were within sight of the idea of the relativity of evil—an idea incompatible with their theology. There is no evil—there are only evils; and what is evil from one viewpoint is good from another. Good and evil cancel out in the infinite.

Let us turn to a Catholic apologist of our own times—a great man, though, as he himself would have readily admitted, of less intellectual caliber than Aquinas—John Henry Newman. The famous Cardinal would not have given a point blank denial to the cogency of "the five ways," but they made little appeal to him. The Angelic Doctor could calmly raise a hundred skeptical ghosts and lay them with the magic of his metaphysics. But Newman was always haunted by his ghosts, even when his faith was most assured. He was a spiritual isolationist. He confessed that for him there were "two and two only absolute and luminously self-evident beings, myself and my Creator."

In one of the most eloquent passages of his *Apologia Pro Vita Sua* Newman reviews the whole tragic course of the world, and concludes that "either there is no Creator, or this living society is in a true sense discarded from his presence." Newman's "whole being" was "so full" of "that great truth" which the nature of the world seemed to deny, and his inability to behold in the flux of painful change a reflection of the Creator gave him the shock that he would have sustained on looking into a mirror and seeing there no reflection of his own face.

Newman's Theism was a matter of intuition. God was for him primarily a moral agent, whose reality is revealed by the conscience. The wicked flees when none pursues him. Why does he flee? We obey our consciences and are happy. Whence this happiness?

Sin seemed to Newman so deep in its roots and so wide in its ramifications that enjoyment of life and its passions was almost a factor of hell. Did he never suspect that his conscience had been shaped by his pious environment? The voice of conscience, far from being a primary inspiration, has spoken a thousand discordant things, echoing the variations of creed and culture that crowd the many centuries of evolving man. The psychology of conscience is not a mystery to the sociologist. Without laws and taboos mankind could never have existed. Morality expresses social needs, whether or not it takes the guise of a divine lawgiver. Ethical codes clash and change. The individual reacts to his ethical inheritance. Great men may revolutionize the ethical outlook of their generation and so produce new gods in their own image. Obedience to the call of the good is not always felt to be obedience to the call of God. Muhammad hears the voice of Gabriel, the angelic spokesman of Allah. St. Paul is subdued by the vision and the voice of the heavenly Christ. But the Buddha is only conscious of his own clarified mind, illuminating the Eightfold Path to a peace no god prescribes and no god can give.

Atheism as a critical rejection of all ideas of deity as unconditioned originator and controller of the world-flux, whose laws science seeks to discover and to apply to the service of mankind, is quite a justifiable attitude for a philosopher to adopt. And yet the mystic may claim to have the last word. The world is many and the world is one. The world is ever changing and the world eternally abides. These two fundamental intuitions cannot be harmonized, but we can escape neither of them. Here we confront the Pantheism of the Upanishads and Spinoza. But we cannot on such a foundation erect liturgies of prayer and praise. No Father in Heaven smiles down on us. There remain the mystery and the splendor and the awfulness of the starry realm that forms the wizard background of "our little life," which is "rounded with a sleep."

SUMMARY OF REPLY TO MR. HOWELL SMITH

Dr. E. L. Mascall

Although a great many modern theists (among whom I would number myself) still consider that the fundamental argument for the existence of God is that which starts from the existence of finite beings, this cosmological argument has in recent years been reinforced by others, *e.g.* the moral argument of A. E. Taylor, the moral-teleological argument of F. R. Tennant, and the argument from religious experience. Furthermore, most modern Thomists would admit that St. Thomas expressed his arguments in terms of the Aristotelian philosophy of his day and would recognize the importance of disentangling them from such contemporary trappings as are not really essential to them. But they would allege that when this work of disentanglement has been done the argument *e contingentia mundi* loses none of its force. Dr. A. M. Farrer's book *Finite and Infinite* is perhaps the most conspicuous example of a presentation of the cosmological argument which takes full account of the movement of philosophical thought since St. Thomas's day. The real heart of the argument consists not in the construction of syllogisms but in acquiring an intuitive grasp of the real nature of finite being; from this point of view, as Fr. M. C. D'Arcy points out in *The Nature of Belief*, the cosmological argument and the argument from religious experience (at least in one of its forms) may be considered as based on the same datum, looked at from outside and inside respectively.

The core of the Thomist position was the fact that the created world is not *necessary*: it need not have existed. We could conceive of its being non-existent, or different. Everything in it does in fact *become* different: nothing endures. The only way by which we could *explain* the existence of such a world was by postulating a being *not* limited in these ways, a necessary non-contingent being. Such a being must be capable of giving effect to acts of choice. The point Dr. Mascall wished to make was that Theism offered the *only* explanation: the non-Theistic position, as exemplified by the Positivists, was that there was *no* explanation, knowable by us. If you rejected Metaphysics completely, then you had ruled out the *possibility* of finding the explanation. It was generally thought that Kant had disposed once and for all of the Thomist cosmological proofs: it was less generally known that Kant's own argument was open to serious logical objections. He confused the cosmological and ontological proofs.

But the heart of the criticism of Thomism in the paper seemed to be that modern science had invalidated the conclusions. Dr. Mascall thought that such problems as the existence of God were outside the scope of scientific researches, which were concerned with empirically tested regularities. Science was not concerned with first causes. To say that science provided no evidence for Theism was like saying: "There's no bread in the larder: I have just searched the bathroom." If you deny metaphysics then you have closed all roads except revelation and mysticism: it was, in Gilson's view, because he had done this that Sir James Jeans found the universe mysterious.

Dr. Mascall made a number of further points briefly: he was not clear how Mr. Howell-Smith meant to use the "Problem of Evil." It proved, or might be held to prove, not so much the non-existence of God as that he was not benevolent. The Christian view of evil was that it was essentially a deficiency in being: it was fundamentally different from good. He could see no reason why the Atheist should be worried by the problem: why should we suppose that a Godless universe would consult our interests? Evil as a philosophical problem is only called into being by the conviction that God is good. The Christian solution of the problem lay in the belief that God could create an end proportionate to the means: the reason why pain created a problem for us was that we could imagine no end commensurate with the appalling suffering witnessed. Thus no one worried about the pain suffered by the boat race crew because it was easy to see it in perspective with regard to the end of winning the race. In the Christian belief God's power and goodness which so infinitely exceeded what we could imagine would put all pains, however great, in the same perspective.

DOES GOD EXIST?

DR. AUSTIN FARRER

[NOTE.—The argument set forth below actually formed only the last half of Dr. Farrer's talk. It was preceded by a long, extempore preamble, which was designed to show the nature of the question being asked, a question which, he said, could only be answered by taking up in imagination the standpoint of the believer. He pointed out the absurdity of first saying that we can give a satisfactory account of reality without God, and then adding a reserve question, by way of postscript, as to whether God exists. Such a God, if established, would be merely marginal, making no difference to existence. But the belief which we are questioning, is in a God who affects and judges the whole of existence, and the proof of *His* existence can only be by a *reductio ad absurdum* of its opposite. To this end, Dr. Farrer distinguished between two kinds of absurdity, formal and material. The former is just logical inconsistency, the latter is that which is absurd in relation to a certain frame of reference, as when a philosopher formally reasonable, like Hume in his account of personal identity, neglects or misdescribes certain obvious facts. Traditional arguments for God's existence have dealt only with questions of *formal absurdity*, showing, for instance, how with closed systems like science or history, God's existence is a necessary hypothesis. But the believer's argument is really based on pointing to the *material* absurdity of his opponent—since we believe in God only by trying to embrace the totality of things.

Dr. Farrer has now replaced this original preamble by a shorter and slightly different one, which is here printed as a further introduction to the argument proper.—EDITOR]

INTRODUCTORY REMARKS

I am asked to state an argument for the existence of God which appeals to grounds of general reason. I will do what I can, even though it is my experience that such arguments are about as likely to weaken as to strengthen belief. For, even granted that the argument is convincing itself, its force lies in many presuppositions which cannot themselves all be stated, still less established, except in a big book. These presuppositions are (in the theist's opinion) natural, and so he puts forward his argument, hoping that the presuppositions will awake in his hearer's mind. But he knows that they may be buried, lost, or distorted: and in that case the argument will fall flat and discredit theism by so falling.

In any case, theistic arguments are not formal demonstrations. Since the Divine Being is unique, he can only be known by a sort of acquaintance: he must impress us *in and through* finite things, very likely, without our fully conscious appreciation of the fact. We can never know the unique by mere inference from other things, nor God by mere inference from the world. What we suppose is that finite-things-enacted-by-God form the proper object of a fully awakened understanding. For a thousand practical purposes we neglect, we abstract from, the God-dependence of things: we may never, even, have become distinctly aware of it. But because it is there for us, we can make ourselves aware of our neglect of it by making ourselves see that a Godless account of things is incomplete. The incompleteness is not logical: what it falls short of is the ideal completeness which is, in fact, present to our minds, however neglected or misunderstood—the activity of God everywhere supporting and inworking his creatures.

So without more ado, let us set forth an argument through which the dependence of the world on God may make itself felt by our minds.

The Argument

The world, so far as I can see, appears to be made up of systems of active process. My conscious being is a system of active process anyhow, a wonderfully balanced interplay of willings and reactings and doings. The existence of living things, my own body for example, is also an interplay of active processes: my body lives as a body only insofar as the heart beats and the blood circulates and the lungs expand and contract and all sorts of other rhythms of digestion and distribution go on, such as physiologists study. There are living bodies of all kinds in the world, vegetable as well as animal, and all are systems of active process. But, if we are to believe the sciences, active process is not the being of living things alone. The apparently solid and stupid lumps of physical matter are, in fact, nothing of the sort: they are really made up of infinitely complicated, minute rhythms of active process, without which process nothing would exist at all.

Active process, then, is a sort of common denominator of all existence known to us, from the lowest to the highest. It seems to be capable of existing at various levels, and in various forms: moreover, it is capable of passing from one level and one form to another level and another form. I am a living and active process when I am half awake, but it only requires someone to apply a suitable stimulus to me, and the slumbering activity which was me a minute ago becomes the highest degree of active attention and perhaps the highest energy of physical action. Lazy daydreaming may transform itself into philosophical contemplation in a moment, so that the active process which constitutes my being may vary its form, e.g., from thought to action, and it may vary its level, e.g., from feeding to reasoning.

These transformations take place within my own conscious life: but consider the transformation by which my conscious life itself arises out of the elementary active process shut up within a germ, or the transformation by which, according to the evolutionists, the rudimentary system of action called an amoeba becomes at last a mammal. We must not, of course, imagine that the transformations are all for the better. On the contrary, species of animals degenerate, individuals die, moral character decays, and as I awake out of sleep into consciousness, so I fall away out of consciousness back into sleep.

I have two points to make here: first, that the common and basic something, active being, takes on an infinity of forms; and second, that all these forms appear to be in a sense arbitrary. None of them is the form of active being as such: they are all particular forms, and they might have been otherwise. We might have had a universe in which physical matter was not organized in the manner in which the atomic theorists say it is, in which there were no oak trees or daisies, no dogs, horses, or men, but completely different systems of active being.

Thus we seem to require an explanation for the fact that existence has taken the shapes that it has. In the ordinary way, when we ask for explanations, we simply go one step, or several steps, back into the history of the process: if we want to know how there came to be those active systems which we call giraffes, we take for granted antelopes, a habitat providing the best fodder on the tops of trees, and the fact of chance variation. From a certain state of affairs we can see another state arising, and we call this "explanation": but the explanation is limited, for there is always some state of affairs presupposed. If we presuppose no state of affairs, no organization of active existence already operative, we can explain nothing. We cannot say: let it be supposed that *active existence as such* is loose in space, and you will get a world. You have to suppose, not active existence as such, but active existence already organized in a particular way: but why in such a way? We always have to suppose active existence running on certain lines: what put it on those lines? If we say, some other finite organization of active existence, the same question crops up about that. We can arrive at no answer which gives final satisfaction, except one. We must step right out of the finite sphere altogether, and conceive of a being who is not just one possible form of active existence, for then we should have to ask "why *this* form rather than another?"—but who realizes in himself the fullest possibility of active existence, in whom Reality has the full status of which it is capable. The notion of such a being is self-explanatory: we do not ask why he is so, rather than otherwise: he is just Himself. Such a Being it must be, therefore, who has laid down the particular lines on which active existence runs in the world we know. He has, to use an ancient phrase, *ordained* it thus. The processes which make up the world cannot be what they are, they are not capable of existing at all, without an infinite ordainer who wills that they should be so.

The argument which I have sketched is based on a survey of everything in general, it argues from the most general facts we can state about the whole range of existing beings in our world. I will now support it by an argument drawn from one very special sort of being, the being that we ourselves are. We can become aware of a whole universe of creatures objectively, but there is only one creature we can experience subjectively, and that is ourselves. I can become aware through outward experience of the patterns of activity which make up many levels and sorts of being, for example, a biologist can examine the activity pattern of the body of a frog. But one cannot taste what it is like to be a frog, one can only taste what it is like to be a man.

Therefore, when we have concluded on grounds of general reason that an infinite and absolute being must have ordained or appointed the forms of finite being, we naturally turn to our own being in order to ask whether, in our own case, finite being tastes as though it had been appointed or ordained: whether we experience our own existence as something for which the lines have been laid down by a higher power. And, I maintain, this is in fact the case. I shall argue as follows:—

We experience our own existence as an activity of self-determination. To be a man is to be the architect of one's own life. We do what we choose to do. The astonishing and almost terrifying fact of our own freedom only throws into higher relief the fact of its limitations. These limitations are of two kinds. On the one hand there are limitations imposed by brute fact. I may try as hard as I will to see into the essential nature of physical being, but I can get hardly any way at all, and never shall, because my faculties don't allow of it: I am a man, and not an angel. I may try as hard as I like to think as well as Aristotle or Kant, but I shall not do it, because I am only Austin Farrer and I haven't got it in me. I may do my best to be in Trinity College to keep an appointment at 10:00 a.m., but even if I defy the traffic lights I can't do it, because it was 9:59 when I mounted my bicycle in Manor Road. I may resolve to remember and do something at a given hour, but for all my resolution an intervening train of thought washes the memory out. All these are cases of brute fact limitation, and they really add nothing to our argument, for we have already seen that every finite existence is limited by the hard fact of its nature and its place. When I find how many things I cannot do, I am simply realizing that I am Austin Farrer, and not God Almighty, not even the Archangel Gabriel, nor even Emmanuel Kant, nor even the captain of university athletics.

But there is another set of limitations which are of more interest here. My free activity is not merely limited by the things I can't do: it is limited also in the doing of the things I can do.

All serious men know that they are limited not only by what they are, but by what they are *called to be*: not by what the human race has attained (which isn't, on the average, anything very grand) but by what the human race in general, and they themselves in particular, are *called* to attain. *Called* to attain: and who does the calling? It is, fundamentally, as simple as that. There is a pattern of our true destiny to which we know that we are called, and to which we are bound to show a measureless respect. Now the more evolutionist we are, the more skeptical about any fixed form called human nature, the more ready to admit that all the forms of finite existence are mere temporary phases in the process of the world—the more we admit these things, the more we ought to be bothered by the question, who or what calls us on into one destiny rather than another? It is vain to talk about "ideals," as though ideals somehow floated about in space or inscribed themselves in the colors of the sunset. Ideals are made by men, or else they are evoked by God. If they are made by men, why cannot we make them what we choose? But we cannot. Old-fashioned philosophy based the stern call to the quest for perfection on a fixed form called human nature, the same in all men from the beginning of the world and on to the end of time. Darwinianism and Historicism have knocked that on the head fairly effectively. Human nature is the form of one particular emergent process. Yet we all know that we are called—not by what man just essentially always was and always will be, nor by what in fact he is going to become in this world, for he may be going to become something not very creditable. Then by what, or rather, by whom, are we called?

Are we not here experiencing God's ordaining in its actual happening? We were previously arguing that it was necessary to suppose that all finite existence is ordained, because it is finite. Then we turned to our own existence, the only existence which we can taste from within, to see whether being a man feels like being under divine ordinance, or no. And it seems that it does, even in our most human, most independent, most godlike aspect, our free will. Precisely at this point at which we are able to make the experiment of playing at being God Almighty, and decreeing what we choose, we find that we cannot, but are under mysterious ordinances. Our free will certainly has great play, it can even reject its true destiny: but that, we know, is a sort of suicide.

Now what can we say of the nature of the being who ordains for us the perfection after which we have to strive? We can say that he is a being to whom none has (in turn) measured out a perfection after which *he* has to strive: he is one who has caught up with his own perfection, who is all the good he sees, and sees all the good he is.

I have put forward these arguments with extreme crudity, and without any of the philosophical caution the matter requires. But I think that some such crude statement may suffice for my immediate purpose, which is not so much to prove God, as to show you what the method of arguments for God's existence is. They simply show how the incomplete and Godless view of the world is supplemented with what it needs by that which believers think God to be. I am well aware that unbelievers can get rid of the whole force of the arguments by denying the meaningfulness of the whole basis from which the arguments start. It is easy, for example, as you very well know, to challenge the whole account of our free will and the claim of our true destiny upon us, which I have so roughly sketched. To which our only reply is, that serious men are forced to think like that in practice, whatever they may pretend to hold in theory. Still, if you deny, you deny, and there is nothing to be done about it, except to cultivate the power of contemplating your own spiritual being, a power which in some otherwise very clever men remains at a rudimentary stage. Cleverness will not take us to the knowledge of God, but wisdom will, and wisdom is a rarer gift.

But the most serious skeptical objection to all arguments for God's existence, is that we have no intelligible notion whatever of God, nor therefore, of the way in which the world depends upon him. To return to our first argument: if we argue that finite existence as such is an arbitrary sort of fact requiring explanation, we are tacitly comparing finite existence, to its disadvantage, with some other sort of existence which would *not* be an arbitrary fact. But this other sort of existence can be none other than the existence of God. The argument cannot stand at all, unless we are catching a glimpse of the Divine Nature out of the corner of the mind's eye. We are really saying: since Divine Nature is the standard of what one might expect being simply to be, how does it arise that what our senses meet on every hand is not God, but finite things? And the argument goes on to answer: it is because the finite things have been ordained by God.

This is perfectly true. If you feel the force of the argument, it is because you are catching sight of the Divine Nature out of the corner of your mind's eye. So much the better for us: that does not help to discredit the argument: it rather helps to suggest that God is there in fact.

Still, if the most rudimentary analysis can show (as many people say) that the idea of God is completely bogus, a piece of unintelligible nonsense: if "infinite spiritual activity" is the description of God, and if "infinite spiritual activity" is a piece of contradictory nonsense like "square circle" or "perfect wickedness," then, of course, the whole argument collapses.

I mention this question because it seems only honest to do so, but I can scarcely handle it here. The most subtle point of theist philosophy is the definition of the sense in which we can think about God. The theistic philosophers are well aware that all our thinking about God is infinitely short of his real nature, and yet they have thought it possible to find a middle position between adequacy and complete frustration. I will not enter into the subtleties of this question: but I will just put before you a train of thought which makes a great appeal to my own mind, and which may show you that the thought of an absolute spirit is far more natural and usual with us than we are inclined to suppose.

I ask you simply to reflect for a moment about your own understanding and will. Simply ask yourself what you mean by understanding, and what you mean by willing. And I think you will find that the first and simplest thing you tell yourself about understanding is that it is a sort of seeing with the mind of how other things are in themselves. But when you turn to look at your own understanding, you will find that it never is in fact this, but at the best a distant approximation to it. When have you understood any being as it is in itself? So you have to say, "*My* understanding is not a pure or proper understanding; it is a limited or diluted understanding." What have you done? You have found it natural, when you begin to think about understanding, to start with what believers suppose the Divine Mind to be: then you have gone on to make the surprising discovery that your mind isn't the Divine Mind. An odd way of thinking, but one which suggests that the idea of absolute or perfect mind is not so completely foreign to us as we were inclined to suspect.

So again with will. What is will? A power freely to frame projects seen to be good, and to execute them because they are seen to be good. What could be simpler—and what could be more divine? We have hardly, ourselves, more than the shadow of such a power. Our rational choice is invaded in every part of irrational impulse, so that we can never perfectly separate the two; we never fully understand the business that we bring about; and we cannot choose what is simply good, but only the best of the possibilities that circumstances open for us. It is because our will is only half a will that the determinist case has any plausibility. So natural it is to us to measure the modicum of will we possess by the standard of this absolute, creative freedom which is what we mean by God.

What I have been saying about understanding and will is no sort of proof that God exists: it is only some indication that the notion of such a being as God is believed to be, plays quite a natural part in our common thinking. If this is so, then we must be overdoing it if we say that the idea of God, or of his creative act, is just meaningless. We measure ourselves by our approximation to the divine. That does not mean that God exists: but it should mean that the idea of God isn't nonsense.

On the other side we must not overdrive the argument. We haven't got "a clear and distinct idea of God" or anything approaching it. If you take the notion of a pure understanding or an absolute will and try to work it out, to conceive such a being in the round, you will quickly fall into an abyss of darkness. But after all, that is what we have to expect. If God might be comprehended, he would not be God. An over-confident dogmatism is as fatal to theistic belief as skepticism itself: it pretends to prove and to define, only to discover that what it has defined and proved is not its Lord and God. You can no more catch God's infinity in a net of words, than (to misapply Housman's poem) you can fish out of the sea the glories of the dying day.[16]

---

[16] Editor's Note (2012): The original spelling in the text, which I have corrected, is Houseman, but the "glories of the dying day" seem to come from a poem by William Cullen Bryant.

PLATO AND CHRISTIANITY

Leslie J. Walker, S.J.

In the course of his long life Plato's philosophy, if we may judge by the sequence of Dialogues which he wrote, underwent considerable development, but all are concerned with one and the same problem: what do we mean when we say that we *know*? After his death, which occurred in the year 348/7 B.C., his philosophy, though in outlook and in substance still the same, became at first somewhat pedantic as expounded by his disciples in the Academy which he had founded; later on passed through a skeptical phase in the New Academy; then acquired fresh life in the new interpretation put upon it by Philo, Plotinus, Porphyry and Proclus in the early centuries of the Christian era, when it came to be known as Neo-Platonism. In this form it was embraced by Augustine, who, at the time of his conversion in 387 A.D. held it to be the true philosophy so far as it went; though that what it taught was much the same thing as Christians were teaching, but that it lacked the power to do what it set out to do, namely, to enable men to control their passions and to lead a spiritual life which should unite them to God. From this time on to the end of the 12th century the influence of Augustine was paramount on Christian thought in the west; and Augustine, alike in his approach to God and in his theory of knowledge, is essentially Platonic. In the stress which he lays on the Trinity, whose semblance he saw everywhere in the created world, he is also following faithfully the Platonic tradition. Even his doctrine of grace which supposes that, if men are to rise the least little bit, or even wish to rise, from the state in which they find themselves, they must draw being from the inexhaustible source of all being, is in strict accord with the Neo-platonic philosophy of being. In the thirteenth century this Platonic philosophy suffered a partial eclipse owing to the fact that Aristotle, somewhat late in life, got baptized. But during the Renaissance, Platonism now become almost synonymous with mysticism, is again in the ascendant. It is less marked in Descartes who devises a new approach to philosophical problems, but again comes into its own in the metaphysics of his disciple, *Malebranche*. In England during the seventeenth century there was a school of Platonists at Cambridge, and in our own day Whitehead, who also devised a new method of approach to philosophy, ends up, as the school of Descartes had done, more or less where Plato had begun.

But let us go back to Plato that we may discover, if possible, the source of that fascination which Platonism has exercised over men's minds.

In one of the earliest dialogues, *Laches,* Socrates discusses with two distinguished soldiers who have just been watching a contest between heavily armed and highly trained warriors, how virtue, and all that virtue connotes, may be imparted to the young. "You must know what you mean by virtue," says Socrates, "and so should be able to tell others what it means." To this they agree. "Well, let us take 'courage,' then, which fighting in armor is supposed to induce. What do you mean by courage?" "A man of courage," says Laches, "is a man who does not run away, but remains at his post and fights the enemy." "But," objects Socrates, "at Plataea the Spartans ran away, and then turned on the Persians and beat them, and one may also be courageous at sea, when faced with disease or poverty, and also in politics. What then is common to all these cases?" "I should say," replied Laches after some hesitation, "that it is the power of endurance." "But," objects Socrates, "endurance may sometimes be foolish and harmful, whereas we look upon courage as noble. So we must rule out foolish endurance." To which Laches agrees, but then has to confess that the trooper who has no knowledge of horsemanship but joins in a cavalry charge, though foolhardy, is more courageous than the trooper who knows how to handle a horse; so that foolish endurance is not incompatible with courage. Whereupon Laches gives up trying to define courage, apologizes for being unable to express his meaning, but adds: *"I still think I know what courage is, but somehow or other it escapes me and I cannot catch it and so cannot put it into words."*

Another early dialogue, *Euthyphro*, is more complex, for in it Socrates criticizes the accepted belief that there are many gods who disagree and quarrel with one another. He nonetheless seeks to drive home the same point. Euthyphro knows what piety is, alike that which one owes to divine beings and that which one owes to one's parents, but he cannot define it in words. Like Socrates he is about to appear in court. "Are you suing or being sued," asks Socrates. "I am suing." "Whom?" "If I tell you, you will think I am mad." "Why? Will he take wings and escape you?" "No! No! He's an old man." "Who is it then?" "It's my own father." "Your father, my dear man, and what, pray, is the charge?" "Murder." "Good heavens, Euthyphro, only the wisest of wise men would dare bring such a charge; but I suppose the murdered man was a relative?" "I am surprised, Socrates, that you should make a distinction between one who is a relative and one who is not, for the crime is the same in both cases. The question is simply whether or not the man was justly slain, and, if unjustly, you must take action even though the murderer shares the same roof and eats at the same table. The man was one of our laborers who got drunk and slew one of the servants. My father bound him up and threw him in a ditch. Then sent to enquire what must be done, and meanwhile the man died of hunger in the ditch. And my family says my father did not kill him, and, if he did, anyhow the man was a murderer, and I ought to take no notice, since it is impious to prosecute one's father."

To which Socrates rejoining: "But aren't you afraid that you may be doing an impious thing?" Euthyphro, however, is quite sure of himself, and since this implies that he knows what the words "piety" and "impiety" mean, he is asked to explain them. At first he answers: "Piety is doing what I am doing, prosecuting someone who is guilty of murder, sacrilege, or any such crime, irrespective of whom they may be." But with this Socrates is not satisfied. He asks, as in the *Laches*, for an idea which shall be expressed in all cases, a standard by which he can measure all actions, by whomsoever they be performed. Euthyphro suggests that piety is that which is dear to the gods, but is soon forced to admit that what he has defined is but an attribute. The gods love piety because piety is good. It is not their love of it that makes it good. So Euthyphro has not as yet stated what piety is. He tries to define it again, but is unable to find a form of words which upon examination does not prove hopelessly inadequate. Yet, though defeated in argument, he goes away, still convinced that he knows what piety is and that it justifies him in prosecuting his father. Nor does Socrates deny this. Men may be quite unable to express in words what they mean by piety and courage, self-control, justice. They may even differ considerably in the way they apply their criteria to particular actions, and hold some actions to be pious which others look upon with abhorrence as impious. They are nonetheless aware that there are criteria of right and wrong, and in some cases are agreed in the way they apply them. For instance, though men commit all manner of crimes and will say and do anything in their own defense, they never plead guilty and at the same time claim that the guilty should go unpunished. Moreover, the trouble men find in defining particular virtues is to a large extent due to the fact that they are all particularizations or partial expressions of one and the same thing, Goodness written with a capital "G" or virtue written with a capital "V."

The main point which Plato seeks to drive home in these Socratic dialogues is that there exist moral criteria of which we are aware not through the senses but by intuition. Dimly at least we are all conscious of them and of the obligations which they impose, but the clarity of this vision differs from man to man, and depends in large part upon the way in which he has been brought up. "*Have we at our age,*" asks Socrates in the *Crito*, "*been discoursing earnestly one with another all our life long in order to discover that we are no better than children? Is not what we used to say assuredly the truth, whether the world agrees with us or not? Namely, that wrongdoing is an evil and a disgrace to him that does wrong?*" "*I agree,*" says Crito. "*Then we must do no wrong, nor repay wrong with wrong, as the world thinks we may?*" "*Clearly not.*" "But, if that be so," argues Socrates, applying the principle to his own case, "must I not suffer death if the state which has nourished me, condemns me to death, rather than wrong the state by refusing to obey, even though the state has wrongly condemned me? Socrates' vision of what ought to be done and of how it applies to his own case, is no less clear than was Euthyphro's, and he cannot but obey its behests.

But what is it that he sees? To this we are given a plain answer in the *Phaedo*, "*Is there such a thing as absolute justice, absolute beauty, absolute goodness?*" asks Socrates. "*Of course there is,*" replies Simmias. "*But, did you ever behold them with your eyes?*" asks Socrates. "*Or did you ever reach them with any other bodily sense—and I speak not of these only, but of absolute greatness and health and strength, and of the true nature of everything. Has the reality of such things ever been perceived by you through the bodily organs? Is it not the nearest approach to knowledge of their several natures made by him who so orders his intellectual vision as to have the clearest grasp of the essence of each thing which he considers?*"

It is not, then, only of moral values that we may attain a clear vision insofar as we set aside and control "*those loves and lusts and fear and fancies of all kinds, which are due to the body and take away the power of thinking at all,*" we also have a clear vision of what the Greeks called τὰ μαθηματικά—numbers and figures and the relations which hold between them each in its own order. For the relations which hold between numbers, given that we know what it is that numerical symbols signify, and the relations which hold between figures and the parts of figures, given that we know what we mean by such words as "triangle," "plane," and "parallel lines" are absolute, necessary, and plain to all, provided they be using symbols for the same purpose and words in the same sense. Whereas in the corporeal world what we call "lines" and "planes" and "triangles" have not these properties, but are ever inexact, and, though they illustrate what we mean when we use the words, never express adequately that about which we are thinking.

The conviction that there exists a realm which is accessible to mind but not to our corporeal eyes or to any other sense organ is basic alike to the philosophy of Plato, to Neo-Platonism, and to the philosophy of Augustine. It prevailed until the early part of the thirteenth century and was the main cause of the strenuous opposition which the revival of Aristotelianism evoked. Man does not derive the whole of his knowledge from sense experience, if indeed the knowledge we derive from this source, which at best is but approximate, deserves the name "knowledge" at all. Man has a twofold vision, it was then said by the opponents of Aristotle. He looks downward with his senses and upward with his mind, and it is by his mind that he acquired knowledge properly so called, though in no case is it knowledge of anything that is perfectly realized or adequately expressed either in the corporeal world or in the statements by which man seeks to formulate it. In the quaint terminology of his age Bonaventure calls attention to this when he criticizes Aristotle's doctrine that there exist but four causes, on the ground that he has left out the most important of all, namely the "exemplary cause," the idea in the mind of God of which created things are but a feeble and inadequate copy, as Plato said.

I pass on to another debt which Christianity owes to Plato, though its indebtedness here is indirect, since in this matter it owes more to Neo-Platonism than to Plato himself. Towards the close of his life Plato wrote a treatise on cosmology, which he called *Timaeus*, since in it Timaeus replaces Socrates as the principal speaker. Than this no work of Plato's was more widely read in the Middle Ages nor more keenly appreciated, for in it there are passages which seem to be describing creation in much the same terms as a Christian would use; but if we examine it closely, not quite the same. In the *Republic* Plato has sought to show that it should be possible in human society to realize to some extent the moral values which Socrates held to be eternal and immutable. The Timaeus opens with the story of an island republic in which these moral values are supposed to have been realized. It then goes on to show how that other realm of eternal objects, τὰ μαθηματικά, come to be realized in the cosmos which we perceive with our senses. Timaeus begins by making a clear distinction between *that which always is and has no becoming*—the realms of perceptible phenomena. He then introduces a δημιουργός—an artificer—who contemplates the realm of mathematical objects in their relations one to another, and, since the cosmos is to be an organic whole the parts of which are ever in motion, in creating it implants therein a world soul which causes it to become the moving image of eternity. The word, δημιουργός, is usually translated by "creator" and is identified with God, and there can be little doubt but that Plato meant his words to be thus interpreted, for he not only believed in God and that God fashioned the world, but he also believed in Providence, as he tells us in the *Laws*. What he says, nonetheless, gives rise to a difficulty. For in the order of being the ultimate reality is not in this case God, but the realms of eternal and immutable objects; and, since in the *Phaedo* and in the *Republic* we are told that the ultimate ground or cause of this realm of eternal objects is the Good, we have two ultimate sources of being: the Good which is the source of all eternal objects of thought, and the Artificer who, by means of life or the world soul, creates a world which is to become the moving but ever imperfect image of the realm of eternal objects.

It is this difficulty which Philo and the Neo-platonists seek to overcome. For Philo God is ultimate, and eternal objects are the product of his thinking, not objects which are presupposed by his thought. For Plotinus the ultimate source of all being is the One or the Good; and from it proceeds νους, i.e., intelligence or thought; and from νους proceeds ψυχή, life or the world soul. These three ultimates, moreover, of which the second presupposes the first and the third presupposes the other two, are by the Neo-platonists called ὑποστάσεις, which is the Greek word for "persons" in the grammatical sense.

Is it any wonder then, that in his *Confessions* Augustine should have written "*In certain books of the Platonists one reads not in so many words, but in many and diverse arguments which convince one that they mean the same thing, that in the beginning was the Word and the Word was with God and God was the Word which in the beginning was with God, and that through the Word all things are made and without the Word nothing is made; and that in what is made there is Life, which is the light of men and shines in a darkness which understands it not. I also read that the Word which is God, is not born of flesh or blood or of man's desire or the desire of the flesh, but is born of God; but that the Word was made flesh and dwelt amongst us, I did not read there.*"

The simplicity of the story of Word made flesh had at first shocked St. Augustine, but he has now come to realize that it is precisely this doctrine which differentiates Platonism from Christianity and accounts for the failure of Platonism to convert men to God, as it set out to do. Without that personal and intimate contact with God which the Incarnation brought about it is impossible to convert souls to God, as St. Anthony had been converted, and Victorinus, the philosopher, the young men at the Emperor's court in Augustine's own day. Philosophies are ephemeral. They come and go. The philosophy of today repudiates with scorn the philosophy which prevailed a few years ago. Furthermore, in itself philosophy is too abstract to bring about a radical change in man's attitude toward God and in his mode of life. Conversion is due to the intercourse of person with person, and the person who is to convert another must be present to him as a vivid and living reality in whom he believes.

That is why, in order to escape the lure of black girls, Augustine became a Christian. But, in becoming a Christian, he did not cease to be a Platonist. Plato taught that the passing show which we call the physical world manifests that ultimate reality of which alone we can have genuine knowledge. Christ taught that in this ultimate reality there is a Father who eternally begets a Son, and a Spirit who eternally proceeds from the Father through the Son, who is to send Him into the world to convert mankind. This doctrine is in accord with the findings of the Neo-platonists and with the teaching of Plato himself. But if this be the nature of that ultimate reality which all thinking men seek to know, in the created world there should be *vestigia* of the Trinity as there are *vestigia* of all else that ultimate reality involves and implies. *Credo ut intelligam*, said Anselm. If I would understand the universe I must start not with some man-made hypothesis, but with what has been revealed, and should then find that in the world of which I have perceptual experience my belief is confirmed in much the same way that a scientific hypothesis may be verified by appeal to perceptual experience. The Platonic doctrine that the created universe manifests the nature of God has survived amongst Christians down to the present day. We are assured that whatever exists perceptually must exist *eminenter* in God; in which case God should be not only intelligence and lover *par excellence*, but also eminently hot, for heat is the clearest case in which like produces like. But amongst the broad and most striking characteristics of the physical universe are many things besides heat: the distinction of thing from thing and of person from person, relation, order, dependence, sequence, society. If we start as natural theologians are wont to do, with the simple thesis that God is one, we can account for none of these broad and striking characteristics of the universe in which we live. But, if with Anselm and Augustine we start with the hypothesis that God is three in one, and that the second person presupposes the first and the third proceeds from both, we begin to realize how it comes about that God creates a universe in which there is distinction, relation, order, dependence, sequence, likeness, and that community to which likeness gives rise, for in God, who is three in one, all these characteristics are plainly to be found.

I submit, then, for your consideration two propositions. The first is that Plato was right in claiming that there exists a realm of eternal objects, alike moral and mathematical, which are neither the projection of man's *libido* nor yet the product of his thought, but are there to be apprehended and explored, and in their systematic wholeness imply a ground which is at once the One and the Good. The second is that the distinctions which Plato adumbrates in the *Timaeus* and which were eventually to give rise to the Neo-platonic distinction between Unity, Mind, and Life, find their full expression in the Christian doctrine of the Trinity, without which it is impossible to account for the outstanding characteristics of the physical universe, which in Christian belief, as in Platonic theory, is an imperfect, but nonetheless a genuine manifestation of the nature of God.

LESLIE WALKER

February, 1948

ARISTOTLE AND CHRISTIANITY

FR. F. C. COPLESTON, S. J.

(*Summary of the meeting held on March 1, 1948*)

The first part of Fr. Copleston's paper was a lucid, historical account of the events which led up to the Aristotelianizing of Christian theology in the 12th Century. He explained how the earlier Christian writers regarded Aristotle only as a logician and a *natural* philosopher, so that from the speculative and *meta*physical standpoint the Peripatetic school was absorbed into the current Neo-Platonism. Further, the speaker described how Aristotle's works, mixed or confused with Neo-Platonic writings, were translated into Syriac, and from Syriac into Arabic, to form the basis of the Islamic philosophy of writers like Avicenna and Averroes. When the Latin Scholastics translated them into Latin, the church at first rejected them as forming an independent, non-Christian system, until, after much dispute, the Scholastics of Paris were able to form a theologico-philosophical system combining Aristotelianism and Augustinianism, chiefly in the work of St. Thomas Aquinas, which has *since* become the most generally accepted basis of Catholic philosophy.

In the second part of his paper, Fr. Copleston presented three problems concerning the relation of philosophy, and in particular of Aristotelianism, to Christian theology. Firstly, is philosophy a *logical* presupposition for the acceptance of revelation? Secondly, is it possible to detach revealed truths from the terms of philosophy, or from the common sense concepts of Aristotle which westerners assume, and could equivalent terms be found in any other system? Thirdly, can there be a Christian philosophy, and, if so, what meaning can we give to that phrase?

In replying to the speaker, Mr. W. C. Kneale maintained that the Church, in taking over Aristotle, had laid a false emphasis on certain of his categories which to him (Aristotle) were just a matter of common sense and of the use of language. Aristotle's chief emphasis was upon the empirical method in science; and if he were living in modern times he would have followed the line of Occam, Bacon, Newton, or even Whitehead and Russell. The Church, for polemical and defensive purposes, had turned Aristotle into a system, which had given rise to counter-systems, and thus acted as a hindrance to progressive, empirical thought, and a stimulus to persecution in politics.

THE DISCUSSION

The main topics of the discussion were as follows:— (1) Certain historical questions about the system of the Peripatetics and its relation to Aristotle. (2) An attack [by Miss D. Hirst] on Mr. Kneale's use of the word "progressive." (3) A question raised by the Secretary as to whether the Bible could be understood without the medium of any philosophy, to which it was answered that the terms of common sense were philosophy in a confused form. (4) In the context of the question of the relation of philosophy to theology, the Chairman questioned the historical accuracy of Mr. Kneale's whole interpretation of Aristotle as a non-metaphysical thinker. According to her, Aristotle's notion of predication, of the act of making a judgment, of attribution and of asserting intellectual knowledge, not to mention his notion of cause, had a metaphysical status such as the modern linguistic analysis will not allow. In replying to the

Chairman, Mr. Kneale took the line that all Aristotle was doing was distinguishing ways in which language could be used for dialectical purposes. A development of this argument took up the rest of the evening's discussion, but was not satisfactorily concluded.

BELIEF AND REASON IN PHILOSOPHY

Mr. M. B. Foster

I will start by giving a provisional sketch of the relation of belief to reason as it might appear to a thinker who admitted the possibility of divine revelation. I don't wish to prejudge the question whether the account contained in this sketch is true or false, adequate or inadequate. I wish to use it in order to introduce the problem, and to give some definition to the terms of it.

It might be held, then, that men have two sources of truth: first, the use of their natural faculties; second, divine revelation.

1. The *Natural Faculties* are sensation and reason. Whatever knowledge men acquire from either of these two sources or from the combination of both of them is acquired naturally. From this naturally acquired knowledge spring both philosophy and science. They are constituted by the use of reason acting either upon its own resources, or upon the data of sensation.

Examples of truths which their authors at any rate claimed to know by the use of their natural faculties are: Descartes' assertion that a world consisting of matter in movement really exists; Voltaire's assertion (which he holds to be self-evident) that there exists one, and only one, God; Copernicus' assertion that the earth moves round the sun; and all the assertions of what we call the natural sciences.

The characteristic of this kind of truth (naturally acquired) is that anybody whatever can be convinced of it, provided that he is equipped with reason and with the normal complement of senses; and that anybody whatever in whatever age of the world he was born and on whatever portion of the earth's surface, could always have been convinced of it, provided always that he possessed the normal human equipment of natural faculties.

2. God has *revealed* to men further truths which they could not have acquired by means of their natural faculties. He has revealed these truths through various channels, through the voice of prophets, through the Incarnation, through inspiration of the church and of its members. Examples of such truths are that there are three Persons in God, and that the dead rise again. These truths men cannot discover by the exercise of their reason; they receive them by belief or faith. To acquire these truths is the task not of philosophy nor science, but of religion.

It is characteristic of these truths that they could not have been discovered by any human being irrespective of the place and age in which he lived; they can be known only by those to whom the revelation has been given. No one who lived before God revealed His own nature in Jesus Christ could have discovered that God is love. Even since Jesus Christ, although this revelation is not exclusive but is intended to be given to everyone, it still cannot be attained by those to whom it has not been given, i.e., by those whom the Gospel has never reached.

I now propose to give a short (and crude) sketch of some views which have been held at different times in the Christian Church about the relation between revealed truth and truth acquired by the natural use of the reason.

The earliest Christians tended to despise and to condemn the pursuit of any truth except revealed truth. God has revealed all that it is necessary for a man to know in order to achieve salvation. Therefore, to concern himself with anything else, with philosophical speculation or with science of nature, is an indulgence of idle curiosity.

The early Christians, therefore, were not interested in science or philosophy; or condemned them as unprofitable. Whether they would also have condemned them as necessarily false, what their attitude would have been if they had been asked whether the natural faculties of men, apart from revelation, were at all capable of discovering truth, I don't know.

Because the Christians renounced science and philosophy, it did not follow that they renounced all methodical reasoning. On the contrary, they had a strong motive for explaining and expounding the content of revelation, for drawing out what was implicit in the truth they had received, and this, of course, had to be done by the use of reason. What was condemned was not the use of reason, but the use of reason in independence of faith. Reason's proper function was to understand what was believed. In order to do this, it had to begin by accepting the belief, and it had to operate throughout under the guidance, direction and government of belief.

This use of reason under the guidance of belief was something new in the ancient pagan world. Unfortunately when the Christian thinkers introduced the new thing, they did not also introduce a new name. It was given the name of theology.

There is an unfortunate confusion in this word, theology, because its original meaning is something different. The original meaning of the word "theology" is "study of God." The pagan Greek philosophers had pursued the study of God, and had called their investigations by this name; and many modern philosophers and theologians have held that there is a study called "Natural Theology," in which reason can discover something of the nature of God independently of revelation. Theology thus can mean two things: (1) it can mean "study of God"; this can be conducted independently of revelation, and it was pursued by the pagan philosophers; (2) or it can mean *the conduct of reason under the guidance of revelation*. This need not be a study exclusively of God; it can include the study of the soul or of the world or of anything about which there has been revelation. This is the thing which was new to the pagan world when Christianity developed it, and this is the thing to which I particularly wish to direct your attention. I wish we had a separate name for it.

I will quote some passages to illustrate how different Christian thinkers conceived this new relation in which reason was subordinated to belief.

i. It was held that faith made understanding possible. *St. Augustine* quotes from the Vulgate translation of Isaiah "*nisi credideritis, non intelligetis*" "unless you believe, you will not understand"; and that is the text of a great deal of his teaching.

[His teaching on this point is illustrated by his life. He had sought truth among the pagan philosophers for many years of his life, but without being satisfied. Then he was converted to Christianity, and his faith gave to his understanding an illumination which it had lacked before.]

ii. *St. Anselm* gave as the sub-title of one of his works (the *Proslogion*) "*fides quaerens intellectum*"—"faith in search of understanding" (which, Gilson says, expresses "the principle of all medieval speculation"). But faith did not seek understanding in order that it might be justified or reinforced by reason, as though it were not quite certain in itself. "I do not apply to you," says a character in another work of St. Anselm, a dialogue, "to remove uncertainty in my faith; but that you may show me the reason of my certitude." The object was not to found faith on reason, but to elicit the rationality implicit in faith.

iii. *St. Thomas Aquinas* took up a position which, as against Augustine and Anselm, allowed a position of relative independence to reason. There are, according to him, certain spheres in which reason is competent to reach conclusions by rational means, without recourse to revelation. One of these spheres, for example, is that of physics, or natural philosophy, in respect of the greater part of which there has been no revelation. In the sphere of those more important truths which a man needs to know for his salvation (about God and about the soul), God has in fact revealed everything which it is necessary to know (because he wished to make the knowledge accessible to the unlearned as well as to the learned); but there are some truths in this sphere which are *also* accessible to reason and can be demonstrated independently of revelation (e.g. the existence of God both has been revealed and can be proved independently). The demonstration of such truths is the business of philosophy.

Above the region accessible to natural reason is the region of other truths which are known by revelation only. In this higher region, reason loses its independence and reverts to the function ascribed to it by St. Augustine or Anselm—of rendering intelligible to the understanding what is known implicitly by faith. This highest region of knowledge is "theology."

The distinctive and characteristic thing about St. Thomas is that he thinks the natural reason has a sphere, that of philosophy, which includes what we call science, in which it can reach truth independently of faith. He recognizes also a sphere ("theology") in which reason is dependent upon faith; but he does not, as St. Augustine and St. Anselm had done, reduce all philosophy to "theology."

Yet even in St. Thomas the independence ascribed to reason in philosophy is not absolute. It is qualified by the two following considerations:

i. Reason, like all the other natural faculties of man, has been vitiated by the Fall. The Fall has injured it in respect of its capacity of attaining truth. In order that the natural reason itself may be restored to soundness, its injury needs to be healed, and this can be done only by the operation of Grace. So that although St. Thomas ascribes power to attain truth within certain spheres to the natural reason, he thinks that the perfect exercise of this power belongs not to the vitiated reason of fallen nature, but, as one might say, to the baptized reason. Grace, and therefore faith, are thus seen to be necessary although more indirectly, to the healthy operation of the natural reason.

ii. Even such a restored reason does not dispense wholly with the support of faith, because even if it proves its conclusions without appealing to faith, still the philosopher, being also a Christian, knows certain truths by faith before ever he starts to prove them by reason, so that faith shows him beforehand in what direction his conclusions have got to lie and to this extent directs his search for reasons.

[Cf. the phrase of the Encyclical "*Aeterni Patris*," that faith is to reason a "*sidus amicum*." It does not propel reason, but points its goal.]

We now come to the Reformation and the Renaissance, the beginning of the modern era.

At this point a split took place between the theologians and the philosophers (philosophy in this age still included science). Both attacked St. Thomas's compromise, but for opposite reasons.

i. The theologians of the Reform (Luther and Calvin), attacked St. Thomas for maintaining that reason was capable of discovering any truth in any kind of independence of faith. According to them, natural reason is, since the Fall, radically corrupt. Men can rely for truth only upon the revelation given by God to faith, and the only legitimate exercise of reason is an exercise under the tutelage of faith. The Reformers thus reverted to St. Augustine's position in an extreme form, and abolished philosophy in favor of theology.

ii. The philosophers protested against any subjection of reason to faith. They did not deny the truth of the Christian revelation; in fact, they believed it. But they said, faith has its own sphere, the sphere of worship on the one hand and conduct on the other. Faith is supreme as a practical guide in those spheres. But from the sphere of philosophy (including science) faith must be entirely excluded. In the sphere of philosophy and science men must rely wholly upon their natural faculties of sensation and reason. Though they possessed faith, they must not allow it the slightest influence upon their reasonings. This is the program proclaimed by Descartes and Locke and the philosophers who succeeded them; more important than that, it is the program taken for granted and acted upon in the making of modern natural science, which was developed at first in part by some of these same philosophers, and disengaged itself entirely from philosophy a good deal later than we are apt to imagine.[17]

In what I am going to say about this modern development since Descartes, I am going to confine myself to considering the philosophy in the narrower sense. I am going to ignore entirely the development of modern natural science; and if you say that is an important omission, I can only reply: Yes, it is.

The distinctive thing, then, about the modern philosophy was that it was to be based solely upon the natural faculties, reason and sensation. You would think (and Locke and Descartes did think) that an advantage to be gained from this new departure would be the removal of disputes. You would think that if you are going to confine yourself to the evidence of reason and experience, then although you would have to extrude from philosophy a good deal of what had previously been believed (you would have to extrude in fact both Aristotelian metaphysics and Christian theology), and would have to start laying foundations anew, *at least* your new foundations would be absolutely immovable. If I am going to start, with Descartes, by retaining in my philosophy only what is evidently demonstrable by my reason, surely I can at least be certain that there will never be any dispute about the truths which I admit? People don't dispute whether $2 + 2 = 4$, or whether the two sides of a triangle are together greater than a third, because these truths are evident to the reason. If the truths of philosophy are to be established on the same basis, we should expect a similar unanimity about them. Or if, with Locke, I am going to confine myself to those truths which I derive from sensible experience, I can surely, at least, be certain that whatever I establish in this way will be agreed by any other human being equipped with similar senses who takes the trouble to verify it.

The remarkable thing in the development of modern philosophy is that the agreement which Descartes and Locke were confident of obtaining, has not in fact been obtained. I think every one of the philosophical assertions of Descartes and Locke has been criticized and rejected by subsequent philosophers. Let us consider what some of the most important of these philosophical assertions were: that I myself am a mind and wholly immaterial; that there exists a real external world of nature, consisting of matter in motion; that God exists (namely an "infinite, eternal, immutable, independent, all knowing, all powerful" substance ... "by which I myself and everything else ... have been created").

All these statements were held to be demonstrable by reason, relying solely upon its own resources and upon the evidence of sense, with no assistance from faith. But a critical reaction soon set in. Berkeley, Hume, Kant, John Stuart Mill, the Positivists of the 19th century, the Logical Positivists of the present day are the representatives of this critical reaction, and philosophy at the present day is deeply under the influence of it. What has this critical philosophy shown? It has shown that the philosophical statements which Descartes and Locke—to use them as typical names—thought they could establish by the evidence of the

---

[17] The distinction between Rationalists and Empiricists, though important for some purposes, is not important for my present purpose. Both schools agreed in relying exclusively upon the natural faculties.

natural faculties, cannot be established on that basis; it has shown, e.g., that you cannot demonstrate the existence of God by bare reason, and that you cannot establish the reality of a material world on the evidence of sensation alone.

It follows that *if* Descartes and Locke were right in including all sources of knowledge except the natural faculties of sense and reason, then we can have no knowledge of anything except sensible objects, neither of nature nor of the self nor of God. "*If* Descartes and Locke were right in that conclusion ..." We—or at any rate some of the older among us—have been so imbued with the intellectual spirit of Descartes and Locke, that it is difficult for us to realize the force of that condition. We tend in all our thinking to start by assuming the principle which Descartes and Locke laid down, and we suppose in consequence that what the critical conclusion involves is that metaphysics and theology are absolutely and unconditionally impossible; and we are uneasy, because although we can see that this consequence cannot be right, we cannot see how it can be avoided.

In reality, the critical philosophy has not shown that truth in morals, metaphysics and theology is impossible to attain; what it has shown is that truth in these matters cannot be attained by a reason which is severed from all attachment to faith. The conclusion, therefore, which we should draw is that Descartes and Locke were mistaken in introducing into philosophy the principle that the natural faculties must work in complete independence of faith. The skeptical consequences follow *if* Descartes and Locke were right in excluding faith from philosophy. The conclusion which I suggest that we should draw is that Descartes and Locke were not right in doing this.

As a matter of fact, the severance of reason from faith, which Descartes and Locke propounded as an ideal, has never been achieved; least of all by Descartes and Locke themselves. For example, Descartes professed to discard from his notion of God all those things which could be known only by faith. He would retain only those attributes of which his reason could assure him. His reason, he thought, gives him the idea of God as "a substance, that is infinite, eternal, immutable, independent, all-knowing, all-powerful, and by which I myself and everything else ... have been created"; and demonstrates to him the existence of such a God with such perfect clarity that he says "I do not think the human mind is capable of knowing anything with more evidence" and "it is at least as certain that God exists as any demonstration of geometry can possibly be." And yet, in the next century, we find Kant denying that the existence of God can be demonstrated at all. Is not the fact of that disagreement very remarkable? How was it possible for Descartes to think that he had demonstrated the existence of God, if he had not? How was it possible for Kant not to see the proof, if he had? Disagreements like this do not occur in mathematics.

There is only one way, I think, of explaining this discrepancy. The conviction of Descartes (the same will apply to Locke) cannot have been, as he thought it was, merely the work of natural reason. If it had been, it must have been shared by Kant. The explanation must be that Descartes had not emancipated his reasoning from the influence of faith so completely as he supposed. That there exists a God infinite, eternal, immutable, all knowing—this is nothing but a residue of Christian faith, which has become luminous to Descartes' understanding. Descartes' reason perceives it to be evident only because it is, in spite of himself, a reason which has been baptized in Christian faith.

A close parallel to this phenomenon (indeed it is really the same phenomenon) is the survival in Victorian England of Christian moral conviction in a generation which had ceased to believe in Christian doctrine. In the first generation or so after belief has been lost, the moral convictions seem to those who hold them self-evidently valid, and not to require the support of any revealed truths of religion. After a lapse of one or two generations, their apparent evidence fades; and although they may continue for a long time to be professed and followed, the profession becomes more and more conventional and hollow, until a sudden puff of skepticism can blow them right away.

In a similar manner, it seems to me, in the first generation of modern philosophy Descartes and Locke held their metaphysical convictions with an unruffled certitude. They seemed to them so clear, that they did not need the support of any revealed truth. They weren't really independent of revealed truth, and therefore when they were severed from their source in faith, they were bound to fade. But not at once; it took some generations for it to happen. It is a remarkable fact that it should take time, but it does seem to be the fact. For the first emancipated generation of philosophers the metaphysical truths retained an undiminished evidence (indeed seemed to shine with a luminous certainty which they had not possessed before). But for later generations the evidence fades. They will go on being held dogmatically so long as they are not disturbed; but an element of the conventional will have entered into them, and they will be ripe for the skeptic's attack. The essence of the skeptic's attack, it seems to me, whether it is Hume, or Kant, or Ayer, in spite of the elaboration with which it is presented, is really very simple. It consists of saying: "Are you really certain of that?" And if we are not really, if we are hollow inside, then, although we may bluster a bit, we have to admit in the end: "No, I am not."

When a moral conviction has lost the self-evidence which it seemed to possess, I don't know that it can be reestablished directly by argument. It may be that we have to go a step further back and reacquire the faith out of which it sprang. Perhaps this also is paralleled in the case of metaphysical convictions. It seems to me that we cannot establish them, or reestablish them, by argument (this is what Idealism attempts to do); but that we have to go one step further back to the faith from which they sprang.

The conclusion which it is the main purpose of this paper to suggest is that Descartes and Locke were wrong and that the Christian tradition from which they departed is right. They were wrong in maintaining that men can discover philosophical truths by the sole use of their natural faculties. The Christian tradition was right in maintaining that reason in philosophy ought to be in some way or other subordinated to belief, and that this subordination is so far from being a restraint or limitation upon reason that it on the contrary enables reason in philosophy to arrive at truth.

I said reason in philosophy ought to be "in some way or other" subordinated to belief. As to the exact method of the subordination, we have seen that there have been variations within the Christian tradition. There is a considerable difference between the doctrine of Luther which reduces all philosophy to "theology" and the doctrine of St. Thomas which allows to the baptized reason a sphere for independent exercise. But important as these differences are, these are still variations within the Christian principle. I am suggesting that the Christian principle is true; but I am not arguing for the adoption of any one of the varying formulations which it has received in the past, I am not saying that we ought to pledge ourselves either to the Thomist or to the Calvinist or to the Lutheran doctrine. Indeed I do not think it necessarily follows that we should revive any one of the theories in which this principle has been formulated in the past. It may be that it now has to take on a new shape.

The principle that reason in philosophy must be subordinated to belief may be called the "theological principle," in the second of the senses which I distinguished in that term. In what form this principle is to be carried out in our age, is a question which I wish to leave open.

In the remainder of this paper I shall not attempt to show how the principle may be carried out, but bring one or two considerations which may make it easier to accept the principle.

1. When we hear of reason being subordinated to belief, we think this is an outrage on the freedom of thought. One synonym of belief is *dogma*; and when we think of our reasoning having to conform to dogma the old Locke in all of us rebels. We think of the attempt of the church to control the conclusions of Galileo, and of religious tests, and of the Thirty-Nine Articles. Here is a modern example of the same repugnance. The Dean of the Harvard Divinity School wrote an article recently, in which he puts the question: "Why does not the Ministry (sc. the Christian ministry) attract students of outstanding ability and promise?" He answers: "Primarily because the student's impression is that his ordination will cost him his intellectual freedom and honesty." And we probably all feel some instinctive sympathy with the student's objection.

There are concealed within this objection some genuine difficulties, which I shall not try to deal with here. I don't pretend that what I am going to say disposes of them. But it seems to me a mistake to suppose that what is really arousing the repugnance is the subjection of reason to belief. What causes the conflict in the case of Galileo is not that he is required to conform his reason to his belief, but that he is required to conform it to a cosmological doctrine which he has ceased to believe. What causes uneasiness to the Harvard students, similarly, is that they fear to pledge their assent to doctrines which they do not wholly believe, or which they fear they may in future cease to believe. I believe that most of our initial repugnance to the conclusion which I am defending is that when we hear talk of subordinating reason to belief, at any rate when it is a question of religious belief, we instinctively suppose that it is a question of submitting our reason to a dogma which we do *not* really believe. That is, of course, something quite different, and something which certainly would be incompatible with the freedom of thought. Therefore, when we imagine to ourselves what is meant by the control of reason by belief, we should take care to think only of examples in which our reason is controlled by what we genuinely and wholeheartedly believe.

2. When we have religious beliefs in mind we tend to think too crudely of the manner in which they exercise control of our reasoning. We think of it as the imposition of an external authority (a prohibition notified to us by a kind of ecclesiastical police), and we protest quite rightly that reasoning cannot submit to such an imposition.

We shall get a better idea of the manner in which belief can exercise control over reason without impairing its freedom if we turn our minds to the beliefs of *common sense*.

Consider, for example, how principles of common sense about the nature of the external world control the reasoning of philosophers in their formulation of a theory of knowledge. The philosopher perhaps first becomes aware of these principles only when his thought collides with them, i.e., when his theory leads to consequences which he recognizes to be absurd.

What is absurd is not what is contrary to reason, in the sense of being logically self-contradictory; the absurd is what is repugnant to the principles of common sense. The philosopher, when he is made aware of this repugnancy in his conclusions, is forced to go back to reconsider his theory and introduce such modifications as he thinks will remove it. Thus common sense, by its sensitiveness to extravagance, keeps theory within bounds and exercises a continual pressure upon the process of its formation. For example, if you find that your theory of perception, though attractive in other respects, leads to the conclusion that there is no distinction of kind between waking and dreaming experience (a thing that is very apt to happen, by the way), that is a point on which you are conscious that you are infringing the principles of common sense, and you go back to your starting point and you see what amendment you can introduce in order to avoid the collision. (The point is that you submit your reasoning to the principles of common sense, and not vice versa. You do not say, for example, "I have proved that the ordinary belief is wrong, and there really is no difference between sleeping and waking.")

Here is an example of the same procedure from a book of Ayer's: He argues in *Language, Truth and Logic* that (with the exception of tautologies) the only propositions which are significant are those which are empirically verifiable; all other propositions are nonsense. And he then raises the question: what sense is to be attached to the phrase "empirically verifiable"? Are we to take it in the strong sense, according to which we should have to say that the only significant propositions are those which are *conclusively established* in experience? Or are we to take it in a weak sense, and to allow significance to any proposition which it is possible for experience to render probable?

Ayer declares for the weak sense, and one of the arguments by which he defends his choice is the following (p. 23):

"It seems to me that if we adopt conclusive verifiability as our criterion of significance, as some positivists have proposed, our argument will prove too much. Consider, for example, the case of general propositions of law—such propositions, namely as 'arsenic is poisonous'; 'all men are mortal'; 'a body tends to expand when it is heated.' It is of the very nature of these propositions that their truth cannot be established with certainty by any finite series of observations. But if it is recognized that such general propositions of law are designed to cover an infinite number of cases, then it must be admitted that they cannot, even in principle, be verified conclusively. And then, if we adopt conclusive verifiability as our criterion of significance, we are logically obliged to treat these general propositions of law in the same fashion as we treat the statements of the metaphysician." (That means saying that science is as much nonsense as metaphysics.)

"In face of this difficulty," he continues, "some positivists" (e.g., Schlick) "have adopted the heroic course of saying that these general propositions are indeed pieces of nonsense, albeit an essentially important type of nonsense. But here the introduction of the term 'important' is simply an attempt to hedge. It serves only to mark the authors' recognition that their view is somewhat too paradoxical, without in any way removing the paradox. Besides, the difficulty is not confined to the case of general propositions of law, though it is there revealed most plainly. It is hardly less obvious in the case of propositions about the remote past. For it must surely be admitted that, however strong the evidence in favor of historical statements may be, their truth can never become more than highly probable. And to maintain that they also constituted an important, or unimportant, type of nonsense would be unplausible to say the very least."

Ayer accordingly concludes against adopting conclusive verifiability as his criterion. The argument, which seems to me a sound one, is that to adopt this criterion involves the consequence that the generalizations of science and the propositions of history are both nonsensical. This consequence is rejected, not on the ground of any logical self-contradiction. It would be no more self-contradictory to conclude that the propositions of science and history are nonsensical, than to conclude that the propositions of metaphysics and theology are nonsensical. The consequence is rejected on other grounds, namely, that it is repugnant to the principles of common sense. (It "proves too much," is "too paradoxical," is "unplausible.") I think common sense will be found exercising a similar control of the argument in any theory of knowledge which we like to examine. Indeed it is only common sense which, by rejecting conclusions which pass the limit of the absurd, keeps the theory in contact with reality. There would be nothing otherwise to prevent the theory from developing into a self-consistent fantasy.

I have spoken as though common sense operated only negatively in the control of a theory of perception, merely posting sentinels, as it were, to keep it within bounds. This negative function is its most obvious one; but I think, in fact, the influence of common sense upon the development of a theory is also more positive than that. It supplies, as it were, the intellectual atmosphere out of which the theory is precipitated. But it is not necessary to argue this point. If we consider only its restraining influence, that is sufficient for my illustration. What I wish to show is that the philosopher, when he submits his reasoning to the control of common sense, doesn't think that he is being restrained from the truth by doing so. On the contrary he is aware that it is only by this submission that he is enabled to reach the truth.

Why should we not take the same attitude when it is a question of the control of reason by religious belief? I believe no reason can be shown why we should not. The reason why we commonly do not I believe to be simply that when we think of the control of reason by common sense, we think of reason as being controlled by something which we believe; when we think of the control of reason by faith, we think of reason as being controlled by something which we do not really believe.

SUMMARY

I will draw together some conclusions of this paper.

(a) We can't build a philosophy without faith. We can't build it by an *a priori* use of reason alone, we can't build it by the use of reason upon experience. The modern metaphysicians, beginning with Descartes and Locke, claimed to do this. But they were really relying on faith for what they claimed to demonstrate by reason; and the critical philosophy, beginning with Hume and Kant and culminating in the critical philosophy of Positivism, has exposed the falsity of their claim. It has shown that what Descartes and Locke thought they could demonstrate by reason, cannot be demonstrated by the unbaptized reason.

(b) But nothing in all this has any tendency to show that we cannot build a philosophy with faith and on faith.

The fact that much modern and contemporary philosophy is skeptical about religious beliefs seems to me no evidence against their truth. It is entirely a mistake if a religious man feels "The philosophers are against me, therefore reason is against me; I must hold to my faith in the teeth of reason." In these matters, the reasonings of philosophers depend upon their beliefs and not vice versa. If a philosopher begins with a belief in the reality of the material world and in the validity of the natural sciences, but without a belief in God (or, if, having a belief in God, he holds that belief apart from his philosophy), then those beliefs and this absence of belief will be reflected in his conclusions. He will reject as paradoxical or absurd all conclusions which are repugnant to the beliefs that he believes in (quite rightly), but he will not possess the corresponding touchstone which would enable him to regret as false the conclusions which are repugnant to belief in God. The conclusions of his reasoning will be skeptical in this regard because he lacked belief. It is not the case that he lacked belief because his reasoning led to skeptical conclusions.

(c) We ought, therefore, to found (or refound) our philosophy upon our beliefs. To make our reasoning thus dependent upon our beliefs does not in any way violate the true freedom of reason, as may be seen if you consider the way in which reason is controlled by common sense beliefs. (Even the philosophers who don't admit that their beliefs ought to control their reasonings, cannot avoid this in practice.)

(d) The important thing is to get our beliefs true. That is not to be done (so far as the most important beliefs are concerned) by purely intellectual means. If it were, the philosopher of the intellectual man would alone be qualified to attain true beliefs. But this is not so. True beliefs on the most important issues are open to all men to attain equally with the philosopher. The philosopher can elicit their implications when he has attained them.

I am not going to touch in this paper upon the way in which true belief may be attained. But I will conclude by mentioning two Socratic precepts, which I believe may be helpful to its attainment.

They are that we should set ourselves (i) to discover what we really do believe, and (ii) when we argue, to say only what we really believe.

i. The first is expressed in the Socratic saying: "The unexamined life is not worthy of a man." In connection with this, we should bear in mind another saying, I have forgotten by whom: "If I want to know what a man believes, I enquire not what he says, but how he acts." We must apply the same principle to the examination of ourselves. The principles which we have to elicit in order to discover what we really believe are not those which we are prepared to maintain in theory, but those upon which we act.

ii. Socrates distinguished two kinds of argument, which he called Dialectic on the one hand and Disputation on the other. (διαλεκτική as contrasted with ἀντιλογική or ἐριστική). He thought that dialectical argument led to the attainment of truth, but that disputatious argument did not. What is the difference between the two?

I can't appeal to any actual passage of Plato which lays down the definition I am going to give, but I think it is the true one and that it represents Socrates' meaning. In dialectic the parties to the argument try to say what they really believe, in disputation they try to say what will gain them a victory.

These are simple recommendations, but if anyone thinks them easy, I can only say that I find them difficult.

Note that, if my interpretation of the second one is correct, *Socrates* is saying that reasoning will not lead to truth unless it is guided by belief. If we were to ponder his saying, we should get fresh light from it on what may be meant by the guidance of reason by belief.

KARL BARTH ON FAITH AND REASON

Rev. Daniel Jenkins

The theology of which Karl Barth is the outstanding exponent is, as might be expected, much more explicit and developed in its analysis of the nature of faith than of the nature of reason. This subject is best approached, therefore, by considering the Barthian definition of the nature of faith. One of the best short summaries of that definition which I know is given in an essay by Dr. H. F. L. Cocks, "Saving faith is the sinner's acknowledgement of the living God who encounters him in His word. It is man's trustful, obedient response to divine grace; the human act that is 'conformed' to God's act of self-revelation."[18] Faith, to Barth, is not merely a virtue of the intellect whereby we are able to believe truths inaccessible to natural reason nor only a disposition of the heart which moves outward in affection towards God, but the fundamental act of committal towards God in which the whole man, mind, heart and will, is necessarily involved. It is the act by which we recover our true humanity by being joined to Christ, who is, in Luther's phrase, "the proper man." Through our identification with Christ, we are covered with His righteousness, holiness and truth, and God, looking at us as we are found in Him, finds us well-pleasing in His sight. But, contrary to much popular belief, this does not mean that nothing takes place in us and that our nature remains fundamentally the same. Justification by faith means that something happens in us, the most radical and decisive thing which can happen. We find a new center for our lives in Christ, so that we can now say with the apostle in the paradox of Christian experience, "I live, yet no longer I, but Christ in me." Faith is the human act which is the proper response to God's revelation in Christ. It is, to use an ordinary word which Barth, in his *Dogmatic* charges with profound meaning, an *acknowledgement* of God in His revelation, that which is called out in us by knowing that Christ died for our sins and rose for our justification. Thus, as Brunner said long ago, we trust God's Word not because we are courageous and try it out for once, but because we can do no other under the constraint of that Word.

Barth would not want to claim any great originality for his teaching. It is a reaffirmation of the Reformer's doctrine of justification by faith, but a reaffirmation which develops that doctrine more thoroughly and less one-sidedly than it frequently has been handled in the history of the Reformed churches. This is not true of Luther, as his great Primary Tract on the Freedom of the Christian Man indicates, but in the history of Protestantism justifying faith has undoubtedly been considered chiefly in moral terms. This is natural and understandable because the very concept of justification has a moral, not to say legal, connotation, and it was inevitable that the theory of the atonement which had the greatest influence on the Reformed churches in particular was the theory of penal satisfaction. The result was, however, that this emphasis on the moral aspect of faith, combined later with the individualistic religion of Pietism, produced an understanding of the doctrine of justification by faith which has been characteristic of, for example, English Evangelicalism to our own day, an undertaking which conditioned the whole of Newman's approach to the doctrine in his "Lectures on Justification." For this point of view, reason is, in effect, not involved in the act of faith at all. Faith is a matter of the resolution of a moral crisis, through a not very closely defined committal to Jesus Christ as Savior and Friend, which provokes intense emotion and great thankfulness and joy at its fulfillment. The relation of this to reason is normally not defined but, where it is, reason is regarded as a critical challenger,

---

[18] *Reformation Old and New* (Lutterworth Press), p. 157.

confronting the believer with doubts as to the validity of his experience, which must, at all costs, be kept at bay. Barth's teaching is to be sharply distinguished from this widely current conception of the meaning of justification by faith. The whole man is involved in faith and that means the mind as much as any other part of him. God's self-revelation in Christ brings the whole man into *krisis*, judgment, including his reason, and reestablishes the whole man, including his reason, in a new relationship with God.

It is, then, in the light of this understanding of the nature of faith that we are to understand Barth's teaching about the nature of reason. As far as I can gather from those writings of his that I have read, I think Barth's work suffers from an inadequately systematic treatment of the place of reason and philosophy in relation to faith and to theology. Many of the best things he has to say in this matter are found in his later *Dogmatic* and are not put in a way easily intelligible to the non-theologian. Barth regards reason as man's highest center of awareness of himself, as one who enjoys the power of self-determination. Because of this, it is in man's reason that his sin, his rebellious attempt to set himself up independently of God, becomes most articulate and precise. Man's nature is a unity. When sin takes possession of the citadel of his being, the whole man is necessarily affected. This, of course, is the meaning of total depravity, which does not mean that we all become very very wicked but that no part of us is free from the taint of sin and that we have no secret hiding place of self-righteousness into which we can safely flee from God. When the whole man is affected, it follows that thought becomes, as Kierkegaard says, original sin as thought. This does not mean that man becomes an idiot. It means that his thinking is the servant of his own sinful purpose, however efficient and reliable it may be within its narrow limits. That is why Luther, with such extravagantly misleading language, used to denounce reason as a harlot. He did not mean by this that he treated man's rational faculty with contempt, but that it had been prostituted by man's sinfulness to base uses. This is not a low evaluation of reason as such but a high one. In itself, the reason is the place where man, being most fully aware of himself, should be most fully aware of God, but because he has deliberately shut out God, reason now radically misunderstands itself and thus becomes the place where man's self-contradiction is most manifest.

When faith comes, however, it marks the beginning of the regeneration of reason. Where the world dwelt the Word, the divine logos, the true source of all order and wisdom, now dwells. Faith means the restoration of right reason, just because it is our identification with Christ, the true Logos of God. This cannot be too strongly emphasized because Barth is frequently criticized as irrationalist, whereas he appears irrationalist only to those who share the Rationalist's misunderstanding of the nature of reason. But as he says, because the Word of God is literally language, therefore, "the communication of it to man must at least also involve a claim upon the intellect, and the experience of it must at least also actually involve the co-option of the intellect."[19] And, in the same place, he denounces what he calls the extraordinary polemic which it has been the fashion in recent years to wage against the so-called "intellect" of man, his powers of comprehension and thought, as a center of possible religious experience of the Word of God. The polemic has been waged by fashionable proponents of the subconscious or the numinous or the mystical.

So rationalistic in this sense is Barth that he insists that unless faith presses forward to the rational task of theology it is unable fully to be realized and appropriated by men, and thus that God cannot be adequately acknowledged and obeyed. He makes great use of Anselm's phrase as a description of the task of theology, *fides quaerens intellectum*. That is to say, the nature of faith

---

[19] *Dogmatic*, p. 231.

is such that it is inevitably driven forward to seek understanding. Man cannot adequately acknowledge God, he cannot make that full response within himself to the self-revelation of the God who is the truth, unless God's Lordship is registered at his place of most intense self-consciousness, his reason. And this it does by overcoming, in a rational manner at the intellectual level, those things which appear to contradict and thus to deny, God's Lordship. Unless that urge to understanding is present, faith is not faith, because faith cannot brook its contradiction.

Thus a living faith will strive always to bring every thought into the captivity of Christ. It will see its task on the intellectual level as one of ceaseless victorious battles against all those ideas which are "high things exalted against the knowledge of God," just as on the moral level, insofar as it can be distinguished, it sees its task as one of ceaseless victorious battles against temptation. This must not be too much externalized. It does not necessarily mean that we must all become truculent and aggressive Christian apologists against all the ideologies which appear to deny the Christian faith. It means primarily that we must bring out into the open our own personal doubts and difficulties and strive to overcome them, by the power of God, in a fair intellectual fight. To suppress our doubts or to try to bypass our difficulties by pious wishful thinking is unbelief, a refusal to accept the fact that, to use Barth's own words, "The Word of God determining man's existence, is strong enough also to deal with man as self-determining in thought."[20] God desireth truth in the inward parts and that is impossible unless faith registers itself in our minds, not merely as edifying or inspiring or encouraging or comforting, but as true. Faith must seek understanding if it is to be the analog in us of God's personal speaking in His Word, Jesus Christ, His expression of Himself in the most precise and articulate form of communication possible to men. Thus, so far from being irrational, faith represents the release of the rational faculty from the distortion of error for the joyful exercise of its true God-given function.

Barth's teaching concerning the relation between faith and reason is far removed from irrationalism, but it is also very different from rationalism. The trouble with rationalism in all its forms is that it overlooks the radical discontinuity which runs through all human experience because man is estranged from God. It does not see that there is a crisis in human reason because there is a crisis in human nature. Professor Hodges has shown, in his essay in the volume presented to Barth, how most philosophy until our own time, and not least the *philosophia perennis*, has contrived to evade this issue. It is this which lies behind Barth's terrific hostility to Natural Theology as a preoccupation of Christian theologians, which is so puzzling to many people. Natural theology, he insists, is an improper activity for the Christian because it is based on a refusal to take God's revelation in Christ seriously. It is as though men said, "Let us look at the world as though God had not really spoken in Christ and brought all our life under His judgment and promise and let us see if we can reach God by some other way than that which He has appointed," forgetting that in His revelation He has shown us how distorted our reason is apart from Him and how it leads us astray. This is not to say that those who lived outside the context in which the historical revelation took place or who do so now are always in every way in error. On the contrary, God had dealings with men before Christ and outside Israel as He has with us and led them in ways they did not understand. Today, also, the Spirit of the risen Christ is shed abroad over the whole world. But that is something we see because He is risen. It is not a justification for looking at the world as though He has not risen, in the hope that in so doing we may find a truth more reliable and incontrovertible than that of faith. God can never be known "in Himself," apart from the knowledge He gives in His works and ways, which reach their

---

[20] *Dogmatic*, p. 232.

climax and fulfillment in Christ. Barth's attitude to natural theology is only an attempt to take seriously the words of the most recent of typical non-Barthian Anglican theologians, Alan Richardson, when he says, "Our knowledge of God in this life is essentially a rational knowing made possible by faith in the Biblical revelation."[21]

If we say, "Yes, but what part does reason play in leading us to our knowledge of God," the answer is, "of itself, it has none." God makes Himself known by making Himself known in Jesus Christ. The retort may then be that that is no answer. But that is not so. The specific mode of the operation of reason is determined by the nature of its object. The mode of apprehension which lays hold of the knowledge of God in revelation will be one which answers to the object given in revelation. And the object of reason here is unique and incomparable, God Himself speaking. Whether that object is real can only be determined *a posteriori*, not *a priori*. But, as Barth warns us, in one sense even that is saying too much. The Word of God can only accredit itself as it is genuinely heard in the personal encounter of man with God. Even theology cannot demonstrate its reality. What theology can do is to exhibit the kind of rationality which corresponds with the object of its thought. When it does so, it not only illumines the meaning of revelation, but in so doing illumines the rest of experience as well. This procedure involves no sacrifice of the intellect, although it may appear from the outside to do so, because, as I have said, the nature of God's self-revelation is such that it drives us forward to authenticate itself as true in our experience. It is the Christian paradox of losing one's life to find it expressed on the intellectual level. And the Christian who seeks first the kingdom of God and His righteousness on this level also, finds that all the rest is indeed added unto him.

For Barth, the reason of the man of faith is a faculty of the greatest dignity and importance. In the first pages of the *Dogmatic* he even goes so far as to say that there is nothing in the nature of things which makes theology itself as a separate science necessary. It is a relative necessity, necessary in practice. Philosophy, and "secular" science generally, really need not be "secular," need not be heathen: it might be *philosophia christiana*.[22] To contest this on principle combines despair of the "world" with overvaluation of the "Christian" world, in a way incompatible either with Christian hope or with Christian humility. I believe, and I think Barth would believe, that we need, in these days of confusion and timidity and genuine irrationalism, to reassert our confidence in the efficacy of the sanctified reason as a means of ascertaining the true and perfect will of God. Certainly, it must be done, as faith seeking understanding has itself taught us to see, with a realization of how subtle and deceptive evil imaginations can be and how easy it is for social and economic and ecclesiastical bias, as well as personal vanity and laziness, to lead us astray. Yet God, in His mercy, has provided a way in which wayfaring men, yea simpletons, need not err, if they possess true faith which seeks understanding. That is to say, if we do the eminently practicable things which he asks of us—studying His Word, maintaining our prayers, caring for one another and the world in which we are set, which means watching and examining and analyzing without ceasing—then we shall find, even in the confusion of today, not only an answer to the relevant intellectual questions but an answer to that deeper question of which the relevant intellectual questions are a preliminary form, "How shall a man live?"

---

[21] *Christian Apologetics*, p. 243.
[22] *Dogmatic*, p. 4.

The Discussion

In opening the discussion, Fr. T. Corbishley, S. J., said that he agreed with nearly all that Mr. Jenkins had said, but that natural theology was necessary as an apologetic technique for making ourselves understood to unbelievers. Although all our good acts are due to grace, God lets us think we are doing something when we use our reason about Him. In answer to this, Mr. Jenkins restated his position in sharper contradistinction to Fr. Corbishley's view. The Christian does not offer to pagans any anonymous God known to natural theology, but the revealed God, Yahweh, known only in Christ. After the crisis of Faith, Christians use dialectical terms with a new weight of their own, quite different from the usages of ordinary theology. Mr. Jenkins had to leave the meeting at 9:30 p.m., but before that time he managed to answer a number of questions fired at him by the Chairman, Mr. V. Rice, Mr. M. Foster, Miss G. E. M. Anscombe and other members. He maintained that God can only be known by His appointed means, in his works and ways: that the God of natural theology was nothing apart from His Life known to us by Faith: that Faith must underlie reason, and not, as Mr. Rice seemed to think, follow on from it. Miss Anscombe asked what he would say of a Greek philosopher who had reached monotheism by natural reason and maintained it courageously in the face of all his contemporaries. This led to a lively DISCUSSION which was cut short by digressions and by Mr. Jenkins' departure, after which there continued a long argument about the nature of Faith and Knowledge. The Chairman, supported by Mr. Foster and others, agreed that faith was cognitive, as it gives a personal knowledge of God, while Miss Anscombe could not understand what seemed to her the unjustified confidence of those members who spoke of faith as if it gave them a direct knowledge of God.

EXISTENTIALISM

Ronald Grimsley

Although there may be some uncertainty about the exact meaning of the word "existentialism" and the identity of the "existentialists," the general spirit of the movement is not in doubt.[23] The situation has been concisely put by Berdyaev: "Existential philosophy is a personalist philosophy; the subject of knowledge is the human person." Or again, in the words of Gabriel Marcel: "There is a close solidarity between existentialist and personalist preoccupations." Whatever their differences, all existentialists seem to be agreed on this: that the search for a purely rational objectivity—whether materialist or idealist—is profoundly mistaken. A man cannot, they think, just put aside his real nature as a human being and then proceed to build up a philosophy out of what is left. He cannot first of all stand outside human experience and then proceed to talk about the ultimate meaning of things, as though that experience were irrelevant.

In other words, we must start, say the existentialists, with the individual man *"en situation,"* in a concrete and particular situation. The significance of such a position is that it is mine and not another's, just as the other's is his and not mine. Now this peculiar "myness" of a situation is what constitutes its importance and uniqueness and what, with all its elusive personal character, we must first seek to understand if we are to talk about reality. It is upon this point that emphasis must be laid if we wish to grapple with "existence." "Existence," says Heidegger, "is the existence which we ourselves are" and though it may be possible to talk about "being in general," it is always, he thinks, with this personal human existence that we must begin. Gabriel Marcel has described this type of existence as an "inexhaustible concrete," a "non-inventoriable," which defies rational definition or analysis.

The source of this particular emphasis in all existential philosophy is undoubtedly the Danish writer Kierkegaard, who has been called the father of existentialism—although he himself certainly had no desire to found a "school." The significance of Kierkegaard's work lies in its powerful affirmation of the unique value of a Christian against the emotional naturalism of the Romantic Movement and the obsession of Hegelianism with the Idea. His protest, however, does not take the form of a restatement of Christian dogmas but of an attempt to explain "what it means to be a Christian." He proposes to call men back to Christianity by first calling them back to themselves. In other words the problem for him is not to define Christianity but to examine the means of appropriating it and so to understand what, from a personal point of view, this fact of appropriation really means.

---

[23] The reasons for the comparatively small space devoted to J. P. Sartre in this paper are as follows: first, Sartre had already been the subject of a paper read at the previous meeting by Mr. C. S. Lewis; secondly, Sartrian existentialism is in many ways the most inexistential of existentialisms. Modern existentialism derives from Kierkegaard, whose influence has developed in two main directions: (1) There has been an attempt to strip his viewpoint of its religious significance and make it serve the purposes of a "philosophical" outlook (e.g. Martin Heidegger tries to combine certain Kierkegaardian concepts with the descriptive "phenomenological" method of Husserl. His influence has been strong on Sartre); (2) other thinkers have tried to interpret the human condition by seeking the philosophical significance of fundamental human attitudes (Karl Jaspers and Gabriel Marcel). Connected with this second group are a number of Russian thinkers (Soloviev, Chestov and Berdyaev), who, though not existentialists in the strictest sense, show affinities with Kierkegaard. Finally the Jewish philosopher Martin Buber has certain "existentialist" features (especially in his strongly marked personalism) without belonging to any school. There are thus two main streams of existentialist thought—the non-religious (even the atheistic and the nihilistic) and the religious (and even Christian). We shall be concerned in some measure with both of them.

There is no inert subject or object, he insists, but a living person who, by concerning himself with the problem of his relation to an eternal happiness or unhappiness, qualitatively transforms himself into a true individual. To do this a man must resist all attempts to absorb him into a false absolute, whether the Church, the State or the philosophy of Hegel. His chief target was Hegel who had turned himself into a "fantastic creature" through his efforts to build a system and think in terms of world history. To the Hegelian system Kierkegaard resolutely opposes authentic human existence. In a sense such an existence can never be defined since it is not a simple empirical entity capable of being conceptualized or universalized. Existence is subjectivity, inwardness—the intimate quality of a man's being that is revealed to none but himself.

Though it cannot be defined, existence has certain marked features which allow its broad characteristics to be indicated.

(1) This living concrete existence that I am is fundamentally *dialectical* or ambivalent in character. As soon as I seize one aspect of myself, I am confronted with another, its opposite, in such a way that I am forced to admit the simultaneous presence of these two contradictory aspects in the same person. Existence is finite and earthly; it is also infinite and eternal. The synthesis of mind, body and spirit is the main source of the paradoxes that seem to inhere in all thinking about human existence.

(2) It follows from this dialectical character of existence that it *cannot be conceptualized*. There is no universal objective quality embracing all types of particular human beings. Every individual human is essentially unthinkable. Thought and being are thus separated and not identified as they are in Hegel. Abstract thought in seeking to conceptualize and objectify human personality merely moves away from the reality it is seeking to grasp.

(3) This contradiction can be overcome only by *passion*—not the wild passion of the senses of the "natural man," but the passionate earnestness and infinite concern of a man for himself and his relationship to God. Such passion has a spiritual value carrying the individual to the deepest levels of existence.

(4) In a sense, therefore, we cannot say that existence just "is," for to say that a thing "is" implies a simple homogeneity and static permanence. The existent, as a synthesis of the finite and infinite, is in a perpetual state of movement and development. "*Existence is not; existence becomes.*"

(5) Finally all the above characteristics serve to emphasize that existence must constantly be understood in terms of possibility. Impelled by the thought of himself as a possibility, man must constantly choose and venture himself. "To venture in the highest sense is precisely to be conscious of oneself." Existence thus expresses itself through decision. We must rise from the lowest state of existence to the highest—from the "natural man" through the "universal human" to the truly religious individual. Man must constantly make a leap—a decisive choice of himself which helps to transcend his antecedent state.

To have meaning, however, such a choice must be founded on a real possibility. Such a possibility is freedom. Hence authentic human existence may be defined as freedom.

A decisive qualitative transformation of myself resists conceptual analysis or definition, but the category of the "leap" is preceded by a psychological state in which the future possibilities are vaguely active. Such a state reveals itself as "dread" (*Angst*)—one of the best known of existentialist phenomena. Dread is not to be confused with fear, the instinctive animal reaction to specific danger. It is something vaguer and yet more fundamental. Briefly it is the first movement of the "spirit" which is "dreaming in man." In a sense it is dread of—nothing—an ambivalent mood which is attracted to and repelled by the impending possibility which as yet, in terms of the immediately real, is—nothing. It is the expression of man's first consciousness of his eternal self, the first apprehension of himself as sinful being.

Most of these fundamental ideas have permeated the thinking of modern existentialists and it is interesting to see what form they take in a philosopher like Heidegger who seems at first sight to have little in common with Kierkegaard's point of view.[24] Like Kierkegaard, however, Heidegger rejects any attempt to grasp existence as a purely static object. This existence "which we ourselves are" (to which he attaches the name "*Dasein*") must always be understood as an existence which is in a perpetual state of mobility with reference to itself. We can never say that existence is finished once and for all, a completed fact. It is constantly tending towards its own possibility—a "*sich vorwegsein*," or being that is always ahead of itself. This is what Heidegger calls transcendence. Existence, therefore, can never be separated from its possibilities. In a sense it *is* those possibilities, since it depends on nothing but itself. It is a kind of auto-determinism whose essence lies precisely in its manner of existing—as possibility, not a logical and negative possibility, based simply on the absence of a contradiction, but a positive possibility existing dynamically.

It will be clear from this that when existentialists say that existence precedes essence or that the essence of *Dasein* lies in its existence they do not mean that *Dasein* exists necessarily or that its function is necessarily to exist. What they mean is that the *Dasein* cannot be provided with an abstract and universally valid definition, because what *is* resides in the *how* of its existence. The essence thus becomes nothing but the way of existing. For the *Dasein* to be this or that is for it to exist in this or that mode. Similarly we cannot separate the essence of man from his concrete existence, for it is precisely this concrete existence which constitutes his essence. In the same way the being of the *Dasein* cannot "have" properties, as though there were first of all a subject which "had" properties capable of being taken on or cast off at will. Such properties are all possible ways of existing concretely, committing the whole of the *Dasein*. *Dasein* cannot be a thing which we objectively contemplate; nor can it be a "substance" which watches all the changes in its "accidents" while remaining itself unchanged.

But this dynamic, projective existence is not an existence in a void. It is Being-in-the-World. Distinct from the world, it is yet inseparable from the world in terms of which it must be understood. The significance of this important assumption will appear in due course. For the moment we may merely say that the world and my being are inextricably bound up with each other.

Next, what constitutes the "*da*," the "thereness" of this being which thus finds itself in the world? Every being, says Heidegger, has a feeling for its original situation, an ultimate feeling beyond which there is nothing. This he calls *Befindlichkeit*, which compels me to become conscious of my precariousness and contingency. I feel that I am "thrown" or "abandoned" in the "thereness" of a situation which is imposed upon me. Such is "dereliction" (*Geworfenheit*). This is more than a simple fact; it is the affirmation of an essential condition of human existence.

The most important derivatives of this basic situation are "fear" and "dread." Through fear I discover the uncertainty of my condition and all fear, however objective its direction, is always fear for myself. It is thus that I am forced to a deeper awareness of my essential contingency. Fear, however, covers a still more fundamental feeling which, though related to it,

---

[24] Heidegger has disclaimed any connection with "existentialism," insisting that he is concerned with the problem of "being in general." His interest for existentialism lies in the fact that he proposes to approach this problem through an analysis of human existence.

is distinguished by the fact that it is never determined by a specific existent. Such is "dread" (*Angst*)—cf. the Kierkegaardian concept of dread mentioned above. The reason for and origin of dread is never clear. It is the strange uneasiness felt by the individual when the environment and its surrounding objects seem to have melted away.

Dread, however, for Heidegger lies neither in us nor in the objects around, but comes from the world as such, from the world as world. When the objects have vanished we are, so to speak, before the world in its pure state (cf. Pascal and the "infinite spaces"). Since the world and our being are inextricably linked together, it is thus our own naked and fundamental "being-in-the-world" that stands revealed to us. Dread springs from our condition and at the same time reveals it to us. Yet again it is the real apprehension of our original situation.

It is thus that we are compelled to face the fact of our own solitude. We are by this means placed in a situation which may reveal to us the true meaning of our existence. This inevitable feeling of dereliction and loneliness imposes upon us a choice—are we to accept this situation or not? In fact it soon appears that within the structure of our being are two possibilities—that of authentic, and inauthentic, being. Authentic being supposes the choice of ourselves as we are in our dereliction. Within us, however, is another tendency, the possibility of inauthentic being. This is expressed by the life of what Heidegger calls "*das Mann*" ("*L'On*" of French existentialists)—the neutral, anonymous everyman who constantly seeks to draw us away from the "dreadfulness" of our condition by filling us with concern over the trivial and commonplace, by engaging us in meaningless chatter and false ambiguity in order to bring false peace and assurance. The secrecy and mystery of true personality are then inexorably destroyed. Yet this mode of existence, though inauthentic, is real in the sense that it is not just subjective illusion, but an actual mode of being on a false level.

The threefold aspect of being thus described—possibility, dereliction and "contingent" or "fallen" being (the constant prey of "*das Mann*") is then united by Heidegger under a single existential which he calls *Sorge*: care, concern, although this single existential does not allow the separation of any of the individual moments thus described (e.g., being is projected and yet *already* abandoned in the world). Care may be summarily defined as follows: a being-in-advance-of-itself-already-thrown-into-the-world-in-which-it-is-lost.

We are here faced with a difficulty. How can we say that this idea of *Sorge* gives us a total view of human existence when that existence is by its very nature incomplete? Heidegger answers as follows: it is true that existence as anticipation is incomplete, yet this anticipation is directed towards an absolute end: death, death which is the end of being-in-the-world. The main fact about death is that it is intensely personal. I must die alone and no man can die for me. Such is the position of every person. In spite of the false comforting of "*das Mann*" (death is something that "just happens" to us—"all men are mortal"), the basic fact cannot be hidden: man is a being-for-death.

Dread thus becomes ultimately dread before a possible being faced by the inevitability of death. Dread is then the awareness of our fundamental situation which tells us that we are cast into the world in order to die there. Through dread we are made aware of our true destiny which would otherwise remain stifled beneath the deceitful mask of *das Mann*.

True existence will thus be marked by a correct attitude towards death, the incessant anticipation of ourselves in our ultimate fate, the true understanding of ourselves as essentially *nothing*. There is no escaping the supreme fact that I am a possibility of myself as nothing—a possibility in which I am immured and isolated and which if I am real person, I shall frankly accept. For by such an acceptance I shall attain to a certain tolerance and a certain power of detachment, a real "freedom-before-death."

All existentialists are not committed, of course, to Heidegger's view or even to his central position. Nevertheless there is an important affinity—and divergence—on one particular point which seems to show very clearly the two main paths open to existentialist thought. This is the idea of "transcendence." By this, Heidegger seems to mean at least three things:—(1) transcendence is the projective, dynamic character of the self developing within the *Dasein*; (2) beings as being-in-the-world means the transcendence of the self over itself and the world. By the same movement that it transcends itself, the *Dasein* transcends the world and so gives intelligibility to the crude existence of the world; (3) human existence is self-transcendent in the direction of its own nothingness.

It is the third idea which is the most interesting, for it appears at once as though this emphasis upon the nothingness of the self's ultimate projection is rather like a smuggling in at the last moment of a quasi-spiritual absolute which the premise (being is being-in-the-world) has absolutely excluded. If being, by its very definition, is capable of no positive, qualitative transcendence, the most it can conceive is a negative absolute. The element of nothingness was already in Kierkegaard, as we have seen, but for him it was an important aspect of the finite-infinite synthesis that composes the human personality. The awareness of our nothingness is the first movement of recoil by which we are brought to a consciousness of our positive possibility as spiritual being. Transcendence for him must mean a genuine qualitative transformation of our existence. For Heidegger this is impossible in any true religious sense. But because he is honest enough to want to do justice to the real elements of the human personality, he is compelled to admit an *inverted* religious element in the form of an absolute negativity.

It is interesting to note that there is the same kind of emphasis in the thought of Sartre. All transcendence is for him ultimately determined by the human reality (the "*pour-soi*") and the fact that this human reality is essentially constituted as a "néantisastion" of the "en-*soi*." To be free is thus to be free-for-nothing, because it is precisely this nothingness which constitutes the significance of that transcendent act.

There is a tendency on the part of the analytical philosophers to laugh away this preoccupation with the "nothing" (which, we are told, is transformed into a mysterious something) as a rather elementary logical error which all existentialists seem unfortunately incapable of avoiding. To reduce the whole problem to one of logic is to misunderstand the real level at which existentialism seeks to discuss the problem—namely at the personalist and not the purely "natural" level. The extreme emphasis laid upon the positive effect of personal negativity may well be mistaken, but it seeks to grapple with a very real element in human experience. This appears very clearly when we realize to what extent it may become a purely demoniacal expression of human possibility. When confronted with the necessity of transcending itself as merely empirical or "natural" being, a subjectivity which refuses to recognize the validity of this movement will find itself turned into a demoniacal and nihilist direction. Man can distort his spiritual possibilities, but he cannot really destroy them. This is very apparent in certain philosophers and writers who have especially interested existentialists. Thus Nietzsche is the example of a man who protests against the false values of a bourgeois culture whose Christianity is merely the form of its own dead materialism. This protest, though it comes from a man in whom a spiritual transcendence is stirring, is forced to express itself in purely naturalistic terms. This is plainly an existential contradiction, since a spiritual movement cannot express itself naturalistically. Hence the impulse of the natural man, mistaking the real significance of its own intensity, takes on a demoniacal character. The torment of a Kafka and a Dostoevsky derives also from the fact that the transcendent character of the inner movement is spiritual in character; and although they, unlike Nietzsche, recognize its religious character, they are haunted by the fear of being immured in the empirical elements of their being. Thus Dostoevsky's characters are both dominated by and afraid of the impulse that wishes to say that "all things are lawful." Yet in men like Ivan Karamazov and Stavogrin even the most intense resolve on the purely human level to put this principle into practice breaks against the fact that they are spiritually transcendent beings. It is because they will not recognize this that they must be destroyed in the end.

In spite of the prominence given by some existentialists to the negative and destructive role of freedom (which thus becomes an expression of the meaningless), other philosophers are anxious to vindicate the more positive and creative possibilities inherent in the idea. Such is the case with Karl Jaspers who lies much closer to the Kierkegaardian tradition. For him the transcendent movement of the self is expressed through the choice of itself as freedom and the ultimate significance of that freedom cannot be explained in terms of empirical being but only as the expression of an existence which emerges as by a leap.[25] Existence springs only "out of possible existence." Freedom, as the expression of existence, cannot therefore be proved. "Either freedom is not or it is already in the question I ask of it." To enquire passionately about one's freedom is in a sense already to be free.

Yet freedom, in Jaspers, though it has this more positive role, does not lose its tragic significance. Even with regard to myself I must realize that there is in me the possibility of non-freedom. Hence the dread that I experience before choosing myself. I can only be free at the moment of perceiving the possibility of not being free. Moreover the whole notion of existence, though linked with this genuinely transcendental element is also inseparable from the realm of empirical being through which it must always express itself. Because the structure of my personality is rooted in empirical being, I can refuse the choice of myself as existence in the fullest sense and choose myself on the level of the things which that empirical being presupposes. It is this recognition of the dual character of man's existence that explains the dramatic—and even tragic—emphasis of Jaspers' thought. All human situations are really "limiting situations" since they presuppose the essentially dialectical character of true existence, which must be understood as genuine spiritual possibility and at the same time a constituent of the empirical and earthly situation.[26]

Freedom is also important for another reason. Through the act by which I choose myself, my transcendence is also a movement towards the reality of another self. The individual person who has escaped from the stupefying influence of the group and has discovered himself in his passion for the absolute, is led, by the very act which reveals to him the meaning of his own existence, to the simultaneous recognition of the Other as person, as existence—though such an existence can no more be proved than he can prove his own freedom.

Once again we have here a profound divergence on the value of the Other Person. Kierkegaard was not greatly concerned with this problem because the Other was identified absolutely with God. Heidegger has insisted that all being is being-with (*mitsein*). This being-

---

[25] The idea is clearer in German which links "*Sprung*" and "*Ursprung*."
[26] Although Sartre denies the spiritual possibilities of freedom and the act of choice, he is almost obsessed with the idea of being "*englué*" and "*empâté*" in the viscosity of the world. Thus "*la nausée*" is provoked by the consciousness of our own bodies whose facticity constantly threatens to swallow up our human existence—our "*pour-soi*." Similarly (as we shall indicate below) the look of the Other is a look which petrifies me and strips me of my true subjectivity.

with, since it expresses itself as concern, is made concrete as far as other people are concerned under the form of solicitude (*Fürsorge*). It is, however, in Sartre that the idea of the relation to the Other takes on such an important role. His argument, crudely expressed, seems to be this: the reality of the other's subjectivity must be admitted as a basic fact, but it is a fact that is, from my own point of view, fraught with danger. Although I know that the other exists as subject, I must, in my relationship with him, constantly try and put aside that knowledge. I can only constitute myself as subject by reducing the other to the level of object. Yet at the same time the other-as-subject sees me as an object, so that the other-object that I see is also the other-subject who sees me. Now this fact of being seen by the other presents an irreducible reality, which, though unpleasant, is inescapable, because the other's look ever strives to deprive me of myself-as-subject. The other's look, by reducing my subjectivity, abolishes the world of my experience. "Suddenly an object appeared to me that stole from me my world." The evil consequences of the other's appearance is that he strips me of my freedom, for when I am no longer subject I am no longer free. The other is a hostile force striving to disintegrate my reality. "Hell is other people." How then can I escape from this situation? By one way only—by objectifying the other in my turn, by a "riposte" which annihilates the other's subjectivity. This I must do at all costs if I am to preserve my freedom. Such is the origin of the different attitudes and ruses I take in order to elude the objectification the other desires to impose on me. Two persons together are two persons who seek to enslave the other, in order to avoid being enslaved.

Such a situation, however, is, as Sartre recognizes, impossible. I cannot seize the other as subject, because as soon as I present myself as subject he is transformed into object and before his subjectivity likewise I can only present myself as an object incapable of touching it. The other would have to be revealed to me as both subject and object at the same time and this is impossible. "The other person can never be seized; he flees from me when I look for him and possesses me when I flee from him."

The religious branch of existentialism has a different answer and here joins the thinkers like Buber and Berdyaev who have insisted upon the primacy of the relation of self to self—of Thou to Thou as a fundamental and valid form of existence. On their view Sartre's conception would be precisely the sign of inauthentic existence. The evil which seems to reside in the other's existence derives in fact not from the other's existence as such but from my own self which has not achieved a proper inner relationship. I am kept from the other by the evil in myself. This is brought out very well in Gabriel Marcel's analysis of the idea of "unavailability" (*indisponibilité*). My own egocentricity develops within me an opacity which I then direct upon others. "*Etre indisponible*; *être occupé de soi*." This "unavailability" is a tense form of possession. The dread provoked by the thought of myself and my goods as the prey of time causes me to turn jealously inward upon myself, makes me greedy of myself. The other is transformed into someone-who-threatens-my-possessions. Thus the grasping of the other as object is derived in the first place not from the view of myself as freedom, but from an apprehensive "*indisponibilité*" which springs from a false relationship of myself to myself.

If, however, I make myself "available," I become "open" to the world and others. I "lend myself" to them and their influence. Such is the source of a feeling like admiration. I offer myself to a feeling whose purpose is to tear me from the thought of myself. A refusal to admire is a refusal to let myself be "lifted up." The look which in the Sartrian world is "bouleversant" is thus transformed. The other's look disturbs me, but only to deprive me of my egocentric preoccupation and my false loneliness. Far from destroying me, the other's look tears me from the prison of myself.

The absolute and irreducible worth of this relationship expresses itself as a dialogue of one existence with another. The discovery of the Thou is a confirmation, not a suppression, of my own freedom.

The general significance of existentialism was already indicated at the beginning of this paper when it was described as an attempt to reinstate the human personality into philosophical thinking. We will conclude by drawing out rather more precisely the consequences of such a view. Existentialism does not and cannot claim to be a new philosophical system aimed at replacing all others. It is content to insist upon the importance of an element that has often been overlooked—the human person. Although it does not try to supersede all other systems, it nevertheless condemns all merely intellectualist systems which refuse to face the reality of human existence—of the human being in his true situation and in his concrete freedom. Perhaps no philosophy attempted hitherto has made a genuine effort to grapple with this fact. Even the medieval ontologies which attempted to give some place to the individual cannot escape this charge. A vast system like the Thomist seems to treat the individual man merely as a particular case in some kind of doctrine of forms and substances—a doctrine which in its turn (no doubt because it is Aristotle-inspired) rests ultimately upon cosmological presuppositions (however cunningly they may be disguised). On the existentialist view we can never reach a doctrine of man by starting with the idea of matter—skillfully "individuated" though it may be—and this is because man is not merely an individual who seeks to understand an object but one who questions, acts and chooses.

Such an existence will not lend itself to treatment by a logic derived entirely from the idea of man considered merely as a detached observer standing before the world of objects. Man can never be an object in this sense. He is his possibilities and the understanding of such possibilities cannot be separated from the experiencing of them. How then can we ever "know" what they really are? In a strictly intellectual sense we can probably never "know" what they are, but there may be, as Heidegger has very interestingly suggested in his idea of "*Verstehen*," a sense in which we can understand and be aware of our possibilities without being them. Such a comprehension cannot simply be added to existence in order to take stock of its possibilities; nor is it a simple introspective analysis based on the idea of a knowing subject before a knowable object. It is a kind of inner response which follows not what is, but what becomes. It is the existential dynamism of the self, reflecting itself back into the consciousness of the subject, whose attempt at rational elucidation is but the final and weakened termination of a deeper process. We repeat: the grasping of myself as existential being cannot be separated from my existence as such and the comprehension of myself as possibility itself represents an attitude of existence, which in turn determines the way I shall exist. Whether we can integrate such a comprehension into a philosophy whose logic is derived from the observation of natural processes is perhaps a question as yet incapable of resolution. Is the difficulty we here encounter similar to that confronting modern scientists who, after being accustomed through centuries of practice to using certain types of static concepts, now find that they must try and form a new mental picture based on a more dynamic conception of the universe? Or is the type of understanding necessary for a detailed elaboration of a philosophy of existence faced with a difficulty more fundamental still?

THEISM AND PERSONAL RELATIONSHIPS

M. Gabriel Marcel

M. Marcel began by distinguishing sharply between Deism and Theism. In the former one tended to identify God with a system or all-inclusive unity, into which personal relationships would necessarily become merged until they were finally banished. In such a system, if we talk about God, it is no longer about God that we are talking—but only a finite thing, an outsider with regard to individual beings, one to whom we could not pray. This is the difficulty of all theology, that, as in human relationships, it may be a kind of betrayal to speak of someone in the third person, so by *talking about* God we consign him to a limbo of neutral objectivity. To say "I love" implies a "sheer somebody else," or a "Thou," and "thouness" can be asserted of anyone from whom we expect an answer. But whereas this empirical "Thou" relationship is one that could be destroyed by an intruder, or by doubt and distress, a relationship with an "absolute Thou" would be such that to turn "Thou" into the third person would be to reject Him altogether. Thus the basic question of M. Marcel's paper was: "How can we conceive a relation between the 'absolute Thou' and the 'empirical thou'?" To this end he described the nature of a personal relationship as a "being" with a life of itself, which can be protected, bruised, murdered, etc., *not* a connection between separate data, or an effect of which God could be said to be the cause. To relate such a relationship to an Absolute Thou, we must ask if it is what Thou expects from me, and the answer can be mediated to our "deepest self-consciousness" so long as we transcend ourselves, our immediate feelings, and our vanishing consciousness of Him. Thus the obligation implied by the Christian sacrament of marriage, for instance, by which we also bear witness to an absolute Thou, enables us to solve problems, such as pain, separation and death, not soluble in the world of unbelief. In that world, transitory feeling allows no unconditionality; the death of God, the modern idealization of the mass, is also the death of man. In words to which no summary can do justice, M. Marcel concluded by showing how personal relationships could point beyond themselves, from the termitary body to the Christian mystical body; so this question of relationships, which abstract Theism leaves insoluble, can be solved when conceived in the light of the revelation of an absolute "Thou," by which ordinary companionships may be part of a superior unity and become immortal.

A REPLY

In reply to the speaker Dr. L. W. Grensted brought out some of the things which M. Marcel had said, against the larger background of the religious consciousness in general, remarking how this fundamental distinction between the "Thou" and the "It" had been perceived by various widely different thinkers, in relation to whom Kierkegaard was not building a new philosophy, but presenting an alive emphasis which Sartre had perverted into the empty assertion that Being *is* Becoming. Against this he quoted Von Hügel's notion of Being *in* Becoming.

The Discussion

The discussion which followed was long and animated, M. Marcel enlarged upon some of his views with extraordinary vigor and fluency. Among others, the following were some of the most obvious points that emerged: M. Marcel believed that to philosophize is not the same as to make a system; it is a search which only aspires towards some sort of synopsis. He distrusted Thomism and Thomist proofs; he was more Platonist than Aristotelian in that he believed we must get back to a certain notion of essence, not as a mental object, but as a subject, like a light or an enlightening. The President asked whether in regarding a person as aesthetically beautiful we were not turning him into an "It." M. Marcel replied that this was neither "Thou" nor "It," but a kind of contemplation, a state of grace, so that aesthetic experience might even enter into the beatific vision. Fr. F. C. Copleston asked what M. Marcel would reply to a person who said that the world and human relationships were an absurdity. M. Marcel replied that he could not *prove* such a man mistaken, but only *show* him or persuade him in an unphilosophical way. To be a prisoner of objectivity, to confuse it with existence, or even to speak of immortality objectively, seemed to M. Marcel senseless. Finally, in reply to insistent questioning, he said that we can take nothing for granted; we must continually go over the ground of our thought again and again, and confessed that if indeed everybody were to become existentialist, he himself would then be bound to react against it.

THE SCIENTIFIC WORLD OUTLOOK

Dr. F. Sherwood-Taylor

(*A summary, by M. G. Brock, of the meeting held on November 18, 1946*)

A "scientific world outlook," in the speaker's view, implied the making of judgments, of decisions concerning what is to be accepted and what rejected; the actual decision or interpretation implied in an "outlook" could not be a part of science itself, and did not merit the confidence we place in the conclusions of science. The distinguishing features of the data and conclusions of science were the community (they were wholly intelligible to anyone taking the trouble to learn the terms) and their certainty. The conclusions of science represented the most probable deductions from the data employed.

Scientific men tended to construct their world outlook according to the positivist attitude of science. Thus the scientists' world had no conscious metaphysic. The scientists' criterion of success was that his science should *work*. Every stage in an investigation was checked by experiment; there was therefore no absolute dependence on a long chain of reasoning. That was why the scientist was in general so little interested in philosophy: all he wanted was to be able to predict phenomena correctly. "This verification of reasoning by experiment" (said the speaker) "is the backbone of scientific certainty, and where it is impossible, the man of science is very much at sea."

Thus all scientific explanations lead in the end to a question. But the modern scientist is not always so clearly aware of what he does not know, and is apt to think of his worldview as more complete than it really is. The speaker then showed that scientists were usually unwilling to adopt as a hypothesis (until all other explanations failed) the existence of what we might call "a vital principle." Science could only deal with determined sequences of cause and effect: the suggestion that physical determinism could apply in the realm of the mind disregarded our direct experience of free will, which put the onus of proving it illusory on those advancing the theory of physical determinism. The positivistic scientific method led to a choice between materialism and a belief in a principle of mind, additional to the principles of physics and chemistry. The former, materialism, was in no sense *the* scientific outlook, since it dogmatized about questions on which it had no scientific data. The worldviews of scientists were important to us all, since they now advised governments on almost every subject: this advice took two forms: telling the government how to do what it wanted to do, and, secondly, telling it what it should do. The first was the legitimate function of applied science; as to the second, science, being a mere classification and ordering of abstractions from sense impressions, could not possibly say that anything *ought* to be done. But attempts to invent a system of scientific ethics had been made by evolutionists from Herbert Spencer to Julian Huxley. Such systems were now less plausible than forty years ago. The speaker hoped in the next decade to see a different development, a realization by scientists that it was not unscientific to refrain from attempting to apply the scientific method to phenomena which were clearly not susceptible to scientific treatment, namely, the higher levels of human mental activity, the regions of those far-reaching integrations which are found in our aesthetic and ethical judgments. He wanted the same attention to be given to arriving at religious truth by the religious method as was given to arriving at scientific truth by the scientific method. The hope for the world lay in the incorporation of the religious, philosophical and scientific outlooks in a single comprehensive view. This incorporation had not yet been accomplished. The

Christian ideal had become separated from the common outlook, which was today a debased form of the scientific. We needed a synthesis such as had been applied in Western Europe in the thirteenth century, when the Church had embraced the Aristotelian writings, and from which the great system of Catholic theology had resulted.

THE DISCUSSION

Mr. P. Medawar, opening the discussion, touched on some minor joints of disagreement, and then attacked the picture put forward of the scientific materialist. He was confident that there was now no such person. It was the efforts of Dr. Sherwood-Taylor and Mr. C. S. Lewis to prop the corpse up into a sitting position which gave it a semblance of life. In the general discussion which followed there was far from general agreement about this: Mr. Atkins thought some elements of present government planning exemplified scientific materialism. Mr. Mascall suggested that the radical distinction was between the immanentist and transcendental views: according to the first all that matters to man is discoverable in the finite realm. Attempts were made to justify ethics based on a scientific evolutionary approach, without much success, since, as Mr. Medawar said, from the evolutionary point of view pain was unquestionably a good. Dr. Sherwood-Taylor further defined the scientific materialist view as being that which grants only those things to be real which will produce a pointer reading on an instrument. A member said that as soon as religious truth was mentioned he ceased to make contact: he appreciated that such truths were incapable of empirical verification: apart from that he could assign no meaning to religious terms. The Chairman said that, in the Christian metaphysic, there was a radical distinction between types of cognition. Spiritual things were spiritually discerned.

RELIGION WITHOUT DOGMA?

C. S. Lewis

In an important and brilliant paper, read before this society last term, Professor Price maintained the following positions: (1) That the essence of religion is belief in God and immortality; (2) that in most actual religions the essence is found in connection with "accretions of dogma and mythology" which have been rendered incredible by the progress of science; (3) that it would be very desirable, if it were possible, to retain the essence purged of the accretions; but (4) that science has rendered the essence almost as hard to believe as the accretions. For the doctrine of immortality involves the dualistic view that man is a composite creature, a soul in a state of symbiosis with a physical organism. But insofar as science can successfully regard man monistically, as a single organism whose psychological properties all arise from his physical, the soul becomes an indefensible hypothesis. In conclusion, Professor Price found our only hope in certain empirical evidence for the soul which appears to him satisfactory; in fact, in the findings of Psychical Research.

My disagreement with Professor Price begins, I am afraid, at the threshold. I do not define the essence of religion as belief in God and immortality. Judaism in its earlier stages had no belief in immortality, and for a long time no belief which was religiously relevant. The shadowy existence of the ghost in Sheol was one of which Jehovah took no account and which took no account of Jehovah. In Sheol all things are forgotten. The religion was centered on the ritual and ethical demands of Jehovah in the present life, and also, of course, on benefits expected from Him. These benefits are often merely worldly benefits (grandchildren and peace upon Israel), but a more specifically religious note is repeatedly struck. The Jew is athirst for the living God, he delights in His Laws as in honey or treasure, he is conscious of himself in Jehovah's presence as unclean of lips and heart. The glory or splendor of God is worshipped for its own sake. In Buddhism, on the other hand, we find that a doctrine of immortality is central, while there is nothing specifically religious. Salvation from immortality, deliverance from reincarnation, is the very core of its message. The existence of the gods is not necessarily decried, but it is of no religious significance. In Stoicism again both the religious quality and the belief in immortality are variables, but they do not vary in direct ratio. Even within Christianity itself we find a striking expression, not without influence from Stoicism, of the subordinate position of immortality. When Henry More ends a poem on the spiritual life by saying that if, after all, he should turn out to be mortal he would be

> ... satisfied
> A lonesome mortal god to have died.

From my own point of view, the example of Judaism and Buddhism is of immense importance. The system, which is meaningless without a doctrine of immortality, regards immortality as a nightmare, not as a prize. The religion which, of all ancient religions, is most specifically religious, that is, at once most ethical and most numinous, is hardly interested in the question. Believing, as I do, that Jehovah is a real being, indeed the *ens realissimum*,[27] I cannot sufficiently admire the divine tact of thus training the chosen race for centuries in religion before even hinting the shining secret of eternal life. He behaves like the rich lover in a romance who

---

[27] Editor's Note (2012): Latin for "the most real being."

woos the maiden on his own merits, disguised as a poor man, and only when he has won her reveals that he has a throne and palace to offer. For I cannot help thinking that any religion which begins with a thirst for immortality is damned, as a religion, from the outset. Until a certain spiritual level has been reached, the promise of immortality will always operate as a bribe which vitiates the whole religion and infinitely inflames those very self-regards which religion must cut down and uproot. For the essence of religion, in my view, is the thirst for an end higher than natural ends; the finite self's desire for, and acquiescence in, and self-rejection in favor of, an object wholly good and wholly good for it. That the self-rejection will turn out to be also a self-finding, that bread cast upon the waters will be found after many days, that to die is to live—these are sacred paradoxes of which the human race must not be told too soon.

Differing from Professor Price about the essence of religion, I naturally cannot, in a sense, discuss whether the essence as he defines it coexists with accretions of dogma and mythology. But I freely admit that the essence as I define it always coexists with other things; and that some of these other things even I would call mythology. But my list of things mythological would not coincide with his, and our views of mythology itself probably differ. A great many different views on it have, of course, been held. Myths have been accepted as literally true, then as allegorically true (by the Stoics), as confused history (by Euhemerus), as priestly lies (by the philosophers of the enlightenment), as imitative agricultural ritual mistaken for propositions (in the days of Frazer). If you start from a naturalistic philosophy, then something like the view of Euhemerus or the view of Frazer is likely to result. But I am not a naturalist. I believe that in the huge mass of mythology which has come down to us a good many different sources are mixed—true history, allegory, ritual, the human delight in storytellings, etc. But among these sources I include the supernatural, both diabolical and divine. We need here concern ourselves only with the latter. If my religion is erroneous then occurrences of similar motifs in pagan stories are, of course, instances of the same, or a similar error. But if my religion is true, then these stories may well be a *preparatio evangelica*, a divine hinting in poetic and ritual form at the same central truth which was later focused and (so to speak) historicized in the Incarnation. To me, who first approached Christianity from a delighted interest in, and reverence for, the best pagan imagination, who loved Balder before Christ and Plato before St. Augustine, the anthropological argument against Christianity has never been formidable. On the contrary, I could not believe Christianity if I were forced to say that there were a thousand religions in the world of which 999 were pure nonsense and the thousandth (fortunately) true. My conversion, very largely, depended on recognizing Christianity as the completion, the actualization, the entelechy, of something that had never been wholly absent from the mind of man. And I still think that the agnostic argument from similarities between Christianity and paganism works only if you know the answer. If you start by knowing on other grounds that Christianity is false, then the pagan stories may be another nail in its coffin: just as if you started by knowing that there were no such things as crocodiles then the various stories about dragons might help to confirm your disbelief. But if the truth or falsehood of Christianity is the very question you are discussing, then the argument from anthropology is surely a *petitio*.

There are, of course, many things in Christianity which I accept as fact and which Professor Price would regard as mythology. In a word, there are miracles. The contention is that science has proved that miracles cannot occur. According to Professor Price "a Deity who intervened miraculously and suspended natural law could never be accepted by Science"; whence he passes on to consider whether we cannot still believe in Theism without miracles. I am afraid I have not understood why the miracles could never be accepted by one who accepted science.

Professor Price bases his view on the nature of scientific method. He says that that method is based on two assumptions. The first is that all events are subject to laws, and he adds: "It does not matter for our purpose whether the laws are 'deterministic' or only 'statistical.' " But I submit that it matters to the scientist's view of the miraculous. The notion that natural laws may be merely statistical results from the modern belief that the individual unit of matter obeys no laws. Statistics were introduced to explain why, despite the lawlessness of the individual unit, the behavior of gross bodies was regular. The explanation was that, by a principle well known to actuaries, the law of averages leveled out the individual eccentricities of the innumerable units contained in even the smallest gross body. But with this conception of the lawless units the whole impregnability of nineteenth-century Naturalism has, as it seems to me, been abandoned. What is the use of saying that all events are subject to laws if you also say that every event which befalls the individual unit of matter is *not* subject to laws. Indeed, if we define nature as the system of events in space-time governed by interlocking laws, then the new physics has really admitted that something other than nature exists. For if nature means the interlocking system, then the behavior of the individual unit is outside nature. We have admitted what may be called the sub-natural. After that admission what confidence is left us that there may not be a supernatural as well? It may be true that the lawlessness of the little events fed into nature from the sub-natural is always ironed out by the law of averages. It does not follow that great events could not be fed into her by the supernatural: nor that they also would allow themselves to be ironed out.

The second assumption which Professor Price attributes to the scientific method is "that laws can only be discovered by the study of publicly observable regularities." Of course they can. This does not seem to me to be an assumption so much as a self-evident proposition. But what is it to the purpose? If a miracle occurs it is by definition an interruption of regularity. To discover a regularity is by definition not to discover its interruptions, even if they occur. You cannot discover a railway accident from studying Bradshaw: only by being there when it happens or hearing about it afterwards from someone who was. You cannot discover extra half-holidays by studying a school timetable: you must wait till they are announced. But surely this does not mean that a student of Bradshaw is logically forced to deny the possibility of railway accidents. This point of scientific method merely shows (what no one to my knowledge ever denied) that if miracles *did* occur, science, as science, could not prove, or disprove, their occurrence. What cannot be trusted to recur is not material for science: that is why history is not one of the sciences. You cannot find out what Napoleon did at the battle of Austerlitz by asking him to come and fight it again in a laboratory with the same combatants, the same *terrain*, the same weather, and in the same age. You have to go to the records. We have not, in fact, proved that science excludes miracles: we have only proved that the question of miracles, like innumerable other questions, excludes laboratory treatment.

If I thus hand over miracles from science to history (but not, of course, to historians who beg the question by beginning with materialistic assumptions) Professor Price thinks I shall not fare much better. Here I must speak with caution, for I do not profess to be a historian or a textual critic. I would refer you to Sir Arnold Lunn's book *The Third Day*. If Sir Arnold is right, then the Biblical criticism which began in the nineteenth century has already shot its bolt and most of its conclusions have been successfully disputed, though it will, like nineteenth-century materialism, long continue to dominate popular thought. What I can say with more certainty is that that *kind* of criticism—the kind which discovers that every old book was made by six anonymous authors well provided with scissors and paste and that every anecdote of the slightest interest is unhistorical, has already begun to die out in the studies I know best. The period of arbitrary skepticism about the canon and text of Shakespeare is now over: and it is reasonable to expect that this method will soon be used only on Christian documents and survive only in the *Thinkers Library* and the theological colleges.

I find myself, therefore, compelled to disagree with Professor Price's second point. I do not think that science has shown, or, by its nature, could ever show that the miraculous element in religion is erroneous. I am not speaking, of course, about the psychological effects of science on those who practice it or read its results. That the continued application of scientific methods breeds a temper of mind unfavorable to the miraculous, may well be the case, but even here there would seem to be some difference among the sciences. Certainly, if we think, not of the miraculous in particular, but of religion in general there is such a difference. Mathematicians, astronomers and physicists are often religious, even mystical; biologists much less often; economists and psychologists very seldom indeed. It is as their subject matter comes nearer to man himself that their anti-religious bias hardens.

And that brings me to Professor Price's fourth point—for I would rather postpone consideration of his third. His fourth point, it will be remembered, was that science had undermined not only what he regards as its essence. That essence is for him Theism and immortality. Insofar as natural science can give a satisfactory account of man as a purely biological entity, it excludes the soul and therefore excludes immortality. That, no doubt, is why the scientists who are most, or most nearly, concerned with man himself are the most anti-religious.

Now most assuredly if naturalism is right then it is at this point, at the study of man himself, that it wins its final victory and overthrows all our hopes: not only our hope of immortality, but our hope of finding significance in our lives here and now. On the other hand, if naturalism is wrong, it will be here that it will reveal its fatal philosophical defect, and that is what I think it does.

On the fully naturalistic view all events are determined by laws. Our logical behavior, in other words our thoughts, and our ethical behavior, including our ideals as well as our acts of will, are governed by biochemical laws; these, in turn, by physical laws which are themselves actuarial statements about the lawless movements of matter. These units never intended to produce the regular universe we see: the law of averages (successor to Lucretius's *exiguum clinamen*) has produced it out of the collision of these random variations in movement. The physical universe never intended to produce organisms. The relevant chemicals on earth, and the sun's heat, thus juxtaposed, gave rise to this disquieting disease of matter: organization. Natural selection, operating on the minute differences between one organism and another, blundered into that sort of phosphorescence or mirage which we call consciousness—and that, in some cortexes beneath some skulls, at certain moments, still in obedience to physical laws, but to physical laws now filtered through laws of a more complicated kind, takes the form we call thought. Such, for instance, is the origin of this paper: such was the origin of Professor Price's paper. What we should speak of as his "thoughts" were merely the last link of a causal chain in which all the previous links were irrational. He spoke as he did because the matter of his brain was behaving in a certain way: and the whole history of the universe up to that moment had forced it to behave in that way. What we called his thought was essentially a phenomenon of the same sort as his other secretions—the form which the vast irrational process of nature was bound to take at a particular point of space and time.

Of course it did not feel like that to him or to us while it was going on. He appeared to himself to be studying the nature of things, to be in some way aware of realities, even supersensuous realities, outside his own head. But if strict naturalism is right, he was deluded: he was merely enjoying the conscious reflection of irrationally determined events in his own head. It appeared to him that his thoughts (as he called them) could have to outer realities that wholly immaterial relation which we call truth or falsehood: though, in fact, being but the shadow of cerebral events, it is not easy to see that they could have any relation to the outer world except causal relations. And when Professor Price, with an eloquence which I sincerely admire, defended the scientists, speaking of their devotion to truth and their constant following of the best light they knew, it seemed to him that he was choosing an attitude in obedience to an ideal. He did not feel that he was merely suffering a reaction determined by ultimately amoral and irrational sources, and no more capable of rightness or wrongness than a hiccup or a sneeze.

It would have been impossible for Professor Price to have written, or us to have read, his paper with the slightest interest if he and we had consciously held the position of strict naturalism throughout. But we can go further. It would be impossible to accept naturalism itself if we really and consistently believed naturalism. For naturalism is a system of thought. But for naturalism all thoughts are mere events with irrational causes. It is, to me at any rate, impossible to regard the thoughts which make up naturalism in that way and, at same time, to regard them as a real insight into external reality. Bradley distinguished *idea-event* from *idea-making*, but naturalism seems to me committed to regarding ideas simply as events. For meaning is a relation of a wholly new kind, as remote, as mysterious, as opaque to empirical study, as soul itself.

Perhaps this may be even more simply put in another way. Every particular thought (whether it is a judgment of act or a judgment of value) is always and by all men discounted the moment they believe that it can be explained, without remainder, as the result of irrational causes. Whenever you know what the other man is saying is wholly due to his complexes or to a bit of bone pressing on his brain, you cease to attach any importance to it. But if naturalism were true then all thoughts whatever would be wholly the result of irrational causes. Therefore, all thoughts would be equally worthless. Therefore, naturalism is worthless. If it is true, then we can know no truths. It cuts its own throat.

I remember once being shown a certain kind of knot which was such that if you added one extra complication to make assurance doubly sure you suddenly found that the whole thing had come undone in your hands and you had only a bit of string. It is like that with naturalism. It goes on claiming territory after territory: first the inorganic, then the lower organisms, then man's body, then his emotions. But when it takes the final step and we attempt a naturalistic account of thought itself, suddenly the whole thing unravels. The last fatal step has invalidated all the preceding ones: for they were all reasonings and reason itself has been discredited. We must, therefore, either give up thinking altogether or else begin over again from the ground floor.

There is no reason, at this point, to bring in either Christianity or spiritualism. We do not need them to refute naturalism. It refutes itself. Whatever else we may come to believe about the universe, at least we cannot believe naturalism. The validity of rational thought, accepted in an utterly non-naturalistic, transcendental (if you will), supernatural sense, is the necessary presupposition of all other theorizing. There is simply no sense in beginning with a view of the universe and trying to fit the claims of thought in at a later stage. By thinking at all we have claimed that our thoughts are more than mere natural events. All other propositions must be fitted in as best they can round that primary claim.

Holding that science has not refuted the miraculous element in religion, much less that naturalism, rigorously taken, can refute anything except itself, I do not, of course, share Professor Price's anxiety to find a religion which can do without what he calls mythology. What he suggests is simple Theism, rendered credible by a belief in immortality which in its turn is guaranteed by Psychical Research. Professor Price is not, of course, arguing that immortality would of itself prove Theism: it would merely remove an obstacle to Theism. The positive source of Theism he finds in religious experience.

At this point it is very important to decide which of two questions we are asking. We may be asking: (1) whether this purged minimal religion suggested by Professor Price is capable, as a historical, social and psychological entity, of giving fresh heart to society, strengthening the moral will, and producing all those other benefits which, it is claimed, the old religions have sometimes produced. On the other hand, we may be asking: (2) whether this minimal religion will be the true one; that is, whether it contains the only true propositions we can make about ultimate questions.

The first question is not a religious question but a sociological one. The religious mind as such, like the older sort of scientific mind as such, does not care a rap about socially useful propositions. Both are athirst for reality, for the utterly objective, for that which is what it is. The "open mind" of the scientist and the emptied and silenced mind of the mystic are both efforts to eliminate what is our own in order that the Other may speak. And if, turning aside from the religious attitude, we speak for a moment as mere sociologists, we must admit that history does not encourage us to expect much invigorating power in a minimal religion. Attempts at such a minimal religion are not new—from Akhenaton and Julian the Apostate down to Lord Herbert of Cherbury and the late H. G. Wells. But where are the saints, the consolations, the ecstacies? The greatest of such attempts was that simplification of Jewish and Christian traditions which we call Islam. But it retained many elements which Professor Price would regard as mythical and barbaric: and its culture is by no means one of the richest or most progressive.

Nor do I see how such a religion, if it became a vital force, would long be preserved in its freedom from dogma. Is its God to be conceived pantheistically, or after the Jewish, Platonic, Christian fashion? If we are to retain the minimal religion in all its purity, I suppose the right answer would be: "We don't know, and we must be content not to know." But that is the end of the minimal religion as a practical affair. For the question is of pressing practical importance. If the God of Professor Price's religion is an impersonal spirituality diffused through the whole universe, equally present, and present in the same mode, at all points of space and time, then He—or it—will certainly be conceived as being beyond good and evil, expressed equally in the brothel or the torture chamber and in the model factory or the university common room. If, on the other hand, He is a personal Being standing outside His creation, commanding this and prohibiting that, quite different consequences follow. The choice between these two views affects the choice between courses of action at every moment both in private and public life. Nor is this the only such question that arises. Does the minimal religion know whether its god stands in the same relation to all men, or is he related to some as he is not related to others? To be true to its undogmatic character it must again say: "Don't ask." But if that is the reply, then the minimal religion cannot exclude the Christian view that He was present in a special way in Jesus, nor the Nazi view that He is present in a special way in the German race, nor the Hindu view that

He is specially present in the Brahmin, nor the central African view that He is specially present in the thigh bone of a dead English Tommy.

All these difficulties are concealed from us as long as the minimal religion exists only on paper. But suppose it were somehow established all over what is left of the British Empire, and let us suppose that Professor Price has (most reluctantly and solely from a sense of duty) become its supreme head on earth. I predict that one of two things must happen: (1) In the first month of his reign he will find himself uttering his first dogmatic definition—he will find himself saying, for example: "No. God is not an amoral force diffused through the whole universe to whom suttee and temple prostitution are no more and no less acceptable than building hospitals and teaching children; he is a righteous creator, separate from his creation, who demands of you justice and mercy" or (2) Professor Price will not reply. In the second case is it not clear what will happen? Those who have come to his minimal religion from Christianity will conceive God in the Jewish, Platonic, Christian way; those who have come from Hinduism will conceive Him pantheistically; and the plain men who have come from nowhere will conceive Him as a righteous Creator in their moments of moral indignation, and as a Pantheistic God in their moments of self-indulgence. And the ex-Marxist will think He is specially present in the Proletariat, and the ex-Nazi will think He is specially present in the German people. And they will hold world conferences at which they all speak the same language and reach the most edifying agreement: but they will all mean totally different things. The minimal religion in fact cannot, while it remains minimal, be acted on. As soon as you do anything you have assumed one of the dogmas. In practice it will not be a religion at all; it will be merely a new coloring given to all the different things people were doing already.

I submit it to Professor Price, with great respect, that when he spoke of mere Theism, he was all the time unconsciously assuming a particular conception of God: that is, he was assuming a dogma about God. And I do not think he was deducing it solely, or chiefly from his own religious experience or even from a study of religious experience in general. For religious experience can be made to yield almost any sort of God. I think Professor Price assumed a certain sort of God because he has been brought up in a certain way: because Bishop Butler and Hooker and Thomas Aquinas and Augustine and St. Paul and Christ and Aristotle and Plato are, as we say, "in his blood." He was not really starting from scratch. Had he done so, had God meant in his mind a being about whom no dogma whatever is held, I doubt whether he would have looked for even social salvation in such an empty concept. All the strength and value of the minimal religion, for him as for all others who accept it, is derived not from it, but from the tradition which he imports into it.

The minimal religion will, in my opinion, leave us all doing what we were doing before. Now it, in itself, will not be an objection from Professor Price's point of view. He was not working for unity, but for some spiritual dynamism to see us through the black night of civilization. If Psychical Research has the effect of enabling people to continue, or to return to, all the diverse religions which naturalism has threatened, and if they can thus get power and hope and discipline, he will, I fancy, be content. But the trouble is that if this minimal religion leaves Buddhists still Buddhists, and Nazis still Nazis, then it will, I believe, leave us—as Western, mechanized, democratic, secularized men—exactly where we were. In what way will a belief in the immortality vouched for by Psychical Research, and in an unknown God, restore to us the virtue and energy of our ancestors? It seems to me that both beliefs, unless reinforced by something else, will be to modern man very shadowy and inoperative. If indeed we knew that God were righteous, that He had purposes for us, that He was the leader in a cosmic battle and that some real issue hung on our conduct in the field, then it would be something to the purpose. Or if, again, the utterances which purport to come from the other world ever had the accent which really *suggests* another world, ever spoke (as even the inferior actual religions do) with that voice before which our mortal nature trembles with awe or joy, then that also would be to the purpose. But the god of minimal Theism remains powerless to excite either fear or love: can be given power to do so only from those traditional resources to which, in Professor Price's conception, science will never permit our return. As for the utterances of the mediums ... I do not wish to be offensive. But will even the most convinced spiritualist claim that one sentence from that source has ever taken its place among the golden sayings of mankind, has ever approached (much less equaled) in power to elevate, strengthen or correct even the second rank of such sayings? Will anyone deny that the vast majority of spirit messages sink pitiably below the best that has been thought and said even in this world?—That in most of them we find a banality and provincialism, a paradoxical union of the prim with the enthusiastic, of flatness and gush, which would suggest that the souls of the moderately respectable are in the keeping of Annie Besant and Martin Tupper?

I am not arguing from the vulgarity of the messages that their claim to come from the dead is false. If I did the spiritualist would reply that this quality is due to imperfections in the medium of communication. Let it be so. We are not here discussing the truth of spiritualism, but its power to become the starting point of a religion. And for that purpose I submit that the poverty of its contents disqualifies it. A minimal religion compounded of spirit messages and bare Theism has no power to touch any of the deepest chords in our nature, or to evoke any response which will raise us even to a higher secular level—let alone to the spiritual life. The god of whom no dogmas are believed is a mere shadow. He will not produce that fear of the Lord in which wisdom begins, and, therefore, will not produce that love in which it is consummated. The immortality which the messages suggest can produce in mediocre spirits only a vague comfort for our unredeemedly personal hankerings, a shadowy sequel to the story of this world in which all comes right (but right in how pitiable a sense!), while the more spiritual will feel that it has added a new horror to death—the horror of mere endless succession, of indefinite imprisonment in that which binds us all, *das Gemeine*. There is in this minimal religion nothing that can convince, convert, or (in the higher sense) console; nothing, therefore, which can restore vitality to our civilization. It is not costly enough. It can never be a controller or even a rival to our natural sloth and greed. A flag, a song, an old school tie, is stronger than it: much more, the pagan religions. Rather than pin my hopes on it I would almost listen again to the drumbeat in my blood (for the blood is at least in some sense the life) and join in the song of the Maenads:

> Happy they whom the Daimons
> Have befriended, who have entered
> The divine orgies, making holy
> Their life-days, till the dance throbs
> In their heartbeats, while they romp with
> Dionysus on the mountains ...

Yes, almost; almost I'd sooner be a pagan suckled in a creed outworn.

Almost, but not, of course, quite. If one is forced to such an alternative, it is perhaps better to starve in a wholly secularized and meaningless universe than to recall the obscenities and cruelties of paganism. They attract because they are a distortion of the truth, and therefore, retain some of its flavor. But with this remark I have passed into our second question. I shall not be expected at the end of this paper to begin an apologetic for the truth of Christianity. I will only say something which in one form or another I have said perhaps too often already. If there is no God then we have no interest in the minimal religion or any other. We will not make a lie even to save civilization. But if there is, then it is so probable as to be almost axiomatic that the initiative lies wholly on His side. If He can be known it will be by self-revelation on His part, not by speculation on ours. We, therefore, look for Him where it is claimed that He has revealed Himself by miracle, by inspired teachers, by enjoined ritual. The traditions conflict, yet the longer and more sympathetically we study them the more we become aware of a common element in many of them: the theme of sacrifice, of rebirth, of redemption, is too clear to escape notice. We are fully entitled to use moral and intellectual criticism. What we are not, in my opinion, entitled to do is simply to abstract the ethical element and set that up as a religion on its own. Rather in that tradition which is at once more completely ethical and most transcends mere ethics—in which the old themes of the sacrifice and rebirth recur in a form which transcends, though there it no longer revolts, our conscience and our reason—we may still most reasonably believe that we have the consummation of all religion, the fullest message from the wholly other, the living creator, who, if He is at all, must be the God not only of the philosophers, but of mystics and savages, not only of the head and heart, but also of the primitive emotions and the spiritual heights beyond all emotion. We may still reasonably attach ourselves to the Church, to the only concrete organization which has preserved down to this present time the core of all the messages, pagan and perhaps pre-pagan, that have ever come from beyond the world, and begin to practice the only religion which rests not upon some selection of certain supposedly "higher" elements in our nature, but on the shattering and rebuilding, the death and rebirth, of that nature in every part: neither Greek nor Jew nor barbarian, but a new creation.

REPLY

Professor H. H. Price

As Mr. C. S. Lewis has done me the great honor of criticizing, in detail, a paper which I once read to this Society, I hope you will forgive me if I reply at some length. But however long my reply was, it could not deal adequately with all the points which he has raised. I shall, therefore, confine myself to five of them. The first concerns immortality: the second, mythology: the third, Psychical Research: the fourth, the self-refutation of Rationalism: and the fifth and most important, the alleged insufficiency of "Minimal Religion." I should like to confess at once that I speak as one who gropes rather than as one who sees. If I sometimes appear dogmatic, it is only for reasons of brevity. I certainly do not feel so. The only thing I feel quite sure about is that all these matters are as important as they are difficult.

1. Is the Belief in Immortality Essential to Religion?

Mr. Lewis quotes two instances in support of the view that it is not[28]: early Judaism, and Buddhism (I fancy he is thinking mainly of the Southern or Hinayana version of Buddhism). Now perhaps what is really essential to religion is something less determinate than a belief in immortality: perhaps it is what is called a belief in the *conservation of values*. But it would appear that the only things in the universe which have either value or disvalue are the acts and

---

[28] Editor's Note (2012): That is, that belief in immortality is not essential to religion.

experiences of living beings and perhaps only the acts and experiences of intelligent beings. If so, it is difficult to see how values can be conserved, unless the beings to which they attach are also conserved.

How then did the primitive Jews continue to believe in the conservation of values without believing in human immortality? I answer, because of their ignorance of science. They believed in what I might call the immortality of the human race, or at any rate in the immortality of the Chosen People. It did not occur to them that the immortality of the human race as a whole might one day cease to exist, because this planet will one day become too cold for complicated organisms to live on it. But in fact there are very strong reasons for thinking that it will cease to exist. Thus they could only afford to disbelieve in personal immortality because they were mistaken about the empirical facts.

As for Buddhism: it is true that in a sense it believes in personal immortality, but regards it as an evil. But that is not the whole story. What it regards as an evil is mere endless continuance in time: the weary whirl of one life after another, some in this world and some in other non-physical worlds. But it regards *Nirvana* as a good, indeed as the highest good. Now I would not like to say dogmatically what the word *Nirvana* means. But it *seems* to mean a state of Being to which the notion of time does not apply, and in which the dualisms we are accustomed to in this life—the dualism of subject and object above all—are somehow abolished. Now whatever this state is, two things seem to be fairly clear about it: first, it is an experience of some kind, even though ordinary language can only describe it in negations: secondly, it is an experience which an *embodied* human being cannot enjoy in its fullness, even though it would be said (as in other mystical religions) that one or two embodied human beings can have an occasional foretaste of it. It is, therefore, essential to Buddhism to maintain that experiences can occur apart from the physical body and brain. This is essential not only to its conception of evil, but also to its conception of good. If you like, it says that there are two sorts of immortality, one which is the greatest evil, and one which is the greatest good. The problem which it professes to solve is how to pass from one sort of immortality to the other. But if we do not survive death at all, as the European Materialist assumes that we do not, there would be no problem to be solved, and the notion of *Nirvana* would make no sense.

I do stick to it, then, that the Apostle was right when he said, "Here have we no continuing city, but we seek one to come"; although the different religions of the world have the most various conceptions of what the "city to come" is like. It seems to me that unless human personality in *some* sense survives bodily death, the universe is indifferent to values altogether (as, of course, the modern agnostic thinks it is). And if it is thus indifferent, then Theism must be false.

2. Mythology

I admit that in my paper I used this word in a loose and popular sense. I was speaking the language of the people whose view I was trying to state. They mean by "mythology," "traditional stories which there is no reason to believe." In other words, they use the term in a dislogistic sense. But, of course, we may use it in a merely descriptive sense, without any depreciation—or laudatory—implication. Let us adopt this usage by all means. We have no right to condemn these stories as mere moonshine without examination.

As a matter of fact, my own view about mythology is very much like Mr. Lewis's, though he has far more right to talk about the subject that I have, since he has studied it closely and I have not. I should be disposed to divide the existing body of mythology into many different strands or strata, as he does. To some parts, I dare say, the Euhemeristic explanation applies. Other parts may be adequately accounted for by the natural human love of tall stories (though it would be interesting to ask why we have this love of tall stories—why in other words the ordinary humdrum everyday world dissatisfies us). Still other parts appear to me, as a student of Psychical Research, to be based upon supernormal experiences which primitive people actually did have, or supernormal happenings which they mutually witnessed—though I dare say they improved them a little in the telling. Clairvoyance, precognition, and telepathy—including the experience of telepathic apparitions, even public ones—are things which do happen. The haunting of a place by a localized apparition (the "ghost" of popular speech) is another thing which does happen, though we are not bound to accept the Spiritualistic interpretation of it. Many of the stories of witchcraft which have come down to us seem to me somewhat distorted and misinterpreted accounts of what we should now call mediumistic phenomena. Perhaps such phenomena were more frequent in primitive people than they are among ourselves; the barrier between the conscious and the unconscious parts of the mind may have been weaker in them than it is in us. Furthermore, at least some of the events commonly called miraculous (and all religious traditions contain reports of them) may have been perfectly genuine supernormal occurrences: not breaches of the laws of nature, but instances of laws which at present we understand very little or not at all.

Finally, the total body of Mythology contains what I may call a *quasi-theological* stratum, and I suppose this is the one which chiefly interests Mr. Lewis. I agree with him in thinking that it is to be taken seriously. But by this I do not mean that it is to be taken *literally* (and I don't suppose that he does either). I think that we should apply the same sort of methods of interpretation to it as Psychotherapists apply to dreams: I do not mean Freud's methods of interpretation only, though these do have their value, but rather those of Jung and his school. Myths of *this* sort I take to be symbolic expressions of the unconscious—whatever exactly we mean by that—just as dreams are. (It seems to me that the natural language of the unconscious is symbolic rather than literal). Now, of course, there is much in the unconscious which is far from edifying. But along with this, and mixed up with it in a perplexing way, there may be insights which our ordinary waking consciousness cannot attain to. I am quite prepared to believe that we are "wiser than we know," however silly that statement may sound: though it may also be true that we are more cruel and more selfish than we know. I will, therefore, go as far as this with Mr. Lewis: I do think that the study of dreams is a serious and not a trivial occupation. By the study of myths we may hope to learn something which it is very important for us to know: something about the more obscure recesses of the human mind to begin with, and perhaps also something about the universe. For we must not assume that the bodily sense organs are necessarily our only source of information about the universe. It may be that in some respects they put blinkers on us, so to speak, by limiting our conscious attention to the physical world which surrounds us. And it may be that there is some deeper layer in our personality which is free from the limitations they impose, and which is in touch with some departments of the universe to which our normal waking consciousness has no access.

3. THE RELEVANCE OF PSYCHICAL RESEARCH

I do think that Mr. Lewis has been a little unfair to me over this; or perhaps it is my own fault for not making myself clear. He seems to equate Psychical Research with Spiritualism; and he seems to think that every Psychical Researcher must believe in the literal truth of mediumistic communications about the next world. This is rather like saying that every astronomer must believe in astrology, on the ground that astronomers, like astrologers, are interested in the movements of the planets. Spiritualism is a creed, or even a church. Psychical Research is *not* a creed, still less a church! It is the scientific enquiry into *prima facie* supernormal phenomena. It is not committed to any particular *conclusion* about them (as the Spiritualist is). Its aim is simply to investigate them in as objective a manner as possible. First it has to ascertain which of them are genuinely supernormal, when the effects of fraud, credulity, and careless observation have been discounted. And then it has to devise a hypothesis which will explain these genuinely supernormal occurrences, and test this hypothesis by further observation and when possible by experiment. Among these genuinely supernormal phenomena, mediumistic phenomena are, of course, included. They do happen, and they do need an explanation. The Spiritualists have an explanation, but it is not necessarily the right one. Indeed, in many cases it is a most unplausible one, if only because the Spiritualists tend to ignore the well-established facts of abnormal psychology. It by no means follows that the study of mediumistic phenomena, including alleged communications from the next world, may not yield valuable material to the student of the human mind, and even to the student of an even more obscure subject, the relation between the human mind and the human body. But anyway, even if there were no mediumistic phenomena, there would be plenty of subjects for the Psychical Researcher to study: for example, Telepathy, Clairvoyance, Precognition, Apparitions. Now the claim I made was that these phenomena (for whose existence there is a good deal of evidence) are very damaging indeed to the materialistic conception of human personality. They are things which *ought* not to occur at all in a materialistic universe; and yet they do occur. Now if we consider the historical situation in which we are, it does appear to me that the materialistic conception of the human personality is the greatest obstacle to religious belief in the minds of educated people. And if Psychical Research—I say Psychical Research, not Spiritualism—can help to remove that obstacle, as I believe it can, religious persons (indeed all persons who have the welfare of our civilization at heart) ought to take Psychical Research seriously. To the Orthodox, Spiritualism naturally appears as an enemy; for it is a creed, as I have said, and a different creed from their own. But Psychical Research, which is a science, though only an infant science as yet, should appear as a friend. If they but knew it, it is almost the only friend they have left in this hostile and materialistic age.

4. THE SELF-REFUTATION OF NATURALISM

This brings me to my next point. Mr. Lewis thinks that Religion does not need this particular ally, because Naturalism—that is the Naturalistic or Materialistic conception of human personality—refutes itself anyway. He uses against it an argument drawn from the theory of knowledge. If Naturalism was true, he says, there could be no rational thinking at all; indeed, there would not be any sense in saying that anyone's thoughts were true or (I suppose) false either. And thus if Naturalism were true, there could be no reason for believing it; indeed the very phrase "reason for" would be without meaning.

Now I admit the force of this argument; indeed, I mentioned it myself in the paper. But I think it is primarily an argument against Materialistic Determinism. And so far as I can see, the Materialist might abandon this part of his doctrine (the part which says that the course of our thoughts is wholly explainable by physical causes), and yet retain other parts. He might maintain that the integrity and healthy functioning of the brain and nervous system is an *indispensable condition* of every occurrence of thought, even though the specific course which our thoughts take is not determined in detail by physical causes. Suppose he did maintain this. Would not experience, on the face of it, support him? However rational I am, I cannot follow a complicated mathematical argument if I am in a state of complete physical exhaustion, nor when I am about to faint, and still less when I have fainted altogether. And, therefore (it might be argued), if my brain were completely destroyed, I could not think at all. Equally, of course, it may be argued, that I could not then perceive or remember. And if so, would not my consciousness have been annihilated altogether? It seems to me that so long as we confine ourselves to the facts of normal experience (among which, of course, rational thinking is to be included) this conclusion is very difficult to escape.

I think then that Mr. Lewis' argument, the argument from the possibility of rational thinking, does *not* show that consciousness can exist apart from the body; whereas some of the supernormal phenomena suggest (I do not say prove) that it can.

5. The Alleged Insufficiency of "Minimal Religion"

I think that Mr. Lewis's discussion of this point is the most important part of his paper; and I admit that his arguments shake me a good deal. I do not pretend that I can produce a "knockdown" answer to them. Far from it! But I will try to mention some considerations which seem to me relevant.

Mr. Lewis rightly says that we must distinguish sharply between two questions: one concerns the truth or falsity of the tenets of "Minimal Religion" or "Bare Theism"; the other concerns its psychological efficacy—its power to influence human will and emotion. Mr. Lewis does not say much about the first question, because he would himself agree that the tenets of "Bare Theism" are true, though he thinks they are far from being the whole truth. He agrees that there is a Supreme Being or *Ens Realissimum* upon whom all finite beings unilaterally depend; and he believes in human immortality. But, he says, these beliefs by themselves—however true—have very little power to influence feeling or conduct. A flag, a song, even the Old School Tie, have more psychological efficacy than they have. Like Pascal, he prefers the God of Abraham, Isaac and Jacob to the *Dieu des philosophes et des savants*. To use another terminology: he thinks that revealed religion (in all its forms, Christian and non-Christian) has a psychological power which the thin and watery abstractions of Natural Religion entirely lack: a power for good—and also, I suppose, for evil. (The advocates of Minimal Religion are not going to persecute anybody, or start any religious wars.)

Now I am afraid that as a matter of Psychology this contention is almost entirely right. Indeed, I said something of the sort myself in my own paper. I am afraid that it is very difficult indeed for any religion to establish itself in the human heart unless it gathers round itself a pretty large body of accretions in the way of dogmas, stories, and—I would add—rituals. (I think that Mr. Lewis might well have said more about ritual than he did). That is why the Quakers and the Unitarians, both of whom try to reduce the accretions to a minimum, are far less numerous than the Catholics or the Greek Orthodox or the Anglicans: and I think they always will be.

What is to be done about this? The only answer I can think of is—toleration. What a dull and flat word that is! In these days, as in the sixteenth and seventeenth centuries, it is thought by many, that unless you are prepared to persecute those who differ from you, you cannot yourself be really sincere in what you believe. And others, who would not go as far as that, nevertheless insist that if you really do believe such and such a dogma, you are logically committed to concluding that the other fellow, who does not believe it, is mistaken.

Now I do not think the issue is really so simple as this. I am not sure that the word "belief" is really the right one to use in this connection—that is, in connection with the dogmas, stories and myths which I called inessential ones. Of course, many people certainly do believe them. But I wonder whether the psychological power which these dogmas and stories (for example, the dogma of the Immaculate Conception) are found to have, really comes from the *believing* of them or from something else—from some other mental attitude which is usually, but not necessarily, *accompanied* by belief. To put my suggestion positively: what is psychologically important is not whether you assent to an idea, but whether your thoughts dwell on it, whether you keep it constantly before your mind. If you do keep it constantly before your mind, it will affect your emotions and your conduct; if you don't, it will not—however much you may assent to it when you get up and recite the creed on Sundays. To put the same thing another way, what is psychologically important is *not* what you assent to, but what you *meditate upon* (cf. the spiritual exercises of St. Ignatius. He also points out the importance of *visual* imagery in this connection). In a civilization such as our own Northern European one, trained for three centuries in the matter-of-fact accuracy which scientific method requires, it is difficult to meditate upon an idea unless you also believe it to be literally true. But I doubt whether this has always been so, or whether it is so now in other civilizations than ours; I doubt whether Hindus or even Southern Europeans have the same difficulty as we do; and in any case I do not think it is so *necessary* that meditating upon an idea, or dwelling upon it in thought should be accompanied by assent. I think that *suspension of dissent* is all that is required.

I am well aware that what I have just been saying sounds idiotic. Imagine a man getting up and saying, "My dogmas are A, B, and C, but I don't believe any of them!" And, of course, if there *is* anything in what I have been suggesting, "dogma" will not be the appropriate word to apply to these ideas. For by the word "dogma" we do commonly mean something which a certain set of people believe. A better phrase would be "secondary theological ideas"—secondary as opposed to the primary ones, which make up the content of Minimal Theism.

However that may be, the point I am coming to is this:—there is no reason why the secondary theological ideas which A's mind dwells upon should not differ in many respects from those which B's mind dwells upon. So far as *these* ideas go, there is room for all sorts of theology in the world. How then are we to choose between them, since it is not a matter of truth or falsehood? It is so tempting to answer, "Choose the ones which suit you best, in view of your temperament and your upbringing." In most periods of history (though not perhaps in this age of unsettlement) they would be the ideas commonly used for this purpose in one's own time and country. But I do not think this answer is quite sufficient by itself; it will not meet the point which Mr. Lewis has made about the creed of the Nazis or other bloodthirsty persons. I think therefore that we must also bear in mind the saying in the Gospel, "By their fruits ye shall know them." As I have remarked before, the psychological power which such ideas have may be a power for evil as well as for good. Persecutions and religious wars, as well as charity and saintliness, come from this source. The criterion we must use, for judging these secondary theological ideas is the effect they have for good or evil upon the minds of those who harbor them. I do not mean merely the effect they have on people's *actions*; of course that is important, but it is not the most important thing. The "fruits" that we must look to in the first place are inward rather than outward. I do not know how to describe them except by the vague phrase "increase in spirituality" or "spiritual growth." Horrid phrases, certainly! A shudder goes down one's spine when one pronounces them. Nevertheless, I think they do stand for something real. Perhaps a better way of putting it would be this:—the reason why we need these secondary theological ideas at all is to train a certain faculty which is present in everyone, but in most people is dormant: the faculty for direct and firsthand consciousness of the Divine (perhaps—but I am not sure—it is this faculty which Quakers call the "Inner Light"). Somehow or other, we have to remove the obstructions and distractions and inhibitions which prevent this faculty from operating in us. By dwelling in thought upon these dogmas, myths, and stories—and also by performing ritual acts of various kinds which are associated with them—we may hope to remove the barriers and obstructions which, as it were, veil this inner light. That is why these secondary theological ideas, as I have called them, are needed. But provided they really do perform the psychological function required of them, it does not greatly matter what they are. There may be ever so many roads up the mountain, and yet they may all meet at the top. Choose the one which suits you, but do not despise the man who chooses a different one, and do not think that yours is the only right one and all the others are wrong. Of course some of the others may be wrong. I think myself that they are; but they are wrong not in themselves, but simply because they lead in the wrong direction. For example, the secondary theological ideas chosen by the Nazi are wrong because they do not in fact have the required effect. They promote a decrease, not an increase in spirituality. Instead of removing the obstructions which prevent our spiritual faculties from working, they add fresh obstructions to those which existed before.

    My tentative conclusion then is this. The tenets of Minimal Religion or bare Theism *are* insufficient, as Mr. Lewis says. They do need to be supplemented by something else. But the insufficiency, in my view, is psychological rather than metaphysical (whereas Mr. Lewis thinks that they are insufficient in both ways). They need to be supplemented by a body of what I have called secondary theological ideas and perhaps by ritual observances also. But the important thing about these secondary ideas is not that they should be believed or assented to, but rather that they should be meditated upon. Their function is pedagogical: it is a matter of what the Germans call Psychotechnics rather than of Metaphysics. By dwelling upon them in thought, and by directing our emotions upon them, we may hope to liberate the faculty of direct spiritual experience which is present in us all. It follows that within quite wide limits, many different systems of secondary theological ideas are possible, and anyone is free—within those limits—to choose the ones which suit him best. There are many different roads, although there is one goal. The only limitation in our choice is that we must choose a road which really does lead there. With the tenets of Theism itself, however, the situation is different. They are not optional, in the way the secondary theological ideas are. They are concerned not with the roads, but with the goal. Indeed, they define the goal itself, so far as the limitations of human thought and language permit.

THE DEITY OF CHRIST

PRINCIPAL NICOL CROSS AND REV. T. M. PARKER

(A summary, by M. G. Brock, of the meeting held on November 11, 1946)

After some introductory remarks on his own position as a Unitarian—a creed sometimes defined as "one God, no devil, and twenty shillings in the pound"—Principal Nicol Cross asked for a reexamination of existing beliefs. Theological heresy had always been part of the Divine method of illumination and salvation. First, the doctrine of the Deity of Christ must not be confused with that of His Divinity, the latter being a quality attributable to angels, and in a sense to men. Secondly, he must allude to the "vulgar nonsense" that "a man who said the things that Jesus said, and was not God would be either a lunatic or a devil." This represented such a simplification of the possibilities as only a naïve person could perpetrate, who combined a triple ignorance of New Testament criticism, of psychology, and of elementary logic.

The speaker started his examination by alluding to the doctrine of the Virgin Birth. It was not found in Mark nor in Paul. In Hellenistic circles the idea was not unknown. There was a climate of legend, superstition and credulity which gravely discounts alleged evidence. If Mary knew that Jesus was begotten of God the whole significance of the *mater dolorosa* theme was destroyed. The silences of Paul and the author of the Fourth Gospel are especially significant. Similar supernatural stories were told of Buddha's birth. To apply a biological analogy, the cross between one species and another produced neither but a *tertium quid*.

Turning to the Resurrection, the speaker asked why Christ's appearance after death was confined to Christian circles. If one were in the position of doubting Thomas, Christ himself was partly to blame. The appearance on the Damascus road to Paul fell into the subjective category. Principal Nicol Cross could not accept the account of the Ascension: were we to believe that the first and third persons of the Trinity were pure spirit, while the second was different and retained some sort of body? The whole story must be taken metaphorically and symbolically: literally believed, it was the same as the belief in personal devils or a devil, to which Archbishop Temple (followed by the Methodists up Manchester way) had so lamentably adhered. The bulk of the New Testament miracles were such as would have been expected of a Messiah, as they were of Moses, Elijah and Daniel. Only in the late Fourth Gospel is the striking miracle of raising from the dead performed.

The palpable contradictions between the meaning of the word God and the facts of Jesus' life were sometimes avoided through recourse to the doctrine of κένωσις. This doctrine was sheer self-contradiction: *credo quia absurdum*.[29] The evidence for Christ's perfection throughout his life was inadequate. Appealing to his followers was asking a packed jury. What about the impression he made on the priests and Pharisees? The historical element in the Gospels was inextricably mixed with the writers' interpretations, set forth for apologetic propaganda and dogmatic purposes.

Obviously the primary conception of Jesus in the apostolic period was that of the promised Messiah. Even the mystical unity between Christ and God in the Fourth Gospel is not identity: the Logos is not God any more than the sun's light is the sun. Naturally in a world which deified its emperors a process of idealization and deification ensued, as it did in Buddha's case.

---

[29] Editor's Note (2012): Latin for "I believe because it's absurd."

If Christ were God, why did he not so declare himself, unequivocally? The doctrine, by making the crucifixion a predestined event, took all the human reality and heroism from the story. You could not run humanity and deity in the same harness. The authority for Christ's deity was not the Bible, but the Church, which had been proved erroneous in the doctrine again and again. The speaker preferred to agree with the Liberal Modernist school of Anglicans, such as Bishop Barnes, that Christ has the "value" of God. His conclusion was that the New Testament evidence was ambiguous, the bias being not towards the deity, but the Messiahship of Christ.

THE DISCUSSION

The discussion was opened by the Rev. T. M. Parker. He said that Christians often fell short of full orthodoxy through not sufficiently examining their faith: he agreed as to the value of heresies, which had often compelled the Church to think out and define her Faith more clearly. Principal Cross had attacked several doctrines which were not those accepted by the Church and which the speaker would not dream of holding. The Virgin Birth was not intended as a proof of Christ's Deity. Godhead cannot be created: Christ's Godhead was not the result of the action of the Holy Ghost upon Mary. The view of the Ascension as Principal Cross had expounded it was Appollinarian, rejected by the Church in the fourth century. Nor were Godhead and manhood two terms which could be put side by side as if they were alternatives. Kenoticism was not a widely held doctrine. The belief in a personal devil had been held by the vast majority of Christian writers: it was not a horrifying belief: as one of the early fathers said, the devil was like a chained dog: it was your own fault if you were bitten.

There were further errors of fact in the paper: the Damascus road vision was perceived in some sense by others than Paul: the story of the widow's son of Nain refuted Principal Cross' statement that there was no raising of the dead recorded before the Fourth Gospel; and what could be the meaning of "Before Abraham was, I am," unless the Fourth Evangelist had believed the Logos to *be* God? Reason could only establish the probability of Christ's Godhead. The principal counter-argument he would bring would be that from Jewish Monotheism. It was from that tradition that the first assertions of Jesus' deity grew. Was there any other explanation possible of this than that it was the result of an overwhelming experience which compelled these monotheists to accept that in Jesus of Nazareth they had seen God personally? The remaining question is: "Was this experience genuine or a delusion?" Ultimately this is a question of faith; but to regard the Apostolic conviction as a delusion is to throw such doubt on human testimony as to make complete agnosticism in the whole field of history almost the only way out.

The speaker could understand three positions: the orthodox faith that Jesus is God, or the complete skepticism which asserts that no evidence can overcome the *a priori* conviction that a Galilean peasant could not be God, or some of the great heresies. What he could not understand was a position like that of Principal Nicol Cross which:—

(1) Denies that Jesus was God in any sense other than that in which we are all divine, *i.e.* spiritual.

(2) Denies even that he was morally and intellectually perfect man.

But (3) while maintaining both these positions, is prepared to accept him as in some sense the unique Savior.

On the DISCUSSION being thrown open, Mr. C. S. Lewis defended his views which had been attacked on grounds both of taste and reason. It was Jesus' *claim* to forgive sins committed again others that was staggering. The Cross was not a tragedy in the ultimate sense in which

173

Aeschylus or Hardy used the word: that did not make any less real the sufferings of Mary. It was suggested that the temptations of Christ would be unreal if his Deity were admitted, since there would then have been no moral struggle, to which the reply was given that to see the temptations primarily as a moral struggle might be taking too narrow a view: perhaps their greatest significance was that they represented Satan's first total defeat.

The meeting was adjourned at 10:30 p.m. and reassembled in Manchester College on Sunday, November 17th, when Principle Cross replied to points made. He reiterated that the earliest bias of the written records was towards Messiahship or Mediatorship. The Nicene Creed had only been agreed on after every kind of political influence and pressure. The discussion centered on the question of the reliability of the sources of information. Father Parker, replying to it, said that all the evidence for Christ's life and teaching came from a tradition that believed in his Deity. He thought that the explanation that Christ combined both natures in one person was less contrary to the evidence than any other. As an historical fact and as the heresy of Docetism showed, the early Church had found it much more difficult to believe that Christ was man than that he was God.

DID THE RESURRECTION REALLY HAPPEN?

Rupert E. Davies

The question is clearly a central one to any Christian; if the Resurrection did not happen, the Christianity which would survive the discovery of the fact, if any form of Christianity did in fact survive it, would be a quite different thing from that which at present goes under that name.

I propose to deal with the question as a historical one, using as far as I am able the methods of historical science. At the end of what I have to say I shall touch on some of the theological implications of my conclusions, but, as far as I know, my only presuppositions in the course of the inquiry are these: (*a*) When considering the historicity of any event of which eyewitnesses' accounts are not available, we must allow for variations from the truth in any account that we have, some due to inaccurate memory, some to unconscious interpretation, some to the necessity, felt by this or that narrator, of combating error; we have to allow for these things in the case of everyone who has taken a part in the transmission of the story. Our assessment of the total variation will be determined by the length of time which elapsed between the event and the account of it with which we are dealing, by the number of intermediaries who have handed on the account, and by their character and intelligence, and by the nature of the event which is alleged to have happened. (*b*) For an event which seems to contradict the order of nature as otherwise observed we require better evidence than for normal events—more, for instance, for the Virgin Birth and the Gospel miracles than for the murder of Julius Caesar. I make this presupposition, not because such events are less likely to have happened, but because God's activities on the whole follow a course which is observably regular, and because very frequently marvelous events which are widely believed to have happened turn out on close investigation to be normal. (*c*) For one extremely unlikely event the evidence is satisfying—the becoming-man of God in the person of Jesus of Nazareth. (*d*) The presupposition (*c*) just mentioned does not necessarily involve us in accepting the accuracy of the miracle stories in the Gospel or of any of the Resurrection accounts; for the Incarnation *may* have been of such a sort that Jesus was entirely involved in human limitations. Such accuracy must be historically investigated without presuppositions either way.

I want to make two further preliminary points: (*a*) The historical method which I propose to use must be used because Christianity is a historical religion—it asserts that God took a publicly visible part in history; and if the evidence for those events which constitute his participation is slight, the whole religion hangs in the air. It is impossible, therefore, to say, though some do, that the knowledge of the Resurrection was granted by revelation to the disciples and is insusceptible to historical investigation. Such a statement tends strongly in the direction of making Christianity non-historical and subjective. (*b*) I mean by belief in the Resurrection as a historical fact, belief that Jesus after His death by crucifixion appeared alive in real, objective, personal presence to His friends and communicated ideas to them. I take this meaning of the phrase because it is the minimum one. Belief in the Resurrection might, of course, include far more than this, and does for most of those who hold it.

I come now to the evidence. The earliest is in the letters of St. Paul. He takes the Resurrection for granted in everything that he writes, and gives the evidence for it explicitly in 1 Corinthians xv, written, as far as we know, in or about 54 A.D. This is what he says: "I delivered unto you first of all that which also I received, how that Christ died for our sins according to the Scriptures; and that he was buried; and that he hath been raised on the third day according to the

Scriptures; and that he appeared to Cephas; then to the twelve; then he appeared to above five hundred brethren at once, of whom the greater part remain until now, but some are fallen asleep; then he appeared unto James; then to all the apostles; and last of all, as unto one born out of due time, he appeared to me also!" This is the statement of a one-time unbeliever who had been convinced by an appearance of the living Christ; and it directly claims to be, at least in great part, derived directly from information given to him by the apostles of Jesus. The possibility of illusion hardly exists in the case of Peter, though it must be allowed to exist; still less in the case of James, the brother of Jesus, who did not become a follower of Jesus, so far as we know, until after the crucifixion; still less in the case of Paul, who was an unbeliever at the time of the appearance to him; and still less by a large margin in the case of the five hundred. For Peter does not seem to have expected the Resurrection. James and Paul certainly did not, and Paul disbelieved in its happening for a considerable time after it was alleged to have happened; and it is not very plausible to suggest that five hundred people were all deceived at the same time.

The next earliest piece of evidence is in St. Mark's Gospel; this account is independent of St. Paul's, and is usually thought to have come ultimately from St. Peter. It was written, probably, about 66 A.D. It describes how Mary Magdalene and other women "came to" or "entered" the tomb of Jesus early in the morning of the first day of the week, and were told by a young man in white—normally taken to be an angel—that Jesus was not there but was risen, and would go before his disciples into Galilee. The women were filled with amazement, and told none because they were afraid—and then the Gospel ends abruptly; but the lost ending of it must surely have included an account of the appearances of the risen Christ to the disciples in Galilee.

The account in St. Matthew's Gospel (80-90 A.D.) is partly derived from St. Mark, partly independent. In the part derived from St. Mark the author—by universal consent not the apostle Matthew—greatly intensifies the marvel of the event: there is for instance an earthquake, and the young man is definitely and vividly described as an angel. He alters St. Mark's last words, and says that the women went off to tell the disciples. Then he adds that Jesus met the women, and that on a mountain in Galilee. He met the disciples and commanded them to preach to all nations. He also adds, in his account of the burial, the setting a watch to prevent the stealing of the body, and describes the panic of the watchmen when the Resurrection happened, and their bribing by the elders to say that the body was stolen while they were asleep.

There is no doubt that St. Matthew's Gospel, for the most part, merely exaggerates St. Mark, and probably we should disregard his additions; the story of the bribing of the soldiers to say that they had committed what must be a capital offence in any army, reads very much like a Christian answer to a Jewish charge. It may be, in fact, that the additions, except for the story of the guard, are merely inferences from St. Mark's account.

St. Luke's Gospel (80-90 A.D., perhaps earlier, perhaps later than St. Matthew's) borrows from St. Mark all that St. Mark has to lend. But he alters and amends what he borrows: one young man becomes two angels, and the instruction to go to Galilee to meet Jesus becomes a reminder of what Jesus had said to them in Galilee. He adds the journey to Emmaus, the reference to an appearance to Peter, presumably in Jerusalem, and an appearance to all the disciples, still on the day of the Resurrection, certainly in Jerusalem; and an ascension, or at least a final departure, still on the same day, near Bethany. (It should be noted that he corrects his account of the Ascension in Acts 1, where it is placed at an interval of forty days from the Resurrection.)

We have particularly to notice in the Lucan account the definite addition of appearances of Jesus in Jerusalem.

St. John's Gospel (90-100 A.D.), almost certainly not written by the apostle John, must be used with great caution in this matter. Throughout his narrative of Jesus there is a tendency to confuse symbolical and historical truth, and the same tendency may be present here. He gives the visit of Mary Magdalene to the tomb, and her finding it empty; her running to Peter, who comes with John, also finds it empty, and goes away with his companion. Then he describes how Mary, who has followed Peter and John back, stays behind near the tomb and sees Jesus in the garden; how Jesus says, "Touch me not, for I am not yet ascended"; how Jesus then ascends (this is implied rather than stated) and later appears twice to His disciples behind closed doors at an interval of a week, the first time in the absence of Thomas, the second time in his presence. Then the Gospel ends. The last chapter of St. John's Gospel in our Bibles is an appendix by another hand. It describes an appearance to the disciples by the Lake of Galilee.

This Gospel, therefore, does not add much to what we have already in the others, except the appearance to Mary Magdalene and a further one in Jerusalem.

Before we pass to the next piece of evidence, I should like to make a general comment on the evidence in the Gospels. It testifies to a large number of appearances, but disagrees freely in detail; the chief discrepancy is, of course, between those who place all the appearances in Galilee and those who place them all in Jerusalem. But these discrepancies, so far from discrediting the general account, confirm it. For if the Gospel writers had been on unsure ground they would have made very sure not to contradict each other at any point.

The final piece of evidence is the history of the Church. You may not think much of the Church's record in some ages. But there is an unbroken succession of men and women of courage, wisdom and love, from that day to this, who ascribe their goodness to the risen Christ; and in particular the whole life and attitude of the disciples was changed in a short space of time from fear to steady courage. None can think that the story of the Resurrection was a deliberate lie. But were those who told it self-deceived? *Some* event is needed to explain what happened afterwards and is still happening. Does a neurosis or an uprush of the unconscious or any kind of hallucination on the part of a few simple people really explain the facts?

I submit to you that for an ordinary event this evidence would be conclusive, and for an event so surprising as this it is all but conclusive. As a Christian I do not myself expect it to be quite conclusive. The truths of religion are not allowed by God to be fully demonstrable, for that would abolish free will. If you believe in the Resurrection you are *bound* to be a Christian. And that would never do.

But what kind of a Resurrection are we to believe in? Two views on the subject are held by Christians and both are in the New Testament. The first is that the risen Jesus was pure spirit, and His body did not rise from the tomb; His real self manifested itself to His disciples in the shapes and sounds to which they were accustomed. The other is that the risen Jesus had a semi-material body, which could eat and be touched, but could also pass through closed doors.

The former is the view of St. Paul. For he speaks only of appearances; he describes the appearance to himself, which must surely have been a spiritual one in any view, in exactly the same terms as he describes all the other appearances; and he goes on to assimilate our resurrection to that of Christ. It is true that, according to him, when we rise we shall have a body; but it will be a *spiritual* one, continuous with the old, but changed out of all recognition, as a plant is from the seed, and no longer consisting of flesh and blood, which "cannot inherit the Kingdom of God." That is, it will be an instrument, the "clothing," of our personality in the next life, but not in any material or physical sense. In fact, when he calls it a "spiritual body" he is clearly struggling with words, trying to express in Jewish terms something which transcends

Jewish thought. He does not mean a body in our sense of the word at all. So with the appearances of Christ; he called the appearances those of the "spiritual body" of Christ. We should call them "objective visions" of Christ.

The second is the view of the Gospels, as is shown by the story of the empty tomb, the eating of fish, and wounds which could be touched.

Which view are we to choose? I prefer the former and will give my reasons.

Firstly it is that of St. Paul, whose account is the earliest that we have. Secondly, if it is right we can easily explain the growth of the other view; if the other view is right we cannot explain the growth of St. Paul's view. It is easy to see how the "spiritual" view would turn into the "physical" view, for in that age the more material the evidence the more convincing it would be, both to believers and to unbelievers. Moreover, the Docetists, who held that Jesus was a wraith both before and after His Resurrection, could be best combated by a doctrine that even after the Resurrection the body of Jesus was partly physical. Thirdly, there are traces of the "spiritual" view even in the Gospels—in the story of Christ's disappearance at Emmaus, the account of His power to come through closed doors, and the notion in St. Luke and St. John that the Ascension took place on Easter Day, extended in St. John to mean that the appearances to the disciples took place after the Ascension.

Fourthly, the discrepancy between the Galilee stories and the Jerusalem stories is most easily explicable if we think that Jesus appeared to many people in many different places at much the same time, and was not bound by the limitations of time and space.

I suggest, then, that the earliest form of the apostolic preaching about the Resurrection was that Jesus rose spiritually, not physically, from the dead; that this grew later into the story that Jesus' body left the tomb and was seen and touched by His friends; and that the destruction of Jerusalem helped this to become the generally accepted view by preventing it from being investigated.

What shall we say about the Empty Tomb? If you accept the Gospel's version of the Resurrection you will accept this, too, though I am not quite sure what you will think happened at the Ascension and what ultimately became of the body, or rather of the physical elements in the "spiritual body" of Jesus. But on the view that I prefer, the story of the Empty Tomb drops out altogether. What is the evidence for it? Solely, as far as I can see, that of the women who visited the tomb in the early morning, who can quite easily have mistaken what they were told by the "young man," or even have gone to the wrong tomb. In any case, according to St. Mark, they did not say anything to the disciples—at least until later—and according to St. Luke, when they told the disciples they were not believed. It is hard to accept the Johannine story of the visit of Peter and John to the tomb, since it contradicts all the other Gospels.

What does St. Paul say of the Empty Tomb? Nothing at all. My own conviction is that he had never heard the story of it, or, if he had, set no store by it. He does not mention it in the chapter of 1 Corinthians where he is stating the evidence for the Resurrection; he simply says that Christ "was raised on the third day according to the Scriptures," and goes on to detail the appearances. But why did he fix "the third day" as the day of the Resurrection? It *may* have been because of the women's story; but equally he may have thought of the fulfillment of Scripture as requiring the third day or he may have known that the appearance to Peter was on the third day. Some argue that (even if he did not believe the women's story), since the Jews always thought of the body as being raised from the dead and then "transubstantiated" for the Resurrection, he also must have done so in the case of Jesus, and so must have believed in the Empty Tomb. But he changes the ordinary Jewish views about the life to come in so many other ways that he may easily have changed them in this respect also.

And the women's story is not really sufficient evidence for so vast a miracle as this. I suggest, therefore, on this point, that the women's story was told from the beginning, and believed by some, but not taken seriously by the Jerusalem apostles or by Paul; but was later accepted by the leaders and so received into the Gospels. From that time forward it has been put forward as the main ground for belief in the Resurrection, and many people think that the Resurrection stands or falls with it. But this is not really so. The evidence for the Resurrection lies in the appearances of Jesus recorded by Paul and the Gospels, and still more in the change brought about in the disciples and in millions of men and women since by the living Christ.

So far our enquiry has been purely historical. I will make a brief excursion into theology, that is, into the interpretation of the history. As I see it, the Resurrection means the vindication of the life and work of Jesus. If He had not risen, we *might* have supposed that He was right in His teaching about God, right in His belief that in His life and teaching and work and passion God's Kingdom had really come and God's redemptive activity was to be seen. But it would have remained pure speculation—and the possibility would have remained that Jesus was just another good man with beautiful ideas that did not correspond with anything in the real world. But the Resurrection shows that He was more than that, that He was what He claimed to be—the Son of God and the inaugurator of His Kingdom.

I take it also that the Resurrection was a "miracle" quite distinct from His other miracles, for (*i*) it took place as a vindication of the claims of Christ to be the Son of God, whereas the other miracles, although they were signs that the Kingdom was at work, were kept as quiet as possible, lest the claim of Jesus be thought to rest upon them, (*ii*) it took place irrespectively of human faith, whereas the others seem to have depended on at least some faith; (*iii*) we are persistently told in the Acts and the Epistles that "He was raised up," that is, by God, or, directly, that "God raised Him up"—which means that the miracle was performed not by Christ, but by God the Father. If we take these differences in conjunction with the fact, which I believe to be established, that it was not the body, but the "spirit" of Jesus, that was raised from the dead, we are led to the conclusion that the Resurrection was not an event in the earthly life of the Incarnate Christ, but took place after it was ended.

This seems to involve the third point that I wish to make, that St. Paul was wrong in thinking that the Resurrection of Jesus is a guarantee of our resurrection—which is the statement that he makes in the latter half of 1 Corinthians xv, though not elsewhere. For He rose in virtue of His deity. The case for our resurrection must rest on other grounds—the love of God, and the present reality of eternal life in Christ, which can be ours.

But, of course, on any view the Resurrection of Jesus Christ remains the most astonishing and the most significant event in history. Jesus, we now know, is not a dead teacher whom we may rather patronizingly admire in the manner of our contemporaries, but a living Lord who rightly demands our obedience and offers this sufficient grace.

A REPLY TO MR. DAVIES

REV. T. M. PARKER

(This is a very brief résumé, by Rev. Parker, of the reply, which he made at the original meeting.)

Let me begin by recording at what points Mr. Davies and I agree, since it is always more pleasant to note agreement than disagreement.

1. We are both agreed that some quite unusual and striking event, occurring after the Crucifixion, is necessary to explain both the Apostolic conviction of the victory of Jesus and the whole history of Christianity.

2. We are also agreed that Christ's death upon the Cross was not the end of His life and that in some sense or other He overcame and survived death.

Here, however, we part company. For Mr. Davies believes that the earthly body of Jesus remained in the Tomb and that "the risen Jesus was pure spirit." I submit that, whether this reconstruction of the event is true or not, it ought not to be called a Resurrection; for the term "resurrection" means, and properly can only mean, some kind of resuscitation of the body. What Mr. Davies contends for is really a doctrine of the immortality of Christ's soul—quite a different matter.

It is impossible in the space at our disposal fully to discuss his analysis of the evidence, which amounts to the conclusion that the stories of Christ's appearances to His disciples after death are true, whereas the story of the Empty Tomb is false or the result of a mistake. I do not see myself how one can easily so separate the early testimony; both affirmations come to us from the early Church and it would seem that they stand or fall together. If the early believers were wrong about one, they could as easily be wrong about the other. But, in any case, I do not think that St. Paul is in fact intending to teach a different idea of the Resurrection of Christ from that described in the Synoptic Gospels. He does indeed insist upon the spiritual character of our resurrection and may be supposed to believe that Christ's resurrection was of the same nature. But to imagine that by a spiritual resurrection he meant merely a doctrine of the immortality of the soul is to ignore the strong Jewish conviction of the importance of the body in human nature. Judaism in its orthodox forms was convinced that man was a being composed of body and soul, not merely a soul imprisoned temporarily in a body, as Graeco-Roman paganism and philosophy for the most part thought. To a Jew—and St. Paul always remained essentially Jewish—an immortality of the soul only would not have been a real survival of man. St. Paul to the end claimed to hold the Pharisaic doctrine of resurrection (Acts xxiii. 6), as against the Sadducees, who probably did hold a doctrine of the survival of the soul only, and he incurred the ridicule of Greek philosophers by preaching a resurrection (Acts xvii. 31-32).

The truth is that a doctrine of a spiritual resurrection does not contradict the idea of a resurrection of the flesh; to imagine so is to fall into the modern confusion of thinking that "spiritual" means "having no connection with matter" instead of "transcending matter." What St. Paul seems clearly to teach in 1 Cor. xv is that the human body will be transformed at the resurrection in such a way that, though still material, it will be henceforth subject to the spirit and not, as now, largely recalcitrant to it. By the term "spiritual body" he does not mean the same thing as "spirit." This, I submit, is in full accord with what the Gospels tell us of the Resurrection Body of Christ, which could be seen and disappear and pass through doors and walls. (The Gospel of St. John implies, upon a close reading, that it passed through the graveclothes as it rose.) I submit that it was from what he knew of these facts that St. Paul formed his doctrine of the spiritual body; he did not invent it *a priori*, nor would it have seemed to him at all inconsistent with the story of the Empty Tomb. There is indeed no strict proof that he knew of this last (though it seems to me inconceivable that he did not), but there is no reason at all to suppose that he would have disbelieved it or thought it contrary to his own conception of the Resurrection. Rather the contrary.

It is indeed to my mind quite impossible to try to trace the growth of alleged legend in the New Testament in the way that Mr. Davies has tried to do unless one dismisses the whole New Testament as legendary. The Christian Gospel never rested upon the ideas or stories of individuals, but upon the consentient witness of a whole community, and the attempts to show that this person or that added something novel or false to a primitive simple tradition all break down upon the simple fact that any such accretions would have had to pass the censorship of a body of people who knew the facts either directly or from a multiple tradition.

Whilst therefore I am glad to express my entire agreement with Mr. Davies that the Resurrection of Christ is an essential part of the Christian Gospel and rests upon solid historical fact, I must hold that his interpretation of what that resurrection was both evacuates the word of its real meaning and is contrary to the evidence of the New Testament. And this is not, be it noted, a mere academic point without theological significance. For only a full doctrine of the resurrection of the flesh can ultimately save us from the heresy that what is material does not matter. It is this heresy which both does violence to the observed fact (which every development of psychology goes to confirm) of the interdependence of soul and body in man and the necessity of both to full humanity. And it can also easily lead to a falsely "spiritual" religion of a Gnostic kind, which ignores the material welfare of men and has nothing to say to tyrants who maltreat the bodies of their fellows.

THE NECESSITY OF CHRISTIAN MYSTICISM

Fr. Conrad Pepler, O.P.

Before I can explain the obvious ambiguities in the title of this paper I must give some explanations of the particular meaning I wish to attach to the very vague and uncertain term "mysticism." The easiest way of doing this is to refer you to Cuthbert Butler's *Western Mysticism*, in which the abbatial author explains that the term itself is a modern invention which has supplanted the Dionysian term "mystical theology." "Mystical Theology" itself is open to some misunderstandings, and Abbot Butler points out that in the West the Latin word "contemplation" held its ground until the later Middle Ages and has in fact never been really supplanted (cf. *Western Mysticism*, Prologue, purpose. 2-3). "Mystical Theology," although a favorite of the now popular St. John of the Cross, may suggest a certain ratiocination in respect to divine things which is the opposite of its true meaning. A λόγος of divine things may be gained either by reason or by mystery, whereas the modern "theology" has come to be largely restricted to the former. We are here, however, speaking of that knowledge of God in mystery which is beyond human knowledge and which yet engages the whole man, the contemplation of God which in some way draws his reality, rather than an abstract idea of him, into the mind; or perhaps it would be truer to say that *the mind* is drawn into God.

A celebrated passage in the *Confessions* expresses very clearly the meaning of "mysticism" as contemplation:

> Step by step was I led upwards, from bodies to the soul which perceives by means of the bodily senses; and then to the soul's inward faculty to which the bodily senses report external things, which is the limit of the intelligence of animals; and thence again to the reasoning faculty, to whose judgment is referred the knowledge received by the bodily senses. And when this power also within me found itself changeable, it lifted itself up to its own intelligence and withdrew its thoughts from experience, abstracting itself from the contradictory throng of sense images, that it might find what that light was, wherein it was bathed when it cried out that beyond all doubt the unchangeable is to be preferred to the changeable; whence also it knew That Unchangeable: and thus with the flash of one trembling glance it arrived at THAT WHICH IS (*Confessions*, 7, 23).

This progress, "step by step," emphasizes the movement of mysticism or contemplation. At its highest point, of course, the mystic contemplates God as He is in Himself "face to face"; in other words the very thought of God is removed from man's mind and is replaced by the increate Word in the perfect fulfillment of the Beatific Vision.

But to say that this summit of mysticism is necessary would be meaningless, for we are speaking of Christian mysticism as being necessary for something, necessary indeed for salvation, and this Vision is salvation. I do not wish to try to prove that Christian mysticism is necessary for itself; nor even that in its complete perfection man finds his necessary end. In order that the title makes sense at all the mystical ascent outlined by St. Augustine must be limited to this life. We must take for granted that man's full perfection lies in the beatific vision and concentrate our attention on the way towards vision, the way without its end. The ascent into contemplation is necessary in the here and now for man to attain his final eternal happiness—that is what I wish to make of the title. It would be possible to show that a certain orientation towards the mystical ideal is necessary for true human living, that society needs its St. Augustines, St.

Thomases, St. Catherines. But I want as far as possible to avoid the sociological craze, for today we fall naturally into the utilitarian error, and it would rob mysticism of its truth to make it useful to society. It is, of course, of the greatest possible service to society, but that is its fruit and not its aim. I will leave it to others to consider the fruit.

To approach the question from a theoretic point of view we must first consider what *ought* to be. If man begins life without the possession of his faculties but in possession of the inheritance of original sin, and if he must grow up from this seminal state until he reach the full perfection of his nature when all his desires will be satisfied, all his love occupied and all his thoughts concentrated in the one infinite Word, he must move from the one point to the other by a progress or development which is a growth of soul. The final vision and the principle means of reaching it depend, of course, upon the direct action of God upon man, and absolutely speaking God could reduce the potency of the newly formed human soul to perfect act without the soul having to pass through any intermediate stages—a sudden and complete conversion. But such a transformation would be scarcely consonant with the divine manner of working through the secondary causes which divine providence has disposed, and it would be in conflict certainly with the spirit of the Gospels where the Word incarnate has insisted that he himself is the Way and to follow that way a man must exercise himself in certain things, denying himself, serving God and the neighbor; in this way grace may grow as the small seed which becomes a great tree. In fact Christ declares that to be perfect, to rise to the heights of union with God, certain individuals must prepare by great austerities—to sell all and to follow the Way.

Conversion from a state of sinfulness to a life of grace is, indeed, instantaneous. Grace itself cannot be acquired by the observance of rules nor by the exercise of natural virtues; grace builds on nature, but is not a steady progression and development from nature. Grace is a new beginning, a new birth into a new life. But even so, once grace has been given the new life develops and grows in normal progression—or should do so. God abhors the *saltus*[30]; conversion itself is a new creation rather than a "jump," and sudden leaps even of a supernatural character would upset the divine harmony so that the supernatural would cease to be an "ORDER." St. Thomas, who is the great apostle of order in thought as in things, takes his stand here when discussing the need for works and progress in the attainment of the Beatific Vision:

> "God could make a will having a right tendency to the end and at the same time attaining the end" (St. Thomas explains later that God did so in fact in producing the first creatures and in making Christ's humanity). "But the Order of divine wisdom demands that it should not be thus ... (For) to possess the perfect good without movement, belongs to that which has it naturally: and to have Beatitude naturally belongs to God alone ... (But) since Beatitude surpasses every created nature, no pure creature can fittingly gain Beatitude without the movement of action (*operationis*), whereby it tends thereto" (I-II, 5, 7).

It is a matter of working with the help of grace in order to merit a supernatural end, and such activity takes, if not time, at least succession through a series. There are people who regard the great mystics as "a gallery of neurotics and psychopaths" (to quote a recent writer on the subject) but the Christian view of mysticism is simply that of orderly progress, in which the soul cooperates with God, preparing for and gradually approaching the fullness of vision in which all perfection is to be found. With such an end as the Beatific Vision to provide the whole process with a unity and a character we should look for the gradual destruction of all that is not in

---

[30] Editor's Note (2012): Latin for "leap."

conformity with God himself, and in some way even the transformation of the material, physical element, which cannot, as it is, be drawn into the union of Vision. First, all the subsidiary functions and activities of human nature must be brought into subjection from the anarchy in which they have existed through sin. The powers which man shares with lowest creation need to be transformed, as weight which when left to its own devices roots a body to the ground can be transformed by impetus into the momentum of flight. Beatitude would be incomplete if the body was permitted to find its own level. The glorious resurrection of the body is one of the final stages of the mystic way.

Then the mind and the will have to be cleared of the obstructions which prevent their being completely occupied by the absolute truth and the absolute good in the Beatific Vision. In this respect it is primarily a question of development of charity or love. If the will is cleared of attachments which are other than God, so that charity may take possession of its every act, then the knowledge of divine things which is born of the affinity of affection rather than of the application to study or the exercise of reason, will increase into wisdom. St. Thomas, following St. Augustine again, describes the growth towards perfection, i.e. towards the heights of contemplation and mysticism, as a growth in charity according to the three stages of beginners, proficients and perfects. In this way the whole man grows in union with God and approximates more closely to the union of beatitude; and he is at the same time meriting, through his cooperation with divine grace, the same beatitude as a reward of his labors. Heaven is not something quite different from the actions which merit it; God does not act like a father giving a boy a box of chocolates for having been good, the reward is rather a development and perfection of that very goodness. St. John of the Cross, who is very much the *Christian* mystic since he attempts always to base his doctrine on the Scriptures rather than on experience, begins to comment on the stanzas of his own *Dark Night of the Soul* with these preparatory remarks:

> Before we enter upon the exposition of these stanzas, it is well to understand here that the soul that utters them is now in the state of perfection, which is the union of love with God, having already passed through severe trials and straits, by means of spiritual exercise in the narrow way of eternal life whereof Our Savior speaks in the Gospel, along which way the soul ordinarily passes in order to reach this high and happy union with God (Peers translation i, 348).

A close analysis of the doctrine of grace as the "seed of glory" (St. Thomas calls it the *inchoatio gloriae*) would reveal the same necessity of development; for the objective indwelling of the Trinity and the subjective perfection of the Gifts of the Holy Spirit are aspects of grace which become increasingly actual as sin and false attachments are discarded and grace is given freedom to operate. The Thomistic doctrine of the new presence of God by grace in the soul makes all this very clear. God by his creative activity is in everything by his essence, presence and power, and in that sense every speck of reality in the world is a sacrament of the divine presence. But in the soul engraced, God becomes present in a new way in that He, in the intimacy of three divine Persons, is the object of a man's knowledge and love. The man gradually *becomes* what he knows and loves, so that this new supernatural knowledge and love embrace more and more of the reality around him, so he comes to be identified with God, every aspect of his day to day life being *informed* by charity and faith. The seven gifts of the Holy Ghost begin to perfect the action of the moral virtues and to strengthen the apprehension of the intellect with divine intuition. In this way a man becomes more and more "as God" (*sicut dii*, even as gods, as the psalmist has it) and there is a true unification of every fiber of his being in this union with God. But there is no time to delve into the spiritual depths of the idea of Christian sanctification. I would, however, draw your attention to the traditional doctrine regarding the relationship between the active life and the contemplative, for it supports the thesis that a man must pass into contemplative stages en route for heaven. It has always been the Christian teaching that virtuous activity, that is, all Christian human action, is primarily a preparation for contemplation, that every Martha must be in training to become a Mary, "Bodily working," writes Walter Hilton, "belongeth to all young beginning men, which come newly out of worldly sin to the service of God: for to make them able to ghostly working, and for to break down the unbuxomness of the body by reason and by such bodily working, that it might be supple and ready, and not much contrarious to the spirit in ghostly working" (*Mixed Life*, Minor Works, p. 4). And St. Thomas puts it in clear, scholastic terms, but recalling St. Augustine and St. Gregory—the active life is a "*dispositio*" for the contemplative, it is "in *via generationis*" to contemplation (cf. II-II, 182, 4).

This teaching, which in our modern activist age has largely been discarded, brings out clearly the fact that although the active or ascetic life of the moral virtues is to be distinguished from the mystic or contemplative life of faith, hope and charity, yet they may never be separated. In a general sense, it is more practical to speak of "mysticism" as embracing also the asceticism which is its necessary prerequisite. If it is necessary to learn Greek and Hebrew before studying Scriptural exegesis, it would not be a misuse of terms to say that a man were beginning his exegetical studies even though he were in fact immersed in Hebrew pointings and Greek paradigms. St. Augustine, in the passage I have quoted from the *Confessions*, shows that a good deal of labor and many ascetical practices were required before he was granted that foretaste of heaven in the "touch" of divine truth. While we stress the necessity for Christian mysticism in the attainment of supernatural Happiness or Beatitude, we must include also Christian asceticism which has constantly to be preparing the ground for the mystic seed.

It will be clear by now that I do not include in this mystical development the extraordinary experiences which sometimes reveal a mystic but may as often conceal a mimic. Ecstasy has always been regarded, even by such ecstatics as St. Teresa herself, as a weakness. All such things as visions, levitations, voices, thought-reading, prophecies, stigmatization, all are at first strongly suspect; they may well be effects of insanity or diabolical possession; they are often used by the devil to deceive; and when they are genuine they are never more than secondary and unimportant. The mystical must be clearly distinguished from the marvelous, from feelings and emotions, and to a certain extent from experience. In the higher reaches of the mystical stream as the soul approaches the clear spring, the Source of grace, there will be experiences. The union which is called transforming, the nuptials of the soul with God, the secret touches by which God communicates himself to the soul in its depths, these will register outwardly as momentary, temporary events which can be recognized by memory and intellect (but not necessarily by the senses). But inwardly the mystic union remains a permanent reality. Bl. Angela of Foligno describes the moment of highest mystical experience, (declaring at the same time that it is blasphemy to put it into words):

> In my soul is a room into which no joy nor sadness, nor pleasure of any kind, neither virtue nor anything else, can enter. But into that room enters that All-Good ... I see myself alone with God, all Purity, all Holiness, all Truth, all Rectitude, all Certitude, and in Him all Heavenliness.

But she adds at the end of the passage:

It is true, when I am out of this greatest state I see myself to be all sin and obedient to sin, dark and impure, entirely false and full of error. But I am quiet, and there remains continually with me a divine unction, which is a supreme unction, and which I may have at all times of the day (*Catholic Mysticism*, Algar Thorold, pp. 158-9).

And the author of the *Epistle of Privy Counsel* is describing what is practically a permanent state—"evermore without ceasing" (c. 13)—when he outlines his conception of the supreme point of contemplation:

In this time it is that thou both seest thy God and thy love, and nakedly feelest him also by ghostly oneing to his love in the sovereign point of thy spirit, as he is in himself, but blindly as it may be here, utterly spoiled of thyself and nakedly clothed in himself, as he is, unclothed and not lapped in any of these sensible feelings—be they never so sweet nor so holy—that may fall in this life (c. 12).

This *simplex intuitus veritatis*[31] engendered by an intensely purified love of God, as described by all these mystical writers, represents the highest point ordinarily attainable by man in this life, and it is evidently only one step removed from the final union of the beatific vision. It is this divine touch in the substance of the soul, beyond feeling and in some ways beyond concepts, which we are maintaining to be of necessity for attaining the final, supernatural goal of human existence. But you will be asking me to come down to earth and to face realities. These transports of union with God are granted, as far as we can gather from experience, to one in a million—certainly only one in many millions ever comes to describe them for the benefit of others. The overwhelming majority of men are too busily engaged in the cares and enjoyments of this life ever to visualize such mystic heights, and their activities—even when of the perfect Christian type—occupy *all* their attention. On this we must agree; but we must remember that it is modern scientific man, not the infinite God, who is impressed by numbers and statistics. Number is essentially bound up with matter, and the things of which we speak are of spirit. Christ himself appeared sometimes indifferent to statistics—"Many are called but few are chosen." Secondly if it is a fact that this life is not only a foretaste of heaven but a preparation for it, then the Catholic doctrine of Purgatory bridges the otherwise unbridgeable gap between the life of the multitude on this earth and their ultimate salvation. Purgatory provides a way of progress through the mystical, dark nights and illumination, a way which is certain and not subject to hazard, but which is the more constrained as it offers no way of escape.

In practice it would seem that the greater part of mankind cannot or will not rise above the active life; men shun contemplation and are not brave or wise enough to face the initial purifications which provide the foothills of the mystical ascent, more precisely named asceticism. There is, however, an increasing number of people who not only admit a *saltus*, a leap, possible for almost every man at death, straight from his state of selfish imperfection into the very lap of God, but who also would encourage a *saltus* during earthly existence. These are the men who indulge in mystical readings and a number of mystical practices, who seek the *simplex intuitus veritatis* without being willing to traverse the grim approach described by such experienced writers as John of the Cross or the author of the *Cloud of Unknowing*. It is possible, I think, to achieve through human effort and ingenuity a certain state of equilibrium and contemplation of absolutes, a state which is in point of fact purely human, and mystical only in

---

[31] Editor's Note (2012): Latin for "simple contemplation of truth," or an act of contemplation.

appearance. The effects of original sin can be counteracted by a sound human culture, particularly one which has grown out of a good Christian tradition. The result is a very highly developed human personality, pervading a gentle atmosphere of peace, descending into humanitarian activities without the flurry of activism. The aim of such a one is not the loving vision of God but the fulfillment of his own person, as far as possible on this earth—and this is the aim of many who are now interested in the subject and the effects of mysticism. In my view this is not supernatural or Christian mysticism: it is, however noble, a counterfeit, a sign of an effete society seeking a way of escape from the horrible effects of dissolution.

If my explanation of Christian mysticism is correct, it is necessary to recall men not to the consideration of the last stages of Mystical Theology which, as St. John of the Cross says, "signifies secret or hidden wisdom of God, wherein without noise of words and without the aid of any bodily or spiritual sense, as if in silence and in quiet, hidden by darkness from all that is of the senses and of nature; God teaches the soul after a most hidden and secret manner, without her knowing how" (*Spiritual Canticle*, 39, 12, Peers ii, 401), but to recall them to the strenuous way of asceticism. The former is too attractive, and may seem to lie within reach of unaided human power, but the first stages of mysticism are hard and forbidding and include all the rougher aspects of the gospels which we are often anxious to forget. Certainly if this mystic ascent is necessary then we must first of all look to its term in order to take our bearings, and it is sometimes useful to draw out some sort of plan or map of the way. The last stages of the journey will remain inevitably hazy to the beginner, and it is more useful if, having made the rough map, he settles down to measure the sharp contours of the first steep ascent which rises up immediately before him.

In other words, if Christian mysticism is necessary for a man's salvation, then the active life, which marks the initial stages of Christian mysticism is immediately and urgently needed, the true active life, that is, which leads on of itself to contemplation and union with God. I may be accused of having changed the subject from the necessity to the possibility of Christian mysticism, but those who are converted by the necessity of the Christian message will always ask the question: "What must we do to be saved?" and some hope must be offered to them. I would therefore conclude with another quotation from St. Augustine which shows the need and the possibility of this true Christian mysticism:

> If we be faithful, we have already arrived at the way of faith; and if we do not abandon it, we shall without doubt arrive at, not merely so great an understanding of things incorporeal and unchangeable as cannot in this life be grasped by all, but even to the height of contemplation, which the Apostle calls "face to face." For some of the least ones, who yet perseveringly walk in the path of faith, come to that most blessed contemplation; while others who have knowledge of what invisible, unchangeable, incorporeal nature is, but refuse to follow the path leading to the abode of such happiness, which seems folly to them—viz. Christ crucified—are not able to come to the shrine of that quiet, although their mind is already, as at a distance, touched by the ray of its light (Ep. 120, 4, quoted Butler, p. 242).

PSYCHIC RESEARCH AND ITS BEARING ON CHRISTIAN FAITH

DR. L. W. GRENSTED

(A summary of the meeting on May 3, 1948)

After defining the limits of his subject, Dr. Grensted gave examples of psychic phenomena, first of a kind which it is difficult to investigate scientifically: of these, the most important are the common belief in communication with the dead, for which the evidence is slender: paranormal phenomena such as table-turning, automatic writing, poltergeists and hallucinations related to distant objects, all of which leave much unexplained material. The supposed messages from the dead show complete agreement about two ultimate things of religious import: firstly, the lasting supremacy and importance of love, and secondly the law that every event works out its own consequences. Dr. Grensted then went on to describe the attempts to obtain controlled, statistical material, in particular Prof. Ryan's experiments in precognition. The more startling, long-range examples of telepathy and clairvoyance have not been statistically examined, but some cases are almost demonstrable. If these facts are reliable, the speaker said, they mean that we shall have to recast our whole theories about time and cognition. Time will no longer be linear, but serial: a single event in time, like death, could then not be determinate of the whole range of its subject. This opens the door to the Christian beliefs about death and immortality. Our time series becomes more like a creative, mental construct than a mechanical system of crude materialism. As regards cognition, it may be that the ground of knowledge is a continuum of cognition, and the unity of all knowledge in God's eternal present may have to be taken for granted, so that the question of philosophers will then be, how *we* come to have a bit of it. Because of these possible implications, psychic research has to be taken seriously by some people, though for the purposes of ordinary Christian living it can and should be safely ignored.

THE DISCUSSION

Opening the discussion, Mr. B. Babington Smith, while agreeing that there were still some unexplainable phenomena, gave scientific reasons for suspecting flaws in Prof. Ryan's experiment, which he explained by describing exactly what are the difficulties of statistical tests.

In the discussion which followed, Dr. Grensted developed further his hypothesis about cognition, with reference to the Fall of Man. The possibility of good and evil being inherent in the fact of Creation, the primary hypothesis of our knowledge must be a condition which is to us inapprehensible, so we must proceed from the unknown to the known in knowledge as well as in faith. This was discussed by the President and the Rev. E. L. Mascall, whose views, and Dr. Grensted's, were fairly well reconciled. Mr. Basil de Mel then put forward a further hypothesis, arguing, from the fact of telepathy, that before the Fall men were not limited to their sense perceptions, but partook in a "cosmic unity" of perception. Mr. Mascall and others argued against him that telepathy implied no unity between the subjects, since the object of the experience was always externalized. The President supported Mr. de Mel in the view that there was a unity among primitive peoples from which we have to emerge in order to reach a higher kind of unity. Finally, the Chairman suggested that this higher unity was already present to us through the acts of Jesus Christ and in Eucharistic worship, and that even our common acts of knowledge and judgment are in fact participations not only in one another's rational experience, but also in the form of the whole act of creation.

NOTE.—Owing to the length of this number of the Digest, publication of Mr. C. G. Hardie's long and interesting paper on "The Oedipus Myth" has had to be postponed till our next issue.

OXFORD UNIVERSITY SOCRATIC CLUB

"Οὗτος μὲν οἴεταί τι εἰδέναι οὐκ εἰδώς, ἐγὼ δὲ ὥσπερ οὖν οὐκ οἶδα οὐδὲ οἴομαι."
—*Socrates*

"Εἴ τις δοκεῖ ἐγνωκέναι τι, οὔπω ἔγνω καθὼς δεῖ γνῶναι."
—*St. Paul*

"La dernière démarche de la raison est de reconnaître qu'il y a une infinité de choses qui la surpassent." —*Pascal*

This Club has been formed for those who do not necessarily wish to commit themselves to Christian views but are interested in a philosophical approach to religion in general and to Christianity in particular, in a spirit of free enquiry and in the light of modern thought and knowledge.

OPEN DISCUSSION follows the introduction of the subjects by speakers who include both Christians and non-Christians.

Weekly discussion meetings have also been held on Thursdays during Term, in which the subjects of the larger meetings have been further discussed among a smaller group of members.

OFFICERS, 1945–48

President: C. S. LEWIS, M.A.

Chairman: STELLA ALDWINCKLE, M.A.

Senior Treasurer: DR. F. PRINGSHEIM

Secretaries:

Michaelmas Term, 1945	P. Macnaughton Smith
Hilary Term, 1946	Helen McGivering
Trinity Term, 1946	E. A. Robinson
Michaelmas Term, 1946	M. G. Brock
Hilary Term, 1947	T. A. Stock
Trinity Term, 1947—Trinity Term, 1948	J. F. Goodridge

Junior Treasurers:

Michaelmas Term, 1945	Caryl Micklem
Trinity Term, 1946	Andrew Mannheim
Michaelmas Term, 1946—Hilary Term, 1947	J. L. Broom
Trinity Term, 1947—Hilary Term, 1948	Elizabeth M. Gibson
Trinity Term, 1948	D. Hunter

MICHAELMAS TERM, 1947

October 13—Does God Exist?	Dr. A. M. Farrer
	Mr. W. H. Walsh
October 20—Toynbee's Study of History	Mr. M. B. Foster
	Mr. J. F. Goodridge
October 27—Design and the Existence of God	Mr. F. L. MacCarthy
	Mr. C. S. Lewis
November 3—A first glance at Sartres	Mr. C. S. Lewis
	Dr. E. L. Mascall
November 10—Existentialism	Mr. Ronald Grimsley
	Fr. F. C. Copleston
November 17—Time	Dr. John Marsh
	Rev. D. Nineham
November 24—Did the Resurrection happen?	Rev. R. E. Davies
	Rev. T. M. Parker
December 1—Values without God	Mr. A. D. Howell Smith
	Mr. Ian Crombie

HILARY TERM, 1948

January 19—Can the Existence of God be demonstrated?	Mr. Vernon Rice
	Mr. G. Somerhoff
January 26—Political Faiths	Mr. T. D. Weldon
	Mr. H. A. Clegg
February 2—"Miracles"—a reply to Mr. C. S. Lewis	Miss G. E. M. Anscombe
	Mr. C. S. Lewis
February 9—Rudolf Steiner and the Scientific Outlook	Dr. A. Heidenreich
	Dr. F. Sherwood Taylor
February 16—Theism and Personal Relationships	M. Gabriel Marcel
	Dr. L. W. Grensted
February 23—Christianity and Plato	Fr. Leslie Walker
	Mr. A. G. N. Flew
March 1—Christianity and Aristotle	Fr. F. C. Copleston
	Mr. W. C. Kneale
March 8—The concept of salvation in analytical psychology and religion	
	Rev. Basil de Mel
	Fr. Leycester King

TRINITY TERM, 1948

April 26—Our political predicament theologically considered	Dr. V. A. Demant
	Mr. T. D. Weldon
May 3—Psychic Research and its bearing on the Christian Faith	Dr. L. W. Grensted
	Mr. B. Babington Smith

May 10—The Necessity of Christian Mysticism   Fr. Conrad Pepler
                                                        Rev. T. M. Parker
May 17—Aesthetics and Moral Standards   Mr. N. J. P. Brown
                                                        Mr. C. S. Lewis
May 31—Karl Barth on Faith and Reason   Mr. Daniel Jenkins
                                                        Fr. T. Corbishley
June 7—Biblical thought and the language of philosophy Dr. A. M. Farrer
                                                        Rev. P. J. Thompson

SOCRATIC DIGEST

No. 5   1949–1952

CONTENTS

FOREWORD: *John Wisdom*   195

INTRODUCING THE CONTEMPORARY DISCUSSION—

    Modern Philosophy and Theology: BASIL MITCHELL   196

CONTINUING THE DISCUSSION—

    Theology and Falsification: I. M. CROMBIE   202

    Analysis, Personality and Religion: GEOFFREY MIDGLEY   214

    A Theologian's Point of View: AUSTIN FARRER   220

OTHER CONSIDERATIONS—

    Is Theism Important?: H. H. PRICE, C. S. LEWIS   223

    The Existentialist Political Myth: IRIS MURDOCH   232

EDITORIAL NOTE

The Oxford University Socratic Club, to which these papers (with the exception of Dr. Farrer's) have been read, is an open forum for the discussion between Christians and agnostics of topics relevant to the claim of the Christian Faith to be *true* in some ultimate sense. But nowadays we have to revert to an ancient problem and begin further back—not with truth but with language and meaning. So here we are concerned with "clarification" rather than with argument: an historical introduction explains the nature of the philosophical developments that have not only outdated arguments for the existence of God with modern intellectuals, but have thrown doubt on whether sentences mentioning God can even have any meaning. There follow various attempts by philosophers to respond to the reiterated request from agnostics for enlightenment as to the kind of significance (the logical status) of talk about faith and about God.

S.A.

THE CONTRIBUTORS

H. H. Price *is Wykeham Professor of Logic in the University of Oxford.*

John Wisdom *is Professor of Philosophy in the University of Cambridge.*

C. S. Lewis, *literary critic, novelist, and apologist, tutors and lectures in English Literature at Oxford.*

Austin Farrer, *the theologian, tutors and lectures in theology, philosophy of religion and New Testament criticism at Oxford.*

Geoffrey Midgley *is Lecturer in Philosophy at Newcastle-on-Tyne.*

I. M. Crombie, Basil Mitchell and Iris Murdoch *tutors and lecturers in philosophy at Oxford.*

Three Shillings and Sixpence

ALL RIGHTS RESERVED

PRINTED IN GREAT BRITAIN FOR BASIL BLACKWELL, PUBLISHER, 1952

FOREWORD

JOHN WISDOM
Fellow of Trinity College, Cambridge

For centuries men have spoken of gods and daemons and God and the Devil. About these things they have agreed and disputed with one another and within themselves.

It often happens that people can do a thing very well without being at all good at describing what it is to do it well; thinking about how to do a thing often makes one do it worse. On the other hand sometimes it enables one to do it better—perhaps after a time of doing it worse. Sometimes it happens that though upon the whole people do a thing very well there are occasions where procedure breaks down, and then often nothing can be done to remedy this without reviewing the whole procedure on all occasions. Sometimes occasions of breakdown are so frequent that many people give the whole thing up as hopeless. Some people began to feel this way about philosophical thought and some have felt this way about religious thought.

At such junctures philosophers may exert themselves to lend a hand in reviewing the whole position and in considering whether, and how far, a whole type of procedure which purports to get at the truth is unsatisfactory, and how far it is not, and if not why not.

The good philosopher in trying to get at "what we really mean" by, for example, "simultaneity," "mind" or "God" does not turn back at every cry of astonishment or protest, and at the same time is ready to give each such protest his serious attention whether it comes from others or from himself. For example, he will not insist and, surely, does not insist, that our language is an exact calculus or that the logic of a chronically elusive gardener or anything else is a perfect model of the logic of God. On the contrary, he remarks—on the contrary.

Amongst the authors of these papers Mr. Crombie, Mr. Midgley and Professor Price may be mentioned as being concerned especially in an effort to reach a better understanding of what it is to believe that God does or does not exist, is of this nature or that. If you read what they have written you will find, I think, that they have worked with acumen, honesty and seriousness. You may not be satisfied with what they have done—they certainly are not, and will welcome help.

MODERN PHILOSOPHY AND THEOLOGY

BASIL MITCHELL
Fellow of Keble College, Oxford

The purpose of this paper is to discuss the attitude of modern philosophy to theology. The sort of modern philosophy I have in mind is by no means the only sort of philosophizing that goes on nowadays. It is the sort of philosophy that is dominant at Oxford and Cambridge and its influence is increasingly felt elsewhere.

There are two things about "Modern Philosophy" so understood which make it worthwhile trying to explain its bearing on Theology. The first is that very little has been published by its exponents and most of that has been in technical journals; so that recent developments are unfamiliar to the educated world at large and are in danger of being misunderstood. The second is that there is a strong impression that such philosophy is inherently anti-religious and as such is to be deplored and attacked in all its forms. There is no doubt some justification for this view. I shall not pronounce upon it, but will endeavor to make clear what the issues are. Inevitably, the account will have to be simplified. One can only hope to indicate trends—bearing in mind that this is not a well-defined school of philosophy, but a general way of approaching philosophical problems.

There has been a change in the relation between philosophers and theologians which may conveniently be represented in a parable:—

Fifty years ago—in the heyday of British Idealism—the Theologian and the Philosopher thought they understood one another pretty well. The Theologian was used to seeing the Philosopher occupying a rival pulpit, from which he expounded worldviews and philosophies of life and elaborated accounts of ultimate Reality. Whether he approved or disapproved of what the philosopher said, he felt he knew what he was at. He was preaching. But one day the philosopher announced that he was going to devote himself to mathematics and the study of language. Philosophy, he declared, was not concerned with problems of ultimate reality, but with devising symbolic systems and analyzing the conceptions of common sense. Philosophy was not metaphysics, but logical analysis. It was not *his* job to preach. Thereupon he descended from his pulpit.

This was disconcerting to the theologian, who thought it a pointless and irresponsible thing to do and from that day on he viewed the philosopher with suspicion.

The philosopher, for his part, was inclined, as a general rule, to let the theologian go on preaching; and was perhaps, if he gave any thought to it, just a little offended at the coolness the theologian displayed towards himself. This was rather disingenuous of him, since he had from time to time interrupted his new pursuits to declare in loud and provocative terms that the theologian was talking nonsense. True, he had later explained that it was only strictly speaking nonsense: that, indeed, it might even be profound nonsense. But these concessions quite failed to allay the theologian's uneasiness. It was difficult to tell which was the more unsatisfactory—these outspoken attacks or the usual indifference. So long as the philosopher declaimed in the old way either for or against him he was at least being contradicted. Now he was not even taken seriously enough for that. It is an ominous sign when a man's friends no longer contradict him.

But the theologian's bewilderment perhaps reached its height when, as occasionally happened, the philosopher would come and sit attentively beneath his pulpit and murmur agreement with his propositions (or at least quasi-agreement with his quasi-propositions).

It is impossible, as I have said, to interpret this parable in straightforward historical terms, without dangerous oversimplification, but the attempt must be made.

The dominant tendency in modern philosophy—which may be roughly called Empiricism—goes back, of course, very much further than the turn of the century, when Russell and Moore gave it a fresh impetus. The empiricist challenge to religious belief has had two (perhaps three) main phases—the first culminated in David Hume; the second in the Logical Positivists; and it is important to appreciate the difference between these two phases if we are to see the point of the contemporary philosopher's difficulties.

The first was directed principally against Natural or Rational Theology, the attempt to demonstrate the existence of God by means of the traditional arguments: which—with the exception of the ontological—started from the existence of the world and argued in different ways to the existence of a First Cause—a necessary being. The ontological argument did without the empirical premise—that the world exists—and argued to the existence of God from his perfection; for if God did not exist he would be less than perfect.

Hume attacked these arguments with the weapon which has been aptly termed "Hume's Fork." Of any argument he would ask, "Is this a piece of abstract reasoning concerning quantity and number?" or "Is it a piece of experimental reasoning concerning matter of fact?" If the former, then it could not prove existence: if the latter, then its conclusion could not be demonstrated. It followed that by no sort of argument could the existence of God be proved. For God was held to exist necessarily. God couldn't just *happen* to exist. But the ontological argument which purported to establish this contained no empirical premise, but started from a definition. It was, therefore, a piece of abstract reasoning and could not prove the existence of anything. The other arguments started, indeed, from an empirical premise, but purported to yield a necessary conclusion. But from such a premise only a probable conclusion could be derived. It follows, then, that Natural Theology is a mistake and Hume himself drew the conclusion that religion finds its "best and most solid foundation in faith and divine revelation."

All this meant was that the Christian could not claim to prove his Faith; and at all times there have been Christians who, far from contesting this conclusion, would welcome it: for whom it was the essence of a "faith" that it could not be proved.

But the next phase of Empiricism challenged even this position. I have called it the next phase—although there are hints of it in Hume and indeed in Berkeley. But it first became central and explicit in the thought of the Logical Positivists. They declared that it was not the function of philosophy to distinguish true assertions from false ones, but to discriminate between the meaningful and the meaningless—or what, for them, amounted to the same thing, between science and metaphysics. Their main interest had been in scientific method and they were primarily—and were proud to be—philosophers of science. In order to make this distinction they armed themselves with a powerful weapon, the "verification principle."

The first formulation of this: "the meaning of proposition is the method of its verification" was paradoxical, and led to such implausible suggestions as that an historical statement about Julius Caesar *meant* something about looking up references in *De Bello Gallico*. This clearly wouldn't do, and the principle was therefore broadened to "A proposition has meaning, if and only if, some possible sense experience is relevant to the determination of its truth and falsehood," in which form it appears in A. J. Ayer's *Language, Truth and Logic* (1936).

A sentence which failed to pass this test lacked "factual" or "literal" meaning and was nonsense: it was a "pseudo-proposition."

It will be clear at once, that on such a criterion of meaning all statements about a transcendent God must be adjudged meaningless: and in *Language, Truth and Logic*, Ayer roundly declared that the statements of Theology, Metaphysics and Ethics were nonsensical pseudo-propositions. In the face of *this* challenge it was no longer any use for the theologians to say "But I don't claim to prove any beliefs: I simply take them on faith" because what was now being assailed was not the arguments by which these beliefs were supported, but their claim to significance. It was not that their truth could not be proved. They could not even be false. This needs understanding. The philosophical critic of Christianity is no more an atheist than he is a believer: for a man cannot disbelieve in God unless he can attach meaning to the statements he is asked to believe. He says "I don't know what you are asking me to believe in."

There were a number of serious objections to the criterion for, theology apart, the criterion as it stood ruled out as meaningless such utterances as commands and moral judgments: which in any ordinary sense are not meaningless. And it was objected that to legislate about the word "meaning" in this way was a highly arbitrary proceeding. It was seen that you do not verify a command or a moral judgment in the way that you do a scientific hypothesis; but you understand what it means. Moreover there were difficulties about the principle itself. How is *it* verified or is *it* also meaningless? Ayer himself in his second edition (1946) recognized the justice of much of this criticism and defended "verifiability" as a methodological principle. Ayer confesses that metaphysicians will not easily be persuaded to accept his "methodological principle" and that it will be necessary to deal with metaphysical statements piecemeal as each is put forward. But it is in itself of little comfort to the metaphysician that he is to be eaten piecemeal, instead of swallowed whole. In fact it was generally seen that there was something pretty objectionable in the arbitrary manner in which the earlier Logical Positivists had restricted the meaning of "meaning." Few, if any, contemporary Oxford philosophers would call themselves "Logical Positivists," and the pure original doctrine is now espoused only by undergraduates understandably concerned to restrict the scope and complexity of the subject they are required to study.

Under fire, the direction of the attack was changed. It was no longer sought to use the verification principle as a device for separating propositions into the sheep and the goats—the meaningful and the meaningless. A more modest program was envisaged: that of classifying "utterances" into different types or categories according to the various ways in which they were used and tested. It was, for example, no longer maintained that moral judgments were meaningless, but it was noticed that they were used differently from statements of fact and that they required to be supported by reasons of a different kind. "This action is right" might look very much like "this apple is red," but it was really a very different sort of proposition—its "logical form" was different. So, in place of the dogmatic *assertion*, "Theological propositions are meaningless," you get the more modest, or at least more cagey *question*, "What is the logic of theological statements?" or, in the self-consciously homespun metaphors of Professor Ryle, "How do theological sentences behave?", "What jobs do God propositions do?"

It is this further development (my possible "third phase" of Empiricism), which is not yet generally familiar. It is characteristic of modern Oxford philosophy and serves to distinguish it from Logical Positivism (to which, however, it is heavily indebted). It is for this reason that a book like Prof. Joad's *Critique of Logical Positivism* is wide of the mark. The target has passed on.

The philosopher is not now going to rule out theological statements from the start. Nor is he going to say that insofar as they are not statements of fact, they have no meaning at all. He is prepared—as in the case of moral judgments—to concede meaning to sentences which do not state facts. What he will try to do is to discover whether they *are* to be taken as statements of fact (i.e. of possible fact) or not; if not, what sort of statements they are—what their function is in discourse. He is interested in logical classification. There is, then, I think he would maintain, nothing inherently anti-religious about his philosophical activities. Indeed, in one sense, it is obvious that there could not be. The philosopher does not, in any ordinary sense, make discoveries. That is the job of the scientist. It follows that there could not be a straight contradiction between philosophy and theology since philosophy, at any rate, does not claim to make assertions which might conflict with the assertions of the theologian. "The result of philosophy," said Wittgenstein in his influential *Tractatus Logico-philosophicus*, "is not a number of 'philosophical propositions,' but to make propositions clear." "The object of philosophy is the logical classification of thoughts—philosophy is not a theory but an activity. A philosophical work consists essentially of elucidations."

The modern philosopher would claim that he is concerned with an entirely neutral analysis, which is preliminary to any examination of the truth or falsehood of theological doctrines.

At this point a certain suspicion may arise. It has been said that we are dealing here not with a "philosophy" but with a number of philosophers who agree in practicing a certain method. But in the past it has been customary for a method to be linked to a metaphysic, and it is natural to suspect that this movement also has its metaphysic, no less powerful through being unformulated. It seems clear to us now that the Logical Positivist had one. Can the Logical Empiricists claim to be without one?

This is not an easy question to answer. It would not in any case be easy to discern a metaphysic which is contemporary and unformulated. But there is this much to be said: this method is practiced by people of contrasting temperaments who vary widely in their attitude to the method itself. Some are excited and elated by the prospect it seems to offer of dissolving the fruitless controversies of the past and of bringing a refined and disciplined language into the service of science and personal decision. There is a "Bliss was it in that dawn to be alive"[32] air about them. Others see it in a plainer, more workaday light, as a patient process of rendering philosophy genius-proof. For others it is a gateway to poetry and mysticism, for so much of what is important can no longer be said, or can be said only in paradoxes. One must tread gently—not too heavily, not too lightly—if the elusive gleam is to be momentarily caught and held. There are striking contrasts here, which throw doubt on the suggestion that this method is any single metaphysic in disguise. It seems in practice to be compatible with a variety of basic attitudes. And this should warn us not to assume prematurely that it cannot consort with Christian Faith.

The question which the modern philosopher asks raises a problem with which theologians are familiar—more familiar than the philosopher often allows—the problem of how we are able to talk about God at all. Other things we are able to talk about because we meet them in experience or because we meet things like them in experience. But we do not, at least in any ordinary sense, experience God, nor is there any like Him. It is sometimes said nowadays that meeting God is like meeting a person. He constantly confronts us through life and in history. We may not talk of God, but we may talk to Him. This analogy is, doubtless, a valuable one, but it must be recognized that it *is* an analogy. Meeting God is not just like meeting a man, as anyone

---

[32] Editor's Note (2012): William Wordsworth, *The Prelude*.

will know who has had to answer a child's questions: "But where is He?" "Why can't I see Him?" "What does He look like?" "How old is He?"

If we are to talk about God, as has been traditionally recognized, we must talk by analogy. Thus if we say "God loves mankind as a father loves his children," we are saying that God's attitude to us is analogous to a human father's love for his children. But we cannot hope to know fully what it is for God to love. Sometimes the inadequacy of the comparison is so evident that it seems more proper to say that God's love is utterly different from man's love. But if we insist on this, then we can no longer justify the use of this word about Him rather than any other. Unless the analogy holds, however tenuously, we might as well say He hates as that He loves.

It is just this danger about analogy that the logical empiricist notices. An analogy can easily get cut off from its base. A. G. N. Flew in a recent article[33] exposes the danger clearly. He says, someone tells us that God loves us as a father loves his children. We are reassured. But then we see a child dying of inoperable cancer of the throat. His earthly father is driven frantic in his efforts to help, but his Heavenly Father reveals no obvious signs of concern. Some qualification is made—God's love is not "a merely human love," or it is "an inscrutable love," perhaps, and we realize that such sufferings are quite compatible with the truth of the assertion that "God loves us as a father (but of course ...). We are reassured again."

But to say "God loves" and then to make this qualification is to take away much of its meaning from the word "love." It is in Flew's expressive phrase to "erode" the analogy.

If this danger is to be escaped, the theologian must be prepared to make a stand somewhere: to say that this or that, if it were to happen or had happened, would count against what he says about God. And then, of course, it would be possible to approach the matter in a truly empirical fashion. We might, for instance, experiment with prayer. But it seems that Christians are not prepared to experiment in this way and to abide by the results. They refuse to admit that anything could count against their beliefs. And yet they insist that these beliefs are to be understood as assertions, as statements of fact. But if the doctrines of theology are compatible with any experience whatever, if there is no testable state of affairs, which they rule out, what can they be asserting?

Thus the verifiability principle is now put forward as a criterion of what constitutes an *assertion*, and the theologian is accordingly confronted with a dilemma: either show how theological statements conform to the logical requirements of an assertion or admit that they are to be understood in some other way—as expressions of attitude, perhaps, or policies for living.

We may be tempted to reply to this dilemma, "If all that is at stake is whether theological doctrines are to be *called* 'assertions,' does it matter one way or the other? *Call* them what you like. Isn't this just a *verbal* question?" It is, of course, a verbal question, but not in any sense that renders it trivial. What is at stake is not simply whether to use the word "assertion" or the word "fact," but whether theological statements are sufficiently like the other sorts of statement we classify as "assertions" to justify their being so called. In order to assert that something or other is the case, you must know what it is that you are asserting to be the case. You must have some idea what it would be like for the statement to be true, and this entails being able to say what situations are, or are not, compatible with its being true (not all of them, of course, but some of them). If I say "the sun is shining now in London," I don't know whether this is true, but I do know what it would be like for it to be true and I do know that if it were overcast now in London that would be incompatible with its truth; and that if the B.B.C. had predicted snow in London today that would constitute evidence against (though not, of course, conclusive evidence).

---

[33] "University," Vol. I, No. 1 (Basil Blackwell): originally given as a fuller paper to the Socratic Club.

It does not fall within the scope of this paper to consider the ways in which it has been sought to answer this dilemma. Any suggested answer must satisfy two conditions. It must meet the dilemma posed by the empiricist, and it must maintain the historic Faith intact. The second of these requirements may prove more difficult in practice than at first appears. It may be that theological statements really *are* more complex than is usually thought and should not be regarded as in any straightforward sense "assertions." On the other hand an analysis tailor-made to current philosophical fashions may prove dangerously constricting. In the interests of logical classification the Faith may be drastically distorted.

The development I have tried to outline has been the concern of professional philosophers and may seem—especially in so condensed an account—to be an esoteric, specialists' affair. But it gives expression to a difficulty that is today far more widely felt—that of giving meaning to the idea of God. In this modern philosophy is representative. So that theologians, in endeavoring to grapple with this philosophical issue, will at the same time be meeting a common need.

I shall conclude, very diffidently, with my own impression of how this philosophical discussion should affect the theologians. It seems to me that it emphasizes once again the fundamental importance, in religious language, of analogy. If the theologian is aware that he is constantly using analogies, he must be alive to the dangers that beset analogical language. Not only must he beware of "eroding" the analogy: he must also reflect carefully on the warrant he has for using a particular analogy (or "image"—this word is, perhaps, less misleading), and for the use he makes of it. He must not assume, for example, that a scriptural image can be removed from its context and retain its significance unimpaired. He should beware of thinking that there is always one analogy which is *the* analogy: it may be that a number are needed, each inadequate in a different way. He would be chary of supposing that he can free himself from the limitations of metaphor by the introduction of clearly defined concepts: for the impression he then has that he has attained, and is communicating, more accurate knowledge, may be dangerously delusive. Finally, he must accept the fact that he can in the nature of the case know very little about the correct application of his analogies—that there must remain always a certain salutary agnosticism.

THEOLOGY AND FALSIFICATION

I. M. Crombie
Fellow of Wadham College, Oxford

There are some who hold that religious statements cannot be fully meaningful, on the ground that those who use them allow nothing to count decisively against them, treat them, that is, as incapable of falsification. This paper[34] is an attempted answer to an article by Mr. A. G. N. Flew in "University" for Winter 1950, and an unpublished paper read by Mr. A. M. Quinton to the Aquinas Society. I shall offer only a very short, and doubtless tendentious, summary of my opponents' views.

Briefly, then, it is contended that there are utterances made from time to time by Christians and others, which are said by those who make them to be statements, but which are thought by our opponents to lack some of the properties which anything must have before it deserves to be called a statement. "There is a God," "God loves us as a father loves his children," "He shall come again with glory ..." are examples of such utterances. *Prima facie* such utterances are neither exhortations, nor questions, nor expressions of wishes; *prima facie* they appear to assert the actuality of some state of affairs; and yet (and this is the objection) they are allowed to be compatible with any and every state of affairs. If they are compatible with any and every state of affairs, they cannot mark out some one state of affairs (or group of states of affairs); and if they do not mark out some one state of affairs, how can they be statements? In the case of any ordinary statement, such as "It is raining," there is at least one situation (the absence of falling water) which is held to be incompatible with the statement, and it is the incompatibility of the situation with the statement which gives the statement its meaning. If, then, religious "statements" are compatible with anything and everything, how can they be statements? How can the honest inquirer find out what they mean, if nobody will tell him what they are incompatible with? Are they not much more like such exhortations as "Keep smiling," whose confessed purpose is to go on being in point whatever occurs? Furthermore, is it not true that they only appear to be statements to those of us who use them, because we deceive ourselves by a sort of conjuring trick, oscillating backwards and forwards between a literal interpretation of what we say when we say it, and a scornful rejection of such anthropomorphism when anybody challenges us? When we *say*: "He shall come again with glory ...," do we not picture real angels sitting on real clouds; when asked whether we really mean the clouds, we hedge; offer perhaps another picture, which again we refuse to take literally; and so on indefinitely. Whatever symbolism we offer, we always insist that only a crude man would take it literally, and yet we never offer him anything but symbolism; deceived by our imagery into supposing that we have something in mind, in fact there is nothing on which we are prepared to take our stand.

This is the position I am to try to criticize. It is, I think, less novel than its clothes; but nonetheless it is important. I turn to criticism.

Let us begin by dismissing from our enquiry the troublesome statement "There is a God" or "God exists." As every student of logic knows, all statements asserting the existence of something offer difficulties of their own, with which we need not complicate our embarrassment.

That being dismissed, I shall want to say of statements about God that they consist of two parts. Call them, if you like, subject and predicate. Whatever you call them, there is that which is

---

[34] In composing it I have also filched shamelessly (and shamefully no doubt distorted) some unpublished utterances of Dr. A. M. Farrer's.

said, and that which it is said about—namely God. It is important to make this distinction, for different problems arise about the different parts. As a first approximation towards isolating the difference, we may notice that the predicate is normally composed of ordinary words, put to unordinary uses, whereas the subject-word is "God," which has no other use. In the expression "God loves us," the word "God" is playing, so to speak, on its Home Ground, the phrase "loves us" is playing Away. Now there is one set of questions which deal with the problem of why we say, and what we mean by saying, that God loves us, rather than hates us, and there is another set of questions concerned with the problem of what it is that this statement is being made about.

To approach the matter from an angle which seems to me to afford a good view of it, I shall make a few observations about the epistemological nature of religious belief. Let me caution the reader that, in doing so, I am not attempting to describe how religious belief in fact arises.

Theoretically, then, religious belief, like all of us, has two parents; and, like some of us, it is nurtured after its birth, both by its parents and by a nurse. The female parent is what one might call *undifferentiated theism*, the male parent is particular events or occasions interpreted as theophanic, and the extra-parental nurture is provided by religious activity.

A word, first, about the female parent. It is in fact the case that there are elements in our experience which lead people to a certain sort of belief, which we call a belief in God. (We could, if we wished, call it rather an attitude than a belief, so long as we were careful not to call it an attitude to life; for it is of the essence of the attitude to hold that nothing whatever in life may be identified with that towards which it is taken up). Among the elements in experience which provoke this belief or attitude, perhaps the most powerful is what I shall call a sense of contingency. Others are moral experience, and the beauty and order of nature. Others may be actual abnormal experience of the type called religious or mystical. There are those to whom conscience appears in the form of an unconditional demand; to whom the obligation to one's neighbor seems to be something imposed on him and on me by a third party who is set over us both. There are those to whom the beauty and order of nature appears as the intrusion into nature of a realm of beauty and order beyond it. There are those who believe themselves or others to be enriched by moments of direct access to the divine. Now there are two things that must be said about these various theistic interpretations of our experience. The first is that those who so interpret need not be so inexpert in logic as to suppose that there is anything of the nature of a deductive or inductive argument which leads from a premise asserting the existence of the area of experience in question to a conclusion expressing belief in God. Nobody who takes seriously the so-called moral argument need suppose that the *prima facie* authority of conscience cannot be naturalistically explained. He can quite well acknowledge that the imperativeness which impresses him could be a mere reflection of his jealousy of his father, or a mere vestigial survival of tribal taboo. The mystic can quite well acknowledge that there is nothing which logically forbids the interpretation of the experience which he enjoys in terms of the condition of his liver or the rate of his respirations. If, being acquainted with the alternative explanations, he persists in rejecting them, it need not be, though of course it sometimes is, because he is seized with a fallacious refutation of their validity. All that is necessary is that he should be honestly convinced that, in interpreting them, as he does, theistically, he is in some sense facing them more honestly, bringing out more of what they contain or involve than could be done by interpreting them in any other way. The one interpretation is preferred to the other, not because the latter is thought to be refutable on paper, but because it is judged to be unconvincing in the light of familiarity with the facts. There is a partial parallel to this in historical judgment. Where you and I differ in our interpretation of a series of events, there is nothing outside the events in question which can overrule either of us, so that each man must accept the interpretation which seems, on fair and critical scrutiny, the most convincing to him. The parallel is only partial, however, for in historical (and literary) interpretation there is something which to some extent controls one's interpretation, and that is one's general knowledge of human nature; and in metaphysical interpretation there is nothing analogous to this. That, then, is my first comment on theistic interpretations; for all that these journeys of the mind are often recorded in quasi-argumentative form, they are not in any ordinary sense arguments, and their validity cannot be assessed by asking whether they conform to the laws either of logic or of scientific method. My second comment upon them is that, in stating them, we find ourselves saying things which we cannot seriously mean. Thus the man of conscience uses some such concept as the juridical concept of authority, and locates his authority outside nature; the man of beauty and order speaks of an intrusion from another realm; the mystic speaks of experiencing God. In every case such language lays the user open to devastating criticism, to which he can only retort by pleading that such language, while it is not to be taken strictly, seems to him to be the natural language to use.

To bring these points into a somewhat stronger light, let me say something about the sense of contingency, the conviction which people have, it may be in blinding moments, or it may be in a permanent disposition of a man's mind, that we, and the whole world in which we live, derive our being from something outside us. The first thing I want to say about this is that such a conviction is to no extent like the conclusion of an argument; the sense of dependence feels not at all like being persuaded by arguments, but like seeing, seeing, as it were, through a gap in the rolling mists of argument, which alone, one feels, could conceal the obvious truth. One is not *persuaded* to believe that one is contingent; rather one feels that it is only by persuasion that one could ever believe anything else. The second thing I want to say about this conviction of contingency is that in expressing it, as Mr. Quinton has admirably shown, we turn the word "contingent" to work which is not its normal employment, and which it cannot properly do.

For the distinction between necessity and contingency is not a distinction between different sorts of entities, but between different sorts of statement. A necessary statement is one whose denial involves a breach of the laws of logic, and a contingent statement is one in which this is not the case. (I do not of course assert that this is the only way in which these terms have been used in the history of philosophy; but I do assert that this is the only use of them which does not give rise to impossible difficulties. I have no space to demonstrate this here; and indeed I do not think that it is any longer in need of demonstration). But in this, the only coherent sense of "contingent," the existence of the world may be a contingent fact, but so unfortunately is that of God. For *all* existential statements are contingent; that is to say, it is never true that we can involve ourselves in a breach of the laws of logic by merely denying that something exists. We cannot therefore in this sense contrast the contingent existence of the world with the necessary existence of God.

It follows that if a man persists in speaking of the contingency of the world, he must be using the term in a new or transferred sense. It must be that he is borrowing[35] a word from the logician and putting it to work which it cannot properly do. Why does he do this, and how can he make clear what precisely this new use is? For it is no good saying that when we are talking about God we do not use words in their ordinary senses unless we are prepared to say in what

---

[35] It might be argued that, historically, the borrowing was the other way round. To decide that we should have to decide where the frontier between logic and metaphysics really comes in the work of those whose doctrine on the relationship between these disciplines is unsatisfactory.

senses it is that we do use them. And yet how can we explain to the honest inquirer what is the new sense in which the word "contingent" is being used when we use it of the world? For if it is proper to use it, in this sense, of everything with which we are acquainted, and improper to use it only of God, with whom we are not acquainted, how can the new use be learnt? For we normally learn the correct use of a word by noticing the differences between the situations in which it may be applied and those in which it may not; but the word "contingent" is applicable in all the situations in which we ever find ourselves. If I said that everything but God was flexible, not of course in the ordinary sense, but in some other, how could you discover what the new sense was?

The answer must be that when we speak of the world as contingent, dependent, an effect or product, and so contrast it with a necessary, self-existent being, a first cause or a creator, we say something which on analysis will not do at all (for devastating criticisms can be brought against all these formulations), but which seems to us to be the fittest sort of language for our purpose. Why we find such language appropriate, and how, therefore, it is to be interpreted, is not at all an easy question; that it does in some way, it may be in some logically anomalous way, convey the meaning of those who use it, seems however to be an evident fact. How it is that the trick is worked, how it is that this sort of distortion of language enables believers to give expression to their beliefs, this it is the true business of the natural theologian to discuss. Dr. Farrer, for example, in *Finite and Infinite*, has done much to elucidate what it is that one is striving to express when one speaks of the contingency of the world, and so to so enlighten the honest inquirer who wishes to know how the word "contingent" is here being used.

What I have said about contingency and necessity applies also to obligation and its transcendent ground (or goodness and its transcendent goal), to design and its transcendent designer, to religious experience and its transcendent object. In all these cases we use language which on analysis will not do, but which seems to us to be appropriate for the expression of our beliefs; and in all these cases the question can be, and is, discussed, why such language is chosen, and how it is to be understood.

That then is the female parent of religious belief; call her natural theism, or what you will, she is a response, not precisely logical, and yet in no sense emotional or evaluative, to certain elements in our experience, whose characteristic is that they induce us, not to make straightforward statements about the world, but to strain and distort our media of communication in order to express what we make of them. In herself she is an honest woman; and if she is sometimes bedizened in logical trappings, and put out on the streets as an inductive argument, the fault is hardly hers. Her function is, not to prove to us that God exists, but to provide us with a "meaning" for the word "God." Without her we should not know whither statements concerning the word were to be referred; the subject in theological utterances would be unattached. All that we should know of them is that they were not to be referred to anything with which we are or could hope to be acquainted; that, and also that they were to be understood in terms of whatever it is that people suppose themselves to be doing when they build churches and kneel down in them. And that is not entirely satisfactory; for while there is much to be said in practice for advising the honest inquirer into the reference of the word "God" to pursue his enquiry by familiarizing himself with the concrete activity of religion, it remains true that the range and variety of possible delusions which could induce such behavior is theoretically boundless, and, as visitors to the Pacific coast of the United States can testify, in practice very large.

The male parent of religious belief, that which brings us on from the condition of merely possessing the category of the divine, into the condition of active belief in God, this consists in

Christianity (and if there is nothing analogous in other religions, so much the worse for them) in the interpretation of certain objects or events as a manifestation of the divine. It is, in other words, because we find, that, in thinking of certain events in terms of the category of the divine, we can give what seems to us the most convincing account of them, that we can assure ourselves that the notion of God is not just an empty aspiration. Without the notion of God we could interpret nothing as divine, and without concrete events which we felt impelled to interpret as divine we could not know that the notion of divinity had any application to reality. Why it is that as Christians we find ourselves impelled to interpret the history of Israel, the life and death of Christ, and the experience of his church as revelatory of God, I shall not here attempt to say; it is an oft told tale, and I shall content myself with saying that we can hardly expect to feel such an impulsion so long as our knowledge of these matters is superficial and altogether from without. Why we feel such an impulsion, it is not of course a logical impulsion; that is, we may resist it (or fail to feel it) without thereby contravening the laws of logic, or the rules of any pragmatically accredited inductive procedure. On the anthropological level the history of Israel, Old and New, is certainly the history of a religious development from its tribal origins. We may decide, or we may not, that it is something more, something beyond the wit of man to invent, something which seems to us to be a real and coherent communication from a real and coherent, though superhuman, mind. We may decide, or we may not; neither decision breaks the rules, for in such a unique matter there are no rules to conform to or to break. The judgment is our own; and in the language of the New Testament it judges us; that is, it reveals what, up to the moment of our decision, the Spirit of God has done in us—but that, of course, is to argue in a circle.

Belief, thus begotten, is nurtured by the practice of the Christian life—by the conviction so aroused (or, of course, not aroused; but then it is starvation and not nurture) that the Christian warfare is a real warfare. Something will have to be said about this later on, but for the moment I propose to dismiss it, and to return to the consideration of the significance of religious utterances in the light of the dual parentage of religious belief.

I have argued that unless certain things seem to us to be signs of divine activity, then we may hope that there is a God, but we cannot properly believe that there is. It follows from this that religious belief must properly involve treating something as revelatory of God; and that is to say that it must involve an element of authority (for to treat something as divine revelation is to invest it with authority). That what we say about God is said on authority (and, in particular, on the authority of Christ) is of the first importance in considering the significance of these statements. In what way this is so, I shall hope to make clear as we go along.

If we remember that our statements about God rest on the authority of Christ, whom we call his Word, we can see what seems to me the essential clue to the interpretation of the logical nature of such utterances, and that is, in a word, the notion of parable. To elucidate what I mean by "parable" (for I am using the word in an extended sense) let us consider Christ's action on Palm Sunday, when he rode into Jerusalem on an ass. This action was an act of teaching. For it had been said to Jerusalem that her king would come to her riding upon an ass. Whoever, therefore, deliberately chose this method of entry, was saying in effect: "What you are about to witness (namely my Passion, Death and Resurrection) is the coming of the Messianic King to claim his kingdom." The prophecy of Messiah's kingdom was to be interpreted, not in the ordinary sense, but in the sense of the royal kingship of the Crucified. To interpret in this way is to teach by violent paradox, indeed, but nonetheless it is to teach. Part of the lesson is that it is only the kings of the Gentiles that lord it over their subjects; if any man will be a king in Israel (God's chosen people), he must humble himself as a servant; part of it is that the Crucifixion is to be seen as Messianic, that is as God's salvation of his chosen people. Now the logical structure which is involved here is something like this:—You are told a story (Behold, thy king cometh, meek and lowly, and riding upon an ass). You will not know just what the reality to which the story refers will be like until it happens. If you take the story at its face value (an ordinary, though humble, king, bringing an ordinary political salvation), you will get it all wrong. If you bring to bear upon its interpretation all that the Law and the Prophets have taught you about God's purposes for his people, though you will still not know just what it will be like until it happens, nonetheless you will not go wrong by believing it; for then you will know that Christ ought to have suffered these things, and to enter into his glory, and so you will learn what the story has to tell you of God's purposes for man, and something therefore, indirectly, of God. If you remember what Isaiah says about humility, and sacrifice, you will see that what is being forecast is that God's purposes will be accomplished by a man who fulfills the Law and the Prophets in humble obedience.

This story is that one that can be fairly fully interpreted. There are others that cannot. There is for example Hosea's parable in which he likens himself to God, and Israel to his unfaithful wife, and expresses his grief at his wife's unfaithfulness. If, now, you ask for this to be fully interpreted, if you ask Hosea to tell you what he supposes it is like for the Holy One of Israel, of whom no similitude may be made, to be grieved, demanding to know, not what would happen in such a case to the unfaithful sinner who had provoked the divine wrath, but what was the condition of the divine mind in itself, then no doubt he would have regarded the very question as blasphemous. As an inspired prophet, he felt himself entitled to say that God was grieved, without presuming to imagine what such a situation was like, other than in its effects. What he said was said on authority; it was not his own invention, and therefore he could rely on its truth, without supposing himself to understand its full meaning. Insofar as Hosea's parable is "interpreted," the interpretation is confined to identifying the *dramatis personae* (Hosea = God, his wife = Israel). It is noteworthy that the interpretation which is sometimes given to the parables of the New Testament is usually of the same sketchy kind (The reapers are the angels). In Plato's famous parable of prisoners in a cave, it is quite possible to describe the situation which the parable seeks to illuminate. One can describe how a man can begin by being content to establish rough laws concerning what follows what in nature, how he may proceed from such a condition to desire explanations of the regularities which are forced on his attention, rising thus to more abstract and mathematical generalizations, and then, through the study of mathematics, to completely abstract speculation. One cannot similarly describe the situation which the parable of the Prodigal Son is intended to illustrate (or rather one can only describe the human end of it); and no attempt is ever made to do so.

I make no apology for these paragraphs about the Bible; after all, the Bible is the source of Christian belief, and it cannot but illuminate the logical nature of the latter to consider the communicational methods of the former. But we must turn back to more general considerations. It is, then, characteristic of a parable that the words which are used in it are used in their ordinary senses. Elsewhere this is not always so. If you speak of the virtues of a certain sort of car, the word "virtue," being applied to a car, comes to mean something different from what it means in application to human beings. If you speak of hot temper, the word "hot" does not mean what it means in the ordinary way. Now many people suppose that something of the latter sort is happening in religious utterances. When God is said to be jealous, or active in history, it is felt that the word "jealous" or "active" must be being used here in a transferred sense. But if it is being used in a transferred sense, some means or other must be supplied whereby the new sense can be taken. The activity of God is presumably not like the activity of men (it does not make him hot or tired); to say then that God is active must involve modifying the meaning of the word. But if the word is undergoing modification, it is essential that we should know in what direction. In the case of ordinary transfers, how do we know what sort of modification is involved? This is a large question, but roughly, I think, the answer is in two ways. Firstly there is normally a certain appropriateness, like the appropriateness of "hot" in "hot temper"; and secondly we can notice the circumstances in which the word gets used and withheld in its transferred sense. If I hear the phrase "Baroque music," the meaning of the word "Baroque" in its normal architectural employment may set me looking in a certain direction; and I can clinch the matter by asking for examples. "Bach? Buxtehude? Beethoven?" But for either of these ways to be of any use to me, I must know something about *both* ends of the transfer. I must know something about Baroque architecture, *and* I must be able to run through musical styles in my head, to look for the musical analog of Baroque features. If I cannot stumble on your meaning without assistance, I can still do so by eliciting from you that Bach and Buxtehude are, Handel and Mozart are not, examples of the sort of music you have in mind. This is informative to me if and only if I know something of Buxtehude and Bach, Handel and Mozart.

Now we all know what it is like for a man to be active. We can quote examples, decide correctly, and so forth. But what about divine activity? Surely we cannot have it both ways. Either God can be moderately like a man, so that the word "active," used of him, can set us looking in the right direction; or he can be quite unlike a man, in which case it cannot. Nor can we be helped by the giving of examples, unless it is legitimate to point to examples of divine activity—to say "Now here God is being active, but not there." This constitutes the force of Mr. Flew's demand that we should tell him how statements about God can be falsified. In essence Mr. Flew is saying:—"When you speak about God, the words which occur in the predicate part of your statements are not being used in the ordinary sense; you make so great a difference between God and man, that I cannot even find that the words you use set me looking in anything that might perhaps be the right direction. You speak of God as being outside time; and when I think what I mean by "activity," I find that that word, as used by a timeless being, suggests to me nothing whatsoever. There is only one resort left; give me examples of when one of your statements is, and is not, applicable. If, as no doubt you will say, that is an unfair demand, since they are always applicable (e.g. God is always active, so that there are no cases of his inactivity to be pointed to), I will not insist on actual examples; make them up if you like. But do not point to *everything* and say '*That* is what I mean'; for *everything* is not *that*, but this and this and this and many other mutual incompatibles; and black and white and red and green and kind and cruel and coal and ink and everything else together cannot possibly elucidate to me the meaning of a word."

As I have said, the answer must be that when we speak about God, the words we use are intended in their ordinary sense (for we cannot make a transfer, failing familiarity with both ends of it), although we do not suppose that in their ordinary interpretation they can be strictly true of him. We do not even know how much of them applies. To some extent it may be possible to take a word like "activity" and whittle away that in it which most obviously does not apply. It is however an exaggeration, at the least, to suppose that this process of whittling away leaves us in the end with a kernel about which we can say that we know that it does apply. A traditional procedure is to compose a scale on which inanimate matter is at the bottom, the characteristically human activities, such as thinking and personal relationship, at the top, and to suppose that the scale is pointing towards God; and so on this assumption the first thing to do is to pare away from the notion of human activity whatever in it is common to what stands below it on the scale—for example actual physical moving about. Taking the human residue, we try to decide what in it is positive, and what is negative, mere limitation. The tenuous ghost of a concept remaining we suppose to be the essential structure of activity (that structure which is common to running and thinking) and so to be realized also in divine activity. Perhaps this is how we imagine our language to be related to the divine realities about which we use it; but such ghostly and evacuated concepts are clearly too tenuous and elusive to be called the meanings of the words we use. To think of God thus is to think of him not in our own image, but in the rarefied ghost of our own image; and so we think of him in our own image, but do not suppose that in so thinking of him we begin to do him justice. What we do, then, is in essence to think of God in parables. The things we say about God are said on the authority of the words and acts of Christ, who spoke in human language, using parable; and so we too speak of God in parable—authoritative parable, authorized parable; knowing that the truth is not literally that which our parables represent, knowing therefore that now we see in a glass darkly, but trusting, because we trust the source of the parables, that in believing them and interpreting them in the light of each other, we shall not be misled, that we shall have such knowledge as we need to possess for the foundation of the religious life.

So far so good. But it is only the predicates of theological utterances which are parabolic; it is only in what is *said about* God that the words are put to other than customary employment. When we say "God is merciful," it is "merciful" that is in strange company—deprived of its usual escort of human sentiments. But the word "God" only occurs in statements about God. Our grasp of this word, therefore, cannot be derived from our grasp of it in ordinary human contexts, for it is not used in such contexts. How then is our grasp of it to be accounted for? In other words, if I have given some account of how, and in what sense, we understand the meaning of the things we say about God, I have still to give some account of how, and in what sense, we know what it is that we are saying them about.

In thus turning back from the predicate to the subject of religious utterances, we are turning from revealed theology to natural theology, from the male to the female parent of religious belief. And the answer to the question:—"What grasp have we of the meaning of the word 'God'?" must be dealt with along the following lines. Revelation is important to the believer not for what it is in itself (the biography of a Jew, and the history of his forerunners and followers), nor because it is revelation of nothing in particular, but because it is revelation of God. In treating it as something important, something commanding our allegiance, we are bringing to bear upon it the category of the transcendent, of the divine. Of the nature of that category I have already spoken. In other words, there must exist within a man's mind the contrast between the contingent and the necessary, the derivative and the underivative, the finite and the infinite, the perfect and the imperfect, before anything can be for him a revelation of God. Given that contrast, we are given also that to which the parables or stories are referred. What is thus given is certainly not knowledge of the object to which they apply; it is something much more like a direction. We do not, that is, know to what to refer our parables; we know merely that we are to refer them out of experience, and out of it *in which direction*. The expression "God" is to refer to that object, whatever it is, and if there be one, which is such that the knowledge of it would be to us knowledge of the unfamiliar term in the contrast between finite and infinite.

Statements about God, then, are in effect parables, which are referred, by means of the proper name "God," out of our experience in a certain direction. We may, if we like, by the process of whittling away, which I have mentioned, try to tell ourselves what part of the meaning of our statements applies reasonably well, what part outrageously badly; but the fact remains that, in one important sense, when we speak about God, we do not know what we mean (that is, we do not know what that which we are talking about is like), and do not need to know, because we accept the images, which we employ, on authority. Because our concern with God is religious and not speculative (it is contemplative in part, but that is another matter), because our need is, not to know what God is like, but to enter into relation with him, the authorized images serve our purpose. They belong to a type of discourse—parable—with which we are familiar, and therefore they have communication value, although in a sense they lack descriptive value.

If this is so, how do we stand with regard to verification and falsification? Must we, to preserve our claim to be making assertions, be prepared to say what would count against them? Let us see how far we can do so. Does anything count against the assertion that God is merciful? Yes, suffering. Does anything count decisively against it? No, we reply, because it is true. Could anything count decisively against it? Yes, suffering which was utterly, eternally and irredeemably pointless. Can we then design a crucial experiment? No, because we can never see all of the picture. Two things at least are hidden from us; what goes on in the recesses of the personality of the sufferer, and what shall happen hereafter.

Well, then, the statement that God is merciful is not testable; it is compatible with any and every tract of experience which we are in fact capable of witnessing. It cannot be verified; does this matter?

To answer this, we must make up our minds why the demand for verification or falsification is legitimate. On this large matter I shall be summary and dogmatic, as follows. (1) The demand that a statement of fact should be verifiable is a conflation of two demands. (2) The *first* point is that all statements of fact must be verifiable in the sense that there must not exist a *rule of language* which precludes testing the statement. That is to say, the way the statement is to be taken must not be such that to try to test it is to show that you do not understand it. If I say that it is wrong to kill, and you challenge my statement and adduce as evidence against it that thugs and headhunters do so out of religious duty, then you have not understood my statement. My statement was not a statement of fact, but a moral judgment, and your statement that it should be tested by anthropological investigations shows that you did not understand it. But so long as there exists no *logical* (or might say *interpretational*) ban on looking around for verification, the existence of a factual *ban* on verification does not matter. "Caesar had mutton before he crossed the Rubicon" cannot in fact be tested, but by trying to devise ways of testing it you do not show that you have not understood it; you are merely wasting your time. (3) The *second* point is that, *for me, fully* to understand a statement, *I* must know what a test of it would be like. If I have no idea how to test whether somebody had mutton, then I do not know what "having mutton" means. This stipulation is concerned, not with the logical nature of the expression, but with its communication value for me. (4) There are then two stipulations, and they are different. The first is a logical stipulation, and it is to the effect that nothing can be a statement of fact if it is untestable in the sense that the notion of testing it is precluded by correctly interpreting it. The second is a communication stipulation, and it is to the effect that nobody can fully understand a statement, unless he has a fair idea how a situation about which it was true would differ from a situation about which it was false.

Now with regard to these two stipulations, how do religious utterances fare? With regard to the first, there is no language rule implicit in a correct understanding of them which precludes putting them to the test (there may be a rule of faith, but that is another matter). If a man says:—"How can God be loving, and allow pain?" he does *not* show that he has understood it.

There *is* a *prima facie* incompatibility between the love of God, and pain and suffering. The Christian maintains that it is *prima facie* only; others maintain that it is not. They may argue about it, and the issue cannot be decided; but it cannot be decided, not because (as in the case of e.g. moral or mathematical judgments) the appeal to facts is *logically* the wrong way of trying to decide the issue, and shows that you have not understood the judgment; *but* because, since our experience is limited in the way it is, we cannot get into position to decide it, any more than we can get into position to decide what Julius Caesar had for breakfast before he crossed the Rubicon. For the Christian the operation of getting into position to decide it is called dying; and, though we can all do that, we cannot return to report what we find. By this test, then, religious utterances can be called statements of fact; that is their *logical* classification.

With regard to the second stipulation, the case is a little complicated, for here we are concerned with communication value, and there are the two levels, the one on which we remain within the parable, and the other on which we try to step outside it. Now, on the first level we know well enough how to test a statement like "God loves us"; it is, for example, like testing "My father loves me." In fact, of course, since with parents and schoolmasters severity is notoriously a way of displaying affection, the decisive testing of such a statement is not easy; but there is a point beyond which it is foolish to continue to have doubts. Now, within the parable, we are supposing "God loves us" to be a statement like "My father loves me," "God" to be a subject similar to "My father," "God loves us" being thus related to "My father loves me" as the latter is related to "Aristotle's father loved him." We do not suppose that we can actually test "God loves us," for reasons already given (any more than we can test the one about Aristotle); but the communication value of the statement whose subject is "God" is derived from the communication value of the same statement with a different proper name as subject. If we try to step outside the parable, then we must admit that we do not know what the situation about which our parable is being told is like; we should only know if we could know God, and know even as also we have been known; see, that is, the unfolding of the divine purposes in their entirety. Such ignorance is what we ought to expect. We do not know how what we call the divine wrath differs from the divine mercy (because we do not know how they respectively resemble human wrath and mercy); but we do know how what *we mean* when we talk about the wrath of God differs from what *we mean* when we talk about his mercy, because then we are within the parable, talking within the framework of admitted ignorance, in language which we accept because we trust its source. We know what is meant *in* the parable, when the father of the Prodigal sees him coming a great way off and runs to meet him, and we can therefore think in terms of this image. We know that we are here promised that whenever we come to ourselves and return to God, he will come to meet us. This is enough to encourage us to return and to make us alert to catch the signs of the divine response; but it does not lead us to presume to an understanding of the mind and heart of God. In talking we remain within the parable, and so our statements communicate; we do not know how the parable applies, but we believe that it does apply, and that we shall one day see how. (Some even believe, perhaps rightly, that in our earthly condition we may by direct illumination of our minds be enabled to know progressively more about the realities to which our parables apply, and in consequence about the manner of their application).

Much of what I have said agrees very closely with what the atheist says about religious belief, except that I have tried to make it sound better. The atheist alleges that the religious man supposes himself to know what he means by his statements only because, until challenged, he interprets them anthropomorphically; when challenged, however, he retreats rapidly backwards towards complete agnosticism. I agree with this, with two provisos. The first is that the religious man does not suppose himself to know what he means by his statements (for what religious man supposes himself to be the Holy Ghost?); he knows what his statements mean within the parable, and believes that they are the right statements to use. (Theology is not a science; it is a sort of art of enlightened ignorance). The second proviso is that the agnosticism is not complete; for the Christian, under attack, falls back not in any direction, but in one direction; he falls back upon the person of Christ, and the concrete realities of the Christian life.

Let us consider this for a moment with regard to the divine love. I could be attacked in this sort of way:—"You have contended," my opponent might argue, "that when we say that God loves us the communication value of the statement is determined by the communication value of a similar statement about a human subject; and that we know the statement to be the right statement, but cannot know *how* it is the right statement, that is, what the divine love is like. But this will not do. Loving is an activity with two poles, the lover and the loved. We may not know the lover, in the case of God, but we *are*, and therefore *must know*, the loved. Now, to say that the image or parable of human love is the right image to use about God must imply that there is some similarity or analogy between human and divine love. Father's love may be superficially very unlike mother's, but unless there is some similarity of structure between them, we cannot use the same word of both. But we cannot believe that there is any similarity between the love of God and human love, unless we can detect some similarity between being loved by God and being loved by man. But if being loved by God is what we experience all the time, then it is not like being loved by man; it is like being let down right and left. And in the face of so great a discrepancy, we cannot believe that God loves us, if that is supposed to be in any sense a statement of sober fact."

I cannot attempt to answer this objection; it involves the whole problem of religion. But there is something I want to say about it, which is that the Christian does not attempt to evade it either by helter-skelter flight, or by impudent bluff. He has his prepared positions onto which he retreats; and he knows that if these positions are taken, then he must surrender. He does not believe that they can be taken, but that is another matter. There are three main fortresses behind which he goes. For, firstly, he looks for the resurrection of the dead, and the life of the world to come; he believes, that is, that we do not see all the picture, and that the parts which we do not see are precisely the parts which determine the design of the whole. He admits that if this hope be vain then we are of all men the most miserable. Secondly he claims that he sees in Christ the verification, and to some extent also the specification, of the divine love. That is to say, he finds in Christ not only convincing evidence of God's concern for us, but also what sort of love the divine love is, what sort of benefits God is concerned to give us. He sees that, on the New Testament scale of values, it is better for a man to lose the whole world if he can thereby save his soul (which means his relationship to God); and that for that hope it is reasonable to sacrifice all that he has, and to undergo the death of the body and the mortification of the spirit. Thirdly he claims that in the religious life, of others, if not as yet in his own, the divine love may be encountered, that the promise "I will not fail thee nor forsake thee" is, if rightly understood, confirmed there. If of course this promise is interpreted as involving immunity from bodily suffering, it will be refuted; but no reader of the New Testament has any right so to interpret it. It is less glaringly, but as decisively, wrong to interpret it as involving immunity from spiritual suffering; for in the New Testament only the undergoing of death (which means the abdication of control over one's destiny) can be the beginning of life. What then does it promise? It promises that to the man who begins on the way of the Christian life, on the way, that is, of seeking life through death, of seeking relationship with God through the abdication of the self-sovereignty claimed by Adam, that to him the right will be hard but not impossible, progress often indiscernible, but real, progress which is towards the paring away of selfhood, and which is often given therefore through defeat and humiliation, but a defeat and humiliation which are not final, which leave it possible to continue. This is the extra-parental nurture of religious belief of which I spoke earlier, and it is the third of the prepared positions onto which the Christian retreats, claiming that the image and reflection of the love of God may be seen not only hereafter, not only in Christ, but also, if dimly, in the concrete process of living the Christian life.

One final word. Religion has indeed its problems; but it is useless to consider them outside their religious context. Seen as a whole religion makes rough sense, though it does not make limpidity.

SOME REMARKS ON ANALYSIS, PERSONALITY, AND RELIGION

GEOFFREY MIDGLEY
Lecturer in Philosophy at Newcastle-on-Tyne

I suggested in my reply to the paper[36] which began all this discussion, Tim Miles' paper on "The Analysis of God-propositions," that, on his account of the matter at least, the techniques of philosophical analysis current now show a bias which can be described as regarding Natural Science as the norm of valid human experience. I also suggested that the techniques as he outlined them must prove inadequate to the notion of personality. The reason I suggested for this is that personality is not a scientific concept. Since reading through Mr. Wisdom's series of articles on "Other Minds," I am not disposed to alter this opinion. On the contrary, I think Mr. Miles correctly revealed a bias present in the enterprise of logical analysis as such. I do not want to read a long paper this afternoon. All I want to do is to throw out for discussion a somewhat uncompromising statement of what I have said before, and to give an indication of the direction in which we might find a clarification of the issues. Let me begin with a few assertions.

(1) The applicability of any contemporary method of logical analysis is based on certain characteristics which verbal language is believed to have in common with deductive symbolic systems like that of Theoretical Physics.

(2) This is not just a peculiarity of contemporary logical analysis, but a necessary feature of logical analysis as such, which it has exhibited in every philosophical epoch, owing to the close connection between the methods of Formal Logic and the methods of Mathematics.

(3) The features of language assumed for the purposes of logical analysis are indeed present, but only where language is used in certain ways, namely as a tool in theoretical thought.

(4) The conception of logical analysis as the principal task of Philosophy is the direct consequence of regarding Natural Science as in some sense knowledge par excellence, and hence of regarding the use of language in theoretical thinking as the only use in which language rises above mere ejaculations, of however complex a kind, to the level of making assertions.

(5) This evaluation of Natural Science is historically and psychologically a peculiar characteristic of the present epoch, and colors our attitude not only intellectually in that it sets our framework of fundamental presuppositions, but also emotionally in that it determines our system of values.

(6) This current attitude is intellectually and emotionally positively hostile to the conception of personality as such.

(7) Religion, in any form familiar to us, simply *is* the taking seriously of the notion of personality.

(8) Hence, though scientific *knowledge* can never be in conflict with anything valid in religion, the scientific *attitude* is in many points incompatible with the religious.

If I am right in these assertions, then there will be an inevitable conflict between Christianity and any school of Philosophy that makes logical analysis a primary part of its program, *insofar as that philosophy concerns itself with matters beyond the criticism of the concepts of Natural Science,*[37] since such a school will inevitably adopt the attitude that all "proper" language is of a certain kind, and will therefore either set, or suggest, limits to what

---

[36] Editor's Note (2012): responses to Logical Positivism.
[37] "Natural Science" is here used to include those statements of common sense which have a theoretical function similar to scientific statements.

may be said, which preclude everything which either is based upon or entails an attitude in opposition to the so-called "scientific attitude." And the focus of this conflict will be the notion of personality.

I think I should begin by making good the statement that Religion is the taking seriously of the notion of personality. To make this clear I would like to direct your attention to the notorious distinction between knowledge by acquaintance and knowledge that is a matter of intellect. It is a matter of regarding certain propositions as true. And what is this? It seems to me that the significance of propositions factual in this sense lies at the foundation of Positivism and Pragmatism.

The function of theoretical knowledge is always the prediction of future events in order that we may cope with them technically. Of course human thought is free to this extent that it may envisage situations which are so wildly improbable that the knowledge of facts relevant to such situations, while undeniably genuine theoretical knowledge, is also undeniably useless, and Pragmatism has been attacked on these grounds. But this is a misunderstanding. For reasons which I cannot go into now it seems to me undeniable that theoretical knowledge consists in being disposed to act in an appropriate manner in the face of some practical situation, whether or not the appropriate situations are likely to arise, and even when we do not know clearly what situations would call upon our theoretical knowledge. For such knowledge the basic tenets of Positivism and Pragmatism seem undeniable. "Knowledge that," in fact, is a species of "knowledge how." The unity of theory and practice is not an ideal, but a logical necessity.

But what of knowledge by acquaintance? It seems to me only proper to use this phrase in the ordinary sense, of knowledge of persons. Now it seems to me that knowledge of persons cannot be regarded in terms of intellectual activity imposed on something merely given, in a passive sense experience. We know persons by having relationships with them, and it seems to me that if we are to extend the term "knowledge by acquaintance" to cover knowledge of other things than human persons, we must suppose that there is some sense in which we can have a relationship with the things in question. We do not "know" green patches or tables; we see them; but perhaps we know places, and perhaps we know the world. Perhaps there is some sense in which there can be a relationship with the inanimate not-self which is strongly analogous to personal relationship. A strong insistence on the immanence of God seems to be allied to such a conception. But at any rate it seems to me to be legitimate to speak of knowledge by acquaintance only where the object of knowledge is in some sense active, and knowledge consists not in theorizing about it, but in being involved in mutual interaction with it. And it seems to me that our ends are set for us in such mutual interaction with something beyond ourselves. Theoretical knowledge is confined to means. It is only in the fundamentally non-intellectual knowledge by acquaintance that we find ends.

Now Religion is essentially the search for a right relationship with one's fellow men and with reality. The scientific quest is concerned with handling reality, the religious quest with loving it. And these two quests are connected with two fundamentally different uses of language, (1) the logical use, in which words are used as symbols in a calculus, and language is the tool by which thought, when expressed in symbols which obey the mechanical rules of formal logic, may be converted into a mechanical operation, and (2) the expressive use, in which the end of language is to establish contact between persons. This distinction is not unconnected with the distinction between descriptive and emotive language,[38] except that the latter tends to debase the expressive use of language to mere ejaculation, and tends to divide words into two separate

---

[38] Editor's Note (2012): These are terms from the field of philosophy known as Logical Positivism.

classes; descriptive and emotive words, which is a false division, for in expressive language the articulation of discourse into discrete words and sentences is not applicable.[39] The permanency of meaning which makes such an articulation significant is present only where language has been intellectualized by exact rules and definitions which turn language from an art into a calculus.

What I am driving at here is that Theology is not descriptive in the sense in which Science is, but it is devotional, that is, in Theology language is being used to establish a relationship with the Supreme Being, and to introduce other humans to the relationship. Theology is the coordination of prayer. It seems to me obvious that an analysis of theological language based on the assumption that all language which is not mere ejaculation is significant only insofar as it is concerned with practical activity at the physical level is bound to find no sense in theological statements, if indeed we can speak of statements in such a connection.

It isn't that I think that religion is not concerned with fact; it is rather that I think Natural Science is not concerned with fact. To say that Science is concerned only with how questions and not why questions is an understatement. The truth is that Science is not at all concerned with what things are but only with what we do with them. But in a genuine personal relationship we are not concerned to exploit a person, but to appraise him for what he is in himself, and this has no analogy in Science.

Now I can say what I wanted to say about the importance of personality in Religion. I want to take four important words and phrases and show how they must be misunderstood if we apply scientific criteria to Religion. (I am afraid this is all very condensed, but I hope the point will get across).

PRAYER:—From the scientific point of view, prayer can only be regarded in two ways. Either it is the attempt to influence some cosmic force with a view to exploiting the power of that force, or it is a technique for the solving of psychological problems. Hence we test the value of petitionary prayer by making a statistical analysis of its results, and test the value of all kinds of prayer by their psychotherapeutic value. God must therefore be regarded either as a scientific concept, which experiments will no doubt show to have no empirical validity, or as a psychological symbol in the Jungian sense, or as a logical construction out of religious experience, with some sort of additional aesthetic value. But prayer is communion with a person valued for his own sake, and the use of language in prayer is expressive.

GOD EXISTS IN SOME SUPREME SENSE:—This looks like a metaphysical statement, and Metaphysics, insofar as it fits in with the scientific scheme, can be nothing but meta-logic. The only element of meaning of this statement that gets across the analytical viewpoint is that we are trying to assert that God is not a hypothesis like an electron. But the important part of the statement is to be grasped only by recognizing the fact of the dependence of one person on another. We can then recognize that the existence of dependent persons involves the existence of an independent person, or at least we can recognize what is meant by this assertion, and it becomes plain that the special sort of existence attributed to God is that of independent personality.

FAITH:—For the scientist all that faith can be is the acceptance of data on the authority of other scientists. To qualify for the status of an authority a person or book must fulfill certain

---

[39] I cannot quite understand what I meant by this remark. I do not suggest that there are no such things as full stops or separate words in expressive language. I think I must have meant that the division of discourse into words and sentences in a scientific use of language reflects the structure of the abstract concepts in terms of which we try to interpret and handle reality, whereas in expressive language this does not occur, since the separate sentences have no determinate stable meaning apart from their context, and so do not represent an articulation of fact into elements.

conditions which are certainly not fulfilled by religious authorities. But faith in the religious sense is simply the achievement of personal relationship. It has no analogy at the level of theoretical thinking.

SIN:—Ethics as an intellectual discipline can be nothing but the formation of rules of conduct and the investigation of the logical structure of such rules. Theoretical knowledge of moral principles is nothing but the formation of empirical generalizations of what turns out to be "right" or "wrong" in certain sorts of situation. But ethics has continually failed to achieve anything of value because it has always tried to find an intellectual account of the origin of rightness and wrongness. The religious conception of Sin is a different sort of thing altogether. Here wrongness is seen as an outrage upon a person, as something that can arise only from personal relationship.

I hope these vague and condensed hints will mean just enough to you to serve as a focus of discussion. What I am saying is that theoretical knowledge consists in having certain rules for the manipulation of language, directed ultimately to the manipulation of things. That therefore theoretical knowledge can be concerned only with exploitation and even there only with the means of exploitation, not its ends. I would maintain that the use of language as a tool in such theoretical thinking is not a primary but a secondary use of language. That the primary use of language is an aesthetic use in which it establishes not rules of procedure, but contact with persons. That in such contact alone are we concerned with real existence as opposed to mere recipes for desirable future experiences. Finally that in all its methods logical analysis, now, and always in the past has been concerned, as it must always be, with the use of language as a calculus, a tool of theoretical thinking, and has nothing to say about the expressive powers of language with which we are concerned in real acquaintance with anything beyond ourselves.

Let us look for a moment at what happens when the procedure of logical analysis is applied to even most elementary aspects of personality, the sensations of others. I will give a very short account of Wisdom[40] on "Other Minds."

His approach is that the aim of logical analysis is to cure headaches. That is to say we start from the tautology that all answerable questions can be answered, and we then concern ourselves with curing whatever disease it is that makes people ask unanswerable questions. One of the main weapons in such a cure is to show that the so-called question is not really a question at all, but a lament. Thus when the philosopher asks "How do I know that there is a chair in the next room?" and we give him the sort of answer that might be expected; e.g. "Why! Don't you remember? You saw it there ten minutes ago, and you know the only way out is through this room, and of course no one would go to the trouble to come in through the window and take a great big chair like that away," he is not satisfied. He knows all this. He has attached such a meaning to his question that any information we can give him can never satisfy him. He is not asking for information; what then is he doing? Simply saying to himself "Oh dear, oh dear, we can never really know whether there is a chair in the next room or not." This is the kind of lament that analysis aims to cure. Now some laments are curable non-philosophically. For example the lament "Oh dear, I can never know whether this ring is really gold or not" is easily cured by the discovery of *aqua regia*.[41] But sometimes a philosopher has more reason to lament than this. He can sometimes prove not merely that there is no known way of finding out what he laments not knowing, but that there *could* be no way of finding out. And then all we can do is to find a flaw in his reasoning. Now the analyst's approach to the lament that we can never really

---

[40] Editor's Note (2012): That is, John Wisdom the philosopher.
[41] Editor's Note (2012): A corrosive acid able to dissolve gold.

know whether there is a chair in the next room is to attempt to show that the sentence "There is a chair in the next room" is not quite the sort of sentence the lamenting philosopher thought it was. That what he is lamenting is not some knowledge he might have had if only it were not such a nasty world, but something that it would be silly to claim to have. And so we get phenomenalism. We try to show that insofar as the lament is justified we do not know what we are lamenting. And when we say that we do not know what we are lamenting when we lament the fact that however much evidence there is for the chair being there, and however often our predictions come right that we make on the basis of this evidence, we still do not know whether there is a chair there or not, we are saying that there is nothing over and above the evidence and the predictions involved in saying that there is a chair there, and this is to lay down as obligatory the scientific use of language.

Now Wisdom's approach to the problem of other minds is quite in this spirit. The question may be put thus: Are there other minds like our own? The answer is Yes. The next question is: "How do we know?" The answer is that people talk to us and behave in various complicated ways. The next question is: "Yes, but how do we know that over and above talking and behaving as they do, other people have experiences like our own?" The answer is that this is a lament like the lament about chairs. What we are lamenting is that we do not know other people's minds as we do our own. But it is silly to suppose that we could, for if we really knew another mind as we do our own, it would be our own mind. Hence we do not know what we are lamenting when we lament that we do not know other minds as we do our own, for we attach no meaning to the phrase "Know another mind as we do our own."

The next step is to ask what sort of knowledge we do have of other minds, and Wisdom's answer, insofar as it is an answer, is significant. For I take his elaborate discussion of a certain Leprechaun-driven watch to signify that the concept of other minds is related to the behavior of their bodies rather as the concept of an electron is related to the observed electrical phenomena.

To put the matter briefly, and hence inaccurately, we are led at first to say that statements about electrons mean the same as statements about the observed effects of electrons, for any other set of hypothetical entities having the same observable effects according to some theory could be substituted for electrons and we would not be asserting any different state of affairs. But this is not quite right, for the conception of electrons leads us to have certain mental pictures which would be different if we substituted any other hypothetical entities. We do not assert that these pictures correspond to the facts, for we never expect to see anything corresponding to them, and if we did we should have to regard our theories as wrong. So the pictures we have are not part of the meaning in the sense of what we assert to be the case, but still they do make a difference between asserting the one thing and asserting the other. Furthermore the pictures are suggestive; they suggest new lines of research, and thus play an important part in scientific theory. Hence statements about electrons do not mean the same as statements about their observed effects; they mean more, and the surplus meaning is all in terms of imaginative pictures which we do not expect ever to see in reality, and of the suggestive power of such pictures. In the same way the function of the picture of what is going on in other people's minds, the images we regard as belonging to their inner experience, play the same part in our thinking and our meaning as the pictures we associate with electrons.

The point of this is that just as it makes nonsense to say that we see all the effects of electrons, and our predictions based on the electron theory are right, yet we still do not know whether there really are electrons, so it makes no sense to say that we see how people behave, but do not know whether they really have experiences like ours. It makes no sense to say either of these things because knowing the facts in question actually consists in knowing their observable consequences, making all the correct predictions, and, perhaps, in having appropriate mental images. To claim to know another mind in any other sense than this is nonsense, for the mind would *ipso facto* be our own.[42]

This seems to be Wisdom's line in treating the problem. But of course it is fatal to any such use of the concepts of personality as we would want to make in saying that God is a person, or in approaching ethical problems from a religious point of view. Yet you have only to expose yourself to Wisdom's technique to feel that really he does make it almost impossible to take any different line. I submit that this is because the assumptions about language underlying his method are assumptions we all unconsciously make because we are so imbued with the scientific attitude. I shall say nothing of the anti-personal tendencies of modern politics, or of the disconcerting nature of the discoveries of psychoanalysis and neurology. I am only concerned with the corruption of language which has taken place since the industrial revolution. Consider the great enrichment of the vocabulary of dead, mechanically defined technical words, words like "frequency," "axis," "energy," "mass," and so on, which are familiar to most of us now in a purely technical sense. Consider what has happened to the word "power." Remember that Dr. Johnson meant something when he called St. Paul's Cathedral "Awfully built and terribly designed." Our attitude is reflected in our language. We have two kinds of language left: technical and merely emotive. Emotive ejaculations like "super," "wizard," and "awful" in our fatuous modern sense have replaced expressive words like "awful" in Dr. Johnson's sense.

I have only one thing to say about the philosophical analysis of personality, and that is that Wisdom has convinced me that traditional Metaphysics sinned just as people like Ryle and Ayer have sinned. It prescribed a talk. And the moment you prescribe a talk, the moment you lay down a set of rules distinguishing good talk from bad talk, you must use language intellectually, and then you should stick to Science. All I can say is: Let us talk about personality naively and simply, just as we feel disposed to talk, and take no notice of these linguistic Highway Codes. But let us talk good English, and don't let us kid ourselves that we are evolving a *Philosophy* of personality. There is no Philosophy of persons, just personal relationships. Philosophy, in the sense of systematic Logic or Metaphysics, has no business outside the sphere of technological Science.

GENERAL NOTE:—I wish to say generally of this paper that it expresses views I no longer hold. It is essential to its main point that language, insofar as its structure is capable of formal analysis, should be concerned solely with handling reality, and not at all with stating what it is in itself. Such reservations as "to some extent" would destroy the argument. But if they are not made the enterprise of scientific explanation is misdescribed. I do not know whether my main point could be reconciled with a more adequate account of scientific explanation or not. It now seems to me that scientific theories are illuminating and make reality intelligible in a way I confess myself unable to explain.

---

[42] I no longer regard this treatment of Wisdom as entirely fair to him. It seems to me now that he was not stating a positive doctrine in the sense in which I have attributed one to him, but simply directing our attention to certain difficulties in our customary ways of speaking.

A THEOLOGIAN'S POINT OF VIEW

AUSTIN FARRER
Fellow of Trinity College, Oxford

I had a dream. There were Theology and Philosophy, clothed in both the moral and the academic dignity of female professors. Theology held several slips of paper in her hand, with a single sentence written upon each: "God exists" on one, "The word was created" on another. Philosophy displayed several baskets on a table, marked with tickets describing sentences of different logical kinds, "Moral Commands," "Empirical Statements," "Truths of Definition," and so forth. "Into which baskets, dear Theology," she said, "would you like to put your statements?"

Theology looked at the baskets and hesitated. "Do I have to?" she replied. "I mean, is it certain that the right basket for my statements is on your table at all? Of course, if it were demonstrable that all the possible sorts of logical baskets were represented here...."

"Dear me, no," said Philosophy, "we can't claim to be sure of that. But don't you find some of these baskets rather alluring? Here is a brand new one, delivered only this morning by Logical Baskets Limited (limited, you know, or virtually so, to Oxford and Cambridge). It is called 'Expressions of Attitude to life.' Isn't that what you want? Now be reasonable."

"No, I'm afraid not," Theology replied. "You see, when I say, 'God loves what He has made,' I do not mean that John Christian takes up, or would be well advised to take up, a benevolent attitude to things in general or to his neighbor in particular; nor that he either does or should view them in the rosy light cast upon them by association with the creator God image. No, I mean what I say; I mean that the actual creator is doing this actual loving."

"Good God!" said Philosophy, "you don't say so! Well, if that's how it is, Basket Four is what you require," pointing to a basket labeled "Statements about Other Persons." "And in that case," she continued, beginning to talk exceedingly fast, "your statements will of course be subject to the routine tests of empirical verifiability and falsificab ..."

"Please, please, not again," said Theology, raising her hands to her ears. "We've had this so many times before. Haven't I told you that statements about God are not statements about a person among persons, but about that transcendent subject to whom our personal existence bears only a distant, though a real, analogy?"

"And so," said Philosophy, "I suppose you are let off any attempt at relating your statements to real life."

"Dear me, no," said Theology, "I don't get off that. Almost all religious thinking relates statements about God with statements or directions concerned with common life. Lots of people know how to do such thinking, but to know what its logical nature may be is a different matter. Perhaps you and I might hold a joint class, to find out how such thinking goes. I fear it will have to be an Advanced Class, for theological talk will turn out to be less simple in its logic, I suspect, than 'It is sweet and commendable to die for our country' or 'This garden is kept by a gardener whom no one has caught at work.'"

"Ah, I dare say," said Philosophy. "But as it would be foolish to anticipate the findings of your Advanced Class, allow me to take up another point here. You were saying that you attach great importance to the literal sense of 'God loves what He has made.' But the next moment you were protesting that the divine person is only distantly analogous to human persons, and so, presumably, that His making is only distantly analogous to human making, and His loving to

---

[43] Reprinted, by permission, from "University," Vol. 1, No. 2. Spring 1951.

human loving. If so, you mayn't seem to be saying anything very literal, or very clear, when you say that God loves what He has made. Are such meager dregs of meaning worth bothering about? You have conceded agnosticism already. Be an atheist and have done with it."

Theology replied: "It isn't only believers in an Unknown God who admit that their talk comes far short of expressing God or His doings. We should all be agnostics if our knowledge of God were our exploration of Him; as though God sat there impassive as a rock-cut Buddha, and we tortoises vainly tried to scale His knees. We cannot aspire to talk about God in (as it were) divine language, but He can stoop, if He chooses, to talk to us in our language and to deal humanly with mankind. When, for example, for us men and for our salvation …"

On hearing these dogmatic words, Philosophy muttered, "We will hear thee another time on this matter," and faded away to tea, followed by the Stoics and Epicureans. Theology was left addressing the empty Areopagus, except that I could see the Areopagite Denys skulking behind a column, and a woman called Damaris looking over the wall.

"Won't you come in, my dear?" said Theology to Damaris. Damaris entered, pulling on a commoner's gown. She produced a pencil and notebook as though from nowhere, but on being assured that the subject in hand was of no Schools value she was persuaded to put them away again and converse like a human being. She had, in fact, thought of an Intelligent Question: "I think I see what you mean," she began, "when you say it doesn't matter so much our not being able to talk straight about God, so long as He talks straight to us. You would say He does that specially in the Gospel?"

Theology assented. "But," Damaris continued, "doesn't that make God talk a terribly incorrect language? I mean, the Jews knew nothing about it really, did they, and they mixed up their logical types like anything. And we find Christ talking just like a Jew. And it isn't only the language, it's the ideas. He said He was Messiah, and you can't understand what that means without a whole lot of Jewish history. And it's the same with everything else, for instance, how He meant the sacrament would be His body and blood."

"I know," said Theology. "But we can't have it both ways, can we? If God comes down to our level and talks to us in our speech, it will have to be the speech of some one time and place. When He was fully grown He had thought-forms of a bible-minded Jew; before that, He had used the broken speech of childhood."

"That sounds all right in theory," said Damaris, "but the Jews' ideas were so queer, and it is all so far away now."

"Queer, if you like," said Theology, "but expressive for the purpose. You could talk vividly about divine things and be understood in the streets of Galilee; just try at our street corners, or—or here in our Areopagus. And as to your 'Far away'—two thousand years are two thousand years, but there is always a bridge. For those ideas you speak of have lived on and partly molded, partly adopted the forms of every age from then till now."

"What should we do then?" said Damaris. "Should we try to strip away the Jewish stuff as much as we can?"

"No, I don't think so," said Theology. "My business anyhow is to understand the Scripture in its ancient dress and see what is signified to us through it. You don't understand Shakespeare by stripping away Elizabethan England: and it is a more weighty matter to understand God. Yet understanding Shakespeare is no unreal dramatization of yourself as an Elizabethan, and to understand Christ is not to dramatize yourself as an ancient Jew.

"Now here is a book," said Theology, rummaging in her briefcase, "called *Revelation and the Modern World*,[44] which I have been given to review. Dr. Lionel Thornton does not get round to saying much about the modern world. He opens his readers' eyes to the way in which Apostles and Evangelists thought. He describes, in our language, systems of imagery and implication which the ancients never dreamt of describing, because they lived in them. After doing this for us, Dr. Thornton does not bring us back to our modern world. He does not need to. We are in it all the time, and if we have been seriously grasping the ancient speech under our author's guidance, and taking it to ourselves, we shall have been making the modern translation for ourselves—if, indeed, it is right to say that we do anything quite for ourselves in the sphere of revealed truth. May I recommend Dr. Thornton as Lent reading for the intelligent? The effort required will be penance enough for the season, and the profit derived an assistance to the enjoyment of Easter."

Denys, feeling these remarks to be unfair, came alive and carried Theology and Damaris off to tea.

---

[44] Dacre Press, 30s.

IS THEISM IMPORTANT?

H. H. Price
Fellow of New College, Oxford

Is Theism important? No man in his senses could answer "No." He may think that Theistic Belief is erroneous, or groundless; but even so he cannot possibly deny its psychological importance, nor its social and historical importance either. So if the question is put in this perfectly general form, there is no profit in discussing it, because the answer is manifestly "Yes."

But I expect that the question you wish me to discuss is a more specific one than this, something like "Is Theism *philosophically* important?" Again, it seems to me that the answer is plainly "yes." The assertion that there is a Supreme Being unlimited in power, wisdom and goodness, upon which all finite things and events unilaterally depend, and that this Supreme Being is a mind, or a conscious being—such an assertion, true or false, *must* be philosophically important.

I shall not waste time on considering the theory, held by the early positivists in the 1930's, that this assertion is nonsensical, neither true nor false (though even if it were, the fact that it was would in itself be philosophically important). For it is a plain matter of ordinary observation that assertions about God *are* understood by a very large number of persons. There may be different sorts of understandability, appropriate to different sorts of assertions; statements about God, perhaps, are not understood in quite the same way as statements about the physical world are. Perhaps they are not intelligible to everyone, but only to people who have had experiences of the appropriate sorts; just as descriptions of a sunset are not intelligible to men who have been blind from birth, and not wholly intelligible to color blind ones. But for all that, it is an obvious empirical fact that statements about God *are* understood by a very large number of people in some good sense of the word "understood." And I do not think that the Linguistic Philosophers of the present day would deny this. We are no longer living in the 1930's.

The interesting question, then, is not whether Theism is philosophically important, because the answer to that is so obviously "Yes." There is no denying that Theism is a subject which philosophers *ought* to discuss, even though in fact they do not at present discuss it very much. The interesting question is *how* ought they to discuss it? And that is the question I shall talk about. What is it that the philosophy of Religion in general, and the philosophy of Theism in particular, should try to do?

As I mentioned just now, present day philosophers, at any rate in English-speaking countries, do not take much interest in Theism, or indeed in any other kind of religious belief, whereas their predecessors right up to the early years of the 20th century took a good deal. Religious people are inclined to complain of this, and of course I agree with them. And yet there are two sides to the question. There *are* reasons why religious people should be rather pleased—relieved at any rate—if philosophers prefer to let the subject alone. There is a certain hostility, "Tension," I believe, is the fashionable word, between the philosophical attitude and the religious attitude; and it is still there, even when the philosopher is arguing in favor of religious belief and not against it. Philosophy is a dangerous friend; and however friendly it tries to be, the religious man may still have some inclination to say *Timeo Danaos et dona ferentes*.[45]

In former times, philosophers busied themselves with devising proofs of the existence of God. It has been said that proofs of the existence of God have made many men Atheists. Perhaps

---

[45] From Virgil's *Aeneid*, "I fear the Greeks, even those who bear gifts."

that is an overstatement, but I think they have made quite a lot of men Agnostics. Why is this? Partly because the "proofs" turn out on examination to be inconclusive. The Ontological Proof assumes that existence is a predicate, which seems to be just a mistake. The Cosmological Proof (the so-called "First Cause Argument") assumes that an inference from effect to cause still makes sense when we ask what is the cause of *all* events, as it does when we ask what is the cause of this or that *particular* event; and this assumption, though not perhaps absurd, is at least highly dubious. The Physico-Theological Proof (the Argument from Design) would only at the most establish the existence of a Finite Deity, a Demiurge or "Architect of the World" who works on pre-existent material; and such evidences as there are of design in the world are at least compatible with the hypothesis that the designer—if there were one—was neither perfectly wise nor perfectly good.

But the real trouble is not with the weaknesses of detail which the traditional proofs appear to have. Even if we could detect no flaw in them, there is something irreligious or non-religious in the whole idea of *proving* the existence of God at all. You remember the exclamation of Pascal: "God of Abraham, Isaac and Jacob, not the God of the philosophers and the scientists!" A God whose existence has to be *proved* is not the God of religion. If he were, the ordinary religious man, who has never heard of these proofs, would be convicted of irrationality. He would be believing something which he, personally, had no good ground for believing. His belief might in fact be true (if conclusive proofs for it could be devised); but he, personally, would be obliged, as an intellectually honest man, to give it up, or at least to suspend judgment on the question, unless and until the requisite proofs were brought to his notice.

But might he not be content with *probable* arguments? Even though he has no proof of what he affirms, might he not still have *evidence* in his favor? Yes, but in that case, if he is a rational man, the strength of his belief should be proportioned to the weight of the evidence, and no stronger. Religious faith, in a rational man, would have to be a kind of *opinion*, comparable to the opinion which one has concerning some unsettled question of science or history—say the historicity of King Arthur, or of Homer, or the origin of the solar system. And if adverse evidence turns up one ought to feel less confidence in one's opinion or even reject it altogether. Now whatever religious faith may be, it is quite different from opinion. In face of adverse evidence, a man sticks to his faith, but he abandons an opinion.

That religious faith is as a matter of psychological fact independent both of proofs and of probable arguments is pretty obvious. As a matter of psychological fact, it is seldom acquired by means of arguments, nor is it often lost because of adverse arguments. "So much the worse for faith," you may say; "if that is the sort of thing faith is, it is just an irrational attitude, which an intellectually honest man will keep clear of, and if he unfortunately finds that he has it, he will do his best to get rid of it." Perhaps. But no religious person will agree to this proposal. Why will he not agree to it? Is he just being obstinately unreasonable?

I think not. There really is something wrong with all those arguments for the existence of God, whether they claim to be conclusive proofs, or only to establish a probability. What is wrong with them is that they attempt to establish a religious conclusion from non-religious premises; the same kind of wrongness as there is in the attempt to establish ethical conclusions from non-ethical premises (which was likewise a favorite enterprise of philosophers at one time). And that is why these arguments fail to establish what the religious man affirms. Even if they were flawless in detail—which they are not—they would still be mistaken in principle. And if "proofs of the existence of God have made many men Atheists"—or Agnostics at least—the main reason for this was not the weaknesses of detail which people have detected in these proofs;

it was rather that even in *hoping* to base their theistic belief upon proofs (or probable arguments on that) they had already lapsed out of the religious attitude.

It does not follow that all the labors which great and good men have expended in devising proofs of the existence of God have been wasted. If I said that, I should be false to the testimony of the religious consciousness itself. From the days of the Fathers onwards, Christian philosophers have rendered most important services to the Christian religion; and likewise Hindu, Buddhist and Moslem philosophers have rendered most important services to *their* religions. But the right way to conceive the labors of these thinkers is summed up, it seems to me, in the phrase *fides quaerens intellectum*—"faith seeking understanding." And the point of this phrase is that the faith is prior to the understanding. For what the philosopher of religion is trying to understand is just the content of faith itself. And the faith is prior to the understanding both temporally and logically. It is temporally prior, because the faith must already be in existence before we can set about understanding its content. And not only temporally. Faith is not like a scaffolding which can be removed when the edifice of philosophical theology has been completed—as if it were just a temporary second best, which we have to put up with until philosophical argument can provide us with something better. That is just the error against which I am contending.

We are indeed told in the Christian scriptures (as in other scriptures) that faith is as it were an *interim* attitude, appropriate to immature creatures. The time will come, we are told, when faith will no longer be needed, though it will not come in this life. Of the three Theological Virtues, Faith, Hope and Charity, it is only charity which "abideth forever." "Now we see as in a glass darkly, but then face to face." Yes, but this seeing face to face is certainly not philosophical thinking, and still less does it consist in entertaining forever and ever the chain of propositions which constitutes the Cosmological Argument. That better thing which is to succeed Faith is described in the Christian tradition as *vision*—the "vision of God"—and in other religious traditions it is described in somewhat similar terms. The word "vision" is of course metaphorical, but whatever it means, it surely does not mean philosophical thinking.

I conclude, so far, that the task of a philosopher of religion is not to try to produce a substitute for faith, but to reflect as carefully as he can on the contents of faith itself.

Now this, I suggest, is precisely what the good philosophers of religion have done—even when they supposed they were doing something else. The so-called proofs of the existence of God are something much better and much more interesting: they are *analyses, or partial analyses of the idea of God*, attempts to make clear to us just *what we are believing* when we believe that God exists. The God in whom Christians and other Theists believe *is* indeed the *Ens Realissimum*, the Perfect and Infinite Being, spoken of in the so-called Ontological Proof (I mean, that is what Theists believe him to be); he *is* indeed the Supreme Being or First Cause, spoken of in the so-called Cosmological Proof, the Being upon whom all finite things and events unilaterally depend; he *is* indeed the Being who orders all things for the best, spoken of in the so-called Physico-Theological Proof (the Argument from Design). These so-called proofs really do give us an analysis or classification of the *content* of Theistic faith. They enable us to see, more clearly than we could before, just what it is that we are asserting when we assert that God exists. They give us a relatively clear and reflective faith in place of the relatively muddled and unreflective one which we had before. What they do not do, and cannot do, and should not even try to do, is to provide a *substitute* for faith, something which will make faith unnecessary for philosophically enlightened persons.

I expect that many of you have listened to me with great impatience, and I am rather surprised that you have gone on listening at all. It may very well appear to you that I have been defending a kind of religious irrationalism. Haven't I been saying that religious faith does not need to be supported by philosophical proofs or arguments; and still worse, that it *cannot* be so supported? Then surely my view must be that religion is just a matter of feeling? *Pectus facit theologum*, it has been said: "it is the heart that makes the theologian." Am I not saying that it is "the heart" which makes the philosophical Theist too, so far as I allow that there is any function for such a person?

Well, I do think that "the heart"—that is, the emotions or emotional dispositions of the thinker—is not entirely irrelevant to philosophical theology. I do think that a philosopher of religion, if he is to do his job, must at least have a strong sympathy with the religious man's attitude. He must at least be able to put himself in the religious man's shoes, look at the world through his eyes. If he cannot do this, he simply will not have before his mind the thing which it is his job to analyze. Indeed, I am inclined to think that a philosopher of religion must be a religious person himself, though I do not think he needs to be supereminent in piety. As a matter of fact, of course, the very greatest philosophers of religion have been St. Augustine, St. Thomas, Sankara.

All the same, I do not really want to maintain that religion, or religious faith, is just a matter of feeling. (Still less do I want to maintain that it is just a matter of conduct.) The two alternatives, that *either* religious faith is capable of being justified by arguments from non-religious premises *or else* it is just a matter of feeling, are not exhaustive. There might be such a thing as *religious experience*, and I believe there is. And I mean by the word "experience" something cognitive, not just an emotion, though doubtless emotion accompanies it. I mean a mode of awareness, a unique one, not reducible to any other—and certainly not reducible to reason of any kind, though some of the thinkers, both Eastern and Western, who have talked about "intuitive reason" may have had this peculiar mode of awareness in mind. If we *must* classify it under one of the familiar heads, I would rather call it "a sense" myself, *a sense of the divine*; for it does have this in common with the ordinary senses, that it is an original source of *data*, though, in other ways it is not at all like them, e.g. no sense organ is connected with it.

Without religious experience, I believe there would be no such thing as religion at all. And that is why an argument from non-religious premises can never establish a religious conclusion, just as an argument from non-ethical premises can never establish an ethical one. From the mere fact that a Negro slave is a human being it will not follow that we have duties to him. The ethical conclusion will only follow if we have, in addition, the *ethical* premise that there are duties which we owe to human beings as such. Moreover, unless I have a *sense* of duty already (a conscience, a moral consciousness) I shall not be able to understand this argument, however valid it may be in itself, because I shall not know what is meant by the word "duty" at all. Similarly, arguments concerning the divine, for example arguments intended to convert a Polytheist to Monotheism, can only be valid if there are propositions about the divine among these premises. And the person to whom they are addressed will not be able to understand them, unless he himself has some sense of the divine to begin with. If he were entirely destitute of religious experience, he simply would not know what one was talking about. I am sorry to use this clumsy phrase "sense of the divine." I might have used Otto's phrase, "sense of the numinous." But I prefer not to, because it seems to me—unless I misunderstand him—that the experience he speaks of is defined in terms of *emotion* (in terms of a mixture of horror and fascination) and is not a *cognitive* experience, an *awareness* of some object. I do so, because I do not want to suggest that this basic and indispensable religious experience is anything so clear and determinate as an awareness of *God*—at any rate in the usual Theistic sense of the word "God.")

Granting that you have this sense of the Divine, *then* you may argue for the existence of the God of Theism, and you can understand and be convinced by such arguments when they are offered by other people. For then they are arguments not for the existence of the Divine as such—that is accepted already—but rather they are designed to support a particular conception of what the Divine is. I think, however, that such an argument would not take the form of the traditional Theistic proofs. It would be more like the argument, or the set of considerations, which leads from Polytheism to Monotheism, through the intermediate conception of a hierarchical or monarchical Polytheism, in which there is a *Jupiter optimus maximus*, or a Zeus who is "the Father of Gods and Men." But this is something very different from the traditional Cosmological Argument or the Argument from Design, which try to argue from more *natural* phenomena—phenomena which we can be aware of *without* having any religious experience—to the existence of God. This road from Polytheism to Theism might rather be described (in the language of the Idealist philosophers) as "the internal dialectic of the religious consciousness itself."

For my part—if you will allow me to express my prejudices for a moment—I have a very warm place in my heart for the Polytheists of old. Disgusting as some of their practices were, I think the Ancient Polytheists were much nearer to Christian Theism—and to the Kingdom of Heaven too—than the enlightened readers of the *New Statesman*.[46] And I would almost venture to suggest that no one can be a genuine Theist unless he has at least some sympathy with Polytheism, and some sympathy with still more primitive religious attitudes, such as Animism and Polydaemonism. (This is one of the unexpected advantages of a Classical Education). For these queer and crude theologies, I suspect, are just the natural phases of development of the religious consciousness itself, and one has to pass through them (or at least understand what it would be like to be in them) if one is to reach something better.

I think that this mode of awareness, which I have called the sense of the divine, exists in all men, though the language in which it is expressed differs very much in different ages and countries. I know that the appearances are against me when I say this. There do appear to be many people, especially in this age in which we happen to live, in whom this awareness I spoke of is wholly absent. They will tell you that they have never had any kind of religious experience at all, and that they simply do not know what you mean when you talk about it. I venture the hypothesis (of course it is no more) that in such men the awareness I speak of is *repressed*, in somewhat the way that desires and memories are repressed according to Freudian psychology,[47] and it is repressed, I think, because it does not fit at all with the conception of the world and of human nature which is commonly accepted in the present Secularistic phase of Western Civilization. To repress it is not very difficult. It does not have the urgency and the forcefulness of our primitive desires and passions. It is described in the Bible as "a still, small voice." All the same I do not think it will remain repressed forever, any more than I think that the present phase of Western Civilization will last forever. The time will come, and I think it may well come quite

---

[46] Editor's Note (2012): Since 1913, the *New Statesman* has been one of Britain's magazines on politics and current affairs.

[47] I have heard the saying: "There is no *innocent* ignorance of God." It seems to me an overstatement, tho' an overstatement of something true and important. I would rather say that there is no ignorance of *the divine without repression*. But I do not think the repression need be morally blameworthy, tho' doubtless emotional and conative factors always play some part of it, i.e. we refuse to admit this awareness of the divine because we do not *want* to.

soon, when our modern Naturalistic *Weltanschauung*[48] will seem topsy-turvy, a systematic attempt to put second things first and first things nowhere.

I am only too well aware that there are many loose ends in what I have been saying, and one of them is so important that I must try, at least, to fit it in before I stop. In the earlier part of this paper, I talked about Faith (I said, you remember, that the business of the philosophy of religion was just to analyze the content of faith). In the latter part, I have not talked about Faith at all, but about religious experiences or the awareness of the divine. What is the relation between the two? That is a very puzzling problem: and the demand for "a plain answer to a plain question" is here even more than usually misleading.

One of the puzzles is this. Faith, you may say, is a form of belief, and belief is something quite different from knowledge; but the sense of the divine, of which I have spoken is surely a form of knowledge, a direct acquaintance with something? Or again, it may be argued, where one has *experience* of the Divine, there is no need, and indeed no possibility, of a mere *belief* in the existence of the Divine. Then shall we say, instead, that Faith is *not* just a form of belief? Shall we say, instead, that Faith and religious experience are two names for the same thing? Yet that would not be quite right either.

I think that many religious people would argue that Faith is *not* just a form of belief—at any rate not in the sense in which the word "belief" is used by philosophers. On the other hand, they would not allow that it is a form of knowledge either,[49] and certainly they would not allow that Faith in the existence of God is a direct acquaintance with God himself. Such an acquaintance, they would say, if it ever exists at all, does not come to us in this present life. It comes to this. If you compare Faith with knowledge, you are inclined to say it is only a form of belief, and unless you are careful you will soon find yourself saying that it consists just in "accepting the Theistic hypothesis." On the other hand, if you compare Faith with belief, you are inclined to say that it is a form of knowledge; and if you are not careful you will find yourself claiming a direct acquaintance with God. And either of these conclusions—that Faith is just accepting a hypothesis, or that it is a kind of direct acquaintance—would be emphatically rejected by the religious consciousness itself.

The answer to the puzzle is perhaps something like this. The attitude called Faith does contain an element of direct and immediate experience; and this is why we refuse to admit that it is just belief, and why we also think that Faith is not to be abandoned in face of "awkward facts"—such as the facts summed up under the name of "The Problem of Evil." For the experience is there, and we do have it (at least religious people do) whatever other facts there may be.

On the other hand, this direct and immediate experience, though cognitive, though not just a form of emotion or feeling, is an excessively dim and confused sort of cognition, at least in most men. It is rather like the visual experience a blind man would have when he was just beginning to be cured of his blindness. Imagine him "seeing as in a glass darkly." He does see, but from his own visual experience, he cannot describe *what* he sees; and his visual experience, though he does have it, cannot be called a *knowledge* of the visible world. It is awareness, but it is much too dim and vague to deserve the name of knowledge. If he wants to have a more clear and determinate conception of what it is that he sees, he will have to ask other people who see

---

[48] Editor's Note (2012): German for worldview.
[49] Of course the Bible does talk of men "knowing" God. But what seems to be meant is that God places them in something most simply described as a "personal relation" with Himself.—Ed.

better than he does (if he can find them) and take their word for it. To abandon the analogy, he will have to find other people whose sense of the divine is more developed or more mature than his own (getting such testimony of their general reliability and trustworthiness as he can), and accept what they say. This *is* belief; it is a special case of belief upon testimony. And that is what tends to make us think, mistakenly, that religious faith is *nothing but* belief. It isn't. Some sense of the divine, some direct and immediate religious experience, however dim and confused, must be there already. Unless it were, you would neither seek the testimony of those who have a clearer and more developed sense of the divine than you have, nor would you understand their testimony when you received it.

I had better stop. I have said quite enough to lay myself open to the most devastating criticism. Nobody could be more muddled about these important questions than I am. But perhaps it is better to be muddled than not to think about them at all.

REPLY

C. S. LEWIS
Fellow of Magdalen College, Oxford

I have lost the notes of what I originally said in replying to Professor Price's paper and cannot now remember what it was, except that I welcomed most cordially his sympathy with the Polytheists. I still do. When grave persons express their fear that England is relapsing into Paganism, I am tempted to reply, "Would that she were." For I do not think it at all likely that we shall ever see Parliament opened by the slaughtering of a garlanded white bull in the House of Lords or Cabinet Ministers leaving sandwiches in Hyde Park as an offering for the Dryads. If such a state of affairs came about, then the Christian apologist would have something to work on. For a Pagan, as history shows, is a man eminently convertible to Christianity. He is essentially the pre-Christian, or sub-Christian, religious man. The post-Christian man of our day differs from him as much as a *divorcée* differs from virgin. The Christian and the Pagan have much more in common with one another than either has with the writers of the *New Statesman*; and those writers would of course agree with me. For the rest, what now occurs to me after rereading Professor Price's paper is something like this.

1. I think we must introduce into the discussion a distinction between two senses of the word *Faith*. This may mean (a) a settled intellectual assent. In that sense faith (or "belief") in God hardly differs from faith in the uniformity of Nature or in the consciousness of other people. This is what, I think, has sometimes been called a "notional" or "intellectual" or "carnal" faith. It may also mean (b) a trust, or confidence, in the God whose existence is thus assented to. This involves an attitude of the will. It is more like our confidence in a friend. It would be generally agreed that Faith in sense A is not a religious state. The devils who "believe and tremble" have Faith-A. A man who curses or ignores God may have Faith-A. Philosophical arguments for the existence of God are presumably intended to produce Faith-A. No doubt those who construct them are anxious to produce Faith-A because it is a necessary pre-condition of Faith-B and in that sense their ultimate intention is religious. But their immediate object, the conclusion they attempt to prove, is not. I therefore think they cannot be justly accused of trying to get a religious conclusion out of non-religious premises. I agree with Professor Price that this cannot be done: but I deny that the religious philosophers are trying to do it.

I also think that in some ages, what claim to be Proofs of Theism have had much more efficacy in producing Faith-A than Professor Price suggests. Nearly everyone I know who has embraced Christianity in adult life has been influenced by what seemed to him to be at least probable arguments for Theism. I have known some who were completely convinced by Descartes' Ontological Proof: that is, they received Faith-A from Descartes first and then went on to seek and to find Faith-B. Even quite uneducated people who have been Christians all their lives not infrequently appeal to some simplified form of the Argument from Design. Even acceptance of tradition implies an argument which sometimes becomes explicit in the form "I reckon all those wise men wouldn't have believed in it if it weren't true."

Of course Faith-A usually involves a degree of subject certitude which goes beyond the logical certainty, or even the supposed logical certainty, of the arguments employed. It may retain this certitude for a long time, I expect, even without the support of Faith-B. This excess of certitude in a settled assent is not at all uncommon. Most of those who believe in Uniformity of Nature, Evolution, or the Solar System, share it.

2. I doubt whether religious people have ever supposed that Faith-B follows automatically on the acquisition of Faith-A. It is described as a "gift." As soon as we have Faith-A in the existence of God, we are instructed to ask from God Himself the gift of Faith-B. An odd request, you may say, to address to a First Cause, an *Ens Realissimum*, or an *Unmoved Mover*. It might be argued, and I think I would argue myself, that even such an aridly philosophical God rather fails to invite than actually repels a personal approach. It would, at any rate, do no harm to try it. But I fully admit that most of those who, having reached Faith-A, pray for Faith-B, do so because they have already had something like religious experience. Perhaps the best way of putting it would be to say that Faith-A converts into religious experience what was hitherto only potentially or implicitly religious. In this modified form I would accept Professor Price's view that philosophical proofs never by themselves, lead to religion. Something at least *quasi-*religious uses them before, and the "proofs" remove an inhibition which was preventing their development into religion proper.

This is not exactly *fides quaerens intellectum*, for these quasi-religious experiences were not *fides*. In spite of Professor Price's rejection, I still think Otto's account of the Numinous is the best analysis of them we have. I believe it is a mistake to regard the Numinous as merely an affair of "feeling." Admittedly, Otto can describe it only by referring to the emotions it arouses in us; but then nothing can be described except in terms of its effects in consciousness. We have in English an exact name for the emotion aroused by the Numinous, which Otto, writing in German, lacked; we have the word Awe—an emotion very like fear, with the important difference that it need imply no estimate of danger. When we fear a tiger, we fear that it may kill us: when we fear a ghost—well, we just fear the ghost, not this or that mischief which it may do us. The Numinous or Awful is that of which we have this, as it were, objectless or disinterested fear—this awe. And "the Numinous" is not a name for our own feeling of Awe, any more than "the Contemptible" is a name for contempt. It is the answer to the question "of what do you feel awe." And what we feel awe of is certainly not itself awe.

With Otto and, in a sense, with Professor Price, I would find the seed of religious experience in our experience of the Numinous. In an age like our own such experience does occur but, until religion comes and retrospectively transforms it, it usually appears to the subject to be a special form of aesthetic experience. In ancient times I think experience of the Numinous developed into the Holy only insofar as the Numinous (not in itself at all necessarily moral) came to be connected with the morally good. This happened regularly in Israel, sporadically elsewhere.

But even in the higher Paganism, I do not think this process led to anything exactly like *fides*. There is nothing credal in Paganism. In Israel we do get *fides* but this is always connected with certain historical affirmations. Faith is not simply in the numinous *Elohim*, not even simply in the holy *Jahweh*, but in the God "of our fathers," the God who called Abraham and brought Israel out of Egypt. In Christianity this historical element is strongly reaffirmed. The object of faith is at once the *ens entium*[50] of the philosophers, the Awful Mystery of Paganism, the Holy Law given of the moralists, and Jesus of Nazareth who was crucified under Pontius Pilate and rose again on the third day.

Thus we must admit that Faith, as we know it, does not flow from philosophical argument alone; nor from experience of the Numinous alone; nor from moral experience alone; nor from history alone; but from historical events which at once fulfill and transcend the moral category, which link themselves with the most numinous elements in Paganism, and which (as it seems to us) demand as their presupposition the existence of a Being who is more, but not less, than the God whom many reputable philosophers think they can establish.

Religious experience, as we know it, really involves all these elements. We may, however, use the word in a narrower sense to denote moments of mystical, or devotional, or merely numinous experience; and we may then ask, with Professor Price, how such moments, being a kind of *visio*, are related to faith, which by definition is "not sight." This does not seem to me one of the hardest questions. "Religious experience" in the narrower sense comes and goes: especially goes. The operation of Faith is to retain, so far as the will and intellect are concerned, what is irresistible and obvious during the moments of special grace. By Faith we believe always what we hope hereafter to see always and perfectly and have already seen imperfectly and by flashes. In relation to the philosophical premises a Christian's faith is of course excessive: in relation to what is sometimes shown him, it is perhaps just as often defective. My faith even in an earthly friend goes beyond all that could be demonstratively proved; yet in another sense I may often trust him less than he deserves.

---

[50] Editor's Note (2012): Latin for "being of beings," entity of all entities, another name for God.

THE EXISTENTIALIST POLITICAL MYTH

IRIS MURDOCH
Fellow of St. Anne's College, Oxford

There are various ways in which one can think of existentialism as being important. One can think of it as a literature, as a morality, as a psychology, or as a piece of academic metaphysics which mixes Cartesian and Hegelian strains. The aspect of its importance which I want to consider now however is its importance as a political myth. That it plays this particular role among others has of course not escaped the attention of either its adherents or its opponents—and many on both sides may well regard this as being its central role. The Hungarian Marxist George Lukacs says of existentialism that it is rapidly becoming the ideology of the European bourgeois intellectual; and the existentialists themselves return constantly, in an uneasy way, to attempt to situate themselves *vis à vis* the Marxists. This problem, the problem of what to think about communism, *how* to think about communism, is the most persistent thorn in their side. And they wage an inconclusive battle of persuasive definitions round about the concepts of Marxism, trying to draw them, as it were, into the existentialist camp.

Now there is a great deal which Marxism and existentialism have in common with each other—and there is even something which they both have in common with contemporary English philosophy. It is worth noticing the common character before going on to consider the conflicts. To indicate this character one might say in an inexact epigrammatic mode of speech: this is an age of anti-essentialist thinking, anti-Cartesian, anti-abstract, dialectical. It is an age when we are both reaping the fruits of Hegel and facing the problem of his break with Kant. Kant was a dialectical but a dualistic thinker; that is, he did not conceive of the mind's relation with its object as being that of static contemplation or the receiving of atomic impressions. He conceived the mind as struggling with reality, as seeking totality, rational satisfaction, within it; on the other hand, Kant distinguished between the shifting phenomenal show, and an unknown, or partially known, transcendent reality that lay beyond it. The task of philosophy was to examine the limitations of our thinking; to show how it was that one could never completely know the reality which nevertheless exercised upon us a constant magnetic attraction. Hegel was a dialectical but monistic thinker. For him there is nothing but the shifting phenomenal show, and this, conceived of as a closely knit rationally developing whole, is truth, reality. There is nothing outside it. Hegel is sometimes wrongly thought of as remote, airy, and metaphysical in the purely pejorative sense of that word. He could more justly be considered as the first great modern empiricist; a dialectical empiricist, as opposed to, say, Hume who might be called a mechanistic empiricist. What Hegel teaches us is that we should attempt to describe phenomena. That he cast the laws governing phenomena in logical terms is neither here nor there as far as the value of his method is concerned. In fact he set about patiently *describing* a vast quantity of human experience, experience of individuals and of societies; and the Marxists had only to drop his logical rubric and turn the thing the other way up in order to have a mode of descriptive analysis which could then be labeled dialectical *materialism*. "Hegel's Logic is the algebra of the revolution." The Hegelian characteristic which Marxists, existentialists, and English logicians (or logical analysts) have in common is a non-dualistic patience with phenomena. What we are all working upon, it might be said, is *le monde vécu*, the lived world, what is actually experienced, thought of as itself being the real, and carrying its own truth criteria with it—and not as being the reflection or mental shadow of some other separate mode of being which lies behind it in static parallel. This is the revolution in philosophic method which is showing us its different faces at the present time. It is a move, one might notice, which brings the activity of the philosopher in some ways closer to that of the novelist. The novelist is *par excellence* the unprejudiced describer of *le monde vécu*—and it is not surprising that a great novelist, such as Tolstoy, found out long ago things which Sartre and Professor Ryle are now offering to us in a philosophical form. With this concentration upon phenomena goes the overcoming of a crude opposition between idealism and materialism; with it goes a sense of the unity of theory and practice, a determination not to say more than we can see: in short an abandonment of the old speculative metaphysics of the Cartesian kind. Of course, one can overdo the attractive business of observing a unity of pattern in an apparently highly various region. If one were to say, for instance, that when Professor Ayer says that much of our mental life takes place in public he is making a Hegelian remark about "objective spirit," this might sound paradoxical and excessive. Yet I think there *is* this unity of pattern, and that it is important.

It is true that the differences are more obvious than the similarities. It is one thing to decide that "explanation" is the orderly observation of experience and not a looking behind experience. One might say, broadly, that the logical analysts describe ordinary language, and behavior so far as it illuminates this, the existentialists describe a range of psychological phenomena connected with private personal experience, and the Marxists describe man's behavior as a social being. Further, the purposes for which the descriptions are used are different. Yet the method has a common character, and even as far as conclusions are concerned, existentialism shares some things with logical analysis and others with Marxism. For instance, Ryle and Sartre both attack, and in very similar terms, the substantial intellectualist picture of the mind; and, if we look on the other side of existentialism, we find Sartre using Marxist categories as soon as he starts to describe man's social existence.

To sum things up in a rather shocking way: as far as method goes, we are all Hegelians nowadays; but the specter which haunts us is Kant. The Cartesian dualism is dead. Hegel killed it long before *The Concept of Mind* was written. The problem of metaphysics today is the problem of the Kantian dualism.

Now it may seem odd, on the face of it, to describe the existentialists as anti-Cartesian, since they are constantly talking about "the *cogito*" and claiming descent from Descartes. When I call them anti-Cartesian I am using this term as Professor Ryle used it, to mean that they are not mind-body dualists. What *is* Cartesian about them is their insistence upon the primacy and the authority of the personal consciousness. Sartre describes the human condition in a terminology and by a method which owes much to Hegel; but he wishes too to stress the solipsistic isolation of each human unit, and here he makes appeal to the Cartesian *cogito*. Yet the isolation which Sartre's man suffers from goes even beyond that of the Cartesian doubter; for it is also the incurable isolation of the man described by Kierkegaard. Sartre attempts both to display the general structure of human consciousness and to indicate its absurd isolation. In attempting the former he is writing in the general tradition of philosophical endeavor which descends from Kant through Husserl; he is attempting a new deduction of the categories. Sartre's deduction has more pictures and conversations about it than that of Kant; it reads more like a psychological myth, and seems closer to Freud than to the *Critique of Pure Reason*. Yet it is a sort of transcendental deduction; Sartre is seeking in the consciousness for the *a priori* basis of objective reality. When he analyzes the structure of our consciousness of others, or our emotional consciousness, he is exhibiting our fundamental categories. These "forms" are regarded as held as it were in common between the objective and the subjective world—and they are laid bare by a technique of description, the phenomenological reduction, which puts the question of the objective reality of phenomena "in parenthesis" so that the essential structure of the phenomena may be investigated. What is supposed to emerge is the nature of human consciousness, or, if you like, the human condition. It is here, in this sort of semi-psychological description and analysis, that existentialist writings are at their most brilliant and illuminating. The new concepts which they invent (such as Sartre's *être-pour-autrui*, Gabriel Marcel's *fidelité*) draw a line round important aspects of experience, naming what has not been named before. I am not concerned here however with the psychological subtlety and finesse of these descriptions, nor with any logical criticism of their more dubious philosophical corollaries. I am concerned with their character as a political myth.

We may notice to begin with how extremely recognizable Sartre's descriptions seem to a great many people—particularly perhaps on the other side of the Channel. People say: yes, this is what we are like. And it is not far from here to: this is what man is like. Well, what is he like? We might contrast the Sartrian man with the Kantian rational being. What Kant describes is an empty consciousness, a structure of intuition, understanding, reason, which is the same in every rational creature. But Kant's man lives in a universe where there is a transcendent objective truth, although it may not be altogether knowable. Similarly the man whom Kierkegaard describes may live plunged in doubt and confusion but he lives in a universe where there is God. Sartre's man is described as an isolated non-historical consciousness, like Kant's man, and as being anguished and doubtful like Kierkegaard's man—but he is unlike both in that he inhabits a universe which contains no transcendent objective truth. Truth somehow depends on him. There is no human nature, Sartre tells us, there is only a human condition.

This condition is not described in abstract philosophical terms. Philosophical jargon sketches a framework, but the detail is filled in by concrete description, of a subtle and compelling kind, of our moment to moment awareness. The scale and method of this description are important. Sartre concentrates attention on the individual consciousness, and its immediate mental behavior, and what emerges is a non-historical, non-social, and non-determined individual. A solipsistic picture. We might compare Sartre's method, from this point of view, with that of the logical analysts. They too look at the moment to moment character of consciousness in order to delineate the concepts used in talk about the mind. The being which they examine is a non-historical specimen. The concepts analyzed are of a completely general character; one would not, for instance, expect to find here an analysis of a concept such as "class-consciousness." They sum up their observations in the view that knowing how has primacy over knowing that; that is, that our nature as rational creatures is best considered in terms of activities and skills rather than in terms of the contemplation of truths or the private manipulation of syllogisms. From this they profess to draw no further conclusions about man's nature; a program which on the whole they carry out more strictly than does Sartre, who makes a similar profession. Their analyses are concerned simply to solve certain philosophical problems, and they make no metaphysical claims. Yet we may notice that in one case at least, political, if not metaphysical, conclusions are to be found connected with an analysis of this kind. I am thinking of Michael Oakeshott, also starting out with epistemological views exactly similar to those of Ryle, makes them lend support to a sort of traditionalistic political liberalism. The argument, crudely put, runs: if man is a knower how and not a knower that, if his rationality expresses itself in non-reflective and non-deliberate modes of activity and not in intellectual apprehension of subsistent truths—then we should not imagine that society ought to be, or can be, changed overnight with the help of a rationalistic political blueprint. Oakeshott is the opponent of everything which he calls "rationalism in politics": and of course the most notorious rationalists are the Marxists.

Sartre is not shy of drawing both metaphysical and political conclusions from his examination of consciousness. But his political position turns out to be very unlike that of Oakeshott. He examines the intellectualist, substantialist, picture of the self and finds it wanting; and instead of saying "then don't let's have a picture," he invents one with the opposite characteristics. Man is not a substance, a something; so he is a *néant*, a nothing. He is a *néant* which aspires toward being, with an aspiration which is subject to no role external to itself or common to others. Sartre is not a dualist in the sense of the dualism which Ryle attacks; but he is a dualist in two other senses. There is, to use his own jargon, the dualism between the consciousness or *être-pour-soi*, and the world of things or *être-en-soi*, and there is the dualism between the consciousness and the ideal totality which the consciousness aspires to be, and which Sartre calls *être-en-soi-pour-soi*. Sartre's first novel, *La Nausée*, is a sort of metaphysical poem on the subject of the two dualisms. The hero, Roquentin, is afflicted with a dreadful sense of the contingency of the world, the brute nameless there-ness of material existence. He feels himself as an empty nothing which has been crowded out of the opaque world of objects. Compared with *them* he is *de trop pour toujours*. On the other hand, he is haunted by thoughts about melodies and circles which seem to have a perfect satisfying intelligible mode of being which lifts them out of the fallen world of existence. Toward this other world Roquentin aspires, and hopes to reach it, it appears at the end of the book, by creating a work of art. This myth, Kantian, sometimes Platonic, in its flavor, perfectly expresses Sartre's view of human life, the view to which he gave a philosophical expression in *L'Etre et le Néant*. Man is an emptiness poised between two inaccessible totalities. The world of objects is impenetrable, the world of intelligible being is unattainable, even contradictory.

This rather bitter view of objective reality as "fallen" is a persistent feature of existentialist thinking; and one which could no doubt be connected, if one cares for this sort of genealogy with parallel or antecedent trends in Protestant and Jansenist theology. The form which this notion takes in contemporary existentialism is interesting however. Roquentin, the hero of *La Nausée*, is not only impressed by the brutish solidity of the stones on the seashore; he feels a similar kind of horror when he contemplates the world of insincere bourgeois banality which surrounds him in the provincial town where he is living. He notices, in this world, the *mauvaise foi*[51] of its inhabitants, the idolatry of state and family, the "justification" drawn from position and wealth, in short the reification of relations and institutions. But, Roquentin thinks, the rationality and solidity of this world is a veneer, just as the rational classification and tame nameability of the world of objects is a veneer. Beneath the latter lies the brute confusion of the contingent world, and behind the former lies the non-rational, non-justifiable absurdity of the lonely consciousness. What is human and real is this lonely, empty aspiration—the bourgeois social world of technical hierarchies and rights and duties is made to conceal this unnerving solitude—and somehow it is the latter which is the true seat of value. The trend of thought is anti-rational, anti-scientific, anti-technical. The world of clearcut rational distinctions, of techniques and positions and institutions and rights is unreal. This is the echo which we hear in the writings of thinkers as apparently far apart as Oakeshott, Camus, Marcel. It is no accident that this term "technique" is used pejoratively by both Marcel and Oakeshott; it may be a long way from the latter's attack on rationalism to Camus' recommendation of the absurd life, but it is down the same road.

---

[51] Editor's Note (2012): French for "bad faith."

Now the comments which a Marxist would make on all this are but too clear. He would say: this is the mythology of those who reject capitalism, with its materialistic values and its deadening of human activity, and who are yet afraid to embrace socialism. They are afraid of the conclusions which a rational and scientific consideration of the scene would force upon them, and so they deny reason, and identify it with the rigid technicalities of the capitalist system. The individualistic outlook natural to capitalism can no longer ignore the rapidly changing social basis of man's life and values. A universalistic Kantian Rousseau-esque individualism is now impossible. So those who are morally sensitive and intelligent enough not to be taken in by capitalism now embrace a solipsistic and nihilistic individualism. Their own lives are absurd and pointless and their society faces annihilation; so naturally they welcome a philosophy which says that all human life is essentially senseless and that man lives *vis-à-vis du néant*.[52] So they feel that their miserable lot is the lot of all humanity, and not just their historical fate—and at the same time, with the help of the theological concepts furnished by their philosophy, they can maintain themselves in a state of doubt and guilt and anguish, thereby both expressing and appeasing the bad conscience which they feel at not being socialists. Such remarks are made, for instance, by the Marxist critic of existentialism, George Lukacs.

Before considering the justice of these comments I want to look at the other side of the dualism. It is here that we must look to see what sort of answer Sartre himself might give to the Marxist charges. Consciousness is negation, nothingness; it makes itself by negating the given, the brute thingy world, on one side—and it makes itself also by aspiring, on the other side, toward an ideal completeness. So consciousness is both *rupture* (the break with the given) and *projet* (aspiration to totality); both these characteristics Sartre equates with freedom and the latter he connects with value. Freedom, considered as negation and project, is the main character of human consciousness. We are condemned to be free. We express this freedom by our inability to be things; however hard we may build up thingy ramparts of institutions and reified values round about us, there is an aspiration which continually breaks down these ramparts in favor of some more distant ideal, which in turn is deadened and reified when we come upon it. What we want is the impossible; that is to be a living transparent consciousness and at the same time a stable opaque being; to be both *pour-soi* and *en-soi* at the same time. This, says Sartre, is the aspiration to be God, to be *ens causa sui*, and it is innately contradictory. This, he says, is the fundamental form of all our particular projects and ambitions. Toward the end of *L'Etre et le Néant* Sartre speaks in characteristically persuasive rhetorical terms about the situation of the being who aspires vainly to be God. The passion of man is the opposite of that of Christ; Christ suffered so that God should be man. Man suffers in order to be God, but since the completeness which he seeks is impossible his suffering is vain. *L'homme est un passion inutile*. Under the form of one object or another, one value or another, man seeks his own Godhead; but no project satisfies him, all tend to fall dead into the region of the reified. From the point of view of their ultimate failure to satisfy, all projects are equally vain and *ça revient au même de s'enivrer solitairement ou de conduire les peuples*.

This has an attractive ring of heroic stoicism and nihilistic despair. So we might be surprised to find Sartre, in another *persona*, preaching the ethics of social democracy and liberal individualism, and talking like any Fabian. In his pamphlet *Existentialism and Humanism* we find Sartre speaking of freedom in much more universalistic and Kantian terms. I cannot choose something as good for myself unless I choose it as good for all men. I cannot will my own freedom without willing that of all. And in *What is Literature?* he tells us that a writer, since his

---

[52] Editor's Note (2012): French for "face to face with nothingness."

work is an appeal to the free assent of his audience, cannot but be an advocate of freedom. Here we see "freedom" being used to mean not the frustrated flickerings of the isolated consciousness, but something much more like what Rousseau meant by it, more like what it means in talk about social democracy and liberalism. This contradiction, which is pointed out by Lukacs, is not an unimportant slip, but represents a real dilemma.

Is it individual choice which founds freedom and value, giving to my actions a meaning which otherwise they would not have and which is *their* meaning? In this sense of freedom stone walls do not a prison make, I am free so long as I am conscious. If on the other hand one thinks of freedom also in the ordinary sense of social, civil, political freedom, as a domain of personal spontaneity which might be infringed and which ought to be respected—then how is *this* to be connected with *that*? They can only be connected by assuming some sort of universal human nature, which Sartre does in *Existentialism and Humanism*, although this contradicts his earlier position. Sartre wants to have the best of both these worlds.

It may be pointed out that the first sense of liberty makes the word so general that it robs it of its meaning. A deterministic theory has the same dazing effect; if one accepts the new use of the terms one has then to think of other terms to indicate the contrast, which still seems to be there, between free and non-free. Yet this theory, is not without point. It emphasizes the absence of any framework which *contains* me, the individual. Neither the institutions and rights of the bourgeoisie, nor the dogma of any religion, nor any conception of historical development can confer sense from the outside upon my actions. Even the psychoanalyst can't. Meaning is egocentric. Yet, as I am infinitely free, I am also infinitely responsible. Simone de Beauvoir depicts this sense of infinite responsibility in her novel *Le Sang des Autres*.[53] The hero of this work is constantly being reminded of the crime of "being another." One cannot but do harm to the innocent—whether it be to the girl one fails to love, or to the hostages who are shot because one resists tyranny. The solution, the author concludes, is to struggle for a kingdom of freedom, where we shall not be forced by circumstance to do violence to each other—and where respect for one another's freedom will render innocent such inevitable conflicts as shall still remain. The novel carries as a superscription a quotation from the *Brothers Karamazov*: I am responsible for everything before everybody. Now one may feel both puzzled and uneasy at the total character of this assertion. Uttered in a religious context it may have a sense. Though one sympathizes with Lukacs who, looking at the works of Dostoevsky, points out how a total responsibility may take the form of a total irresponsibility. In Simone de Beauvoir's novel the sense of total responsibility does seem to lead to a certain clouding over of the notion of the ordinary virtues. The cardinal virtue for her, and for Sartre in his more Fabian *persona*, is sincerity, the exercise of one's own freedom, and a respect for and defense of that of others. This latter idea is tied onto the lonely self-justifying individual by means of an implicit notion of human nature, or else with the help of an emotionally attractive idea of responsibility. Thus Sartre is able to preach social democracy as if it were deducible from existentialism, and complain in *What is Literature?* that people are wasting their good will in personal relationships instead of setting about the task of setting humanity free, which seems to impose itself because we are what we are.

What form, one may go on to ask, can a metaphysic of social democracy take in a world such as ours where it is increasingly impossible to think in terms of the *Contrat Social*? It has been said of existentialism that it is a myth of the Resistance. This is superficial if it means that it is a matter of momentary fashion or slogan. But it may have a deeper sense. The picture of man which Sartre offers is of a being constantly threatened by a deadening and solidifying of his

---

[53] Editor's Note (2012): French for *The Blood of Others*.

universe—a fall into the banal, the conventional, the bourgeois, the realm of *Mauvaise foi*—who may rise out of this in search of a living totality but forever in vain. Such a being is at his best, his most human, when he is by an effort of sincerity breaking his bonds; yet such a moment can never be held or stabilized. What is the political cash value of such an idea? Simone de Beauvoir sums up the existentialist position when she says: *seule la revolte est pure*. All achievement deadens and corrupts—living value only resides in active affirmation or the rebellious struggle. Sincerity is not a state of being. This viewpoint, plausible in a personal psychological context, has its political counterpart. It fits perfectly the ethos of a resistance movement. But once the comparative simplicity of this situation is removed, it shows itself as a fear of authority, conformity, achievement. The pure moment is something which is poised between the dead conventions of capitalist society on the one hand and the rigid dogma of the Communist party bureaucrat on the other. There is something typically existentialist about this position. We find the same principle in Marcel and in Berdyaev. The latter, as Miss Judith Macdonald recently pointed out to me, gave significant expression to it when he valued courtship above marriage and held that there should be divorce if ever the living flame should die down. In the political field this viewpoint may issue in a sort of romantic Trotskyism. It is this which George Lukacs calls the politics of adolescence. It's interesting to note in passing that almost the same phrase is used by Oakeshott, for an opposite purpose, that is to describe the rationalist approach to politics. One can, I think, say what is appropriate about the label in both cases. This romantic Trotskyism, which consorts with Marxism for purposes of revolt but not for purposes of achievement, may be seen in particular in the work of Simone de Beauvoir and Maurice Merleau-Ponty, and also, though less markedly perhaps, in Sartre. Volumes III and IV of Sartre's novel *Les Chemins de la Liberté* contain a curious and touching fable about this matter, where the friendship is described of the communist Bouvet with the mysterious Schneider—Schneider, who turns out to be a discredited ex-party member pointedly called "Vicarios" and for the sake of whom Bouvet eventually breaks with the Party, with whose immediate doctrines he is in conflict. The question is: should the personal and the immediate values be preferred to the long-term workings of a machine in which one can but have faith? Is the scapegoat rightly branded and excluded, and even if he is not, what is the sense in taking his part if one has nothing but an individual gesture to oppose to a planned and organized intention for good? How is one to know, after how much incursion of evil, that planned intention must be regarded as irrevocably corrupt? The (I think) deliberately Christ-like figure of Sartre's Vicarios may make one think of the great prototype of this kind of fable: the story of the Grand Inquisitor in the *Brothers Karamazov*.

I have been suggesting that existentialism can be seen as a mythological representation of our present political dilemma. I think the Marxists are right when they say that a powerful reason for the popularity of existentialism is that it makes a universal myth of the plight of those who reject capitalism but who cannot adjust themselves to the idea of socialism, and who seek a middle way. They seek it, the Marxists might add, in doubt and despair, finding no genuine political road in the center, but only turnings away to the left and the right. To put it in Sartrian jargon, they reject the opaque brutish world of capitalist institutions and values, they are outside, or conceive themselves as outside, this *être-en-soi*; yet the ideal totality which they yearn for, the *en-soi-pour-soi* of socialism, is impossible, since all achievement corrupts and the dead hand extinguishes the pure flame. So they are left in the middle, empty and lonely and doomed to continual frustration.

Now one may ask: should we reject this myth as simply not representing how we are situated, or if we do accept it as having a political significance, is there any answer which can be made to those who are drawing extremist lessons from it? The existentialists, while possibly even accepting much of the Marxist analysis of their picture, would resist the Marxist conclusion. How is one to see this? One could think again of the Grand Inquisitor fable and, put in these terms, it seems clear that one must answer: I must side with Christ against the Grand Inquisitor. But what is it to side with Christ? Putting Stalin in the place of the Inquisitor and Marx or Trotsky in the place of the Messiah will not help us here.

This myth raises empirical and moral questions which, as so often in the field of politics, merge into each other. The question "Are the Marxists right?" can up to a point be regarded as an empirical question. We may ask: did Marx not underestimate the ideological power of the middle class? May it not be possible for the capitalist system to readjust itself and survive its internal contradictions? If the class struggle in England and America seems to be losing its sharpness, is this only a temporary phenomenon? One could attempt to answer these questions by examining facts. Yet the empirical answer does not seem to give the moral answer. Even if one were to see what History were doing, one might still decide to let it get along without one. In any case, it seems clear to me that the empirical answer is clouded in such obscurity that although we must not cease to look for it, we cannot do the looking without raising the moral questions at the same time. The problem which the existentialist myth puts before us is a problem about time, about the value of the present and of the personal. If we decline to valorize the historical process, or if we cannot understand it, can we morally contract out, and what would this mean? Marxism stands for, and is, an incarnation of ideas and values. The social values of capitalism are also incarnate, but those of the Middle Way are at present not. It may be well to say: believe only in a *living* future, a future that belongs to existing human beings, and not in a rational ideal of a politically deduced future time. Do not sacrifice a human present for a problematic inhuman future. But does this leave one with only a personal morality, and with no political morality or only a negative one?

An anti-rationalist historian such as Butterfield reminds us too that every generation is equidistant from eternity, and adds as a final piece of advice that we should hold to Christ and let the rest take care of itself. But he does not tell us what this means or what attitude to the historical process it would involve for us at present. This was what I had in mind earlier when I spoke of the Kantian dualism. Here one's values seem not to be incarnate, either in the old or the new morality, but present themselves as transcendent. What is it to choose in this way, and may one not after all be rejecting the flesh and blood in favor of the shadow? The answer to the empirical question about History does not seem to me to be clear enough to enable one to avoid the moral, or if you like, metaphysical question. Belief in God may affect how one thinks about the matter but will, I think, not give one any easy way out of the dilemma. We seemed to be faced, as Pascal was, with the necessity of betting.

This presentation may seem to an English audience utterly unreal. History condemns us to be metaphysicians or even Trotskyists? Come now! And it is true that the existentialist picture of the dilemma is one which has power on the continent but, on the whole, and for a variety of reasons, not over here. Yet I think that whether we recognize it or not, and whether or not we enjoy these romantic and dramatic pictures of it, we are in some such dilemma. The dilemma of deciding what it is the rejection of Marxism condemns us to. Here again it may be said: why put it so intensely? Let us not try to jump out of our skins. Let us go along as we have always done, making *ad hoc* moral choices and pursuing a politics of compromise. This would be all right if it were not for the fact that the present tempo of politics means more than ever that he who hesitates is lost. The only recorded remark made by the American novelist William Faulkner during his recent visit to Europe was one to the effect that: now there are no spiritual problems, there is only the problem when shall I be blown up. But indeed it is just this, the imminence of being blown up, that makes there to be spiritual problems for those who otherwise could have got along without them.

To put it at last in concrete terms: there are certain features about Marxism as it is lived in Soviet Russia which make it morally unacceptable to many of us. There are certain *facts*: the existence of forced labor camps, the insecurity of the individual, the authoritarian direction of thought, which we find intolerable, and to which we can only say no. On the other hand, I take it for granted that any intelligent moral being will say no also to what I might call the morality of Macarthur, or the notion of a self-righteous crusade against Communism in defense of "Western values." What are the alternatives? One may adopt a sort of total morality of refusal, a deliberate washing of the hands, which would involve, for instance, complete pacifism. This is a perfectly intelligible position and one which must be respected. On the other hand, one may tag along, accepting the sins and the morals of one's civilization, and waiting for the slippery sidestep into war, where it will inevitably appear that the other side is the aggressor. Meanwhile, one may devote one's time to attacking such manifestations of the Macarthur morality as one encounters in public or private life. This sort of compromise is, I suppose, the one which many of us are adopting. Finally, one might make the moral effort to embrace Marxism nevertheless, accepting the forced labor camps and so on. Whether one can do this will depend partly on one's estimation of the empirical arguments and on one's view of the capitalist alternative. The one thing we cannot with honesty say, armed with the atom bomb, is: I shall simply wait and defend England from invasion when the time comes.

If this is how we are placed, and I think it is, the existentialist mythology can be seen as, among other things, a picture of our dilemma. We want to think morally about politics but our moral categories are confused and our political categories are empty. What answer does existentialism offer? It offers no answer. Its concept of value is problematic, a question mark. But it is an expression of a passionate and sincere desire to keep to the middle way, to preserve the values of an innocent and vital individualism in a world which seems to menace them from both sides. We may well feel sympathy with this passion, and with the cry of distress which accompanies it. It is not yet clear what will show whether or not the myth represents a tragic delusion.

OXONIAN PRESS
QUEEN STREET, OXFORD
ENGLAND

www.ingramcontent.com/pod-product-compliance
Lightning Source LLC
Chambersburg PA
CBHW081128170426
43197CB00017B/2789